CAMBRIDGE STUDIES IN EARLY MODERN HISTORY

Editors

J. H. ELLIOTT   H. G. KOENIGSBERGER

THE ARMY OF FLANDERS
AND THE SPANISH ROAD
1567–1659

CAMBRIDGE STUDIES IN EARLY MODERN HISTORY

*Edited by Professor J. H. Elliott, King's College, University of London, and
Professor H. G. Koenigsberger, Cornell University*

The idea of an 'Early Modern' period of European history from the fifteenth to the eighteenth century is now finding wide acceptance among historians. The purpose of Cambridge Studies in Early Modern History is to publish monographs and studies which will help to illuminate the character of the period as a whole, and in particular to focus attention on a dominant theme within it – the interplay of continuity (the continuity of medieval ideas, and forms of political and social organization) and change (the impact of new ideas, new methods and new demands on the traditional structures.

The Army of Flanders and the Spanish Road
1567–1659

The Logistics of
Spanish Victory and Defeat
in the Low Countries' Wars

GEOFFREY PARKER

Fellow of Christ's College, Cambridge

CAMBRIDGE
at the University Press
1972

Published by the Syndics of the Cambridge University Press
Bentley House, 200 Euston Road, London NW1 2DB
American Branch: 32 East 57th Street, New York, N.Y. 10022

© Cambridge University Press 1972

Library of Congress Catalogue Card Number: 76–180021

ISBN: 0 521 08462 8

Printed in Great Britain
by Alden & Mowbray Ltd
at the Alden Press, Oxford

CONTENTS

v

ILLUSTRATIONS

Illustrations

FOREWORD

A locomotive is moving. Someone asks: 'What makes it move?' The peasant answers, ''Tis the devil moves it.' Another man says the locomotive moves because its wheels are going round. A third maintains that the cause of the motion lies in the smoke being carried away by the wind...

The only conception capable of explaining the movement of the locomotive is that of a force commensurate with the movement observed. The only conception capable of explaining the movement of peoples is that of some force commensurate with the whole movement of the peoples.

Yet to supply this conception various historians assume forces of entirely different kinds, all of which are incommensurate with the movement observed. Some see it as a force directly inherent in heroes, as the peasant sees the devil in the steam-engine; others, as a force resulting from several other forces, like the movement of the wheels; others again, as an intellectual influence, like the smoke that is blown away.[1]

Tolstoy's derogatory description of the three main schools of history contains a measure of truth whether the 'locomotive' happens to be the long war between Spain and the Dutch or Napoleon's invasion of Russia in 1812. Many historians of both these events have considered only the devils and the smoke, the heroes and the intellectual influences. The present writer belongs in Tolstoy's second category and he feels that, at least in the case of Spain and the Dutch Revolt, the 'wheels', the mechanics of the conflict, have been somewhat neglected.

This study is concerned with a basic question of historical mechanics: how Habsburg Spain, the richest and most powerful state in Europe, failed to suppress the Dutch Revolt. What were Spain's aims and policies in the Netherlands after 1567? How did she seek to implement them? Why did they fail?

Historians have tended to avoid these questions. Most accounts of the historical evolution of the Netherlands in the century 1550–1650 concentrate upon the internal dynamics of the Revolt, on the character of the opposition to Spain, on the leading events and personalities in the struggle

[1] L. N. Tolstoy, *War and Peace*, tr. R. Edmonds (Penguin, 1957), pp. 1408–9 (*Epilogue*, part II, §3).

– in other words, on why the Dutch won. Few writers at the time (and even fewer since) considered the Revolt from the other side, from the point of view of Spain faced with an embarrassing revolt in a distant province of her empire. There are good reasons for this one-sidedness. Spanish historians have not been attracted to study a war which caused the prolonged sacrifice of men, money and prestige, and produced only humiliation, impoverishment and defeat. Likewise, the Eighty Years' War brought so little political credit or economic profit to the Spanish Netherlands that 'Belgian' historians since the 1580s have concentrated almost exclusively on the religious aspects of the struggle, on how their country became the 'Catholic Netherlands'. The Dutch, on the other hand, have treated the Eighty Years' War as an essentially domestic affair, thus ensuring that the native policies and personalities of their country dominate the story. Spain has ignored the Netherlands, and the Netherlands have ignored Spain.

If the neglect of political historians is thus readily explicable, the lack of interest among military historians in the conduct of the Eighty Years' War is at first sight more surprising. The haughty dismissal of Major-General Fuller, a well-known authority on military history, is all too typical: 'Militarily, little is to be learnt from the French Wars of Religion (1562–1598). And not much either from the Revolt of the Netherlands (1568–1607)...'[1]

The professional soldier likes his wars clean, short and decisive. The Eighty Years' War, like most conflicts which involve large-scale foreign intervention, was the antithesis of this tidy pattern. The 'Military Participation Ratio', as so often in a civil war, was extremely high, and therefore the distinction between the poorly-armed, reluctant soldiers and the militant, determined civilians, between regular and guerilla warfare, is difficult to determine. The *Hauptschlachten*, the 'big battles' beloved of military historians were singularly few and the messy, interminable conflict provided little scope for the emergence of a romantic 'military genius'. Those who ascribe historical importance to Bruce's spider or Cleopatra's nose are doomed to be disappointed by the history of the Eighty Years' War: personal initiatives and good luck were quickly neutralized by the stultifying conditions of warfare. The war, after all, was fought for eighty years before the victor clearly emerged. Small wonder, then, that those reared on Clausewitz, the *Führereigenschaft* and trench-warfare should dismiss the clumsy military marathon in the Netherlands as an unimportant aberration.

[1] J. F. C. Fuller, *Armament and History* (London, 1946), p. 98.

Such, however, was not the view of those who witnessed the long struggle for the mastery of the Low Countries. The wars which began in earnest in 1572 and continued until 1659 were the seminary in which generations of military commanders and entrepreneurs served their apprenticeship. It was there that many of the generals of the Thirty Years' War – both Catholic and Protestant – learnt their profession. The armies locked in conflict in the Netherlands were the mirror in which other forces of the day adjusted their techniques, the yardstick by which they measured their military effectiveness.

Fortunately we can still see today why the Spanish army, at least, was so influential. Thanks to the abundance and variety of its surviving archives we can establish with precision the methods by which an army in early modern Europe was mobilized and maintained; we can reconstruct the way of life of the common soldiers through their wills, their wage-sheets and their writings. Because of this wealth of information we can observe at close quarters the rich tapestry of military life in the sixteenth and seventeenth centuries and we may gain a greater understanding of the technical, economic and fiscal problems which every government bent on victory in war was obliged to surmount.

Yet the Army of Flanders, however influential and interesting, must not be considered in isolation. Military history has been treated for too long as a self-contained compartment. The suitability of the Army to the war it was fighting and to the empire it defended requires discussion and analysis; so does the question of why Spain was prepared to fight in the Netherlands for eighty years. Moreover these are issues of a general relevance because Habsburg Spain was by no means the last imperial power to court ruin by waging a war abroad which it could not manage to win but could not bear to abandon. Nor was it the last empire to believe (erroneously) that the best troops, armed with the latest equipment and backed by the resources of the greatest state in the world were equal to any military challenge.

In part, Spain's undoing was a failure to adapt to change. War in the sixteenth century, as we shall see, was totally different from war in the middle ages: military organization and strategy were transformed in the years around 1500. The Spanish Habsburgs coped well with this challenge at a technical level: the size, organization, armament and morale of their forces were far in advance of anything the middle ages had known. At a theoretical level, however, there was little change: the political principles and assumptions which underlay the use of the new armies were still rooted in the world of chivalry and the crusades. War remained to a certain extent the 'sport of kings', fought for personal reasons – honour vanity, cupidity, the fear of humiliation. Spain's reaction to the revolt of the Netherlands was thus an aspect of the interplay between medieval and modern, between continuity and change, with which the series *Cambridge Studies in Early Modern History* is especially concerned.

One of the very few writers who made a serious attempt to explain and understand the perplexing oscillations of fortune in the Low Countries' Wars, Michael von Aitzing (d. 1598), could only make sense of the struggle by invoking astrology. For him, history moved in a circle governed by the movements of the heavens; the various changes of fortunes in the Homeric duel between Spain and the Dutch thus became explicable in terms of the stars. This engaging but somewhat extravagant determinism saved Aitzing from that pitfall which has claimed almost every subsequent writer: partiality for one side or the other. Even today it is hard to avoid becoming a partisan – of Spain, of the Dutch, even of Queen Elizabeth. Although my own historical prejudices will inevitably have coloured this account of Spain's unsuccessful attempts to suppress the Dutch Revolt, if I have avoided the sin of one-sidedness it will perhaps justify the loosing of an English bull in an essentially Spanish and Netherlands china shop.

ACKNOWLEDGEMENTS

Collecting the evidence for this study has involved extensive and prolonged travel and research in western Europe. Nothing could have been achieved without the generous financial assistance of a large number of bodies, public and private. The Department of Education and Science awarded me a State Studentship for 1965–8; the 'Twenty-seven Foundation' of the Institute of Historical Research made me a most handsome award for my research in 1969; the British Academy and the Houblon–Norman Fund of the Bank of England provided the means for my further study abroad in 1970; and the Leverhulme Research Awards Committee elected me to a European Studentship for 1970–1 which permitted me to complete my investigations abroad. In addition I have received considerable aid over the past five years from the Ellen McArthur Fund of the University of Cambridge and from the French Centre Nationale de la Recherche Scientifique. Above all I thank the Master and Fellows of Christ's College, Cambridge, for awarding me the A. H. Lloyd Research Scholarship for 1965–7 and the Bottomley Travelling Scholarship in 1967, and for electing me to a four-year Research Fellowship in 1968 which has provided me with unique facilities for study and travel. To these several bodies this book is gratefully dedicated: I hope that they will all find it an acceptable monument to their generosity.

I first became interested in Spain and the 'Spanish Road' when, as an undergraduate at Cambridge in 1964–5, I attended Professor J. H. Elliott's stimulating lectures on early modern Europe. Since then his patient and wise advice, generously given, has been of the greatest help to me. I am likewise indebted to Professor J. H. Plumb and Professor Charles Wilson for their encouragement, assistance and advice over a number of years.

I have derived particular benefit from the interest and detailed knowledge of three foreign scholars: M. Fernand Braudel, professor at the Collège de France and dean of sixteenth-century historical studies, took an early interest in my work and procured some vital advance information for me on the contents of certain French and Italian archives; M. Henri Lapèyre fortified my flagging resolve to consult the *contaduría mayor de cuentas* series at Simancas and gave me much useful advice; Mlle Lucienne Van Meerbeeck, Head of the First Section at the Archives Générales du Royaume in Brussels, introduced me to the complex records of the archive and secured permission for me to consult them on the stacks. Many other scholars, archivists and friends have given me help and hospitality at different turns, and I have made reference to their assistance in the text. Finally, I wish to express my gratitude to all who have read this book at some stage of its life and have laboured to improve it: my editors, Professors J. H. Elliott and H. G. Koenigsberger, and also Professor Michael Roberts, Dr I. A. A. Thompson, Dr J. M. Winter and, most of all, my wife. My thanks go to all of them.

NOTES ON SPELLING AND CURRENCY

Where there is a recognized English version of a foreign place-name (Venice, The Hague, Brussels, etc.) I have used it. Otherwise, I have preferred the style used in the place itself, thus 's Hertogenbosch and Aalst, not Bois-le-Duc or Alost. The only exception is 'Flanders', which is occasionally used to refer to the whole of the Netherlands. I have followed the same guide-line with personal names: where there is an established English usage (William of Orange, Don John of Austria, Philip II...) I have adopted it. In all other cases the style and title employed by the man himself have been used.

To avoid unnecessary confusion and to make comparisons possible, all sums of money mentioned in the text have been converted into florins of 20 pattards, the principal money of account used in the Netherlands at the time. There were 10 florins to the £ sterling (also a unit of account then). The commonest coin used by the Army of Flanders in the sixteenth century was the gold *escudo*, but there were three main types: the *escudo* of Spain, of Italy and of France – and each was of slightly different weight and was therefore valued slightly differently (in the period 1585–90, for example, the *escudo* of Italy was worth 57 pattards, the *escudo* of Spain 59 and the *escudo* of France 60). In addition the Army used the *escudo* as a money of account, but again its value changed. From 1560 until 1578 the unit of account was the *escudo* of 39 pattards, rising in stages to 57 pattards by 1585. In 1590 a new system was devised: the normal unit of account in the army became the *escudo* of ten *reales*, a money of account based on silver instead of gold, worth for most of the seventeenth century just 50 pattards (each *real* was valued at 5 pattards).

GLOSSARY

alferez: company lieutenant or 'ensign'.
asiento: contract with a banker (the *asentista*) for a short-term loan.
auditor: judge-advocate.
barracas: huts made by soldiers for shelter.
bisoño: Spanish raw recruit.
brandschatting: the practice of extorting payments from civilians under threat of burning down their property.
cabo de escuadra: corporal, chief of an *escuadra* (q.v.).
cartel: fly-sheet, poster.
consulta: written recommendation of a Spanish council sent to the king.
contador: an accountant; *contaduría* – his department.
contaduría mayor de cuentas: the audit office of the Spanish exchequer.
corselete: pike-man with body-armour; his body-armour (corselet).
decreto: decree of the Spanish crown suspending all payments from the treasury connected with bankers' loans – the 'decree of bankruptcy'; *decretados* – the bankers whose loans were frozen by the decree.
depositario general: the officer appointed in 1596 to administer the wills of all soldiers of the Army of Flanders.
electo: the elected leader of a mutiny.
entretenido: soldier in receipt of a permanent monthly salary (an *entretenimiento*) from the military treasury.
escuadra: 'section' of twenty-five men under a *cabo de escuadra* (corporal).
escuadrón: a large body of soldiers.
étape: a 'staple' where food and goods were collected; a provisioning centre for troops on the march.
juro: a government bond in Castile yielding permanent interest.
laufgeld: the money paid to German troops to cover the cost of their journey to the Army.
leva: recruiting a complete unit for the Army (cf. *recluta*).
libranza: a warrant of the captain-general ordering the paymaster to issue money from the military treasury.
limosna: charitable donation; *real de limosna* – the monthly payment of 1 *real* by each soldier to the military hospital.
maestre de campo: the commander of a *tercio* (q.v.).
medio general: the agreement which followed a *decreto* (q.v.) restoring dealings between the Spanish crown and its bankers.
pagador: a paymaster; *pagaduría* – his department.
pan de munición: government bread.
pica seca: a pike-man without body-armour (also *piquero seco*).

Glossary

recluta: recruiting reinforcements for an existing unit (cf. *leva*).

reformación: the amalgamation of several units of the Army into one in order to reduce cost; *reformado* – an officer who had lost his post through *reformación*.

remate: the final payment of arrears made to a soldier for his service.

santelmo: a man falsely presented as a soldier at a muster in order to draw pay.

tanteo: estimate (of cost, expenditure, revenue etc.).

tercio: a unit comprising about 12 companies and about 2,500 men, commanded by a *maestre de campo* (cf. Appendix B, p. 274 below).

veedor: inspector of the forces; *veeduría* – his department.

ventaja: a wage-supplement granted to a soldier for long or valiant service; *soldado aventajado* – soldier with a *ventaja*.

visita: a tribunal appointed by the king to investigate the conduct of a public department.

wartegeld: money paid to German troops to keep them in readiness for mobilization as soon as need arose.

ABBREVIATIONS

AA	Archivo de la Casa de los Duques de Alba, Madrid (with the *caja* and folio of each document).
AC	Archives Communales.
AD	Archives Départementales.
AE Geneva *PH*	Archives de l'Etat, Geneva, *Portfeuille Historique.*
AE Geneva *RC*	*ibid., Registre du Conseil.*
AGRB *Audience*	Archives Générales du Royaume, Brussels, *Papiers d'Etat et de l'Audience.*
AGRB *CC*	*ibid., Chambres de Comptes.*
AGRB *Contadorie*	*ibid., Contadorie des Finances.*
AGRB *CPE*	*ibid., Conseil Privé, Régime espagnol.*
AGRB *MD*	*ibid., Manuscrits Divers.*
AGRB *SEG*	*ibid., Secrétairerie d'Etat et de Guerre.*
AGS *CJH*	Archivo General de Simancas, Spain, *Consejos y Juntas de Hacienda.*
AGS *CMC*	*ibid., Contaduría Mayor de Cuentas* (with *época* – 1a, 2a or 3a – and *legajo*).
AGS *E*	*ibid., Secretaría de Estado* (with *legajo* and folio of document).
AGS *EK*	*ibid.,* series *K.*
AGS *GA*	*ibid., Guerra Antigua* (papers of the Spanish Council of War).
AGS *MPyD*	*ibid., Mapas, Planas y Dibujos.*
AHE	*Archivo Histórico Español* (a collection of documents published at Valladolid).
AHN	Archivo Histórico Nacional, Madrid.
AM	Archives Municipales.
ARA	Algemeen Rijksarchief, the Hague.
AS	Archivio di Stato.
BAE	*Biblioteca de Autores Españoles.*
BCRH	*Bulletin de la Commission Royale d'Histoire.*
BIHR	*Bulletin of the Institute of Historical Research.*
BM *Ms.*	British Museum, London, *Department of Manuscripts.*
BNM *Ms.*	Biblioteca Nacional de Madrid, *Sección de Manuscritos.*
BNP *Ms.*	Bibliothèque Nationale de Paris, *Cabinet des Manuscrits.*
BPU *Ms. Favre*	Bibliothèque Publique et Universitaire, Geneva, *Collection manuscrit Edouard Favre.*
BRB *Ms.*	Bibliothèque Royale de Bruxelles, *Section des Manuscrits.*
Co.Do.In.	*Colección de Documentos Inéditos para la Historia de España.*
Epistolario	Duque de Alba, *Epistolario del III Duque de Alba, Don Fernando Alvarez de Toledo* (3 vols, Madrid, 1952).
HMC	Historical Manuscripts Commission Reports.

Abbreviations

IVdeDJ   Instituto de Valencia de Don Juan, Madrid (with *envío* and folio of each document).

KB 's Gravenhage *Hs.*   Koninklijke Bibliotheek, 's Gravenhage, *Afdeling Handschriften.*

MDG   *Mémoires et Documents publiés par la Société d'Histoire et d'Archéologie de Genève* (periodical).

Nueva Co.Do.In.   *Nueva Colección de Documentos Inéditos para la Historia de España y de sus Indias.*

RA Arnhem *Archief...Berg*   Rijksarchief in Gelderland, Arnhem, *Archief van het Huis Berg.*

RAH   Real Academia de la Historia, Madrid, Manuscript Department.

RBPH   *Revue Belge de Philologie et d'Histoire.*

Introduction

The character of
the Low Countries' Wars

Some time in 1614 a complete set of toy soldiers, made of wood, was presented to the young prince of Spain, later King Philip IV. There were regiments and companies with their various banners, weapons and equipment, there were horses and cannon for the artillery, even the distinctive shops and tents of the armourers, sutlers and barbers who followed every army. Special materials were included for the construction of artificial lakes, forests and pontoon bridges, and there was a toy castle for the 'army' to besiege. And this, the first child's 'war-game' known in Europe, was proudly described by its inventor in a special publication in Spanish and Latin. The toy was no less grandiose in intention than in execution: it was to give education as well as enjoyment. 'This army will be no less useful than entertaining' the designer, one Alberto Struzzi, wrote to the prince. 'From it one may observe the expenditure which is necessary if a King is to emerge victorious, and how if money (which is the sinews of war) fails, the prince's intentions cannot be achieved.' Armies which are not paid invariably fall prey to disorders, desertion and defeat, warned the inventor.[1]

The ultimate aim of this war-game was to make Prince Philip aware of the existence of the Spanish Netherlands and of the army which defended them. The prince's splendid toy was in fact a perfect replica of the most famous army of the day, the Army of Flanders, maintained by Spain in the Low Countries since 1567. It was never too early to teach a future king of Spain that his power was underpinned largely by military strength and that his armies could function only for as long as they were paid.

The Army which served as a model for Alberto Struzzi's toy was a fighting force at its zenith. In 1604, after a siege lasting three years, the

---

[1] Albertus Struzzus (= Alberto Struzzi), *Imago militiae auspiciis Ambrosii Spinolae, belgicarvm copiarvm dvctoris* (Brussels, 1614, 12 pp.; Latin and Spanish). Struzzi was only paid for his labours in 1630: AGS *E* 2044/192, order of Philip IV to pay 'Alberto Struçi que truxo el exercito de figuras'.

troops of Spain in the Netherlands had forced the surrender of the important Flemish port of Ostend. In 1605 and 1606, with enviable ease, the Army crossed the Rhine and Maas (the so-called 'Great Rivers Barrier') in order to campaign nearer to the enemy heartland, and they captured several towns in the teeth of Dutch resistance. In 1614 the Army again rolled forward across the rivers, this time to occupy the vacant Rhenish duchies of Cleves and Jülich and thus prevent a Protestant from becoming duke. Fifty-five towns and forts were captured and garrisoned without effort. The tide of victory continued. In 1620 the Army of Flanders marched into the Rhine Palatinate and crushed all opposition within a matter of weeks. Although the siege of Bergen-op-Zoom was a failure in 1622, the Spanish army forced the surrender of Breda in 1625, the family seat of the redoubtable enemy commander, Maurice of Nassau. At the end of the year Maurice died, partly, it was said, through chagrin at his defeat over Breda.

The toy army of Alberto Struzzi was not accompanied by a fleet, a remarkable omission considering that it was modelled on an army locked in war with a maritime republic whose chief strength was its seaborn commerce. But there was no mistake; the Army of Flanders was indeed exclusively a landbound force. There had once been a powerful navy in the Low Countries, based on the naval arsenal at Veere in Zealand, but in 1572 the Dutch rebels had captured the arsenal, with the 2,000 or more naval guns and all the munitions it contained, and thereafter the royal fleet lost one vessel after another in action or by treachery until by the summer of 1574 the government had hardly any ships left. In 1576 it lost all the seaports too.

In 1583, the Army of Flanders recaptured the port of Dunkirk. At once a board of admiralty was established and orders were issued for a number of new warships to be constructed. This was the beginning of the 'Flanders flotilla' (the *armadilla de Flandes*) which for the rest of the war operated against the Dutch, captured prizes, protecting Spanish merchantmen and ferrying troops between Spain and the south Netherlands. Yet despite these useful and profitable activities, the Dunkirk fleet was of little use in winning the war. At most times the Dutch navy, vastly superior in numbers, kept a tight blockade on the ports of the Flemish coast, preventing the *armadilla* from ever putting to sea. When a vessel did escape to the open sea, the Dutch were always prepared to lose ten of their own ships in order to destroy it. It was worth any sacrifice to maintain their absolute naval control of the North Sea.[1] All attempts by

[1] AGS *E* 634/64, 'Discurso del estado de la guerra de Flandes', by Juan Bautista de Tassis

Spain to challenge Dutch superiority by sending warships from her own Atlantic fleet ended in disaster: the *armada* of 1574 never set out, the fleet of 1596 was wrecked, those of 1588 and 1639 were destroyed in battle.

This failure to maintain a North Sea fleet was critical to Spain's efforts to subdue the rebellion of the maritime provinces of the Netherlands because in the course of the sixteenth century a number of profound changes and innovations in European military organization and military practice made victory on land increasingly difficult to achieve. Above all, it became almost impossible to win a land war *quickly*: years, perhaps decades, might be necessary for outright victory. As one of Philip II's naval advisers put it in 1577, without a fleet in the Low Countries it could take fifty years to reduce the 'rebels'.[1] This, of course, proved to be an underestimate.

The first important break from the conventions which dominated medieval warfare was the triumph of the Swiss pike-squares over the mounted knights of Burgundy in a series of pitched battles (1475–7). The lesson of Morat, Grandson and Nancy was immediate, important and ineluctable: victory in battle could be won by infantry over cavalry. This shift in military effectiveness removed a crucial restriction on the scale of warfare in Europe. Since a warhorse was not only expensive but also a mark of social rank the size of a cavalry-based army was necessarily circumscribed by the dimensions of the social class which was entitled to go through life on horseback: the knights. There was no such bar to the number of men who could be recruited and issued with a helmet and sixteen-foot pike. Accordingly the eclipse of cavalry by infantry meant that victory in war after the 1470s came to depend not on the quality of the combatants nor on the excellence of their armament, but on their numbers. A government bent on war had now to mobilize and equip every man who could be found.

The logistic consequences of the defeat of the knights of Burgundy were fully grasped and given an enormous diffusion by Niccolo Macchiavelli. In his *Discourses on the First Decade of Titus Livy* (written in 1513) and in his *Art of War* (1520–1) Macchiavelli preached the two clear lessons of the Swiss victories: infantry had defeated cavalry, quantity had over-

---

(1601): 'If we bring out 100 ships they bring out 400, and if more, more; and they are always happy to lose ten of their ships if they can sink one of ours.' On the profits of the Dunkirk fleet, mainly confined to the years 1629–37, cf. H. Malo, *Les corsaires: les corsaires dunquerquois et Jean Bart*, I (Paris, 1913), pp. 333–5 (between 1626 and 1634 the Dunkirkers lost 120 ships and sank or captured 1,835 enemy vessels).

[1] BNM *Ms.* 1749/361–79, memorial of Alonso Gutiérrez to the king, 23 Oct. 1577.

whelmed quality, and they would do so again. Macchiavelli's works were couched in a persuasive, appealing style, and the renown of his name ensured a wide dissemination for his ideas. Translations were made into many languages and exerted a powerful influence on military thinking. In the words of Professor Hale: 'Respect for Macchiavelli's military ideas continued to increase as his political reputation became more alarming.'[1]

In fact, although Macchiavelli's assessment of the changed military situation was correct, few of his plausible predictions for the future of European warfare were vindicated. He foretold greater armies, more battles, battles fought on a larger scale, and consequently shorter and more decisive wars. Only the first of these forecasts came true – and even then not for the reason Macchiavelli had postulated, and not in his lifetime!

The jungle warfare of the Franco–Spanish struggle for Italy which followed Charles VIII's invasion in 1494 was bitter and bloody, but there is no evidence that any one state fielded more than 30,000 effectives before the Peace of Cambrai in 1529. It was only in the 1530s that the size of European armies began a marked and sustained growth. In 1536–7 the Emperor Charles V mobilized 60,000 men in Lombardy alone for the defence of his recent conquest, Milan, and for the invasion of French Provence. In 1552, assailed on all fronts at once – in Italy, Germany, the Netherlands and Spain, in the Atlantic and in the Mediterranean – Charles V raised 109,000 men in Germany and the Netherlands, 24,000 more in Lombardy and yet more in Sicily, Naples and Spain. The emperor must have had at his command, and therefore at his cost, about 150,000 men. The upward trend continued. In 1574 the Spanish Army of Flanders alone numbered 86,000 men, while only half a century later Philip IV could proudly proclaim that the armed forces at his command in 1625 amounted to no less than 300,000 men. In all these armies the real increase in numbers took place among the infantry, especially among the pike-men.[2]

Here then was Macchiavelli's prophecy come true: armies had grown enormously in numerical strength and the growth had taken place among the foot-soldiers. Yet it cannot be said that the 'puissant pike' in any sense *caused* the increase. It was a transformation of the art of defensive

[1] J. R. Hale in *The New Cambridge Modern History*, III (Cambridge, 1968), p. 181.
[2] S. M. de Soto, conde de Clonard, *Historia orgánica del Ejército*, III (Madrid, 1887), pp. 326–9, estimate of Charles V's army in 1536; AGS *E* 1199/2 and 1201/112, *relaciones* of the imperial army in 1552; IVdeDJ 68/309*ter, Relación de bilanço* of Mar. 1574 – 86,235 men; BM *Egerton, Ms.* 338/136–51v, 'Resuemen' of Philip IV, 1627 (on f. 145).

warfare, barely apparent when Macchiavelli wrote, which actively compelled every major state to double the size of its forces.

In the fifteenth century, military architects evolved the bastion. This awesome projection from the line of the walls, provided with a platform upon which artillery was mounted, had four faces: two pointed outwards towards the enemy and two were at right angles to the main wall to provide a cross-fire in the event of an assault (cf. Figure 1 and Plate 1). At the same time, other changes took place. Both bastions and curtain wall

Figure 1. The bastion (*top*) and the new defence-works

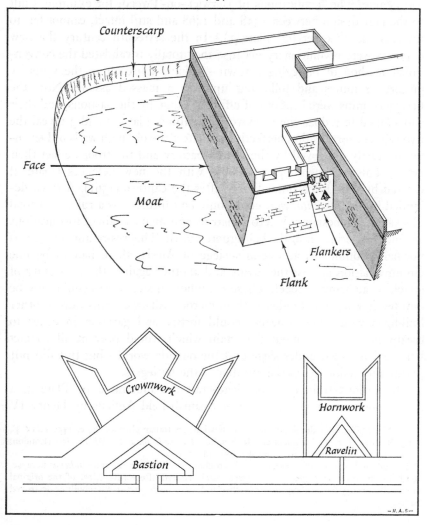

came to be built much lower and much thicker than before, constructed of brick and rubble rather than of stone. Brick, it was discovered, absorbed the enemy's cannon-shot instead of fracturing on impact like stone, while a squat design for the walls proved more resistant to artillery fire. To complete the new defensive system, walls and bastions were surrounded by a wide and deep moat, often defended by further constructions (cf. Figure 1). These developments, and in particular the bastion, 'revolutionized the defensive–offensive pattern of warfare'.[1]

Even today the *trace italienne* (as the new style was known) looks formidable. The fortifications of Berwick-on-Tweed, for example, built to the new design between 1558 and 1568 and still intact, cannot fail to impress the observer (cf. Plate 1).[2] In the sixteenth century the new defences were revolutionary because they totally invalidated the conventional method of besieging a town – making a breach in the walls by gunfire or mines and following up with a massed assault. Now the besiegers' guns were kept out of effective range by the bastions, and their shots failed to reduce the brickwork to rubble. Plates 2 and 3 reveal the two types of fortification perfectly: in Plate 2 the old high walls of Deventer are easily destroyed by the Dutch battery and the troops effect their entry. This was no longer possible with the new defences (Plate 3) erected by the Dutch immediately after the capture (1591). A town defended by the *trace italienne* could only be captured, as a rule, by a total blockade. The besiegers had to construct and man a chain of fortifications around the perimeter of the beleaguered town. This restraining circle was normally double: as at Caesar's siege of Alesia, there had to be one circumvallation against the towns and another against the possibility of attack by an army of relief. These complicated siegeworks could only be omitted in a terrain studded with numerous villages, farmsteads or other buildings which the besiegers could fortify and garrison in order to create an effective armoured curtain which would prevent all contact between the town under siege and the outside world – but this did not permit any reduction in the number of the besiegers.

The various techniques of siege-craft are illustrated by Plate 4, a contemporary print of the siege of Spanish-held Amiens by Henry IV

[1] J. R. Hale, 'The early development of the bastion: an Italian chronology, c. 1450–c. 1534', in J. R. Hale, J. R. L. Highfield and B. Smalley, *Europe in the Later Middle Ages* (London, 1965), pp. 466–94 (on p. 466) – a most important article.

[2] The walls and bastions of Berwick have been chosen to illustrate the *trace italienne* because, built in one piece in 1558–68, they were barely altered afterwards. Most of the original sixteenth-century fortifications of the Netherlands have been extensively rebuilt or destroyed since.

in 1597 together with an aerial photograph of the surviving imprint of the siege-works as modern cropmarks. Amiens was a town defended by a high, thin medieval wall punctuated by round towers. A number of bastions had been grafted on to the ancient defences to protect their weakest points, either abutting directly on to the medieval walls (the true bastions) or else constructed across the moat (the ravelins – cf. the left side of the print). The earthworks of the besiegers are clearly shown in the lower part of the print, *tranchées* and 'sconces' made of earth and joined to form a continuous chain sealing off the town and protecting the main camp of the besiegers (the cluster of stylized tents at the bottom right of the print). It is these earthworks which have produced the cropmarks. At the other side of the town – the south side towards France which was considered safer from attack by a relief army from the Netherlands – the besiegers fortified only the outlying buildings, mainly churches, and the bridges (cf. the top half of the print). The pattern of siege-works at Amiens in 1597 typified the standard procedure adopted against any town defended by the new-style fortifications: blockade and attrition.

The superiority of the *trace italienne* over all previous defensive systems was so obvious that it spread rapidly to all the sensitive frontier-zones of Europe. The magnificent defences built at Verona after 1527 by Michele Sanmicheli served as an advertisement and often as a blue-print for the new style. It was not long before Francis I invited Italian-trained builders and architects to work on the fortifications of France's northern frontier. By 1542 they had constructed bastions all along the border with the Netherlands and Francis was able to mount an invasion of the Netherlands in joyful awareness that his own defences were proof against counter-attack. In fact this proto-Maginot line proved to be a failure. Like the great French hope of the 1930s, Francis I's defences only went as far as the nearest neutral territory. In 1544 Charles V was able to turn the French flank merely by marching into the neutral duchy of Lorraine and invading France through her undefended eastern provinces. One town after another was assaulted and captured. Francis was compelled to conclude a hasty peace. But the emperor learnt his lesson and he ordered his own architects to intensify their efforts: Italian-style defences were erected at all strategic points – along the coast, around certain key towns inland, and all down the Netherlands' border with France. The bastions of Francis I at Doullens, La Capelle and Thérouanne were quickly matched by those of Charles V across the frontier at Charlemont, Philippeville and Mariembourg.[1]

[1] For the spread of the new defences in the Netherlands cf. M. Van Hemelrijk, *De Vlaamse*

Wherever war seemed likely, the new defences sprang up. From Lombardy, the battleground of Europe in the 1530s, they spread to the Netherlands and England in the 1540s. When the outbreak of civil war in France and the Low Countries after 1560 brought large armies to areas which had previously been peaceful, bastions and citadels were swiftly constructed.

The 'revolutionary' character of the new fortifications lay in their stultifying effect on the pattern of warfare. The triumph of the pike-men already guaranteed the superiority of defensive over offensive tactics in mobile operations; now defence became superior to offence in siege-warfare too. When even a small, unimportant town might resist capture for several months provided it had the *trace italienne*, battles became of far less consequence. This realization consoled a dispirited English observer in the Low Countries on the morrow of the rousing and seemingly complete Spanish victory at Gembloux in January 1578. Don John might have won a battle, William Davison observed with grim satisfaction, but he had still to:

> Expugne one towne after another, the least of a nomber wherof cannot cost him less than half a yeres siege with an infinite charge, loss of men and hazard of his fortune and reputation bycause (as men of warr are wont to say) one good towne well defended sufficeth to ruyn a mightie army.[1]

The Low Countries' Wars after 1568 were fought largely in the land of the *trace italienne*. Although in the early years some towns were unprotected by bastions (Oudewater and Buren in Holland, for example, which were taken by assault in 1575) the vast majority of the main actions in which the Army of Flanders was involved were starvation-blockades. In relatively few cases did the besiegers make a charge at a breach in the walls. The spectacular (and unsuccessful) Spanish assault on Maastricht in 1579, commemorated in a play of Lope de Vega (*El asalto de Mastrique*), was one of the last such occasions in the Eighty Years' War. By 1600 the important towns were almost all fortified in the new style and the war therefore became an annual trial of strength to starve out one or more towns of the enemy.

Krijgsbouwkunde (Tielt, 1950), pp. 131–95 (for the south) and C. A. De Bruijn and H. R. Reinders, *Nederlandse Vestingen* (Bussum, 1967 – for the north). The new fortifications were certainly built to last: Willemstad, overlooking the Hollands Diep, fortified in 1583 and perfectly preserved, only ceased to be scheduled as strategically important in May 1928 . . .
[1] Kervijn de Lettenhove, *Relations politiques des Pays-Bas et de l'Angleterre sous le Règne de Philippe II*, x (Brussels, 1891), p. 380, Davison to Burghley, 29 Mar. 1578. The perceptive military commentator, Fourquevaux, writing in 1548, also recognized as a general rule that no town defended by the *trace italienne* could be taken other than by blockade: G. Dickinson (ed.), *The 'Instructions sur le Faict de la Guerre' of Raymond de Beccarie de Pavie, sieur de Four-quevaux* (London, 1954), bk. iii. 2, e.g. f. 85.

This degeneration of the war into a series of long sieges, often of towns which were in close proximity, naturally produced important changes in the size and composition of armies. In the first place it completed the eclipse of the cavalry as an important fighting force. As soon as the Spanish army entered Holland in the autumn of 1572 all heavy cavalry units were paid off. An English soldier serving in the Army of Flanders correctly observed that the duke of Alva 'needed no great cavalry, by reason he was assured there would be but few against him. Also those grounds did not serve for great troops of horsement to fight in'.[1] Heavy cavalry was only mobilized when a campaign was undertaken in the south or east Netherlands where the great towns were further apart and there was more likelihood of a pitched battle. The composition of the Army of Flanders varied with the theatre of operations. 'We need more infantry if we invade the rebel provinces and more cavalry if we campaign in France', observed a prominent Army minister in 1637.[2] Cavalry, therefore, was only recruited *en masse* when it was urgently needed. This system saved money – cavalry was ruinously expensive – but it could prove a dangerous economy: inevitably the cavalry raised suddenly for service against France was untrained and often unreliable. The Spanish defeat at Lens in 1648 was largely caused by the flight of the cavalry before a shot was fired. Even this sobering experience failed to change the Army's ways. On the whole the only cavalry to be permanently retained in the Army of Flanders were the companies of light horse: a few thousand troopers, mostly from Spain and Italy, armed with either lance and pistol or with a horse-arquebus. Their vital function was to patrol the country-side (the *platteland*) and protect loyal communities.

The Eighty Years' War was above all an infantry duel. The foot-soldiers of both sides had to beleaguer enemy towns and defend the strong-points of their own side. Cities, rural towns, villages and small forts: all had to be garrisoned in order to guard against a surprise attack. Throughout the war, upwards of 30,000 men of the Army of Flanders were tied down in garrison duty. In 1639 no less than 208 places in the Spanish Netherlands required permanent garrisons: in all 33,399 men were involved, from 1,000 men stationed in the port of Dunkirk (the

[1] Roger Williams, *The Actions of the Low Countries*, ed. D. W. Davies (Cornell, 1964), p. 83. The same observation was made by the French ambassador in the Spanish camp: 'la cavallerie ne servant de riens audict pays, il n'en fault point faire estat' (L. Didier, *Lettres et négociations de Claude de Mondoucet*, 1 (Paris, 1891), pp. 119–22; Mondoucet to Charles IX, 9 Dec. 1572). For the exact number of cavalry in the Army of Flanders, cf. Appendix A, pp. 271–3 below.

[2] AGS *E* 2051/225, Don Miguel de Salamanca to the king, 8 Feb. 1637.

largest garrison) down to 10 men in the fort called 'La Grande Misère' near Ghent.[1]

These expensive precautions were vital. When every siege became a major, protracted affair, small towns and even villages, especially those with walls or a moat, acquired a considerable strategic importance. Time and again the successful blockade of a great town hinged upon the control of the outlying villages. Moreover from 1572 until the 1590s innumerable small communities far from the main sieges became military objectives in their own right. Although military historians have tended to confine their attention to the formal engagements of the war, to the sieges, battles and major manœuvres, these events formed only the tip of the iceberg of military conflict. Beneath the interplay of the big battalions, at least until 1590, smaller parties of troops fought, intrigued and killed ceaselessly for the control of villages. Spain's piecemeal reconquest of the areas in rebellion in the first phase of the war created a jagged 'floating' frontier, running from one fortified town to another, from one village to the next. Until 1594 the frontier ran from Groningen in the north down to Liège and then westwards to the Flemish sea-coast. All along this invisible line hostile parties of troops conducted a gruelling war of skirmish and surprise. In this situation, as Monluc observed, war became a matter of 'fights, encounters, skirmishes, ambushes, an occasional battle, minor sieges, assaults, escalades, captures and surprises of towns'. It resembled a series of uncoordinated guerilla conflicts rather than a single full-scale war.[2]

---

[1] AGS *E* 2247, unfol., 'Relación de la gente efectiva que es menester para asegurar de surpressa las plazas siguientes'. Most of the strong-points in the province of Flanders are shown in the precise maps of A. Sanderus, *Flandria Illustrata* (Cologne, 1641).

[2] Blaise de Monluc (d. 1577), quoted J. Boudet (ed.), *Histoire Universelle des Armés*, II (Paris, 1966) p. 185. For a magnificent first-hand account of one of the guerilla-actions in the Netherlands, cf. Francisco Verdugo, *Comentario de la Guerra en Frisa*, ed. H. Lonchay (Brussels, 1899). For a parallel distinction between *'guerra'* and *'guerrilla'* in the French Religious Wars, cf. the magisterial study of H. Drouot, *Mayenne et la Bourgogne . . . 1587–1596* (Paris, 1937), especially I, pp. 327–33. The importance of the guerilla warfare in early modern and medieval conflicts has been almost entirely overlooked by military historians. Today, when 'warfare' is so easily identified with the trenches of Belgium and Verdun, it is perhaps difficult to appreciate the contrast between the 'stable front' of the First World War and the 'open fronts' of other wars where neither side commanded enough troops to be able to dig in along a line. The Eighty Years' War resembled, in this respect, the 'Hundred Years' War' between England and France: the multiplicity of fortified points gave rise to innumerable local wars producing a situation of permanent insecurity over a wide area (cf. P. C. Timbal, *La Guerre de Cent Ans*, I (Paris, 1961) p. 105). There is also a similarity between these two conflicts and the German invasion of Russia in 1941–3. Over two winters the frontier between the two sides lay largely in the villages which held a garrison of one side or the other. Outside the village, the frontier was entirely 'open' and there was no security for those 'behind the lines' because, of course, 'lines' did not exist. Such was the situation of the Netherlands during the first thirty years of the Low Countries' Wars.

These localized dog-fights, this *guerre aux vaches*, was a highly intensive and exhausting form of warfare. It called for troops with an unusually high degree of endurance and experience. In battles or mass manœuvres a commander required from his men corporate discipline, good order, careful drilling in certain collective movements and above all stoicism under fire. By contrast, for the skirmish and surprise of guerilla fighting, discipline and unit-organization hardly mattered: the critical qualities were independent excellence and complete familiarity with weapons.[1]

Sixteenth-century commanders and military commentators naturally realized that these different forms of warfare required different types of soldier: one for routine garrison duty and mass manœuvres, the other for guerilla action. On the whole they agreed that it was more difficult to find troops who excelled in skirmish-and-surprise, in what the English called the 'actions' of war. For that veterans were required. The duke of Alva always insisted that some trained troops were indispensable for success in the Low Countries' Wars because 'One cannot fight any "actions" with other troops – unless it comes to a pitched battle where entire formations are engaged.' To the duke's mind (and he had a lifetime of experience to draw on) any troops could fight a battle but it required trained veterans to win a skirmish.[2]

The premium on 'irregular' warfare had an important impact on the organization as well as on the personnel of the armies involved. The basic unit of European armies from the fourteenth century until the present day has been the 'company'. Until 1600 anything larger than a company tended to be only an administrative convenience, not a tactical unit. The size of the regiment and *tercio* was flexible throughout the sixteenth century (anything between 10 and 20 companies or 1,000 and 5,000 men) and they rarely operated as a single command. For active service a completely flexible tactical organization was called for. In the Army of Flanders, when something more than a single company was required, the most experienced companies from the various 'nations' of the Army (Spanish, Walloon, German, Italian, Burgundian and British) were informally combined into a single force. A heterogeneous but highly-

---

[1] For a repetition of this view as late as 1756, cf. P. Paret, 'Colonial experience and European military reform at the end of the eighteenth century', *BIHR*, xxxvii (1964), pp. 47–59, quoting an English officer from the Indian wars (p. 47), who felt that soldiers 'require no Exercise but to be perfectly acquainted with the use of their Arms, that is to load quick and hit the Mark, and for Military Discipline but this one rule: if they are attacked [by enemies] . . . to rush to all parts from where their fire comes'. The duke of Alva could hardly have put it better.

[2] AGS *E* 571/57. 'Del Duque de Alva sobre lo de flandes' (Sep. 1577).

Figure 2. The Netherlands frontier, *c.* 1600

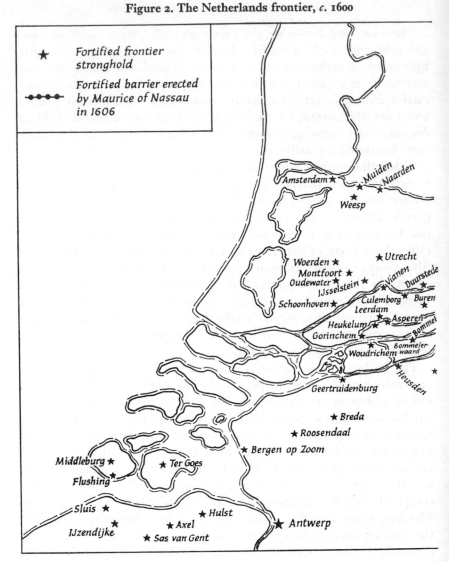

The Dutch made good use of natural geography: their defences were largely clustered along the rivers IJssel, Lek, Linge, Waal and Maas. Between 1590 and 1648 most of the fighting between Spain and the States General centred on the control of these riverside towns, and most of them changed hands at least twice during the course of the war. The strategic importance of the duchy of Cleves–Jülich as a means of side-stepping the 'Great Rivers Barrier' is obvious.

trained force of between 1,000 and 3,000 men could thus be assembled, normally numbering more arquebusiers and musketeers than pike-men. It was known as an *escuadrón*. Such flexibility presented obvious advantages: Walloon musketeers were generally reputed the best marksmen; the Germans were absolutely reliable in adversity; the Spaniards were always acknowledged the bravest and most furious in attack, as well as the most pitiless. A combination of these various skills in a single corps or *escuadrón* produced a fine blend and balance. Above all it produced a suppleness which was ideally suited to the 'irregular' skirmish-and-surprise of the Netherlands wars.[1]

The character of the Low Countries' Wars changed somewhat around 1600. The root cause of the shift lay in the straightening out of the frontier between the two sides. After 1587 the Army of Flanders was diverted from the consolidation and continuation of the reconquest of the 'rebel' provinces first by Philip II's project to invade England (the 'Invincible Armada', 1587–8) and then by the escalating programme of military aid to the French Catholic League (1589–98). Spain's preoccupation with these two enterprises took the pressure off the Dutch Republic. Starting with the surprise of Breda in 1590, the Army of the States methodically reduced all the Spanish outposts north of the Rhine and Maas. Since all Spain's forces were either committed to the French Catholic cause or else locked in mutiny for their wages, no relief army could be spared for the north and the Dutch were able to effect notable conquests with the very small forces at their disposal. The capture of Groningen by Maurice of Nassau in July 1594 completed the process. The frontier was thus dramatically shortened, running from the sea south of Sluis to the neutral duchy of Cleves south-east of Nijmegen (cf. Figure 2).

A further factor in stabilizing the frontier was the defensive construction erected by the Dutch behind the great rivers. In the winter of 1605–6 a chain of 'sconces', blockhouses and redoubts, connected by a continuous earth rampart, was constructed from Zwartsluis on the Zuider Zee to Zwolle and thence along the west bank of the IJssel to Arnhem, on the west bank of the Neder-Rijn to its confluence with the Waal at Schenkenschans and finally along the north bank of the Waal right through to Tiel (cf. Figure 2).[2] This remarkable defence system, which successfully withstood attack in 1606, did not stand alone. The Dutch towns along each of the 'great rivers' (the Maas, Waal, Linge and Lek) were heavily fortified, forming four solid ranks to withstand any invasion. It was not, as so often stated, just the 'great rivers' which constituted the divisive barrier, for the armies of both sides could and did cross them

---

[1] The term *escuadrón* appears prominently in all the Spanish military writers. The usage even passed into the Dutch army, cf. J. W. Wijn, *Het Krijgswezen in den tijd van prins Maurits* (Utrecht, 1934), p. 424. For the exact size and chain of command in the company, *tercio* and regiment cf. Appendix B, pp. 274–7 below.

[2] P. Giustiniano, *Delle Guerre di Fiandra, libri VI* (Antwerp, 1609), pp. 228–9 and figs. 14 and 25, gives a full description, visual and verbal. Cf. also ARA *Staten-Generaal* 4748 for correspondence about the erection of the 'redoubten' as quickly (and as cheaply!) as possible.

with ferries or bridges of boats; it was a combination of geography and Dutch military engineering. The rivers were certainly wide and deep, which had a restrictive effect on military movements; more important, the land surrounding the rivers was thinly populated and often difficult to penetrate. Thick woods alternated with marsh and heathland; there were few villages and the very presence of the 'frontier' along this line after the 1590s tended to depopulate and devastate the area even further, constituting a real no-man's land. In this situation the heavily-fortified river-towns and the rampart barrier after 1606 made the Dutch Republic almost impregnable to attack by land.[1]

Naturally this development 'limited' the extent of the conflict in the Netherlands. Before 1600 no part of the Low Countries was entirely free from the incursions of enemy raiders (the *vrijbuiters* or freebooters), many of them scarcely controlled by any government. The bands of soldiers and irregulars quartered on each town or village (for its defence) would penetrate deep into enemy territory in a sort of *chevauchée*, burning and looting, killing and destroying, amassing booty and prisoners for ransom. The daily organization of the war in this situation devolved upon the local commanders: they organized and planned operations, they sold letters of protection and licences to trade with the enemy, and they raised as much money as they could in ransoms and contributions. The autonomy which a handful of commandants managed to usurp is illustrated by the career of Martin Schenck, a military entrepreneur of ability, who throughout the 1580s transferred his services from Spain to the States and back again with the ease of a shuttlecock until in 1589 he set up on his own. He was reported to be waging:

> Some sort of private war [*une guerre à part*] rather than recognize any master. His soldiers and the costs of his war are paid mostly by the extortions he exacts from the merchants and other ships which have to pass his fortress [Schencken-schans, a fortified spur of land between the Waal and Neder-Rijn]. But he does not omit to undertake various exploits, more to raise some money or to take a good prisoner than for any other reason.[2]

[1] The idea of a 'Great Rivers Barrier', given such wide currency by the works of the late Pieter Geyl simply does not square with the facts. Leaving aside its complete irrelevance for the period before 1585 when the frontier was nowhere near the rivers, the ease with which Spinola and other generals crossed the Rhine and Maas seems to disprove Geyl's claim that *on their own* the rivers presented any insuperable military obstacle to a resolute general (cf. Charles Wilson, *Queen Elizabeth and the Revolt of the Netherlands* (London, 1970), pp. 7–12). The importance of the rivers by themselves was commercial: when the Spaniards advanced to the Rhine it put an end to the riverine trade on which the Dutch depended. Cf. p. 82 n. 2 below for the techniques of getting an army across a river in the sixteenth century.
[2] BNP *Lorraine Ms.* 524/240–1, Gherard Gitinzing to the marquis of Varembon, 28 Apr. 1589.

The independence of Schenck, which only ended with his death in action later the same year, was typical of the condottiere-mentality favoured by the wide diffusion of the war-effort, by the 'floating' frontier, of the first phase of the Eighty Years' War.

The stabilization of the frontier after 1590 stopped all this. With the localization of the conflict, government control over frontier commanders and over other aspects of the war was established for good. Ransoming prisoners was arranged unilaterally in the seventeenth century (the *canje general* – an annual exchange of prisoners of war); the plundering raids of individual garrisons on their own initiative were superseded by a formal system of letters of safeguard and regular protection payments.[1] In time, every military activity came to have its price. In the words of the marquis of Aytona, a disillusioned minister in Brussels in 1630:

> The manner of making war at the present time, and especially the one we are fighting now against the rebels, is reduced to a sort of traffic or commerce, in which he who has most money wins.[2]

The limitation of the area of conflict between the two sides thus resulted in a drastic reduction in the amount of irregular, guerilla action in the Low Countries' Wars. The various local conflicts which had grown up since 1572 over such a wide area were simplified into a single struggle within a confined area. The 'mannerist' style of warfare of the sixteenth century gave way to a more 'baroque' or 'classical' style after 1600. This, of course, did not mean that all fighting ceased. As guerilla activity decreased there was a marked upsurge of actions involving the main field armies of the antagonists. Although the bastion remained impregnable there was an immense improvement in siege techniques. At last the value of artillery was recognized: when the Dutch laid siege to 's Hertogenbosch in 1601 they brought only 22 cannon with them (the siege failed); in 1629 they collected 116. At Grol (Groenlo) in 1595 the Dutch besiegers had only 16 guns, and only 14 in 1597, but in 1627 they had 80.[3] Even so,

---

[1] There is a list of the contributions for safeguards paid by Dutch villages to the archdukes and by the archdukes' villages to the Dutch in 1608 in Wijn, *Krijgswezen*, pp. 524–5. Cf. more lists in ARA *Staten van Holland* 2591 and 2592. By 1659 half a year's contributions from 'Belgian' villages to the French was estimated to be worth about two million florins (AGRB *SEG* 266/92, Caracena to the king, 17 Mar. 1660.) One advantage of purchasing letters of protection was that it served to increase a village's population. A settlement under safeguard attracted an influx of peasants in search of security: letters of safeguard were the peasant's only guarantee that he would be able to harvest his grain or sell his livestock, his only insurance that his property would not be burnt down.

[2] The marquis of Aytona, Spanish ambassador at Brussels, quoted L. P. Gachard, *Les Bibliothèques de Madrid et de l'Escurial : Notices et extraits des Manuscrits qui concernent l'Histoire de Belgique* (Brussels, 1875), p. 487.

[3] J. W. Wijn in *New Cambridge Modern History*, IV (Cambridge, 1970), pp. 222–3.

Plate 1. The new fortifications, Berwick-on-Tweed, 1558–68: *above* aerial view; *below* a bastion with flankers

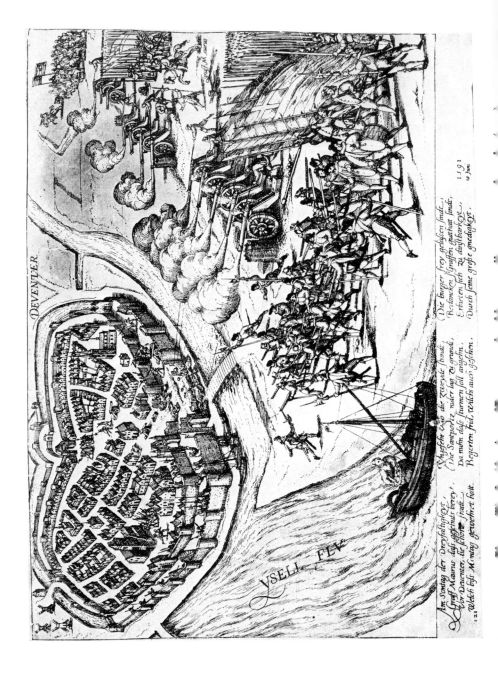

Plate 3. The fortifications of Deventer – the new defences (1648)

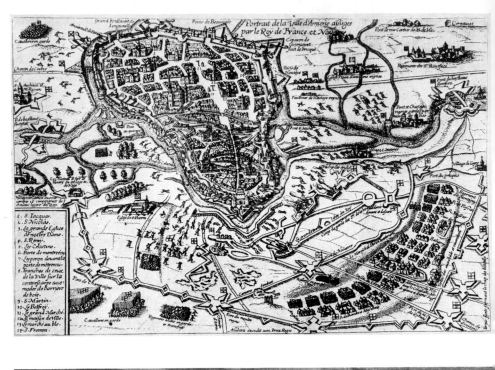

Plate 4. The siege-works of Amiens: *above* in 1597; *below* today (aerial photograph revealing cropmarks) (*Antiquity* 150 (June 1964), Plate 19)

towns under siege continued to fall (if at all) to hunger, not to assault. Complete encirclement of besieged towns was still essential. Siege-works were therefore scientifically improved until they too could resist almost any attack. In the words of one experienced commander: 'No matter what town the enemy wants to besiege, if he is given ten days [to dig in] and decides to defend himself, the town cannot be relieved.'[1] There were very few unsuccessful sieges in the Netherlands wars after 1622.

This development undoubtedly increased the incidence of battles. Since the besiegers felt more confident in the face of an enemy army of relief, a pitched battle was often fought between the relief force and the besiegers. Even Rocroi (1643), one of the more important battles of the war, was fought between the Spanish forces besieging Rocroi and a French army of relief.

Yet even Rocroi did not end the war. After the battle only 2,000 Spanish troops were left together and the Army of Flanders lost most of its papers and a large sum of money, but Spain staggered on and peace was not made with the Dutch until 1648, not with France until 1659. Although defeated in battle, the Army of Flanders still controlled numerous fortified towns, each of which had to be starved into surrender. Warfare thus remained in some parts of Europe what it had been since the advent of the new fortifications: a war of attrition, a stalemate.

> If we put an army of 40,000 men in the field [wrote one disillusioned minister] they bring out as many and more. With that they prevent us from doing anything. If we want to cross a river with all our main army, they cross another with theirs. If we lay siege to one place, they lay siege to another of ours. In this situation, Sir, in order to get anywhere in this war it is necessary to have two armies...[2]

These important changes in the character of the war naturally produced complementary changes in the composition of the armies involved. The increase in formal confrontations made it imperative to overhaul the unit-organization of the forces. Companies were reduced in size and standardized into regiments, the regiments became smaller, more manageable tactical commands. (Cf. Appendix B, pp. 274–7 below.) Even the cavalry companies of the Army of Flanders were grouped into regiments of horse in 1642.[3] The soldiers were now given standard equipment, a uniform, more drill. Each man was expected to be a cog in a vast machine,

---

[1] AGS *E* 2322, unfol., Count Henry van den Berg to the king, 4 Jun. 1629.
[2] BRB *Ms.* 16147–48/86v–88, marquis of Aytona to Olivares, 17 Jun. 1631.
[3] The change, however, was more in response to outside pressure than through internal conviction: regiments of light horse were to be formed 'because they are used today by our enemies, who hold them to be more serviceable'. (AGRB *MD* 3842/33–4, copy of an order of the captain-general, 1 Aug. 1642.)

not an individual of prodigious resourcefulness and valour. Armies became more 'modern'.

Perhaps the verdict on the character of sixteenth-century warfare pronounced by Professor Michael Roberts, by far the most perceptive writer on the subject, is a trifle harsh: 'Strategic thinking withered away; war eternalized itself.'[1] One must not generalize from the conditions of warfare in the Netherlands or in Hungary or Lombardy, the areas where the bastions lay thick, to other theatres with more room for manœuvre. Army commanders had to face facts. If their enemies happened to live in towns defended by bastions, as the Dutch did, the towns had to be taken; the improvements in military architecture after 1520 made the capture of such towns a lengthy business. The two crucial military problems in such situations were first to mobilize enough men to encircle the main enemy towns and second to collect enough money to pay the army until all resistance collapsed. There was simply no way of effecting a quick capture; fighting a battle was often irrelevant. As Montaigne put it with brutal simplicity: 'It isn't a victory unless it ends the war.' Few isolated battles in the sixteenth century did that.

A great deal has been made of the undoubted improvements in drill, discipline, armament and tactics effected by Maurice of Nassau and Gustavus Adolphus of Sweden in the early seventeenth century. Their reforms have even been hailed as a 'military revolution'.[2] Such purely technical improvements, however, could do nothing to overcome either the *trace italienne* or the crippling financial consequences of a war of long sieges. Even Gustavus Adolphus, chief architect of the 'military revolution', proved unable to establish adequate financial support for his great army in Germany. Only five months after the king's death, in February 1633, there was a mutiny in the main army for pay arrears; in May 1633 Chancellor Oxenstierna admitted that the wages of the Army in Germany cost 900,000 *rixdaler* a month, while local receipts (contributions) provided only 200,000.[3] In 1634 the defeat of the Swedes by the Spanish

[1] M. Roberts, 'Gustav Adolf and the Art of War', in *Essays in Swedish History* (London, 1967), p. 60.
[2] The reforms of Maurice, and the parallel but more thorough reforms of Gustavus Adolphus of Sweden receive masterly treatment from Professor Roberts in his essays 'The Military Revolution' and 'Gustav Adolf and the Art of War', in Roberts, *ibid.*
[3] *Rikskanslaren Axel Oxenstiernas skrifter och Brevväxling*, VIII, pp. 306–7 and 682–5, memorial of Oxenstierna to the Riksråd in Stockholm. (Since I do not read Swedish I am grateful to Mrs Sissel Collis for help with the *Brevväxling*.) The situation of the Swedish army in Germany after 1632 resembled that of the Army of Flanders in 1573–6 in a number of ways: both armies,

tercios at Nördlingen demonstrated that even the new tactical organization was not proof against bad generalship and a resolute enemy, while in 1635 the entire Swedish army mutinied again for its pay. The exponents of the 'military revolution' stood in as great a need of money as any other army.

The predicament of the Swedish army in Germany and of the Spanish Army of Flanders was basically the same. Military intervention overseas on such a scale was hampered at every turn by two overriding problems in the early modern period: the distances involved and the cost. The delays and difficulties caused by distance (with which the first part of this study is concerned) complicated the formation of all armies for foreign service – how to assemble an army capable of victory, how to reinforce it, how to control the high command and direct the campaigns of an army hundreds of miles away across hostile territory. Yet these obstacles paled before the equally pressing need to provide the troops abroad with all the money and munitions they required. Failure to supply the soldiers with their food and at least some of their pay inevitably led to military collapse: either mutiny or mass desertion. Adequate financial support, moreover, had to be provided not just for one campaign or two but for ten, even twenty, until all enemy strongholds had fallen or until financial exhaustion forced a compromise peace. This is the theme of the second part of this book. Most wars in the century 1550–1650 were in fact decided by the relative financial strength (or weakness) of the various antagonists: it was very often a case of 'he who has most money wins', as the marquis of Aytona put it. In wars where the resources of the two sides were fairly equal, and the combatants obstinate, it might even take eighty years for a victor to emerge...

having won great victories, mutinied for their pay-arrears and by so doing alienated many neutrals or former supporters; when peace was eventually discussed (1576–7 in the Netherlands, 1644–8 in Germany) it was the need to pay the veterans their due which constituted the major obstacle to a settlement. The governments which controlled the armies were caught in the classic dilemma of imperialism: they could not win a peace through victory, and they were too deeply committed to their cause to cut their losses and simply evacuate.

Part I

Assembling an army:
the problem of distance

One cannot doubt that the Spaniards aspire to universal domination, and that the sole obstacles which they have encountered up
to the present are the distance between their dominions and their
shortage of men.

> Cardinal Richelieu to Louis XIII, May 1624, in G.
> Hanotaux, *Histoire du Cardinal de Richelieu* (Paris, n.d.),
> III, p. 5

To understand the importance of distance is to see in a new light
the problems of governing an empire in the sixteenth century.
Above all, the immense Spanish empire...

> F. Braudel, *La Méditerranée* (2nd ed., Paris, 1966),
> p. 341

CHAPTER 1

MOBILIZATION

The rapid expansion of the scale of military operations in Europe after 1530, transforming the size and composition of armies, compelled all governments involved in war to recruit roughly twice as many men as before. Governments had to experiment with new methods and in new areas if they were to mobilize effectively and rapidly.

One obvious response to the problem was to keep a certain nucleus of trained, equipped troops in permanent readiness, to maintain a standing army. Many states in the sixteenth century, even Tudor England, adopted this expedient and paid a number of companies to garrison important frontier strongholds; some went further and retained a corps of elite troops, a sort of Praetorian Guard, at the centre. In the Habsburg Netherlands 3,200 men served permanently in the fortresses along the French frontier, supported by fifteen *bandes d'ordonnance* (companies of heavy cavalry, all knights and nobles, with foot-soldiers and pages attached. These *bandes* were of doubtful military value in the later sixteenth century, but they provided a little outdoor relief and some harmless and prestigious employment for the Netherlands nobility and for that reason they survived). The ordinary garrisons and the *bandes* could hardly be said to constitute an effective standing army: their numbers were too few, their equipment was outdated, and the taxes allocated for their upkeep were inadequate. One of the duke of Alva's first priorities when he arrived in the Low Countries was to remedy these deficiencies. In 1569 he hectored and threatened until the Netherlands Estates voted a permanent revenue of two million florins to support a standing army of 13,000 men: the *bandes* and the *garnisons ordinaires*, plus 4,000 Spaniards in garrison, 4,000 more Spaniards as a central reserve, and 500 light horse.[1]

With the exception of 1577, when the Army of Flanders was totally demobilized, there was always a permanent corps of between thirteen and fifteen thousand soldiers serving in the Spanish Netherlands, even during the Twelve Years' Truce (1609–21) and after the Peace of the

[1] AA 165/44, 'Tanteo del gasto ordinario para el entretenimiento destos estados de Flandes.'

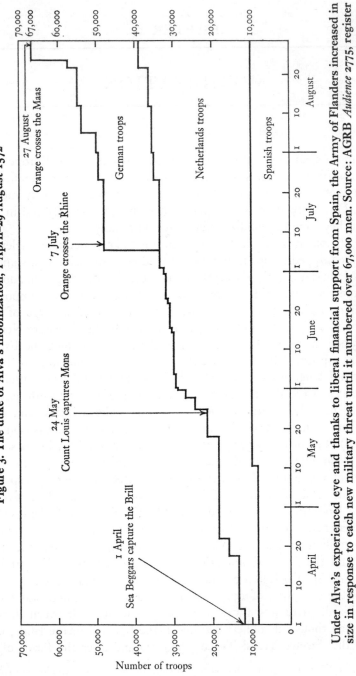

Figure 3. The duke of Alva's mobilization, 1 April–29 August 1572

Under Alva's experienced eye and thanks to liberal financial support from Spain, the Army of Flanders increased in size in response to each new military threat until it numbered over 67,000 men. Source: AGRB *Audience 2775*. register of patents despatched in 1572.

Pyrenees (1659). Of course this was only a peacetime force. Although it was the largest standing army of its day, these permanent units only served as a nucleus; they were quite inadequate if the Netherlands became involved in open war. For that, large numbers of troops were required urgently.

Figure 3 clearly shows the mobilization procedure of the Army of Flanders in action. Between 1 April and 31 August 1572 the duke of Alva was able to increase the forces at his command from the permanent defence corps of 13,000 men to a full war-time establishment of 67,000: in response to each new crisis of that fateful year – the capture of the Brill, the siege of Mons, the invasions of Genlis and Orange – new units were called up. About 65,000 men remained the average nominal strength of the Army of Flanders for most of the Eighty Years' War, although there were further increases to bring Spain's military strength in the Netherlands up to about 85,000 men when a second front was required: against Count Louis of Nassau in 1574, in preparation for the Invincible Armada (1587–8) and during hostilities with France (1589–98 and after 1635).

Spain never seemed more magnificent or more powerful than at those moments when, at her command, tens of thousands of men rallied to the standard of St Andrew, Burgandy's device. Alva's achievement in 1572 and others like it aroused the fear and admiration of contemporaries. How was it done?

*   *   *

The total number of troops who could be mobilized at any one time, and the duration of the procedure, was controlled by three variable factors: the size of the area in which recruiting was permitted, the actual availability of men within those areas, and the minimum age and condition of recruit which could be accepted. Perhaps the most important variable was the first. In the sixteenth century it was common for governments to recruit some of their soldiers abroad, either because the foreign troops were better trained, or because they were more reliable, or perhaps just to prevent a rival government from making use of them.[1] As Sir George Clark has observed: 'The map of the sources of man-power in a war did not normally coincide at all closely with a map of the political components

---

[1] Cf. the epigram of the maréchal de Saxe in 1748: 'A German in the army serves us as three soldiers: he spares France one, he deprives our enemy of one and he serves us as one.' (Quoted by A. Corvisier, *L'Armée française de la fin du XVIIe siècle au ministère de Choiseul*, 1 (Paris, 1964), p. 260.)

Figure 4. The size and composition of the Army of Flanders, 1567–1665

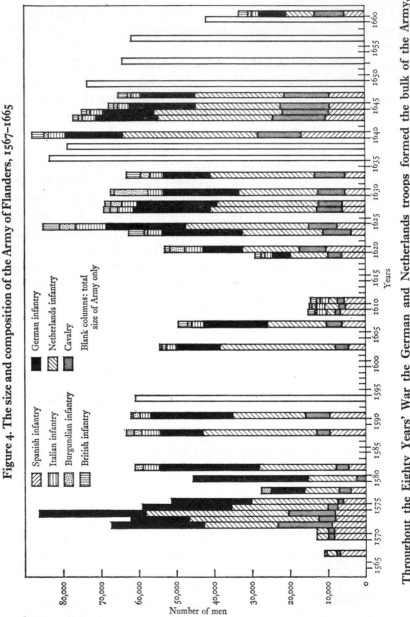

Legend:
- Spanish infantry
- Italian infantry
- Burgundian infantry
- British infantry
- German infantry
- Netherlands infantry
- Cavalry
- Blank columns: total size of Army only

Number of men

Years

Throughout the Eighty Years' War the German and Netherlands troops formed the bulk of the Army, although the Italian, Burgundian and British infantry played a prominent role between 1582 and 1640. The number of cavalry units was low between 1574 and 1635 (the outbreak of war with France). Source: Appendix A.

28

of the two sides.'[1] Thus the Tudors employed Albanian cavalry and a regiment of Spanish infantry against the Scots between 1544 and 1551, while as much as 20 per cent of the French armies of the period consisted of Swiss and German troops. In both cases, the foreign troops tended to form the elite, serving in the forefront of all action 'as those whom one trusts more than anyone and without whom we would not have the courage to undertake the least thing'.[2] The Habsburg armies depended yet more on foreign troops; the Army of Flanders, for example, included the troops of no less than six different 'nations'. As Figure 4 shows, units from Spain, Italy, Burgundy, Germany and the British Isles served by the side of the troops raised locally, the Walloons. To reduce friction the troops were kept as separate administrative units: only Spaniards could serve in or command Spanish contingents and so on (this rule even required that Englishmen could not command Scottish or Irish units and forbade Milanese or Roman troops to serve in contingents from Naples).[3] However, the foreign troops in the Army of Flanders were seldom mere mercenaries like the Tudors' Spanish auxiliaries or the Valois' Swiss. The vast majority were the subjects as well as the soldiers of the king of Spain. The Spanish, Burgundian and Netherlands troops, also the Italian troops raised in Spanish Lombardy, Naples or Sicily, were all serving their own sovereign prince. The Germans were carefully recruited from the patrimonial estates of the Habsburg family, Austria, the Tyrol and Alsace, in the hope of assuring their political and religious conformity. Even the British troops before 1605 were either the traitors who betrayed the Dutch towns in their keeping to Spain, or else Catholic recusants who sought an asylum from persecution; in both cases they were deeply bound to the king of Spain and his cause. Before the 1640s few were simply mercenaries.

The attraction to all governments of recruiting men who would 'serve not only as soldiers but also as vassals wherever they are commanded, not where they choose', is obvious.[4] Such troops were clearly more reliable,

---

[1] G. N. Clark, *War and Society in the Seventeenth Century* (Cambridge, 1958), p. 61. For a 'manpower map' of the Army of Flanders cf. Figure 6.

[2] Sr de Fourquevaux, *Instructions sur le Faict de la Guerre* (1548), ed. G. Dickinson (London, 1954), f. 6.

[3] Most cases of troops serving in the wrong 'nation' concerned the Spanish units, because they were the best paid (cf. Appendix B, p. 277). In 1613, for example, it was discovered that 7 per cent of the Spanish infantry (369 men) and 26 per cent of the Spanish light cavalry (458 men) were not Spaniards at all but Walloons. The Council of State in Madrid ordered them to be discharged forthwith. (AGS E 2027, unfol., *consulta* of the Council of State, 17 Jan. 1613.)

[4] Quoted from AGS E 1258/95, military ordinance of the Spanish governor of Lombardy, 1 Jun. 1583. The high command frequently appealed to this double obligation as vassals and soldiers in time of crisis; cf. p. 178 below.

more devoted, more involved. The fact that the army thus produced was a jumble of different nationalities, none of them at home in the Netherlands, was no disadvantage; indeed it was a strength. Experience had shown that the military effectiveness of most troops increased in direct proportion to the distance of the theatre of operations from their homeland. Even the Spanish infantry, which was lauded excessively when it served in Italy or the Netherlands, was accounted an indifferent fighting force on its home ground. As early as 1521 the Spanish regency government demanded German troops to defend the frontier with France because 'our infantry does not perform as well in its native country as abroad or in Italy'; the same lament was heard in the war of Granada: 'One cannot expect the same from new recruits in their own country as from veterans abroad.'[1]

The great divide between the various 'nations' of a Habsburg Army came between the 'native' troops, and the rest. No one placed a high military value on the soldiers recruited locally, since desertion was too easy and the risk of defection greater. 'The principal strength of this Army is the foreign troops', wrote the commander-in-chief of the Army of Flanders in 1595. 'At the moment no war can be fought in these provinces except with the foreign "nations", because the local troops disintegrate at once', echoed his successor in 1631.[2] The Walloons were despised in the Netherlands but they were highly prized when they went to serve in Italy or Spain. In 1630 the marquis of Aytona wrote to the king:

> If there should be war in Italy, it would be better to send Walloons there and bring Italians here [to the Netherlands], because the troops native to the country where the war is being fought disband very rapidly and *there is no surer strength than that of foreign soldiers.*[3]

In 1631 the king asked for some Walloon troops to serve in Spain, the first of a long series of similar demands.[4] After the outbreak of war with France in 1635 German and Irish as well as Walloon troops were shipped

---

[1] AGS *E* 8/132, Licenciado Vargas to Charles V, 9 Sep. 1521; IVdeDJ 46/50, Don Luis de Requesens to Cardinal Espinosa, copy, 5 Feb. 1570. The duke of Alva, whose contempt for his men was unlimited, lamented that the Spaniards 'take such a long time to reach military proficiency, especially in peace-time'. (KB's Gravenhage, *Hs* 78 E. 9, f. 17v–23v, Memorial of 1560.)

[2] AGS *E* 609/88, Instruction of the Archduke Ernest to Don Diego Pimentel, envoy to the king, 30 Jan. 1595; BRB *Ms.* 16149/53v–4v, Marquis of Aytona to the king, 2 Apr. 1631, copy.

[3] BRB *Ms.* 16149/41v–45, Aytona to the king, 19 Dec. 1630.

[4] AGRB *SEG* 204/167, Philip IV to the Infanta Isabella, 2 Nov. 1631, the first request. For details on some later transfers of Walloons and Germans to Spain, cf. AHN *E libros* 963, 966 and 973, the correspondence of Olivares and Haro with Don Miguel de Salamanca, the minister in the Low Countries responsible for the levies, 1638–49.

to Spain, while Spaniards and a few Italians were sent by sea to the Army of Flanders. In both theatres the foreign troops served as the elite force; Spain had created a system of military expatriation.

In the Army of Flanders, the five foreign 'nations' were by no means regarded as equal. The German troops were rated only slightly higher than Walloons. The duke of Alva was scathing about their military usefulness even before he left for the Low Countries in 1567. The French ambassador reported:

> I know from the duke of Alva's own lips that he does not place any trust in the said Germans if it should come to a fight with the heretics, because he told me that if that came about he would do as he had done in the Schmalkaldic war: carry out the 'actions' with the Spaniards and use the Germans...merely for display and numbers [*pour parade et pour nombre*].

The war against the German Protestants in 1546–7 had certainly been a sobering experience for Alva; he had placed his trust in the German troops only to find that they were quite unreliable because 'many of them were the relatives, servants, neighbours and friends of his enemies'. The troubles of the Netherlands in 1566–7 seemed uncannily like those of Germany twenty years before, and Alva was not the man to make the same mistake twice. The Germans were relegated to ancillary duties in the Army.[1]

Actually, the German troops proved loyal, stubborn, stoic fighters (they did not desert the king even in 1576–7) but their long and faithful service, often unpaid, never succeeded in gaining the complete confidence of the Spanish high command. Perhaps the government was unnerved by the presence of equally large German contingents in the armies of their enemies, the French and the Dutch.

The British and Burgundian troops were rated more highly in the Army, although again the presence of British troops in the Army of the States was worrying (and the British had already betrayed the Dutch), but neither 'nation' equalled the favoured position occupied by the Italians. Like the Germans, the first Italian units to serve in the Army of Flanders were the subject of misgivings. In fact they were only used because immediately after the revolution of 1576 there were not enough Walloons available.

> Up to now [wrote Philip II] it has not seemed that they [the Italians] were suitable for those provinces, because they are disorderly and on a long march would disintegrate unless great care was lavished upon them. But seeing that the Walloons cannot now be trusted as they used to be, and in order that there should

---

[1] C. Douais, *Dépêches de Monsieur de Fourquevaux*, I (Paris, 1896), pp. 237–9, Fourquevaux to Charles IX, 17 Jul. 1567. The incident of 1547 is quoted from a contemporary letter by E. S. Arnoldsson, *La Leyenda Negra* (Göteborg, 1960), p. 196 (= note 4 to chapter 4.)

be troops available to guard the reconquered towns without tying down the Spaniards (who are the men who have to fight the campaign)...they may prove more valuable than the soldiers of any other nation except the Spaniards.

The king's expectations were fully realized. Gradually the Italian troops revealed themselves to be wholly reliable and courageous warriors. Within ten years they were indeed acknowledged to be the most valuable troops in the Army after the Spaniards.[1]

The Spanish troops, and particularly the Spanish infantry, occupied a unique position, however. They were always referred to in the most glowing eulogies – 'the sinews of the army', 'the sole foundation of the Monarchy', 'the defence of Christendom' and so on – and they were always accorded the highest pay, the best living conditions, and the richest rewards.[2] There was, of course, an element of chauvinism in all this (praise of another nation has never come easily to Spanish lips) but it was indeed true that the Spanish *tercios* were the best troops by far in the Army of Flanders. Their excellence derived from the fact that they were serving 700 miles from home and that they were already fully-trained soldiers, for the most part, before they came. In the words of the prince of Parma, they were 'veteran troops, well-disciplined, born to suffer and to fight against the Netherlanders'. This combination of qualities explains the unstinted praise of the generals and the extraordinary and boundless hatred of the Low Countries for the Spanish *tercios*.[3]

Some of the Spaniards sent to the Netherlands were in fact veterans discharged from a campaign elsewhere. The *tercios* who arrived in 1584 and 1585, for example, had conquered Portugal and the Azores (1580–3); the *tercio* of Don Agustin Mexía which arrived in 1593 came direct from the chastisement of Aragon after the *alteración* of 1591–2. But the majority of the Spanish troops sent to the Low Countries came from Italy. After 1535 a standing army of about 3,000 Spanish foot and 500 light horse was maintained by Spain in each of her three Italian dominions: Lombardy, Sicily and Naples. This permanent Spanish presence in Italy was intended to guarantee the government against rebellion and protect the peninsula

[1] AGS *E* 571/113, Philip II to Don John of Austria, 11 Sep. 1577.
[2] For a random sample of the eulogies (and examples could be multiplied almost indefinitely) cf. three letters written by the Archduke Albert to the king in 1596: AGS *E* 611/61–3, 1 May 1596 ('Infantería española que es la essencia y nervio principal de esta guerra'); *ibid.*, f. 96, 9 Jun. 1596 ('El nervio principal destas fuerzas es la infantería española'); and f. 171, 4 Oct. 1596 ('La infantería española, que es el nerbio principal del ejército'). Cf. also the unequivocal and prophetic opinion of the Spanish Council of State: 'Experience has shown that Spanish troops are the real sinews of the army, without whom no successful action has taken place in the past *and none will take place in the future*' (*AHE* III, p. 229, *consulta* of 28 Sep. 1602).
[3] AGS *E* 584/28, Parma to the king, 8 Feb. 1581 ('La infantería española...milicia vieja, disciplinada, hecha a padescer y a pelear con la gente de aquí').

against any attack, whether by the French or by the Turk. For most of the century after 1535 Italy was at peace; the Spanish garrisons had only the *razzia* warfare against the pirates of the Barbary coast to occupy them for most of the time. Such a situation was ideal for training troops. Military service in Italy was therefore popular with the soldiers and valued by the government; for the one it represented the good life with women, wine, wages and booty, for the other it provided an assurance of Spain's continuing domination of Italy.[1]

The Spanish garrisons in Italy, the *presidios* as they were known, also served another politico-military role. The reserve of trained soldiers was too valuable to leave idle in time of war; when the Turkish fleet came west, when the French invaded Italy, when Spain intervened in the empire, the Spaniards from the *presidios* were invariably in the forefront. These trained troops formed the strike-force of the Spanish Monarchy. Above all, the *presidios* provided troops for the Army of Flanders after 1567, and the places they vacated were taken by new recruits (the *bisoños*) from Spain. The system worked smoothly because service in Italy was so popular: levies for Italy were always successful. After they had been trained to obey and were accustomed to military life, the trained men could be safely transferred to a less attractive theatre of operations. The procedure was correctly described and justly praised by an English soldier with experience of service in the Army of Flanders, Sir Roger Williams:

> Their order is, where the Warres are present, to supplie their Regiments being in Action, with the Garrisons out of his dominions and Provinces; before they dislodge, *besonios* supply their places, raw men, as we tearme them. By these meanes he [Philip II] traines his *besonios* and furniseth his Armies with trained Souldiers.[2]

In 1632, the system noted by Williams was given the force of law by the military ordinances of Philip IV; official recognition was given to the fact that the *presidios* of Italy were the seminary in which the invincible Spanish *tercios* were made.[3]

[1] Charles V's 'Instruction' to his son Philip in January 1548 was explicit and emphatic concerning the importance of the Spanish garrisons in Italy. 'Even if you are compelled to look where you can reduce expenditure, should you be in debt and your estates exhausted, you must not for that reason cease to maintain some Spanish troops in Italy at all times... because it will be the true restraint which will stop all fresh outbreaks of war and prevent attempts to recover territory.' (C. Weiss, *Papiers d'Etat du Cardinal de Granvelle*, III (Paris, 1842), p. 290.) For the troops' addiction to the good life of Italy, particularly in Naples, cf. p. 213 below.
[2] Roger Williams, *A Briefe Discourse of Warre* (London, 1590), p. 12.
[3] AM Besançon, *Ms. Chifflet* 63/6v, part of the *Ordenanzas Militares* of 28 Jun. 1632. The duke of Alva himself initiated the system. He took 8,652 Spanish infantrymen with him to the Netherlands in 1567, most of them from the garrisons of Spanish Italy, and he brought with him from Spain 7,614 Spanish recruits, most of whom went into the places vacated by the veterans.

It was not always possible to send troops from Italy, however. Sometimes none could be spared from the defence of the peninsula or of the Mediterranean; instead raw recruits had to be sent. The duke of Alva never ceased to complain about the poor quality of the Spanish *bisoños* who were sent to him in 1568 and 1572.

> New recruits fare very badly in this country [he announced to the king]. Even though I have cherished the companies of the twelve captains who were sent in 1568 and kept them well in reserve, up to now I have been unable to derive any profit from them; and [he continued sourly] we cannot ever expect anything from those brought by the duke of Medina Celi.

He returned to the same theme only a fortnight later:

> In the present state of affairs here, I cannot make any use of inexperienced or exhausted [*roto*] Spanish troops because they have to be sent immediately into the fighting (and for the past ten months not a day has passed without action) and men like these are no use unless they are billeted and well cared for, at least for a year or two.

The duke was right: it saved lives and money if recruits raised abroad were first sent to serve in a garrison for a few years. There they could familiarize themselves with military life and learn obedience away from the firing line.[1] Attempts were made from time to time to apply this precaution to other nations in the Army. The 3,200 Walloons who had manned the fortresses of the south Netherlands for years were called out in 1572 to join the field army, new recruits taking their places in the garrisons.[2] In 1593 the count of Fuentes, commander-in-chief in the Low Countries, proposed that the king should send a thousand Spanish recruits to the Netherlands by sea each winter; the new men could go straight into garrison duty, freeing the more experienced troops there for the 'actions' of the war.[3]

This proposal was a good one, but the organizational effort involved proved too great. In particular it was impossible to move troops out of a garrison into the field without paying them, and in wartime the treasury could rarely mobilize enough money to pay the arrears of large bodies of troops. On the whole, to its great regret, the high command was obliged to let sleeping dogs lie: troops in garrisons normally stayed put, troops in

---

[1] *Epistolario*, III, pp. 289–91, Alva to the king, 12 Feb. 1573 (N.B. that the printed version, like the original decoded letter – AGS E 556/75 – gives '1548', which is clearly a mistake, probably in the decipherment, for 1568); *Epistolario*, III, pp. 294–7, Alva to the king, 24 Feb. 1573.
[2] AGRB *Audience* 1690/1, calculation of 16 April 1568: 'L'intention du duc [of Alva] semble estre que l'on lève de nouveau aultant de gens, que portant les vieulx ordinaires que sont de 3200 testes, comme dict est, pour au besoing pouvoir tirer les vieulx et laisser en leurs lieux les nouveaulx.'
[3] AGS E 604/124, Fuentes to the king, 6 Jul. 1593.

the field were often raised specially for each new campaign. By the 1630s each March and April saw a massive recruiting drive to raise Germans, Walloons and British troops to form new units or to reinforce the old, and most of the new levies went straight into the field army. Few of them were left in the autumn.

In the early modern period, a government could employ three different methods to recruit its armies: commission, compulsion or contract. Recruiting by commission was superbly suited to the needs of the early modern state. All power remained in royal hands, vested in the Council of War in Spain and in the captain- and governor-general in the Low Countries.[1] The central authority decided who should receive a commission (and issued the patent), scheduled the areas in which recruiting might take place, the number of men to be raised, the time which might be taken and the destination to which the troops were to march. Under the commission system, the principal recruiting officer was always the captain and the principal unit the company. The regimental cadres were fixed arbitrarily by the crown: the king himself named the captains, the colonel and all other staff officers.

Each captain, armed with a royal patent, first named his junior officers (cf. Appendix B, p. 274 below) and ordered colours (a *bandera*) to be made for the company.[2] Then with colours, a drummer and his corporals (*cabos de escuadra*) he would visit the various towns and villages specified in his patent. These normally bore some relation to the destination of the troops. In Spain, for example, if the men were bound for service in Italy, recruiting often took place in eastern Castile and the crown of Aragon; if the men were to sail to the Netherlands, most recruits were raised in Old Castile and the Cantabrian provinces, near the ports of embarkation; for the Indies, recruiting tended to be concentrated in Andalusia, La Mancha,

---

[1] Cf. AGS *GA* 80/145, *consulta* of the Council of War, 28 Feb. 1575: 'en estos reynos nunca se suele hazer gente sin noticia del Consejo de Guerra y por aquel'. In the Low Countries there was a division of labour on linguistic grounds. The French- and Flemish-speaking troops took their orders from the *audiencier* (First Secretary of State), the German troops from the German Secretary of State, the Spanish and Italian troops from the Spanish Secretary (*secretario de estado y guerra*). This division did not imply any dilution of powers.

[2] For two regiments of German infantry raised in 1575 to serve with Don John of Austria 'His Majesty will provide the *banderas* at his cost...in yellow, blue and white, which are the colours of Don John' (AGS *E* 1068/42, Order of the duke of Sessa, 3 Mar. 1575). The *banderas* of the Army of Flanders normally included red – Spain's colour – and often a red St Andrew's cross, the device of Burgundy. Cf. the colours illustrated in the beautiful volume of miniatures, BRB *Ms.* 15,662, 'Costumes des troupes pendant la Revolution belgique...1580–1620' by Willem de Gortter, poet of Malines.

Figure 5. The age of troops in the Army of Flanders

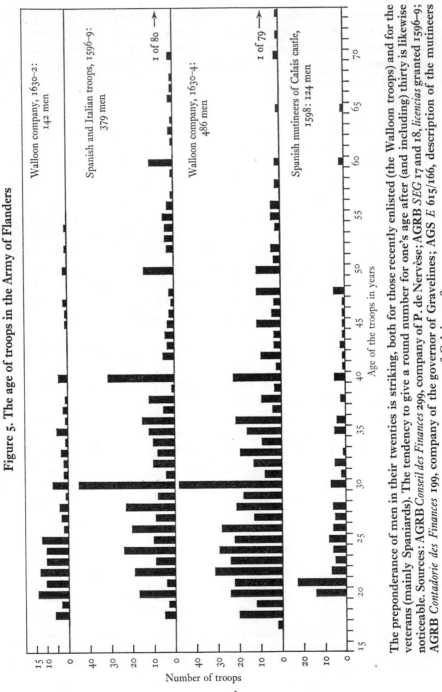

The preponderance of men in their twenties is striking, both for those recently enlisted (the Walloon troops) and for the veterans (mainly Spaniards). The tendency to give a round number for one's age after (and including) thirty is likewise noticeable. Sources: AGRB *Conseil des Finances* 299, company of P. de Nervèse; AGRB *SEG* 17 and 18, *licencias* granted 1596–9; AGRB *Contadorie des Finances* 199, company of the governor of Gravelines; AGS *E* 615/166, description of the mutineers of Calais, 1598.

36

Estremadura and New Castille.[1] Upon arrival in the specified areas, the captain would present his patent to the local magistrates and demand their assistance in his levy. They would be obliged to allocate buildings for the captain to shelter (and if necessary lock up) his men until his quota was filled. Normally an inn or an empty house was offered for shelter, and there the captain set up his colours while his drummer beat a tattoo. From those who came to volunteer their services, the captain chose men who were able-bodied, over 16 and under 50, single and sane.[2] Figure 5 shows that the majority of the troops, not surprisingly, were between 20 and 40 years old, the largest age-group being men in their twenties. The names of the recruits were entered on the company's list (they 'enlisted') and they received a cash payment, free shelter and daily bread, and perhaps a suit of clothes. Naturally, the inducements offered at enlistment varied with the availability of manpower. If recruits were plentiful, as in a year of poor harvest or low wages, men would join up anyway; at other times a *douceur* of between one and three *escudos* was required. In no circumstances, however, was the captain legally entitled to use force to procure recruits. The system was, in the sixteenth century at least, entirely voluntary.

All captains had to present their levies within a few weeks to a special muster-master appointed by the king. The time allowed for a levy rarely exceeded six weeks and it was considered unwise for a captain to remain more than twenty days in one place, because by then the recruits began to desert faster than new men could be persuaded to join.[3] The muster-master examined the company's list, scrutinized every name and every man to ensure that the recruit was really a soldier and not a page or a suborned peasant, and finally signed a declaration at the end of the list certifying the number of men present. Next the Articles of War were read out to the troops, stating the penalties which would attend their misconduct; the men were required to raise their right hands and swear to accept these ordinances, the most important of which concerned the

---

[1] Cf. the remarks and documentary evidence in I. A. A. Thompson, 'War and Administrative Devolution: the Military Government of Spain in the Reign of Philip II' (Cambridge Univ. Ph.D. thesis, 1965), pp. 183–5. For the geography of English recruiting at the same time, cf. C. G. Cruickshank, *Elizabeth's Army* (2nd ed., Oxford, 1966), pp. 63 and 290–1.

[2] As late as 1647, at least in Castile, the government tried to protect married men from the recruiting captains. Attention was to be paid that recruits 'no sean cassados ni hijos solos que hagan falta a sus padres ni a los lugares' (AGS *GA* 1616, unfol., *consulta* of the Council of War, 2 Oct. 1647).

[3] 'As Your Majesty knows, in Spain in the twenty days following the arrival of a captain in his recruiting area with his Paymaster, he will raise his men; and if he stays longer he will ruin the country and lose his men so that not a half will leave.' (AGS *GA* 80/286, *consulta* of the Council of War, 11 Dec. 1575.)

soldier's duty to carry out every order he received without question, not to leave the service until he was formally discharged, and not to mutiny for his wages. By this act the recruits formally entered the service of the state which recruited them, and in token thereof they received their first month's pay. These wages, like later payments, were normally made over to the captain on the basis of the number of men present, and he deducted any advances already made before he gave each man his due. After this the company was guided by more royal commissioners to the theatre of operations or to a port of embarkation.

The success of this system of recruiting, which combined a maximum of state control with a minimum of compulsion, depended on the number of men required at one time. Provided the state's demands did not exceed the reserves of manpower available, the voluntary system seems to have served most governments admirably. However, no state could issue commissions to recruit troops outside its territorial boundaries – that would infringe the sovereignty of another prince. In the empire, in the British Isles or in non-Spanish Italy the Army of Flanders had to raise its troops through contractors. The political implications of raising soldiers for a foreign power were less obvious if a neutral or native agency acted as intermediary, as entrepreneur.

It was extremely easy for a state to engage the services of a military contractor or entrepreneur. A simple agreement, the *Bestallung* or *Accord*, bound the government to pay a certain sum of money to the contractor at once with the promise of regular fixed wages thereafter; in return the contractor undertook to present a given number of men within a certain time at an agreed place. The contractor's chief asset was speed: because he kept a skeleton force of his best men permanently on call, ready to raise the rest when need occurred, he could have a whole regiment ready within three or four weeks. Speed was further increased when the contractor had been fighting in the recent past. For instance, the duke of Alva's mobilization in 1568 against William of Orange's invasion was facilitated by the availability of the German troops raised to fight the iconoclasts in 1566 and only disbanded at the end of 1567. The contractor, finally, not only raised his regiment or company, he also acted as its commander and he named its officers.

In most cases the *Bestallung* was by no means the first contact between a military entrepreneur and a government. Contractors who provided troops in a war were often rewarded with a state pension after demobilization which was taken, at least by the government, to mean that the contractor would raise troops again whenever need arose. It was in this belief that Philip II distributed pensions to German colonels worth some 50,000 florins every year during the 1560s.[1] Some colonels, of course, took a less restrictive view of their pensions, accepting money indiscriminately from various governments in the hope that they would not be forced to fight for one against the other. In 1572, for example, Duke Adolph of Holstein, who had long been a pensioner of Philip II, obeyed the summons to raise a regiment of heavy cavalry for service in the Low Countries. He took an inordinate amount of time to present his men for muster, but they arrived at length and thus Spain was satisfied. Elizabeth of England, however, felt cheated. Duke Adolph had also accepted pensions from her and his participation in the duke of Alva's army was the last thing she wanted.[2] It was to avoid disappointments like this at the critical moment that most governments, when they had the slightest reason to suspect that they might become involved in war, paid their military pensioners a further sum known as *wartegeld* (waiting money). This was intended to allow the contractor to prepare his men and equipment and to hold them in readiness for any emergency. *Wartegeld* was expensive, but it still came to less than half the cost of full mobilization and it provided a sure reserve of manpower: troops held in *wartegeld* could not take service with any other prince. Quite often troops were kept in readiness for several months in this way but were never actually mobilized.

For most of the sixteenth century, when manpower was plentiful, it seems that the contractor raised his men in little less time and at little more expense than the commissioned captain. The normal recruiting period for both was about twenty days. The two methods were therefore used according to the dictates of political geography: recruiting by commission on the government's own territory, recruiting by contract elsewhere.

Such was the fully-fledged mobilization system of the Spanish Habsburgs. The combination of six 'nations', some recruited both through commissioned captains, others through contractors, made possible Alva's rapid mobilization of 1572 and permitted him and his successors to maintain the Army of Flanders at the level they chose with relatively little effort.

It is something of a problem to know where these recruits were raised. Certainly the king could only raise troops on crown land: ecclesiastical

---

[1] AM Besançon, *Ms. Granvelle* 58/134–6, 'Liste des pensionnaires allemans de Sa Majesté Catholique' (*c.* 1564). Almost every pensioner was a military entrepreneur and the total was 51,345 florins.

[2] G. Groen Van Prinsterer, *Archives ou Correspondance inédite de la Maison d'Orange-Nassau*, 1ère série (Leiden, 1836), III, p. 492.

and seigneurial estates were exempt. Within this restriction it seems that the main recruiting effort was concentrated on the towns, and in Castile upon those towns where a *corregidor* (chief magistrate appointed by the king) could support the levy. Although literary tradition in Spain and elsewhere insists that all recruits were 'up from the country', the documentary evidence suggests that the recruiting captain based his activity, and hoped to find most of his men, in the large towns. Of course any country people who wanted to enlist would hear of the levy from local merchants or from the visit of a corporal to their village (if it belonged to the king), and they could easily go to the town to join up and receive their enlistment money. We can be more certain that, whether from town or country, the majority of the recruits were poor, like the volunteer for Italy who sang as he met Don Quixote:

> I was driven to the wars by my necessity;
> If I had money truly I would never go.[1]

Not all recruits were destitute or base-born, however. The Army of Flanders, especially in the sixteenth century, needed quality as well as quantity; men who excelled in single combat, in the 'actions' of the war, were required as well as cannon-fodder for the great battles. Every captain therefore tried to enlist a number of gentlemen (*particulares*) to serve as common soldiers in his company, offering a bonus-pay (*ventaja*) to every gentleman who agreed to do so. Some of these volunteers would be the relatives of the captain, others would no doubt be poor gentry unable to gain a living in other ways (Spanish gentlemen were not supposed to demean themselves by manual labour or commercial transactions), others still would be aspiring noblemen who began their military service in the ranks and hoped before long to rise to a position of command.

Most army commanders set the highest value upon these gentleman-rankers. The duke of Alva, for example, was overjoyed to find that a large

---

[1] Cervantes, *Don Quixote*, II, xxiv:
> 'A la guerra me lleva, ni necesidad;
> Si tuviera dineros, no fuera en verdad.'

I have to admit that I have found no evidence which establishes beyond all doubt that the soldiers of Spain's armies were recruited more from the town than the country. In the few surviving muster-rolls it is true that most men gave a town as their 'place of birth', but was this only their place of enlistment? Was it just the name of the nearest town? The records of the town council of Valladolid (Archivo Municipal, *Libros de Actas* 10–11) suggest that the captain, at least in Spain, was firmly based on the town, although he was *allowed* to recruit in the villages under the town's jurisdiction. The records of the paymasters who accompanied the recruiting captains (AGS *CMC* la/1175–1180 and 1270–1277) confirm this view. In evaluating this indirect evidence I am most grateful for the helpful comments of my colleagues, Dr I. A. A. Thompson and Dr Michael Weisser.

number of *particulares* had volunteered to serve in the Spanish infantry which he led to the Netherlands in 1567.

> Soldiers of this calibre [wrote Alva] are the men who win victory in the 'actions' and with whom the General establishes the requisite discipline among the troops. In our nation nothing is more important than to introduce gentlemen and men of substance into the infantry so that all is not left in the hands of labourers and lackeys.

Throughout the Eighty Years' War the same sentiment was expressed in remarkably similar terms. As late as 1640, for example, a Netherlander – and a civilian at that – could write:

> Gentleman-rankers...are the people who bear the brunt of the battles and sieges, as we have seen on many occasions, and who by their example oblige and enliven the rest of the soldiers (who have less sense of duty) to stand fast and fight with courage.[1]

Service as a volunteer among the infantry was particularly popular among the Spanish gentry, but *particulares* were also to be found in considerable numbers in the ranks of other 'nations'. The English units in the Army of Flanders, for example, regularly included Catesbys, Treshams and other members of the leading recusant gentry families – including Guy Fawkes.[2] Not all these gentleman-rankers were poor. On one celebrated occasion the Emperor Charles V lent additional dignity to the military profession by himself taking up a pike and marching with his men; later, in the 1590s, the dukes of Osuna and Pastrana and the prince of Asculi, scions of the most illustrious houses of Spain, were all to be found serving as simple soldiers in the Army of Flanders. Naturally these volunteers, especially the nobles, aspired to an eventual position of command, but they first received an admirable apprenticeship and, in addition, their presence in the ranks helped to maintain morale and reduce insubordination. In this way the Spanish Habsburgs assembled armies which were supremely capable of victory without resort to any compulsion.

The voluntary recruiting system, however, like capitalist enterprise, obviously demanded a fairly large surplus of cheap labour if it was to work

---

[1] *Epistolario*, I, pp. 525–7 (no. 500), Alva to the king, 27 Apr. 1567; AGRB *CPE* 1574/81–99, Roose's *memorial* of 28 Jan. 1640.
[2] AGRB *SEG* 7–87, the registers of orders issued by the generals of the Army of Flanders, detail the grants and patents issued to, among others, the English troops. In Feb. 1595, 'Guido Fauques, ingles' was awarded a *ventaja* (bonus-pay) of 6 *escudos* each month while he served in the Irish infantry (*SEG* 15/268) and on 16 Feb. 1603 'el alferez Guido Faulkes, ingles', then in the English infantry, received permission to go to Spain (*SEG* 21/129). The English Gunpowder plot of 1605 of course involved a number of other veterans of the Anglo-Irish forces in the Army of Flanders.

in the employer's favour. This surplus, which had existed throughout the sixteenth century, was savagely reduced in the 1590s. On the one hand the population was seriously diminished by natural causes; on the other, several states were suddenly obliged to intensify their military demands. Philip II's mounting intervention in the French religious wars after 1589 eventually involved him in war on six fronts: in Languedoc, Brittany, Lombardy, Franche-Comté and at sea as well as in the Netherlands. Troops of all 'nations' had to be raised in unprecedented numbers. At the same time war broke out in central Europe: the emperor and the Turkish sultan began a prolonged struggle for control of Hungary (1593–1606). The composition of the Habsburg army in Hungary closely resembled that of the Army of Flanders, with Italians, Walloons and Germans as well as troops from other central European 'nations', and serious competition therefore sprang up between the two armies for recruits. The Army of Flanders came off worst.[1] It proved almost as hard to raise enough Spaniards. In the words of a perceptive French military writer, Blaise de Vigenère (d. 1596):

> As for the Spaniards, one cannot deny that they are the best soldiers in the world, but there are so few of them that scarcely five or six thousand of them can be raised at a time.[2]

Even this number often proved beyond Spain's capacity. As early as 1575 an attempt to raise 2,500 men for service in Italy produced only 1,750 recruits (70 per cent of the quota) and the Council of War endorsed the duke of Alva's judgement that the cause of the shortfall lay in the excessive levies of past years: 'Over a period of nine years, almost 80,000 men – not counting those who go to the Indies – have been sent out of Spain.'[3] The pressure of the crown's military needs increased even further after this. The conquest of Portugal in 1580, the Invincible Armada in 1587–8 and

---

[1] The composition of the Army of Hungary is described by A. Randa, '*Pro Republica Christiana*': *die Walachei im 'langen' Türkenkrieg der katholischen Universalmächte, (1593–1606)* (Monachü, 1964). For two complaints about Spain's lack of German recruits due to the war in Hungary, cf. AGS *E* 607/39, Archduke Ernest to the king, 21 Jun. 1594, and BNM *Ms*. 904/173, *Recuerdo* of Ramon Ezguerre to the king, 28 Nov. 1596. The same thing had happened during the previous phase of the war in Hungary, in 1564–8: Spain could not raise enough Germans (for the Mediterranean war).

[2] B. de Vigenère, *L'art militaire d'Onosender* (Paris, 1605), f. 170v.

[3] AGS *GA* 80/286, *consulta* of the Council of War, 11 Dec. 1575. This is an interesting example of Alva's formidable techniques of argument. The duke claimed, and no one contradicted him, that 'en termino de nueve años casi lxxx°U hombres' were sent out of Spain, excluding those bound for the Indies. However, a detailed calculation made for Alva's own use, and possibly for this very council meeting, showed that between 1567 and 1574 only 42,875 men had been sent abroad (to Italy and the Netherlands). A serious drain of men, but not quite of the alarmist dimensions which Alva stated! (AA 166/2, 'Relación de la infantería que desde el año de 67...se a mandado hazer en estos reynos y se a embarcado y ydo a Italia y Flandes.')

intervention in France after 1589, all involved extensive new levies of troops. The towns began to protest, opposing the recruiting officers' attempts to raise men in their area. Time after time the captains failed to fill their quota.[1]

The maximum pressure of military demand in the 1590s coincided with a grave demographic crisis in Spain and the Spanish Netherlands. Between 1598 and 1602 the Iberian peninsula was ravaged by a fearful epidemic of plague which ended and probably reversed the upward demographic trend of the sixteenth century. An estimated 8 per cent of the population was wiped out. The 'year of the plague', long remembered in Spain, marked the culmination of a series of harvest failures.[2] In the Low Countries too the harvests were disastrous for most of the 1590s, causing famine in most of the southern (Spanish) provinces. Many people migrated; many people died. Soldiers became harder to find; Spain's diminished armies were defeated.

The crisis of the 1590s exposed the fragility of the military base upon which Spanish power was founded. Without powerful armies Italy, the Netherlands and the Indies could not be held; without a plentiful supply of men, there could be no powerful armies. Spanish power was only saved by the peaceful resolution of most European conflicts in the decade following 1598.

A *pax hispanica* was maintained until 1618. After the coming of civil war to Germany, a conflict which lasted thirty years and eventually ranged France, England, the Dutch and the Baltic powers with the German Protestants against the Habsburgs, the Army of Flanders experienced increasing difficulty in maintaining its numbers. As in the 1590s, war in Germany interrupted the supply of German recruits. This time the alternative was far more attractive than Hungary; service with Wallenstein or Tilly offered better pay and plunder than fighting in the south Netherlands. After 1632, when the conditions of service in Germany became perhaps less attractive, military manœuvres often made it impossible for recruits from Spain's traditional recruiting grounds in the empire to reach the Low Countries. Spain and Italy could not make good this shortfall. In Italy the appalling mortality caused by the plague of 1630–1, the *peste di Milano*, cleared Lombardy of every potential recruit while the great plague which ravaged Spain between 1647 and 1652, 'the worst

---

[1] Cf. the quotations in Thompson, 'War and Administrative Devolution...', pp. 171–6.
[2] B. Bennassar, *Recherches sur les grandes épidemies dans le Nord de l'Espagne à la fin du XVIe siècle* (Paris, 1969), passim.

demographic catastrophe to strike Spain in modern times', put the finishing touches to the depopulation of Castile.[1]

Demographic and political changes on this scale compelled Spain to adapt her methods of mobilization to the new manpower scarcity. There were a number of changes in the geography of recruiting. To offset the loss of German troops during the Thirty Years' War, more Walloons were raised. Figure 4 (p. 28) shows that the Walloons became the largest single 'nation' from 1621 onwards. The German troops themselves were recruited nearer and nearer to the Netherlands, in the Rhineland or in the lands of the Catholic princes near to the Netherlands border, Munster, Cologne, Trier...Later still the Army of Flanders was even compelled to authorize levies of German contingents in those areas of the Low Countries 'where they speak German'.[2] The Army was also obliged to accept more troops from Spain's allies: more British volunteers after the Anglo-Spanish peace of 1630, the private army of the disinherited duke of Lorraine after 1633, the troops of the exiled prince of Condé (1653–9). No sooner had hostilities ended with the Dutch and in Germany than Spain began to recruit the troops of her former enemies. Lutheran troops were openly recruited in Hamburg in 1647, although there were some misgivings:

> The troops to be raised there [wrote a minister to the court] will be excellent, except that they will be heretics to a man; but this was realized when the levy was ordered, and the extreme shortage of infantry in all parts will compel us to take them wherever they may be found.[3]

In 1649, two years later, Don Ambrosio Mexía secured permission from the States General to levy a regiment of infantry in the United Provinces. Although he concentrated on Limburg, North Brabant and the other areas which had been Spanish, and therefore Catholic, until the 1630s, he recruited many Calvinists. These troops were accepted. There could be

---

[1] AGS *E* 3336/138, governor of Milan to the king, 12 Apr. 1631: 'The plague has left [this province] so reduced in population that it is impossible to raise any levies'; for Spain, cf. the dismal views of the Council of War, which had to organize recruiting: AGS *GA* 1034, unfol., paper of the marques of Castrofuerte, 10 Mar. 1631 ('está el Reyno muy apurado y falto de gente'), *GA* 1076, unfol., duke of Béjar to the king, 27 Nov. 1633 ('la gran falta que ay de gente en estos reynos') and many, many more. For more general remarks cf. J. Nadal, *La población española, siglos XVI a XX* (Barcelona, 1966), pp. 53–61.

[2] E.g. AGRB *SEG* 57/1v, order of 16 Mar. 1659 to recruit 'German' troops in Limburg, Luxemburg and Gelderland 'donde se habla alemán'. In the sixteenth century, when real German recruits were plentiful, soldiers raised in these provinces were classified as 'Low Germans' and paid the same as Walloons.

[3] AHN *E libro* 964/4–8v, Don Miguel de Salamanca to Pedro Coloma, secretary of state in Madrid, 11 May 1647.

no clearer indication of Spain's desperate shortage of troops in the mid-seventeenth century.[1]

Even this unwelcome extension of its recruiting-grounds could not satisfy the Army's full manpower needs after 1621. The actual techniques of recruiting also had to be changed. Generally speaking, where the contract system was already in use, its cost rose enormously; where the commission system had sufficed in the sixteenth century, either the voluntary element was sacrificed or else contractors were employed.

In the Netherlands, the first Walloon regiments to be supplied to the Army under contract were those of the 'Malcontents', the Walloon nobles who in 1579 left the service of the States General with their troops to become an independent third force before finally joining the Army of Flanders. Several, though not all, of the later regiments raised in the Netherlands were recruited by prominent noblemen acting as contractors. Only after 1600 did the levy by commission finally disappear. In the Iberian peninsula a Portuguese *tercio* was raised by contract as early as 1592 (not for the Netherlands in fact) but the example was not followed in Castile until after the outbreak of open war with France in 1635. Sufficient troops simply could not be raised in any other way. The shortage of recruits also increased the price which had to be paid to each man upon enlistment. In the sixteenth century it had been three *escudos* for an infantryman; by 1641 it was ten and in 1647 eighteen. (A cavalry recruit, fully equipped, then cost sixty.) Moreover the contractors demanded a minimum of sixty days to complete their levies.[2] Finally the companies raised by contractors were allowed to become permanent. Unlike the units raised by commission, which were broken up when their numbers fell below a certain level, the contractors were allowed to keep up their strength by recruiting reinforcements every year (these were known as *reclutas*, distinct from *levas* or levies of entire units).

[1] Cf. the interesting story of Mexía's Dutch levy told by a Calvinist recruit from Deventer; he was eventually sent to Spain and converted to Catholicism there: AHN *Inquisición libro* 994/172v–7v. (I owe knowledge of this document to the courtesy of M. Maurice Van Durme.) The Dutch levy was proposed as soon as the Peace of Munster was signed but the poverty of Mexía ('as poor as a church mouse', admitted one Spanish minister) delayed the consent of the States General: AHN *E libro* 973, unfol., Alonso Martínez to Don Miguel de Salamanca, 23 Jul. 1648.

[2] Information from the recruiting contracts registered in AGRB *SEG* 40/67v, 95 and 46*bis*/47 and 109. It has been estimated that some 300 military enterprisers were at work in Germany alone between 1631 and 1634: cf. the standard account, F. Redlich, *The German Military Enterpriser and his Workforce* (Wiesbaden, 1964), I, p. 171. Even paying the increased enlistmen *prime* (the *Laufgeld*) proved a strain for the Army of Flanders in its later days. In 1647 the government felt it prudent to take out an insurance policy to guarantee payment of the *Laufgeld* on the date agreed with the contractors: it cost no less than 9 per cent... (AHN *E libro* 964/2–3v, Don Miguel de Salamanca to Pedro Coloma, 20 Jun. 1647.)

It was the prohibitive cost of using contractors which, above all else, reinforced the resolve of governments to keep on recruiting by commission wherever possible, even if this could only be done by accepting recruits in their teens and employing force and threats to compel others to enlist. The Italian *tercios* which crossed the Mt Cenis pass in 1620 included boys of sixteen, badly dressed, without hats or shoes. An English observer who saw them cross the Alps estimated that barely half would reach their destination; in fact two-thirds did – but over a thousand men were lost.[1] In Spain after 1620 compulsion was used to press the able-bodied unemployed, the 'masterless men', into service; after the outbreak of war with France in 1635 whole regions were systematically combed by crimping-gangs. In 1639, for example, the naval expedition of Don Antonio de Oquendo, which was intended to seek out and destroy the Dutch navy before arriving in the Netherlands, was only manned by embarking 'two thousands fathers and husbands' of the Corunna area at gunpoint. Meanwhile, in Madrid:

> A woman of good family was scourged with rods for helping a certain captain, her lover, to recruit soldiers. She enticed the poor ruffians with food, then she shut them up by surprise in a cellar and left them there without food until they enlisted and accepted their wages. In this way she had already caught a multitude.[2]

In 1647 Spanish captains were informed by the government that if troops could not be raised in any other way:

> If there are any men in the prisons of the Kingdom of a suitable age for service, provided that they are not there for heinous offences [*delictos atroces*] they may be set free, commuting their sentences to service in these companies for a limited period.[3]

Bandits and vagabonds were also fair game for the king's recruiting officers. On one famous occasion a *tercio* was raised in Catalonia from brigands and bandits who received a free pardon in return for their en-

[1] AE Geneva *PH* 2651, unfol., Isaac Wake to the Council of Geneva, 4 Jul. 1620; AGS *E* 1924/120 (muster of 20 Jul. – 3,399 men) and *E* 2309/335-6 (muster of 20 Aug. – 2,333 men).

[2] There is an eye-witness account of the 'day of tears and tribulations' at Corunna by the Portuguese luminary Don Francisco Manuel de Melo, *Epanáphoras de Varia Historia Portuguesa*, ed. E. Prestage (Coimbra, 1931), pp. 308–9; the Madrid incident is quoted by J. Deleito y Piñuela, *El declinar de la Monarquía española* (2nd edn, Madrid, 1947), p. 197.

[3] AGS *GA* 1616, unfol., *consulta* of the Council of War, 2 Oct. 1647. Before condemning such devices out of hand, one should perhaps bear in mind that in the Second World War at least one of the major powers (Soviet Russia) raised penal battalions of political prisoners. The men who served in these suicide units eventually earned their pardons (if they survived). For an identical recruiting repertory in the English Army, cf. Cruickshank, *Elizabeth's Army*, chap. 2, and R. E. Scouller, *The Armies of Queen Anne* (Oxford, 1966), chap. 3.

listment. They went straight to the Netherlands, intended to form part of the Army prepared for the invasion of England in 1587–8.[1] At other times, the brigands seem to have abducted more recruits than they provided. In 1646, for example, Philip IV decided to take action over the army of villains and vagabonds who thronged the streets of Madrid – a good number of them, as he realized, 'soldiers who have left the army without leave'. Ministers prepared complicated plans for a swoop on all the brothels, taverns and other havens of these potential recruits. The raid went well and the victims were bundled into carts, manacled, and trundled off to the Catalan front under an escort of armed guards. The ministers had reckoned without the *bandoleros*. As one of these convoys, consisting of twelve 'recruits' under as many guards, moved slowly through Murcia a bandit gang swept down from the hills and carried off the vagabonds – an equally welcome reinforcement for their own numbers.[2]

Since even these falling standards failed to raise enough men to ensure the defence of the Spanish Monarchy. There were only two artifices left: the ancient obligations of feudal service from the nobility and militia service from the rest. In fact the former brought little benefit to the Army of Flanders since, although great military pressure was laid upon the Castilian aristocracy in the 1630s, they were only obliged to serve within the kingdom, while the Walloon nobility already played a prominent part in the wars. There was, however, room for a more effective use of the Netherlands militia. At the end of the sixteenth century companies of peasants and townsmen were organized into 'rural companies' and 'urban companies' (civil defence units). The piecemeal nature of the Spanish reconquest of the Netherlands in the 1580s, discussed above, made local defence of paramount importance. In the Oudburg district of the province of Flanders, for example, the surrender of Ghent to the Army of Flanders in September 1584 inaugurated a nightmare period in which partisans (*vrijbuiters*, freebooters) based on the Dutch enclaves of Ostend, Sluis, Axel and Terneuzen ravaged the province time and again. In the end the

---

[1] The Catalan *bandolero tercio*, raised by Don Luis de Queralt, was known in the Netherlands as the *tercio del papagayo* because, according to the Castilian troops, when the Catalans tried to speak Spanish it could only be compared to the screech of parrots. (See Alonso Vazquez, *Los Sucesos de Flandes y Francia*, Co.Do.In. LXXIII, pp. 320–2 for an amusing account of these troops.) Remarkably few troops were raised by the crown in Catalonia: the presence of numerous Gascon and French immigrants made Catalan troops a security risk. (The same suspicion was harboured about Valencian troops on account of the dense morisco population in the province.) Cf. the numerous quotations in Braudel, *La Méditerranée*, I, pp. 381–2 and Thompson, 'War and Administrative Devolution...', pp. 185–6.

[2] AGS *GA* 1615, unfol., *consulta* of the Council of War, 15 Jan. 1646; *GA* 1616, unfol., Don Diego Zápata to the Council of War, 3 Feb. 1646.

district had to organize a defence militia of some 400 men, a town guard and a chain of forts along the dikes to contain the raiders.[1]

Not all of these civil defence units were paid. In 1597, for instance, the governor of Hesdin was provided with a patent to raise 700 volunteers for the region's defence. The despatch of the patent was preceded by some official discussion about the company's financial footing. The *audiencier*, who drew up the patent, enquired of his more experienced colleague, Moriensart: 'Sir, I will have to know whether these soldiers will be paid and at what rate, also who will pay them. Please advise me.' The wily Moriensart replied: 'The troops will serve without pay, but it would be better to write in the patent that it will be "at the ordinary and accustomed rate".' One did not serve in the government of Spanish Flanders for twenty years without learning a few tricks![2]

Less ingenuity was required to find weapons and armour for the Army of Flanders' recruits. Many of the foreign troops were already fully equipped when they reached the Netherlands. The Spanish and Italian troops were provided with arms by the government arsenal at Milan or by the many armourers of Lombardy; the German troops were armed either by the contractors who recruited them or by the arsenals of Innsbruck, Nuremburg or some other city. For the rest, the armourers of the Low Countries, particularly those of Liège who supplied the army of the States as well as Spain, could easily provide all the military equipment that the Army could afford. But it had to be paid for. The great limitation on the equipment of the Army of Flanders in the sixteenth century was financial: a pike and body-armour (the *corselete*) cost 30 florins in the 1590s, a musket cost 10 florins, a 24-pounder cannon cost 1,000 florins.[3] With prices like this, there was never enough money to arm all of the soldiers all of the time. There was only limited concern about this: sixteenth-century strategists believed that wars should be fought with men, not material (a belief which appears to have survived until the

---

[1] A. de Vos, 'De strijd tegen de vrijbuiters binnen de kasselrij van de Oudburg (1584–1609)', *Handelingen der Maatschappij voor Geschiedenis en Oudheidkunde te Gent*, XI (1957), 131–75.

[2] AGRB *Audience* 2780, unfol., minute of patent to Antoine de la Coquelle, governor of Hesdin, 30 Apr. 1597. Verreycken: 'Monsieur, il sera besoing scavoir si ces gens auront gaiges et sur quel pied, aussi qui les payera, dont il vous plaira m'esclaircir.' Moriensart: 'Ces gens serviront sans gages, mais il conviendra narrer par la patente que ce sera aux gages ordinaires et accoustumez.'

[3] Calculations from the 1590s in the bundle AGRB *Audience* 1639. For the reluctance to use siege-artillery, cf. p. 18.

suicidal massed assaults along the Somme and Aisne in 1916–7)[1] and faced with a choice between feeding their men or equipping them, they always chose food. Eight hundred men could be fed for a month with the money required to cast one cannon; a pike-man could be given bread for two years with the price of his corselet.

Only gradually did the Army systematize the supply of weapons to its men, deducting the cost of arms, powder and shot by instalments from their future wages (cf. pp. 158–67 below). By 1600, the soldiers of the Army of Flanders were decently armed. As Plate 6 shows, the troops of 1641 were ragged, almost bare-footed in the snow, but they all carried a sword and most of them had an arquebus or pike; a few had a musket. It was a far cry from the gold-inlaid breast-plates and swords of the Negroli or della Cesa of Milan, far even from the spruce and sober figures of Jacques de Gheyn's manual of weapon-handling, but it was better than nothing.[2]

The besetting problem of mobilizing a Habsburg army thus remained a geographical one. There was nothing wrong with Spain's military organization in a technical sense – the multi-national army remained the hallmark of the Habsburgs right up until 1918 when the last army of the dynasty, mobilized with the aid of recruiting posters in no less than fifteen languages, continued to fight even after the empire which it defended had collapsed.[3] But the system revolved around the use of troops raised in one area to fight in another. The vital question was therefore whether the foreign troops who were to form the nucleus and elite of the Army could reach the Netherlands in large numbers. There had to be safe ways of moving units recruited in Germany, Italy, Spain and the British Isles to the Low Countries. The defence of the Spanish Netherlands depended on it.

[1] G. Pedroncini, *Les mutineries de 1917* (Paris, 1967), Chap. IV and conclusion.
[2] The body-armour of sixteenth-century princes was often a work of art in its own right; there are many splendid examples in the major armouries of Europe – Turin, Madrid, Brussels, London and so on. For the everyday equipment of armies, cf. J. de Gheyn, *Maniement d'armes, d'arquebuzes, mousquets et piques en conformité de l'ordonnance du prince Maurice de Nassau, representé par figures* (Amsterdam, 1608 and many subsequent edns).
[3] On the twilight of Habsburg military power, cf. N. Stone, 'Army and Society in the Habsburg Monarchy, 1900–1914', *Past and Present*, XXXIII (1966), pp. 95–111.

CHAPTER 2

THE MILITARY CORRIDORS OF THE ARMY OF FLANDERS

In the sixteenth century, wrote Professor Braudel, distance – *l'espace* – was 'public enemy number one'. The delays and disruptions caused by distance complicated every act of government, from the ceaseless transmission of orders and items of news to the despatch of bullion and the continual movement of troops. The greater the distance, the greater the disruption and the longer the delay.

The need to combat the challenge of distance produced a number of important administrative responses, both by governments and by merchants. Orderly systems of couriers and post-stations spread across the continent, linking capital cities and commercial centres, transmitting letters, conveying news. To transport bullion and merchandise, carters and convoys were organized into a regular service; caravans of mules or long carts moved continually between the centres of trade. Moving an army presented problems of a very different magnitude, however. Where the post-couriers passed in ones or twos, and the mules or carts filled with merchandise in hundreds at the most, troops travelled in thousands. They passed through lands at peace; they moved slowly, irregularly; they demanded shelter and food.

These mass movements posed many trying problems of a purely technical nature, which will be dealt with at length in the next chapter; they also gave rise to a number of less obvious but equally intractable political difficulties. The soldiers needed diplomatic protection against the risk of attack or provocation while they marched to the front. Speed had to be combined with safety. Accordingly, a network of what might be called 'military corridors' was developed by the various states of Europe: recognized itineraries which connected an army on active service with its distant recruiting grounds. The military corridors marked an important step towards solving both the technical and the political problems which surrounded military movements in peacetime, since they regularized the displacement of troops, enabling the necessary basic services to be prepared in advance with a guarantee of permanent diplomatic protection.

Figure 9. The military corridors of the Army of Flanders

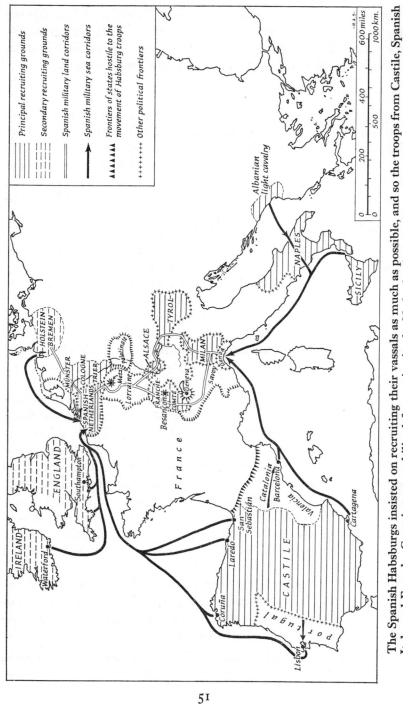

Principal recruiting grounds

Secondary recruiting grounds

Spanish military land corridors

Spanish military sea corridors

Frontiers of states hostile to the movement of Habsburg troops

+++++++ Other political frontiers

IRELAND

Waterford

ENGLAND

Southampton

HOLSTEIN
BREMEN

MÜNSTER
COLOGNE
SPANISH
NETHERLANDS·TRIER
Lorraine
Metz Palatinate
ALSACE
FRANCHE-
COMTÉ
Besançon
Geneva
Savoy
MILAN
TYROL

France

Coruña

Laredo

San
Sebastián

Barcelona
Catalonia
Valencia

CASTILE

Lisbon

Portugal

Cartagena

NAPLES

SICILY

Albanian
light cavalry

N.A.S.

0   200   400   600 miles

0   500   1000 km.

The Spanish Habsburgs insisted on recruiting their vassals as much as possible, and so the troops from Castile, Spanish Italy and Franche-Comté were mobilized for service in the Netherlands as well as men from the Austrian Habsburg dominions of Alsace and the Tyrol. The problem was to get the loyal troops to the front.

Because so many of its troops were recruited outside, far outside the Netherlands, the Army of Flanders was uniquely dependent on its military corridors. There were in fact four of these arteries which brought the army its manpower, two by sea, two by land (see Figure 6).

Perhaps the least important of the four itineraries was the sea route from the British Isles. In the first place the initial contingents of English, Irish and Scots soldiers to join the Army of Flanders were already in the Netherlands. The British garrisons which betrayed Lier, Aalst, Deventer and Zutphen to Spain in the 1580s had all been sent to the Low Countries by the English government. Many of the reinforcements which reached these units were English recusants who organized their own crossing. Direct recruiting for the Army of Flanders began only with the Anglo-Spanish peace of 1604. Almost immediately a whole regiment was raised in England by Thomas, Lord Arundel and another in Ireland by Henry O'Neill. This sudden exodus alarmed Protestant England. In May 1606 Parliament made it a felony for Englishmen to serve a foreign prince unless they first took an oath of allegiance to James I and gave a bond against reconciliation with the Church of Rome. In fact this restriction hardly took effect before the cease-fire in the Netherlands (April 1607) made further recruiting in England superfluous. When the Twelve Years' Truce expired in 1621, the English situation was far more favourable to Spain and intensive recruiting for the Army of Flanders raised the British contingent to 4,000 by 1623. This number fell while England and Spain were at war (1625–30) but soon recovered after the Peace of London: throughout the 1630s about 4,000 British troops served in the Army of Flanders. The position was again transformed in the 1640s when the Confederation of Kilkenny in Ireland and the outbreak of the English Civil War (1641–2) reduced the manpower available for the Low Countries' Wars. No more British troops came over until Parliament's victory first in England and then in Ireland produced the migration of many defeated Royalist and Catholic units, to the benefit of Spain, France and the Spanish Netherlands.[1]

All British contingents after 1605 were raised by contract, and the transportation of the troops was arranged either by the English government or by the contractors. Indeed, part of the money paid to the contractor for each man brought to the Low Countries was intended to cover

---

[1] On all aspects of the Irish troops in the Army of Flanders, cf. the repertory of sources prepared by B. Jennings, *Wild Geese in Spanish Flanders, 1582–1700* (Dublin, 1964).

the costs and risks of his transport.[1] Only rarely were the ships of the Netherlands navy used. Normally coasters from Waterford, Southampton or some other port shipped the recruits either direct to Dunkirk or else to a harbour in northern France (Calais, for example) leaving the soldiers to complete their journey on foot – a procedure no doubt welcome to the men themselves many of whom never recovered from the appalling conditions on the overcrowded troopships.

Although, as we have seen, the Spanish authorities had little more trust in their German troops than in the British, the numbers involved were far greater. There were always numerous regiments of Germans serving in the Army of Flanders and the routes between their recruiting grounds and the Netherlands were well-trodden. The Army of Flanders preferred to raise its Germans in the Habsburg domains of Alsace, Austria and the Tyrol; when these areas could not satisfy the Army's needs recruiting was authorized in the Rhineland. In real emergencies, troops might also be raised in the north of Germany, in Holstein or around Hamburg. In diplomatic terms, obviously the areas nearest to the Netherlands presented the least problem. Münster and Cologne were only separated from Spanish territory by the duchies of Cleves and Jülich; the archbishopric of Trier fronted directly on to the duchy of Luxemburg. In these cases the only diplomatic formalities which necessarily preceded the movement of recruits to the Army of Flanders were the consent of the local ruler and of the emperor (without whose approval no troop-movement within the empire was legal).

Despite the greater distance, it was scarcely more difficult in diplomatic terms for the troops from Alsace and the Tyrol to reach the Netherlands. In the course of their patient empire-building the Habsburgs had acquired an almost unbroken chain of territory from Vienna through to the Rhine. Troops could usually be found in the highland regions north and east of the Alps and they marched to the Low Countries through the Allgäu, passing along the northern shore of Lake Constance and the north bank of the Rhine (the Habsburgs owned the 'vier Waldstädte': Rheinfelden, Säckingen, Laufenburg and Waldshut – cf. Figure 8). The next stage of the journey was less straightforward. From Basel the swiftest way to the Netherlands was to sail down the majestic Rhine by

---

[1] For an example of these risks, cf. the contract of the Army of Flanders with the earl of Antrim to raise an Irish regiment which made provision for the possibility that 'the captains of the ships might be obliged by the soldiers' threats to put into some enemy port' (AGRB *SEG* 45/116–7).

boat, but the way was obstructed by the implacable hostility of the elector palatine to the House of Habsburg. The Lower Palatinate and the duchy of Zweibrücken (ruled by a cadet of the Palatine family) controlled the Rhine valley from near Speyer to Mainz. Contingents marching to serve the king of Spain in the Low Countries entered the Palatinate at their peril. As early as 1568 the Palatine government showed the cloven hoof by seizing without provocation a convoy of 150,000 *escudos* (about 300,000 florins) in cloth and specie, bound for the bankers of the Army of Flanders. In 1572 the elector palatine's allies from the bishopric of Strasbourg surrounded the regiment of Baron Polwiller, raised in Alsace and marching to the Spanish Netherlands, and confiscated their equipment and weapons. In November 1573 vassals of the elector burnt 500 quintals of powder sent by the emperor himself to the Army of Flanders, while in 1574 some 200 Gascon horsemen retained by the elector ambushed Count Hannibal von Hohenems, colonel of another German regiment newly raised for the Low Countries, and prevented him from collecting the arms he had purchased for his men in Strasbourg.[1] Until 1618, the government of the Palatinate sheltered Calvinist exiles from the Low Countries, sent troops from time to time to fight openly in Holland for the States, and molested the passage of any pro-Spanish troops in the Rhineland.[2]

The Palatine nuisance was only ended by direct Spanish retaliation. In 1619 the elector, Frederick V, accepted the invitation of the Protestant Estates of Bohemia to become their king. The emperor, who had also been elected king of Bohemia, defeated Frederick and declared him an outlaw. His lands were confiscated and execution of the Imperial ban was entrusted to the Army of Flanders. The alacrity with which the Spanish forces occupied the Rhine Palatinate in 1620 is only intelligible when one considers the half-century of provocations suffered by Spain and her deep-seated desire to use the coveted Rhineland corridor for her military communications. In 1631 it was even possible to sail an army of Spanish and Italian troops down the Rhine – the first time since 1543. It was also the last. In the same year the victory of Gustavus Adolphus at the Breitenfeld brought Swedish troops into the Rhineland. Based on Mainz, the

---

[1] *Epistolario*, II, pp. 48–9, Alva to the emperor (?), 15 Apr. 1568; *ibid.*, III, pp. 163–7, Alva to the king, 18 Jul. 1572; IVdeDJ 67/197, Requesens to Zuñiga, 15 Nov. 1573; AGS *E* 557/166, Hannibal von Hohenems ('Altaemps' to the Spaniards) to Requesens, 6 May 1574.
[2] On the foreign policy of the Palatinate, cf. B. Vogler, 'Le rôle des Electeurs palatins dans les Guerres de Religion en France, 1559–1592', *Cahiers d'Histoire*, x (1965), pp. 51–85, and the useful booklet of C.-P. Clasen, *The Palatinate in European History, 1555–1618* (Oxford, 1966), especially pp. 5–19.

Protestant forces were able once more to close the Rhine to all troops in Habsburg service.[1]

Fortunately for Spain there was an alternative route open to the troops from the Tyrol which led to the Netherlands but avoided the Rhine Palatinate. By crossing the Rhine at Breisach in Alsace, the troops could pass into the pro-Habsburg duchy of Lorraine by Colmar, Kaysersberg, the Bonhomme pass and St Dié; alternatively, by continuing down the Rhine a little further they could cross the river at Strasbourg and then march through Lorraine by Saverne and Sarrebourg to Spanish Luxemburg (cf. Figures 6 and 8).

This military corridor of the Army of Flanders was doubly important because it was used, on occasion, by Spanish and Italian troops as well as Germans. They crossed from Milan over the central Alps, as we shall see, to join the Rhine either at Bregenz or at Waldshut, reaching the Low Countries via Alsace and Lorraine. Alsace was the hinge of this military corridor; Alsace was indeed more important to Spain than the Palatinate.[2] Accordingly determined diplomatic manœuvres were initiated by Spain in order to secure it from the Austrian Habsburgs. The uncertainty of the imperial succession after 1612 (which could only be decided by the majority vote of the seven electoral princes of the empire) made it important for the Habsburg family to agree upon their candidate. Eventually Philip III and the Archduke Albert (who ruled the Spanish Netherlands) consented to waive their own excellent claims to the imperial dignity and support the Archduke Ferdinand of Styria. But in return they demanded the cession of Alsace to Spain. In 1614 negotiations along these lines proved inconclusive: Ferdinand felt confident of his election even without Spain's blessing. By 1617, however, the Emperor Mathias was clearly a dying man and there was still no agreement on a successor. Ferdinand reluctantly agreed to Spain's harsh terms and signed a treaty which ceded Alsace to Spain. As it happened the outbreak of civil war first in Bohemia and then all over Germany prevented Spain from ever reaping the full fruits of her diplomatic agility and tenacity.[3]

---

[1] For the organization of the 1631 expedition, cf. BNP *Lorraine Ms.* 598/132–157v.

[2] AGRB *SEG* 188/65, Philip IV to the Infanta Isabella, 28 Jul. 1622: 'Aunque es bien conservarlo todo, me ha parecido poner en consideración a V.A. que las cosas de la Alsatia...de por si y en orden a los estados de Borgoña y Italya, son de mas momento y ymportancia que las del Palatinato inferior.'

[3] The original treaty, dated 29 Jul. 1617, signed by Ferdinand and beautifully bound in red velvet, is in AGS *Patronato Real* 56/54. The archduke ceded Alsace, Finale Liguria and Piombino to Spain, recognized that a male heir of Philip III should be preferred to any female heiresses of his own and promised to aid Spain in Lombardy whenever asked to do so. Ferdinand renewed his promise on 20 Oct. 1631, but again it never took effect.

D

The Spanish Habsburgs nevertheless continued to send troops through Alsace until 1631. Here, as in the Palatinate it was the Swedish victory at the Breitenfeld which deprived Spain of her precious military corridor. Things were never the same again. Although the crucial bridgehead at Breisach was saved from the Protestant avalanche for a time it was lost irretrievably in 1638. The same decade saw the Dutch capture Maastricht (1632) and the French extend their 'protection' over the archbishopric of Cologne (1635). As the Infanta Isabella lamented to her nephew Philip IV, their enemies occupied not only the military corridors but also Spain's very recruiting grounds![1] Even recruits raised in Cologne for the Army of Flanders could not cross to the Netherlands in safety. Parties of recruits in the 1640s were frequently attacked and captured as they crossed from Jülich to Roermond and Diest by Dutch scouting units based on Maastricht. By that stage of the war, of course, everything was recognized to have its price and the soldiers were ransomed almost immediately, but still most detachments of recruits required an escort of veteran troops if they were to reach the Low Countries in safety.[2] After the end of the war with the Dutch in 1648 it became possible to raise recruits in north Germany and ship them down to the Netherlands via Hamburg.

It was more difficult to find reliable itineraries for the elite forces of the Army of Flanders: the Spanish and Italian troops. During the 1540s and 1550s Spain had regularly put men and money aboard merchant convoys bound for the Netherlands whenever there was war with France. Spain had command of the Ocean Sea and she enjoyed the hospitality of English harbours, including the deep port of Calais, for shelter or disembarkation. These crucial advantages were all lost after 1558. The security of the sea-link between Spain and the Spanish Netherlands was rapidly eroded.

The first reverse in Spain's maritime position was the French capture of Calais from the English in January 1558. The port of Calais had a special importance for Spain. It was a far better harbour than those of the Flemish coast for landing soldiers and supplies because it was easy to reach for ships sailing up the Channel. Above all, its approaches were unencumbered by the vast sandbanks which stretch for miles before the continental coast from Dunkirk to the Scheldt – *los bancos de Flandes*, the sandbanks of the Low Countries, a graveyard of ships all-too-familiar to

[1] AGRB *SEG* 204/333, Infanta Isabella to the king, 16 Apr. 1632.
[2] AHN *E libro* 973, unfol., Don Francisco Semple to Don Miguel de Salamanca, 7 Sep. 1642.

Spanish mariners. Besides the inconvenience of losing a good harbour, it was unfortunately true that, from the south, the easiest way into Dunkirk (the next best port) was to cross before Calais in order to sail inside the off-shore sandbanks. Spanish shipping bound for Dunkirk, Gravelines or Mardijk was thus at the mercy of the French as it passed through the Calais roads.[1]

The loss of Calais was a deep humiliation for England, and Spain inevitably received a measure of the blame, but Queen Elizabeth preserved an uneasy peace with Spain until December 1568. Then, on the eve of the Northern Rebellion, Spanish ships with a cargo of specie bound for a consortium of Genoese bankers in the Netherlands, were driven by a storm into Southampton. The queen ordered them to be seized.[2] A campaign of muted aggression followed and, although peace was patched up in March 1574, Spanish shipping sailed in constant fear of piratical attack from England as long as Elizabeth lived.

The year of 1568 also saw the emergence of a second maritime threat to Spain: a Huguenot navy (the *armée sur mer*) of about 70 vessels was formed at La Rochelle to assist the cause of the French Protestants by piracy. The pirates prospered principally from the booty captured from Spanish merchantmen in the Bay of Biscay. They were soon joined in this lucrative work by the 'Sea Beggars', Netherlanders exiled for their part in the Troubles of 1566–7 who organized themselves as a regular fleet in the service of the prince of Orange. Based on La Rochelle, Dover, and any other port which would have them, they too harried Spanish shipping mercilessly.[3]

Sending troops or money from Spain to the Netherlands by sea after 1568 thus became an extremely hazardous affair. Almost every expedition, whether major or minor, ended in disaster. In 1572, after long delays and a false start, the fleet bearing 1,200 Spanish recruits and the governor-

[1] Information on this point is available in the *North Sea Pilot* (1963 ed.), IV, pp. 2–3 and *The Channel Pilot* (1965 ed.), II, pp. 411–16, both published by the Admiralty (HMSO). There is also an Admiralty chart and a description of Dunkirk and Calais and their sea-approaches in the impeccable study of C. R. Boxer, *The Journal of Maarten Harpertszoon Tromp, Anno 1639* (Cambridge, 1939).

[2] Conyers Read, 'Queen Elizabeth's seizure of the duke of Alva's Pay-ships', *Journal of Modern History*, V (1933), pp. 443–64.

[3] There are two good studies of the Huguenot war-fleet: J. de Pablo, 'Contribution à l'histoire des institutions militaires huguenotes. I. L'armée de mer huguenote pendant la 3e Guerre de Religion', *Archiv für Reformationsgeschichte*, XLVII (1957), pp. 64–76; and M. Delafosse, 'Les corsaires protestants à La Rochelle (1570–1577)', *Bibliothèque de l'Ecole des Chartes*, CXXI (1963), pp. 187–217. From the second article, a meticulous piece of work, it emerges that there were about 70 pirate ships at La Rochelle in the 1570s, each of them of about 75 tons, manned by some 75 men and armed with 10 light cannon. A comparable study of the Sea Beggars' fleet would be of great interest.

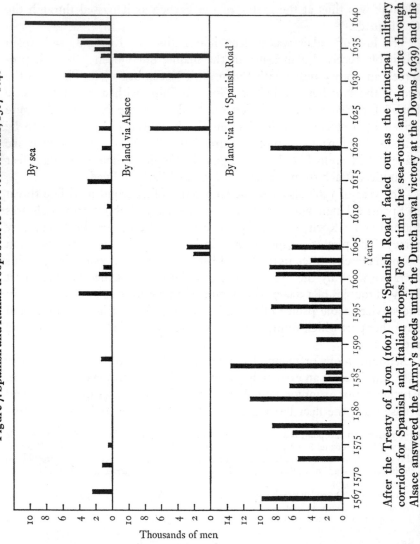

Figure 7. Spanish and Italian troops sent to the Netherlands, 1567–1640

After the Treaty of Lyon (1601) the 'Spanish Road' faded out as the principal military corridor for Spanish and Italian troops. For a time the sea-route and the route through Alsace answered the Army's needs until the Dutch naval victory at the Downs (1639) and the French occupation of Alsace (1632) destroyed their security too. Source: Appendix C

general-designate of the Low Countries, the duke of Medina Celi, entered the Channel. Immediately the waiting warships of the Sea Beggars closed in. The Spaniards were able to run their smaller vessels over the sandbanks and beach them off Blankenberg, although most of them were wrecked in the process, but the larger ships, which attempted to force their way down the Scheldt to Antwerp, were all captured or sunk. Another attempt to send Spanish troops to the Netherlands by sea a few years later proved an even more spectacular failure. The expedition incorporated all that storms and plague had left of the great fleet collected by Philip II to sail to the North Sea and exterminate the Sea Beggars; after a delay of two years, in November 1575 the ships prepared to put to sea. At once the soldiers mutinied for their wages. Chanting 'Money, money, pay, pay' they extorted a settlement of part of their arrears and some of the ships set out, only to be convulsed by a violent storm in the Bay of Biscay. Some ships were crippled, others lost, and those which weathered Cape Finisterre were nevertheless forced to return to Spain when their crews mutinied afresh through fear of an attack by the Sea Beggars. In the end only 430 Spanish soldiers reached the Army of Flanders.[1]

It was clearly essential to discover some other way of sending Spanish men and money to the Netherlands. If the sea was closed to Spain, they would have to go by land. As Figure 7 shows, most of the Spanish and Italian troops who reached the Army of Flanders came by land, the largest number travelling by the famous route known then, and even now in places, as *le chemin des espagnols*, the 'Spanish Road'.[2]

The 'Spanish Road' was first devised in 1565–6 by Philip II himself in anticipation of the journey he intended to make to the Netherlands. Although the king would have preferred to travel through Germany, a route which he knew personally from his voyage of 1548, he ordered the Army which was to precede him to the Low Countries to march through Piedmont and Savoy, Franche-Comté and Lorraine, passing from Spain to Lombardy via Genoa aboard his fleet of Mediterranean galleys. Such an itinerary was distinguished in Philip II's mind by one outstanding advantage: it ran 'quasi sempre su'l suo', almost entirely on his own land.[3]

---

[1] *Co.Do.In.* xxxv and xxxvi contain much information on Medina Celi and his voyage; for the 1575 *débâcle*, cf. AGS *E* 564/139, 'Relación de cartas de Juan Martínez de Recalde', 27 Nov. and 2 Dec. 1575; *ibid.*, f. 141, 'Relación de carta del comisario Juan Lopez de Moscoso', 26 Nov. 1575; AGS *GA* 80/96–9, Reports to the king from Santander concerning the fleet, Dec. 1575.

[2] Cf. this title on Sully's map of 1606, Plate 5. The name is still current in the Val de Chézery and in parts of Lorraine.

[3] The 'Spanish Road' was accurately described by the Genoese ambassador in Spain as early as

The king of Spain was duke of Milan by virtue of the emperor's permission and he ruled the Low Countries and Franche-Comté as sovereign prince. Throughout the Habsburg period Spain patiently concerted close alliances with the rulers of those territories which separated her own. Since 1528 Spain had been the chief strength of the ruling patriciate at Genoa, the *nobili vecchi*, providing them with support against the machinations of opposing factions in the city, and against French-backed rebels on the Genoese island of Corsica (in the 1550s and after 1564). In return for this invaluable assistance the Genoese magnates not only financed Spanish imperialism with their enormous wealth, they also allowed Spain to use the Ligurian ports as the gateway to Lombardy and therefore to northern Europe.

Beyond Spanish Lombardy the duke of Savoy, whose estates had been occupied by France between 1536 and 1559, was a long-standing ally of Spain. The memory of French conquest and occupation was bitter, and the weakness of the Valois Monarchy after the death of Henry II permitted the dukes the luxury of neutrality and even, after 1589, of aggression at French expense. The legal foundation of Savoy's alliance with Spain was the Treaty of Groenendaal (26 March 1559) but the lasting *entente* of the two powers was rooted in Savoy's desire to acquire French territory (for which Spanish aid was necessary) and in Spain's need for a military corridor between Milan and Franche-Comté. The estates of the duke of Savoy straddled the Alps and linked the two Spanish dominions perfectly. The territorial integrity of Savoy, as one minister observed to Philip II, 'matters more to Your Majesty for the passage to the Netherlands, than it does to the Duke'.[1]

Franche-Comté, 'The oldest possession of my dynasty' as Charles V once put it, was governed from the Netherlands but, unlike them, it was committed to neutrality with France. The severed inheritance of Duke Charles the Bold of Burgundy ultimately left France in possession of the duchy of Burgundy while the county (Franche-Comté) went to the Habsburgs. From 1508 it was agreed that the two halves of the inheritance should maintain strict neutrality and refrain from mutual hostilities. This treaty, renewed at measured intervals and guaranteed by the Diet of the

November 1565: AS Genova, *Archivio Segreto* 2412a (*Spagna* 3a), Tommaso Sauli to the Doge and Council of Genoa, 6 Nov. 1565. Philip II received detailed reports about the route from the duke of Savoy and from his own agent in Savoy, Don Juan de Acuña Vela, in December 1566: AGS *E* 1208/52 and 53. The king only abandoned all hope of passing through the Swiss cantons and the empire when he received an unusually crisp letter of dissuasion from the emperor, dated 7 March 1567 (printed by E. Poullet, *BCRH*, 4e série, v (1877), pp. 351–63).
[1] AGS *E* 1269/27, governor of Lombardy (Terranova) to the king, 19 Jan. 1591.

Swiss Confederation, was respected until 1595 and again from 1598 until 1635. There was, however, a special clause which permitted the 'harmless' passage of troops – the *transitus innoxus* – through the region. Spanish troops could thus cross the Comté without compromising its neutrality.[1]

The dukes of Lorraine and Bar, whose lands stretched between Franche-Comté and Luxemburg and from the Meuse to the Rhine, had painful memories of the military movements of the House of Burgundy. In 1475 Charles the Bold had occupied a number of strongholds in Lorraine in order to form a corridor which would connect his territories 'de par deçà' (the Netherlands) with those 'de par delà' (Burgundy). However, after the 1550s and the occupation of three major towns in Lorraine by France (Metz, Toul and Verdun), the duke was prepared to forgive and forget his ancestral quarrel with Burgundy and to balance his favours between Habsburg and Valois in order to obtain rewards from both. His own position was admirably safeguarded by a treaty of neutrality similar to that of Burgundy: France and Spain agreed to guarantee Lorraine's neutrality in 1547 and the treaty was frequently renewed, although in 1589 the duke himself broke it by intervening in the French wars of religion, and Louis XIII ignored it in 1632–3. As in the Comté, the terms of Lorraine's neutrality permitted troops of all powers free passage provided they did not stay more than two nights in one place.[2]

After Lorraine, the troops marching from Italy to the Low Countries entered Spanish Luxemburg. They had still to cross one more small, independent state before they reached the Army: the prince-bishopric of Liège. Completely encircled by Habsburg land, this state was the most dependable of all Spain's allies – especially after Spanish troops helped the bishop to defeat a ham-fisted invasion by the States General in 1595. Again there were formal treaties of neutrality which limited the troops to no more than two nights in one place.

Although Spain thus enjoyed firm friendship with all the powers which constituted her stepping-stones to the Netherlands, the states were in all respects independent and the passage of any troops had to be preceded by respectful diplomatic overtures. Late in 1566 special ambassadors were sent by Philip II to Lorraine, Savoy and the Swiss cantons to solicit permission for the passage of Alva's army, the first military users of the 'Spanish Road', and to reassure everyone that the troops were destined

---

[1] There are copies of all the treaties of neutrality concerning Burgundy in the manuscript BRB *Ms.* II. 1452, 'Traités de paix, 1549–1666'.
[2] Copies of these little-known treaties of 1547, 1557 and 1596 may be found in AD Meurthe, *3 F* 438, ff. 92–109 and *3 F* 439, ff. 310–37.

solely for the castigation of the Netherlands rebels. These emissaries were recalled after the duke reached Brussels.

The need for further military movements along the 'Spanish Road', unforeseen in 1567, helped to establish more permanent diplomatic arrangements. A regular Spanish ambassador had resided at Genoa after 1528, and in 1571 Philip II decided to open permanent embassies in Savoy and the Swiss Cantons. Both these new posts were directly supervised by the Spanish governor of Lombardy. Curiously, no resident Spanish ambassador was ever sent to Lorraine; instead, every request for permission for troops to cross the duchy was made through a special envoy despatched from Brussels. The same was true of Liège.

Although a formal request for passage from the king of Spain was seldom if ever refused, Spain's allies were not pawns. They had their pride and they rarely suffered their sovereignty to be slighted. In 1622 some Spanish soldiers arrived off Genoa and disembarked without any move by the Spanish ambassador to ask permission: the Council of the Republic, filled with righteous indignation, summoned the negligent envoy and delivered a crisp rebuke. In 1577 when the Spanish veterans returning from the Netherlands arrived on the borders of Savoy before troubling to ask permission to cross, the duke preserved his dignity by making the troops wait for several days before giving his consent. Later in the same year the French governor of Toul in Lorraine wrote a sharp note of complaint to the Netherlands government protesting that the bills for the recent crossing of Spanish troops were still unpaid and that, worse still, a regiment of Burgundian infantry marching to the Low Countries had passed a mere half-league from the town without permission and without paying for the victuals they had seized on the way. The governor hinted strongly that unless apologies and compensation were forthcoming there would be serious trouble when the next expedition attempted to reach the Netherlands.[1]

This was the trump-card held by all of the sovereigns and independent communities along the military corridors of the Army of Flanders: Spain would always need their services again. Spain had therefore to respect their autonomy and humour their pretensions. There were, however, three trouble-spots along the Spanish Road which did not possess this safeguard; three city-states, archaic survivals of the middle ages, which

---

[1] These three examples are taken from: AS Genova, *Archivio Segreto* 2747 (*Spagna* 1), f. 25v (a register of the interviews between the Doge and Council of Genoa and the Spanish ambassador), 3 Aug. 1622; AGS *E* 574/144 and 579/57, Count Mansfelt, commander of the Spanish expedition, to the king, 24 May and 9 Jun. 1577; and AGRB *Audience* 1743/3, unfol., governor of Toul to Don John, 6 Nov. 1577.

had good reason to fear that the Spanish troops which passed beneath their walls harboured treacherous designs against their independence – Geneva, Besançon and Metz.

On 28 March 1567 the august Council of the Genevan Republic, an independent, Calvinist city-state, heard certain news of the duke of Alva's march. They therefore resolved to increase the city's garrison and augment its food reserves 'while the enemy is passing through this land'. The Spanish Road was thus branded from the first as the highway of *the enemy*. On 1 April the city fathers heard that Alva's army would comprise 15,000 foot and 6,000 horse (a massive exaggeration) and three days later, with regret, the council delegated its executive powers to a secret war committee which was to coordinate the Republic's defence during the approaching emergency. The council levied new troops in France and elsewhere and it raised a loan of 300,000 florins to pay for them. Geneva refused to demobilize its emergency forces until the duke of Alva and his men were safely in the Netherlands.[1]

No later march along the Spanish Road excited the same degree of terror in Geneva but, conversely, few expeditions failed to provoke a crisis of some sort. Spain continued to be 'the enemy'. In 1577, for example, the return of the Spanish *tercios* from the Low Countries to Italy found the city paralysed with fright: the Spaniards were reported to be coming armed with 'ladders, hooks and other instruments to scale a city'. These, and countless other ill-founded rumours which surrounded every movement of Spanish troops, were based on the reports filed by the army of spies retained by Geneva abroad, tempered by the more level-headed letters sent to the Republic by friendly Protestant states, Bern, Württemburg, Montbéliard and so on. In 1620, detailed news of Spain's preparations for an expedition was sent to Geneva by the English ambassador at Turin, Dr Isaac Wake and, at the Republic's request, he persuaded the Spaniards to change their itinerary from the Little St Bernard pass and Faverges to the Mt Cenis and the Combe de Savoie, to keep them further away from Geneva.[2]

---

[1] AE Geneva, *RC* 62/32v, 33v, 36 and 38v. The first news of Spain's intention to send an army of Spaniards via the Spanish Road reached the city on 1 Nov. 1566 (*RC* 61/105v). On the fiscal consequences of Alva's march, cf. W. E. Monter, 'Le change public à Genève, 1568–1581', in *Mélanges...Antony Babel*, I (Geneva, 1967), pp. 265–90. In fact 124,083 florins were spent in preparations against Alva's arrival, but the rest of the loan was used as capital to float a public exchange in the city.

[2] AE Geneva, *RC* 72/74v, deliberation of the City Council 24 May 1577. No less than sixteen separate, and often contradictory reports reached the Republic concerning the intentions of the Spanish expedition of 1577. There were ten concerning the march of 1584 (cf. *RC* 79). The reports of Isaac Wake in 1620 are in AE Geneva, *PH* 2651.

It is tempting to poke fun at the fear and trembling of the Genevan Council: we know now that the commanders of all Spanish expeditions were under the strictest orders to leave Calvin's city alone. It was not common knowledge at the time, however. The Republic was uncomfortably aware of the friendship of Spain and Savoy; the duke married in 1584 one of Philip II's charming and able daughters, Catalina Michaela. There was also the undeniable fact that the duke of Savoy's serious and almost successful attacks on Geneva in 1582, 1597 and 1602 were secretly prepared under the disguise of arranging the Spaniards' marches in those years. Finally, it was true that Philip II did offer to assist his son-in-law, the duke, with very considerable aid should he attack Geneva. The king of Spain was certainly anxious to see the citadel of Calvinism destroyed – but he was not prepared to delay the despatch of his elite troops to the Netherlands for the sake of Geneva.[1]

The city of Besançon, although it lay in the heart of Franche-Comté, did not belong to the king of Spain. Until 1653 it was an imperial free city, independent and anxious to avoid ties with the rulers of the Comté. In 1575 it lost an important measure of autonomy because, as a result of a surprise assault and occupation by a band of French Huguenots, it could no longer refuse to admit a Spanish garrison. This change, not surprisingly, did nothing to diminish the city's distrust and hostility towards the passage of King Philip's troops through the Comté. In 1567 Besançon would not raise a finger to aid the government's preparations for the duke of Alva, looking rather to its own defence lest the duke should purpose a surprise attack. Likewise in 1577 the news that Spanish troops were marching back to Italy led the town council, fortified with Classical wisdom, to decide:

> Because of the impending passage through Burgundy of the Spanish troops returning from the Low Countries, and because NULLA FIDES VIRIS QUI CASTRA SEQUUNTUR, MM. Doissans and La Tour are appointed to see to the defence of the city with full powers during the passage.

Besançon continued to exhibit this timorous reaction to later expeditions along the Spanish Road although, as we now know, it was in even less danger than Geneva.[2]

---

[1] AGS *E* 1261/90 and 105, the king to Terranova, governor of Milan, 22 Aug. and 12 Sep. 1586. Six thousand men, either Spaniards or Italians, were to support the duke of Savoy's laudable efforts against Geneva 'for the sake of the Faith and to recover his patrimony'. For other examples of Spanish aid cf. AGS *E* 1255/48 and 1256/103 (for Savoy's *empresa* of 1582) and *E* 1263/3 (surprise attack in Jan. 1588).

[2] All Besançon's moves to guard against a surprise attack in 1567 were noted by L. Febvre, *Philippe II et la Franche-Comté* (Paris, 1911), p. 523, n. 6. For the decision of 1577 cf. AM Besançon, *BB* 36/205, Deliberation of the magistrates 18 May 1577.

Henry II's attack on Charles V in 1552 secured for France the three imperial enclaves in Lorraine: Metz, Toul and Verdun. France immediately fortified her conquests, the 'Three Bishoprics' as they were invariably known. At Metz an imposing citadel was completed in 1564 and a garrison of 1,040 men was maintained; Henry II even installed a special civil and judicial administration to provide French government for his new conquests (and this survived until the rest of Lorraine was annexed in the eighteenth century). The continual protests of the emperor and of the imperial Diet at French occupation of the 'Three Bishoprics' achieved nothing.

The duke of Alva's advance through Franche-Comté in 1567 prompted an increase in the garrison of Metz and repairs to the defences of Toul and Verdun. Alva, after all, had besieged Metz once before, unsuccessfully, in 1552. The expedition of 1567, however, and most others, avoided the bishopric with great care, passing either far to the east or west. This was inconvenient, because Metz straddled the most direct and most commodious route to the Netherlands – down the Moselle valley – but France made it very clear that she would not tolerate any violation of her sovereignty at that point. The troops had to find another way.

Fear and uncertainty concerning the true destination of the troops using the Spanish Road was by no means confined to the privilege-jealous citizens of the three city-states. The duke of Alva's march, for example, caused a serious international crisis. As late as 5 July 1567 (when Alva was just crossing into Franche-Comté) the Spanish ambassador in France passed a difficult hour convincing Charles IX that the duke's passage to the Low Countries was not the prelude to a new Habsburg–Valois war. Taking no chances, France made military preparations in feverish haste all along Alva's route. More troops were rushed into the marquisate of Saluzzo, France's precious enclave in Piedmont; 6,000 Swiss mercenaries were hired to shadow the progress of the Spanish Army; the garrisons of Lyon and other frontier posts were increased. On the other side of the Road, the lords of Bern (the largest canton, staunchly Protestant) likewise raised some troops and strengthened a few garrisons, while Strasbourg increased its garrison by 4,000 men.[1]

After the rebellion of Holland and Zealand in 1572 the expeditions along the Spanish Road provoked far less international tension. Governments could accept Spain's assurances that the columns plodding north-

[1] AGS *EK* 1508/7, 18, 27 and 31, Don Frances de Alava (Spanish ambassador in France) to the king, 7 and 25 May, 30 Jun. and 5 Jul. 1567; *ibid.*, f. 24, Don Antonio de Mendoza (Spanish envoy to Lorraine) to the king, 24 Jun. 1567.

wards were destined only for the juggernaut of the Low Countries' Wars. They could therefore be tolerated if not ignored.

Paradoxically the less alarming the Spanish Road became in political terms, the more it provoked religious agitation. That curious internationalism which makes the sixteenth century (in Hauser's phrase) so 'modern' prompted the most diverse and improbable elements in Europe to see in the Spanish Road a personal threat and led them to take action about it, against it.

As early as 1566, according to rumour, some ardent enemies of Spain went so far as to enter Savoy armed 'with ointments to spread the plague' in all the areas through which the duke of Alva was expected to pass. Cardinal Granvelle, who heard and believed the rumour, concluded that such determined and precocious protagonists of biological warfare came from that seminary of revolution and heresy, Geneva.[1] All through the winter of 1566–7 stories flew from mouth to mouth that the French Huguenots were mobilizing forces to block Alva's route to the Low Countries and thereby save the Calvinist cause. The duke of Savoy was quite convinced that there would be some major confrontation between Alva and the Huguenots. He was proved wrong.[2] Similarly grandiose plots to waylay other expeditions using the Spanish Road were reported in later years, but all failed to materialize: Louis of Nassau could not intercept the new governor-general of the Netherlands, Don Luis de Requesens, as he rode through the forests of Lorraine; the duke of Alençon, brightest hope of the Huguenot cause who was thought to be preparing to invade Franche-Comté and cut the Spanish Road in 1578 and 1582, failed to achieve anything.[3]

If this military corridor of the Army of Flanders was to be blocked effectively, the challenge of geography had to be overcome. Only a major undertaking could be successful, and that required money. Discussing the reported preparations of the Huguenots against Alva's troops in 1567, Don Fernando de Lannoy, who knew Franche-Comté better than anyone,

---

[1] E. Poullet, *Correspondance...de Granvelle*, II, pp. 167–77, Granvelle to the king, 23 Dec. 1566. There may have been no substance to this rumour, but the story is not *a priori* impossible: there *was* plague in the region of Geneva at the time (it broke out in the city itself on 2 May 1567: AE Geneva *RC* 62/52) and Alva's army certainly contracted plague and dysentery somewhere along its route.

[2] AGS *E* 1219/163, Duke Emmanuel-Philibert of Savoy to the king, 30 Nov. 1566, holograph.

[3] Van Prinsterer, *Archives*, IV, p. 278, Count Louis of Nassau to William of Orange (undated letter: December 1573); AGRB *Audience* 1706/2, unfol., various papers of 1578 about calling the *arrière-ban* in the Comté against the threatened French invasion; AM Besançon *BB* 38/199v, 24 Aug. 1582, a report received from the Swiss cantons that 'Le capitaine Beaujeu avoit offert son service à Monsr. d'Alençon et aux Estatz des Pays-Bas pour empescher les passaiges des gens du Roy Catholique en Bourgogne.'

wrote: 'They [the Spaniards] will be marching through a country strong in mountains and woods. It will be hard to stop them...without a great deal of money.' If the Huguenots were ever to make their plan effective they had to enlist the support of a government with the power, wealth and strength of purpose necessary to create a complete barrier across the difficult terrain of the Vosges and Jura.[1]

On 24 April 1584, Philippe Duplessis–Mornay, a Huguenot gentleman fertile in ideas and projects, presented a paper to his king entitled 'Discourse to King Henry III on the means of diminishing the Spaniard (*l'Espagnol*).' One of his principal recommendations concerned the Spanish Road:

> The King of Spain has nothing in all his possessions that is fairer, richer or esteemed more highly than the Low Countries...They are sustained with men and maintained with money by Italy and by Spain, for which the only passage is the Franche-Comté. If His Majesty were to set loose some of his subjects, who could be named by the King of Navarre [i.e. the leader of the Huguenots, later Henry IV] they would capture the best places in the Comté – and just one would suffice for the purpose: with just one captured there can be no more communication, except with the greatest difficulty, between the Low Countries and Italy and Spain.[2]

This advice was certainly attractive to the French king. The Spanish Road was used by the bankers of Philip II as well as by his troops. After 1578 in particular large convoys of bullion (mostly gold until 1590) passed close to the French border under only nominal escort. Each was a tempting target. However, Henry III, his kingdom on the brink of another civil war, his authority rapidly dwindling, was hardly in a position to take action. It was left to his successor, the same Henry of Navarre mentioned by Duplessis-Mornay, to implement the excellent suggestion.

At the end of 1592 the governor-general of the Low Countries reported an attempt by French and Dutch detachments to capture a number of towns and valleys in Lorraine in order to make:

> a sort of barrier [*barrière*] across the said duchy in order to close the routes to Italy, Burgundy and Lorraine and from Germany to the Low Countries, and thus to prevent all access here by land from Spain, Italy, Savoy, Franche-Comté and Lorraine.[3]

This determined effort was largely provoked by Spain. The Spanish Road assumed an additional strategic importance during the French

[1] AM Besançon, *Ms. Granvelle* 24/247–8v, Lannoy to Cardinal Granvelle, 19 Apr. 1567.
[2] The Discourse is printed in S. Goulart, *Mémoires de la Ligue* (3rd edn, Amsterdam, 1758), I, pp. 596–601.
[3] AGRB *Audience* 204/124, Count Mansfelt to the king, 22 Dec. 1592. Spanish troops were sent into Lorraine to keep the Road open (*ibid.*, ff. 153–7).

Religious Wars; it became a sort of 'Ho Chi Minh Trail', bringing men and money through neutral territory to reinforce the French Catholics in their struggle against Henry of Navarre. With Spanish aid, the Catholic *Ligue* came within an inch of victory. In 1593–4, however, the tide turned. Henry IV's position strengthened dramatically and he declared war on Spain. Neglecting the traditional theatres of Franco–Spanish conflict, Picardy and Piedmont, Henry opened hostilities in the east. He invaded and overran Burgundy, destroying at one blow the power-base of his principal opponent, Mayenne (the governor of French Burgundy, and leader of the *Ligue*), and damaging the pipeline which supplied Mayenne and his Spanish allies, Franche-Comté (1595). The Spanish Road was not actually cut by this action, but the troops and the bullion convoys were forced to travel further east, even via Saarbrücken, in order to reach the Low Countries in safety. In 1597 Henry IV's troops returned to the attack on the Spanish Road. His lieutenant in Dauphiné, Lesdiguières, invaded the duchy of Savoy and occupied the Maurienne and Tarantaise valleys, the crucial arteries which connected Franche-Comté with Italy. No more soldiers or specie could pass to the Low Countries until France withdrew her troops after the Peace of Vervins (2 May 1598).

Vervins restored a degree of safety to the Spanish Road, but it left unsettled the possession of Saluzzo, a small French enclave in the Piedmontese Alps occupied by the duke of Savoy in 1588. Henry IV demanded the restitution of Saluzzo at Vervins, but negotiation failed to produce the desired result. In 1600, his patience exhausted, Henry invaded and occupied all Savoy with disquieting ease. A peace conference to discuss the dispute opened at Lyon. France offered an alternative to the duke of Savoy; either to return Saluzzo to France, or else to retain Saluzzo and surrender to France all the territories of Savoy (already occupied) west of the river Rhône. This choice involved Spain because if France annexed all the land between the Rhône and the border of Franche-Comté (over twenty miles from the river at its closest point) the Spanish Road was lost. The duke of Savoy, however, was not willing to restore Saluzzo. The delegates at Lyon recognized the justice of Spain's demand for a secure military highway, and proposed one running from Milan through the Swiss Cantons via the Simplon pass, Martigny and Lausanne to Pontarlier in Franche-Comté (cf. Figure 8). This plan was on the point of acceptance when the representative of the city of Geneva at the conference protested that such a plan would expose the Republic to attack by the Spanish troops on its undefended eastern side. He pointed out to the delegates that there was one narrow defile which connected the

Rhône valley with the Franche-Comté: the Val de Chézery or Valserine, close to Geneva but on the west side and separated from the city by a high mountain range. He argued that if just this narrow valley were left to Savoy (together with Saluzzo) it would satisfy Spain's military needs without jeopardizing Geneva's independence. The proposal was accepted, despite Spanish opposition, and it was embodied in the Treaty of Lyon, signed on 17 January 1601. Savoy retained Saluzzo and the Val de Chézery but lost all other territory west of the Rhône.[1]

The Spanish Road was thus confined to one narrow valley and to a single bridge over the Rhône, the *pont de Grésin*. The valley and the bridge were but a stone's throw from the French frontier. France thus acquired the power to deny or delay the passage of any Habsburg troops to the Netherlands and it was not long before she tried out her new opportunity to twist the tail of the Spanish lion. In 1602, Henry IV claimed to suspect that the Italian troops of Ambrosio Spinola, marching through Savoy to the Army of Flanders, were intended to aid the dangerous conspiracy of Marshal Biron. Accordingly the *pont de Grésin* was broken. The Spaniards protested hotly to the pope, guarantor of the Treaty of Lyon, complaining that:

> Their troops could only pass through the territories which had been left expressly for that purpose to the duke of Savoy by the Treaty of Lyon, and that no one could stand in the way of their passage without revealing openly the desire to break the peace.

The papal mediator, sympathizing with Spain, did his best to secure the immediate reconstruction of the broken bridge, but in vain. Spinola was not allowed to cross the Rhône until Biron was executed and his conspiracy entirely crushed.[2]

The Spanish Road never recovered from the Treaty of Lyon. After 1601 it depended absolutely on French goodwill, and France never forgot her advantage. In the detailed maps of France's frontier areas drawn up for Henry IV's minister Sully in 1606 the Spanish Road was labelled and

---

[1] For the Saluzzo affair, cf. J. L. Cano de Gardoqui, *La cuestión de Saluzzo en las comunicaciones del imperio español, 1588–1601* (Valladolid, 1962). The route via Lausanne preferred by the Spaniards is noted in AGS *E* 1291/149, and the counter-proposal of the Genevan representative, François de Chapeaurouge, is in AE Geneva, *RC* 96/209 (Chapeaurouge's report to the Council of the Republic, 22 Dec. 1601); it is given in précis by F. de Crue, 'Henri IV et les députés de Genève', *MDG*, XXV (1901), pp. 471–2.

[2] J. E. M. Lajeune, 'Correspondance entre Henri IV et Philippe de Béthune, Ambassadeur de France à Rome, 1602–1604', *MDG*, XXXVIII (1952), pp. 189–475, letter of Béthune to Henry IV, 19 Aug. 1602 on pp. 270–1. Cf. also AGS *E* 1291/177, Don Mendo Rodríguez de Ledesma (Spanish ambassador to Savoy) to the king, 5 Aug. 1602.

picked out in red (cf. Plate 5). France had the principal supply-route of the Army of Flanders at her mercy.

To those with their eyes open, the unfavourable terms accorded to Spain by the Treaty of Lyon were an early manifestation of the waning of Spanish power. They signalled a significant shift in the relative power of France and Spain which no state whose position depended on playing off one against the other could afford to neglect. The duke of Savoy was one of the first to trim his sails to take full advantage of the change in the prevailing wind. He and his predecessors had always aimed at territorial expansion by all possible means. In the later sixteenth century it was clear that this could best be achieved by enlisting Spanish support against France, but the loss of so much land under the terms of the Treaty of Lyon revealed brutally that the situation had changed. While the humiliation of Henry IV's victory was still fresh in his mind, Duke Charles-Emanuel kept to his Spanish alliance, even admitting a *tercio* of Spanish infantry from Milan to garrison the crucial towns along the Savoy section of the Spanish Road after 1602. Before long, however, the duke began to see that if he secured French aid instead, it might be possible to annex some Spanish lands in Lombardy. In 1609 the Spanish garrisons were expelled and in 1610 the duke concluded an offensive alliance with France against Spain. In 1613, even without French aid the duke fought with Spain over a dynastic claim and withstood with ease every Spanish assault. After four years of desultory and inconclusive fighting the French mediated an uneasy peace between the former allies (Asti 1617). Although a large Spanish and Italian army was allowed to cross in 1620, the entente was short-lived. Savoy made a new anti-Spanish treaty in 1622. The Spanish Road was never used by Spaniards again.

The coming of French control to the Spanish Road in 1601 gave new impetus to Spain's attempts to find an alternative itinerary between Lombardy and the Low Countries. Negotiations were already far advanced in two areas. In 1593, after nearly thirty years of preliminary discussion, the Grey Lords or Grisons who controlled the Engadine and Valtelline, two valleys which linked Lombardy with the Tyrol, concluded an alliance which conceded to Spain the right to move her troops through their territory.[1] Shortly before this diplomatic coup, in 1587, Spain's

---

[1] There is a draft copy of the treaty (27 Jul. 1593) in AGS *E* 1272/160; *ibid.*, f. 134 the governor of Milan told the Spanish ambassador in Rome, 2 Jul. 1593, that the treaty was signed mainly to facilitate the passage of Spanish troops to Lombardy. Cf. also *E* 1221/198 and 274 on the

Figure 8. Lombardy: communications centre of the Spanish empire in Europe

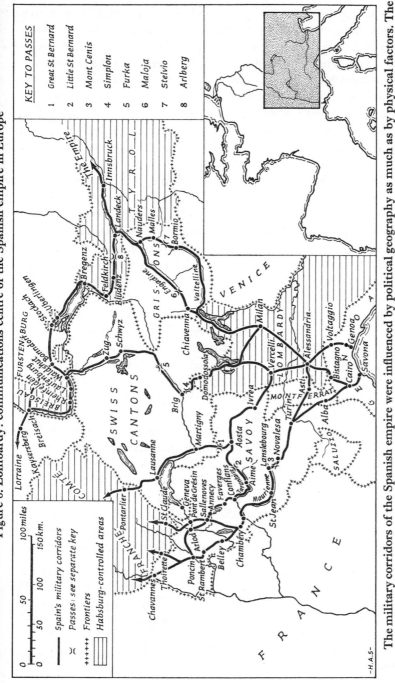

KEY TO PASSES

Passes: see separate key

1 Great St Bernard
2 Little St Bernard
3 Mont Cenis
4 Simplon
5 Furka
6 Maloja
7 Stelvio
8 Arlberg

Spain's military corridors
Passes: see separate key
Frontiers
Habsburg-controlled areas

0 100 miles
0 150 km.

The military corridors of the Spanish empire were influenced by political geography as much as by physical factors. The Alps constituted an important barrier to contact between Lombardy and northern Europe, but the real obstacle to Spanish communications in this area was the attitude of the states which controlled the Alpine passes: Savoy, the Swiss and the Grisons. Sources: The Spanish Road – BNM *Ms.* 3827/175, AGS *E* 1208/52–3 and 1290/42, and BM *Addl. Ms.* 21,117/33 and 34v. The Grisons route – AGS *E* 3338/31 and 3340/86. The Swiss route – AGS *E* 1923/23. The route through Martigny and Lausanne was proposed in 1601 but never materialized (cf. p. 68).

71

ministers in Italy secured a treaty of friendship with the Catholic cantons of the Swiss confederation. These cantons controlled an unbroken corridor of territory between Lombardy and Alsace (via Domodossola, the Simplon pass and Zug). When the possibility of an alliance with the cantons was first discussed in Madrid in 1584 Cardinal Granvelle, who had crossed the Alps himself on a number of occasions, was enthusiastic. He realized that the route through the Catholic cantons 'although shorter, is neither as commodious nor as safe as the Savoy route', but he knew that it was essential for Spain to have an alternative to the Spanish Road in case of need.[1]

The advent of the Treaty of Lyon, which made an alternative route imperative, found a new and energetic Spanish governor in Lombardy: Don Pedro Enríquez de Acevedo, count of Fuentes. The most daring and the most successful of Spain's proconsuls, Fuentes was just the man to bully and cajole the Swiss into permitting the passage of Spanish troops: he was Alva's nephew and a formidable soldier in his own right, and he knew from first-hand the Army of Flanders' dependence on Spanish reinforcements (he had commanded in the Netherlands 1592-6). Fuentes typified the strong viceroy who, under the aimless, vacuous rule of Philip III, tended to forge Spain's foreign policy independent of the court. He lost no time in working on the Swiss and the Grisons.

In 1604 Fuentes managed to re-negotiate Spain's treaty of friendship with the Swiss Catholic cantons, this time with the coveted clause which authorized the passage of Spanish troops through to the Rhine (provided the soldiers moved in small groups and were unarmed: weapons and munitions had to be sent separately in boxes). Cynically, but with obvious success, Fuentes worked on the assumption that 'self-interest is the best hold one can have over that nation' and he arranged to deliver a subsidy of 33,000 *escudos* (82,500 florins) annually to the Swiss leaders and to divert the convoys of merchandise which plied between Italy and the Netherlands to pass through (and therefore to pay tolls to) the Catholic cantons.[2] The new route was used successfully by Spanish expeditions in 1604 and 1605 but after Fuentes' death in 1610 the subsidies fell into

negotiations of Don Sancho de Londoño (of *Discurso* fame) with the Grisons in 1564-5 and *E* 1258/55-6, the Treaty of Spain with the Grisons signed in Sep. 1583 but repudiated by the Grey Lords in Jun. 1584 (*E* 1259/45).

[1] A draft copy of the treaty, dated 12 May 1587, is preserved in AGS *E* 1262/8. Under its terms, a subsidy of 66,500 *escudos* (about 166,000 florins) was paid to the cantons on 27 June (*E* 1263/37). On the discussions of 1584 cf. BRB *Ms.* 9471-2/374-5, Granvelle to the king, 28 Oct. 1584.

[2] AGS *E* 1293/25, Fuentes to the king, 5 May 1604. (The overland trade between Italy and the Netherlands had formerly passed along the Spanish Road.)

arrears and in 1613 the French (by means of an equally liberal distribution of gold) persuaded the cantons to repudiate the treaty. Although the Catholic cantons solemnly renewed their alliance with Spain in June 1634, French diplomatic pressure prevented further detachments of Spanish troops from marching to the Low Countries by this route.[1]

The count of Fuentes also took characteristically decisive steps to consolidate Spain's diplomatic foothold in the Grisons. In 1603, without warning, his engineers and soldiers built a fort on an impregnable promontory right at the mouth of the Valtelline: the Forte di Fuentes on the hill of Montecchio.

This solution to the Grisons problem proved modestly successful: the Grey Lords became more obliging. The revolt of the Catholic inhabitants of the valleys against their Protestant masters (21 July 1620) provided an ideal opportunity for further encroachment. In November 1620, invited by the Catholics, Spanish troops entered the Valtelline. Unexpectedly they built a castle at Bormio, right in the Grisons heartland, and further garrisons were rapidly introduced from Lombardy and the Tyrol to form a chain of strong-points which could guarantee the security of the new military corridor. By 1622 there were 3,626 Spanish and Italian troops in Alsace and 4,290 more in the Grisons valleys.[2] Under their protection, armies were sent from Lombardy to the Low Countries via the Valtelline, Tyrol and Alsace in 1623 and 1631, while imperial regiments marched through the valleys to Italy in 1629 and 1630 to aid Spain in the war of Mantua. Spain's imperial communications thus functioned adequately without either Savoy or the Swiss cantons. The Valtelline itinerary was long, but in the 1620s it was safe.

In autumn 1631, however, the Habsburgs lost Alsace. It was a terrible blow for Spain: no safe 'military corridor' remained beyond the Alps. In 1634 the cardinal-infante of Spain, Don Fernando, assembled another great army in Lombardy ready for the Army of Flanders, but before he set out he was warned that the only feasible route from Milan to Brussels was to march into Germany, join forces with an imperial army, and fight a way through the Protestant states in his path. Miraculously, in September 1634 the joint Habsburg army routed the Swedish and Protestant forces which blocked the road to the Netherlands at Nördlingen. It was a

---

[1] BNM *Ms.* 18,718 n. 81, 'Liga renovelada entre la magestad del Rey de España y los cantones católicos squizgaros...' 20 Jun. 1634. It was signed in Milan by the cardinal-infante; cf. clause 6.

[2] AGS *E* 1926/128, '*Relación*' of Philip IV's troops in Alsace and the Grisons, Jan. 1622. Cf. also the interesting study of A. Giussani, *Il forte di Fuentes. Episodi e documenti di una lotta secolare per il dominio della Valtellina* (Como, 1905).

73

great victory, and it opened the way to the Low Countries for the cardinal-infante, but it could not create a new military corridor. The year after Nördlingen, the French invaded Germany and the Grisons. Neither Spain nor the emperor had any more armies to drive them back.[1]

To a considerable extent the negotiations with the Catholic cantons and the military occupation of the Grisons, Alsace and the Palatinate in the early seventeenth century were the product of Spain's anxious search for sure military corridors to the Netherlands. The late Professor Geisendorf was very near the mark when he attributed the troubles of the Valtelline to the Treaty of Lyon and the fragility of the *Pont de Grésin*.[2] This was not the only cause however. Spain had already made purposeful moves to establish her mastery over the lords of the Alpine passes long before 1601; the unfavourable terms at Lyon led to the intensification of negotiations already afoot. The domestic peace of the valleys was shattered because Spain was no longer the only power with an active interest in sending troops through the Alps. The Grisons were, in the real sense of the term, a crossroads of power. Spain's military corridor ran through the Valtelline and Engadine, linking Lombardy with the empire and the Netherlands; in the Grisons it crossed with France's military corridor, over the Julier pass and through Camonica valley to Venice, her only reliable Italian ally (Figure 9). Savoy was a fickle ally for France as well as for Spain: if French armies were to intervene effectively in Italy there had to be an alternative to the route controlled by Savoy. The Grisons' corridor was used by Strozzi and Guise under Henry II; it was used again by Coeuvres and Rohan under Louis XIII. It was as vital to France as it was to Spain. Any alliance of Spain with the Swiss, with Savoy or with the Grisons, and any Spanish military presence in the Alpine regions, was thus immediately a target for French diplomacy to destroy because, as one lugubrious ambassador to the cantons wrote: 'it runs directly counter to the end they [the French] have always had – to close to His Majesty the passes from Italy to the Netherlands and from Germany to Italy'.[3] In addition, at least after the fall of the Brûlarts and their conciliatory foreign policy in 1624, it was not enough for the passes to be closed to Spain; they had also to be secured for the use of French

---

[1] AGRB *SEG* 2289, unfol., marquis of Aytona to the cardinal-infante, 3 Jun. 1634. The exact itinerary of the 1634 expedition is given in *SEG* 34, the cardinal-infante's order-book on the march.

[2] P.-F. Geisendorf, 'Le Traité de Lyon et le pont de Grésin, ou d'une cause parfois méconnue des troubles des Grisons au 17e siècle', *MDG*, XL (1961), pp. 279–86.

[3] AGS *CJH* 522, unfol., 'Relación del estado que tiene las cosas de S.M. en Esquizgaros' by Alfonso Casati, 3 Apr. 1613. (This document was kindly brought to my notice by Mr P. L. Williams of University College, London.)

Figure 9. The Valtelline: crossroads of power

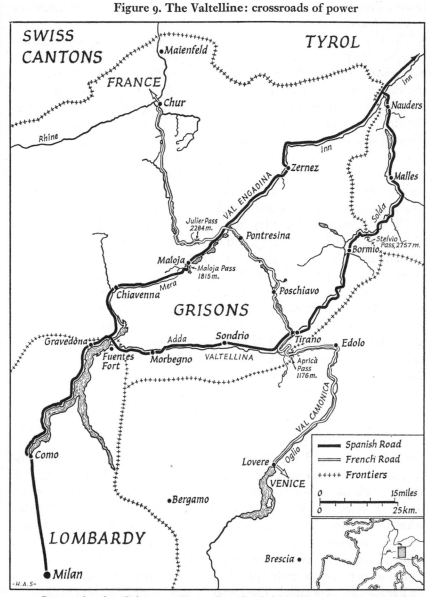

It was in the Grisons valleys that Spain's military communications between Lombardy and the Empire crossed those of France leading to Venice. Both powers needed absolute control of the valleys if their foreign policy was to be successful: hence the misfortunes of the Grisons in the first third of the seventeenth century. Source: AGS *E* 1221/274 and 1239/36.

troops. This alone explains the presence of a French army in the Valtelline in 1624–6 and 1635–7.

There was a similar clash of interests in Alsace. The province was occupied by French forces after 1638 because it commanded the surest passage from France into south Germany. As the perceptive historian of the French conquest has written: 'For Richelieu, Alsace represented less a territorial reality than a crossroads.'[1] Breisach in particular, commanding the only bridge over the Rhine between Strasbourg and Basle, carried the 'French Road' from Saverne through the Black Forest to Pforzheim as well as the Spanish thoroughfare from Italy to the Netherlands. As control of the Valtelline guaranteed French intervention in Italy, so mastery of Breisach and Alsace underpinned French aggression in the empire. Alsace, like the Valtelline, had to be occupied.

The same military logic lay behind the French invasion of Savoy in 1630–1 and Lorraine in 1632–3. Although there was an element of personal vendetta in both actions – the two dukes had tried to dethrone Henry IV in the 1590s, invading France in support of the *Ligue,* and the duke of Lorraine at least had given overt support to Louis XIII's turbulent brother, Gaston of Orleans ('Monsieur') – Richelieu's motives for occupying the two duchies were overwhelmingly strategic. Savoy was the gateway to Italy and Richelieu had to be sure of his supply-line from France as long as his armies were fighting across the Alps; Lorraine was no less the gateway to Germany and its control was the necessary prelude to effective French intervention in the Thirty Years' War. Neither conquest was relinquished until France had achieved her purposes.

These French successes completely disrupted most of Spain's military corridors. The French occupation of Savoy was the least damaging to Spain because it had been long foreseen; the loss of the Valtelline and Alsace were more serious; but the invasion of Lorraine by Louis XIII in 1633 cut all the major military supply-routes of the Spanish empire at one blow, since the routes from the Tyrol and from the Valtelline together with the well-trodden Spanish Road all depended on the right of passage through Lorraine. Even before the fall of Nancy France made it clear that she would not respect that right: in April 1633 an expedition of 3,000 Burgundian recruits marching to the Netherlands was forced to turn back by French threats of attack. The loss of Nancy later in the year (20 September) meant that 'Communications between the Low Countries and Franche-Comté, Italy and Germany remain cut and at the mercy of the French.'[2]

---

[1] G. Livet, *L'Intendance d'Alsace sous Louis XIV, 1648–1715* (Paris, 1956), p. 26.
[2] AGRB *SEG* 207/293–4v, Infanta Isabella to the king, 24 Oct. 1633.

To an extent the destruction of the overland military corridors of the Army of Flanders was inevitable. Their availability to Spain was essentially the consequence of the internal weakness of France after 1559. Once France resumed her traditional foreign policy, after 1595 under Henry IV and after 1628 under Louis XIII, French aggression was bound to concentrate on mastery of the bridgeheads into Italy and Germany. French success in these objectives necessarily meant that Spain forfeited her military highways.

The Army of Flanders coped surprisingly well with these tremendous changes in the balance of power in Europe. The closing of the route from the Tyrol was compensated by an increase of recruiting in: Rhineland. Only the Burgundians were completely cut off: the merciless guerilla warfare which followed France's declaration of war on Spain in May 1635 put an end to all possibility of further recruiting in the Comté – even had Lorraine remained neutral. The Italians and Spaniards, by contrast, who had made such intensive use of the Spanish Road, found another way of reaching the Army of Flanders, at least in the 1630s.

It was the hostility of England which, above all else, made the Channel unsafe for Spanish shipping after 1568. The few attempts to run the gauntlet of enemy fleets and transport Spanish recruits directly to the Netherlands (1598, 1601 and 1602) all ran into difficulties because, when the Dutch attacked, the Spaniards were unable to shelter in any English port. The situation was changed by the Anglo–Spanish Treaty of London in August 1604. Thereafter Spanish troopships could count on English protection. Only the truce with the Dutch (1607–21) restrained Spain from using the sea-route more often. Then in 1625, England declared war on Spain again; once more the Channel was closed to Spanish shipping. It was only in 1630, with the second Treaty of London and the Dover Composition Trade, that England offered positive assistance to Spain over the transportation of her troops and specie to the Army of Flanders. Since the land corridors were blocked, Spain made full use of the new route. Larger and larger expeditions left the Cantabrian ports for the Netherlands, counting on a sure refuge in England should need arise. In all some 27,000 troops were sent to the Low Countries by sea from Spain between 1631 and 1639 (cf. Appendix C). Carriage was normally provided by frigates of the Dunkirk fleet, but on a number of occasions English merchants in Spain offered to ferry troops for the Spanish crown.

It all came to an abrupt end in 1639. Five ships of a leading English merchant in Spain, Benjamin Wright, left Cadiz with 1,500 Spanish recruits on 18 May bound for the Netherlands. Thirty Dutch warships were waiting in the Channel under Admiral Tromp, having been forewarned of the ships' cargo, they surrounded Wright's vessels. The English sailors refused to fight. Who would compensate them, they asked, if they lost life or limb defending the Spaniards? Anyway the Dutch were their friends. In this way the Dutch fleet captured 1,000 of the Spaniards; the rest found asylum in Portsmouth. The same year saw an even greater disaster for the Spanish supply-route. In August 1639 the Spanish government prepared a fleet of sixty vessels to carry 14,000 men to the Netherlands and to seek out and destroy the entire Dutch navy. Admiral Tromp was not hard to find; he was waiting in the Channel with his fleet. Swiftly he outmanœuvred the Spanish commander, Don Antonio de Oquendo, and forced him to seek shelter in the roadstead of the Downs, off Deal. There, despite English protection, Oquendo's fleet was annihilated by Tromp on 21 October.[1]

Not even a defeat as complete as this could stop Spain. After all, as Olivares was quick to point out, the survivors of the battle of the Downs, about 5,000 of them, did escape to England and were eventually shipped over to Dunkirk and the Army of Flanders. In addition and more important, there was no alternative route. Therefore, despite the risks, small vessels continued to ferry unwilling detachments from Spain to the Netherlands throughout the 1640s. Often foreign merchantmen were hired for the purpose; indeed after the peace of 1648 even the Dutch began to participate in this commerce. The numbers, however, were always small; a few hundred at a time was the maximum, and many of them arrived in the Netherlands more dead than alive thanks to the notorious overcrowding on the troopships. The Army of Flanders was forced into even greater dependence on the troops recruited locally.[2]

[1] AGRB *SEG* 369/292–5, Reports of the commander of the Spanish recruits, Don Simon Mascarenhas, to the cardinal-infante (from England), heavily critical of Benjamin Wright ('Ruit' to the Spaniards). Wright, for his part, claimed to have spent £100,000 (about 1 million florins) in transporting Spaniards to the Netherlands between 1630 and 1644. Nothing had been repaid by Philip IV in 1655 (BNM *Ms.* 9405/116, memorial of Benjamin 'Ruit', 23 Feb. 1655). The Oquendo-Tromp duel is superbly narrated by Boxer, *Journal of Tromp*. The king of Spain stated that the fleet would carry 14,000 Spaniards, 9,000 of them for the Army of Flanders. (BM *Addl. Ms.* 14,007/71–5v, Philip IV to the cardinal-infante, 30 Aug. 1639, copy.)

[2] AHN *E libro* 963 contains a number of papers from 1640–1 about hiring foreign frigates to transport troops between Spain and the Low Countries. The letter on f. 76 is particularly informative. Cf also *ibid.*, libros 955, 964 and 973. The number of troops embarked on individual ships is given for several voyages of German troops to Spain in the 1640s: a frigate of about 70 tons transported about 100 soldiers (excluding the crew) and a warship of 500 tons

Such were the vital military corridors which, until 1640 and the final collapse, provided the Army of Flanders with its foreign troops and permitted Spain to mobilize its great armies with such startling rapidity. Yet surmounting the political obstacles, difficult as they were, constituted only half the battle. Diplomatic protection secured, the troops had still to be assembled, armed and fed along their route, whether by sea or land. It proved easier to make these preparations for a sea voyage, but paradoxically the indifferent marine technology and above all the treacherous weather of the Bay of Biscay, the Channel and the North Sea made it extremely difficult to predict how long the voyage would take. All too often a fleet left with adequate provisions for three weeks, but was kept out of harbour for six. The expeditions by land were not influenced to the same extent by climatic conditions, but they had more than their fair share of administrative and technical problems on their march – which might be 700 miles and upwards.

carried about 700 men. In general, the number of men carried varied between one and two men per ton of the ship's displacement. It was customary to embark more troops in winter than in summer.

CHAPTER 3

THE SPANISH ROAD

There are many proverbs in Spanish which relate to the Low Countries' Wars. 'Poner una pica en Flandes', to get a soldier (a pike-man) to 'Flanders', is one of the better-known; it means 'To do the impossible'. It is indeed a marvel that any Spanish troops ever reached the Netherlands, especially overland. Geography, climate and the primitive agrarian structure of Europe all hindered movement. Travellers were confronted by mountain passes which were too high or too narrow for comfort, by rivers which were too wide to ford, by forests which were too dense or too dangerous to penetrate, by highways infested with robbers. There was much room for improvement. In fact the technical knowledge and skill necessary to overcome almost every physical obstacle was available from the fifteenth century onwards. In 1480, for example, the first Alpine tunnel was opened. It was cut under Mount Viso in the western Alps at a height of 2,900 metres. It was 72 metres long, $2\frac{1}{2}$ metres high and $2\frac{1}{2}$ metres wide – just large enough to permit the passage of a loaded pack-mule. It was constructed by order of the Marquis of Saluzzo who wanted to attract the merchant convoys travelling between France and Italy and, with them, their tolls.[1] This remarkable feat of engineering was not repeated until the nineteenth century. In the early modern period, expensive and permanent improvements in communications were undertaken solely in the interests of commercial profit, if at all. The technical competence was available but the incentives to use it were not. Until Louis XIV and Louvois, military convenience was seldom held to justify permanent changes in roads or routes. Although soldiers constituted the majority of road-users until the late seventeenth century any improvement of only military value to roads had to be effected by the soldiers themselves. Even the Spanish Road, probably the busiest of Europe's military supply-routes, was little better when the last army passed along it (in

---

[1] Yves Renouard, *Etudes d'Histoire médiévale*, II (Paris, 1968), pp. 715–16. On the general nature of roads in the sixteenth century cf. the excellent remarks of G. Livet, 'La route royale et la civilization française, 1500–1750', *Les Routes de France* (Colloques 'Cahiers de Civilization', Paris, 1959), pp. 57–110.

1620) than when it was first used by the duke of Alva in 1567. Its history illustrates the full range of practical problems inherent in the Habsburgs' military expatriation system and the technical and administrative devices which were employed to surmount them.

*   *   *

The Spanish Road was neither discovered nor monopolized by the Spaniards. Parts of it were regularly used by merchants: traders and their wares moving between France and Italy normally used the Mt Cenis and the Maurienne in winter and the Little St Bernard and the Tarantaise in summer. Both routes were suitable for pack-mules and were furnished with a number of fully-equipped resting places.[1] Nevertheless in 1566–7, with their customary thoroughness, the duke of Alva and his commissary-general, Francisco de Ibarra, sent a qualified engineer and 300 pioneers to build *esplanadas* (widened tracks) in the steep valley leading up from Novalesa through Ferreira to the Mt Cenis pass. A painter accompanied the pioneers, by royal command, to paint the countryside so that the government might plan more effectively. Thanks to these preparations the expedition crossed the mountains smoothly, despite difficult weather. Exactly the same combination of engineer, pioneers and artist was sent to the Val de Chézery and its approaches in 1601 to establish a new route for the troops. A panorama of the Valtelline and a written description were provided for Philip II as early as 1574 to help him to assess its military usefulness, and in 1620, after the valley had been occupied, engineers were sent to widen the existing tracks so that men and packmules could pass with ease along the Habsburgs' new military corridor.[2]

Roads outside the Alpine areas might also be renovated for a military expedition, although rain, frost and ordinary use soon eroded any improvement. Surviving sections of paved road could be refurbished in

---

[1] Cf. the description of Don Juan de Acuña Vela in Dec. 1566, AGS *E* 1208/53, 'Relación'. The advantage of the Mt Cenis was that it was clear of snow about one month earlier than the Little St Bernard; for this reason it was the favourite itinerary of the Spanish and Italian troops, who were needed urgently in the Netherlands each spring.

[2] AGS *E* 1219/259 and 261, the king to the governor of Lombardy, 27 and 30 October 1566 for the preparations for Alva; AC St Claude (Jura) *BB* 6/83 records the arrival of military engineers in 1601, preceding the first Spanish expedition through the Val de Chézery. They spent eight days preparing and reconstructing roads from the Pont de Grésin to St Claude. The new route, partly illustrated in Plate 5 and Figure 8, is described in AGS *E* 1290/42, 'Relación del paso de Flandes', by Juan de Urbino, 12 May 1601. Unfortunately the panorama which accompanied this description has been lost. The Valtelline panorama is AGS *MPyD* ix–53, the written description which was attached *E* 1239/36. News of the improvements of 1620 are in AGS *E* 3335/114–16, Juan de Ayzaga to the king, 15 Nov. 1620.

readiness and difficult passages across a marsh might be made easier with a bridge or a causeway made of bundles of faggots and stone. Each expedition was preceded by an advance-party 'to visit the *grands chemins*' and to see that all rivers in the Army's path were provided with a ferry or a bridge.[1]

Contrary to the assertions of many historians, bridges in the early modern period could be constructed and removed with great ease. Both for campaigns and for peaceful military movements, bridges could be assembled inexpensively and quickly. Local shipping could be commandeered to form a bridge of boats; special machines were available to drive piles for a free-standing bridge into deep water.[2] But even the most solid constructions built solely for the troops rarely proved permanent: the interests of commerce again overrode those of strategy. If the river was wide and deep enough to require a major bridge, it was normally navigable, and a bridge constituted a hindrance to navigation. Bridges built to meet a sudden military need were therefore destroyed, as a rule, as soon as the need passed. It is perhaps surprising to find that it was still cheaper to build and dismantle a bridge than to hire ferries when an army was on the move, but against the 70 florins paid to erect a bailey-bridge to take a Spanish army across the Saône at Grey in 1582, and the $7\frac{1}{2}$ florins to destroy it, it cost 275 florins to hire boats to transport an equal number of Spanish veterans across a smaller river, the Ain, in 1577. Moreover, crossing a river by bridge was much quicker.[3]

Naturally the expense of constructing a bridge or improving a road was

---

[1] For example, AD Vosges, AC Rambervillers *CC*34 (account of the commune for 1585): a cartload of planks was transported 'devant l'estang d'Aunoye pour faire des pontz pour passer les espagnolz'. *Ibid.*, *CC* 28 (account for 1578) notes the purchase of *fagotz* to make up roads for the passing Spaniards. In 1604, also in Lorraine near Dieuze, the Spanish troops were routed 'sur la chaussée de l'estang de la Gardie, puis sur la pontu de la chaussée de l'estang de Lindre' (BNP *Lorraine Ms.* 598/2–4, *capitulation* of 11 Sep. 1604).

[2] There are illustrations of these implements in the excellent textbook of J. Besson, *Théâtre des Instruments mathématiques et méchaniques* (Lyon, 1578 – first published 1569), Plates 22 and 23. The machine used by Pierre le Poivre to build his famous siege-bridge across the Scheldt below Antwerp in 1584–5 (the piles were 75 feet long) is illustrated in his notebook, BRB *Ms.* 19,611 no. 64. 'Pontoons' (barges for ferrying troops across rivers) apparently came in two sizes: one large enough to carry 80 men, or 2 carts, and the '*demi-ponton*' large enough to carry 6 horses or 30 men. The pontoons required to ferry the Army of Flanders across the Great Rivers in the Netherlands were usually constructed and collected at Namur or Maastricht (for the Maas) and at Cologne or even in Luxemburg (for the Rhine). At the appropriate time the barges were floated downstream to a pre-arranged spot to meet the Army. (Cf. AGRB *Audience* 1953/1, unfol., with full information on the '*pontons*' collected at Cologne and elsewhere for Spinola's invasion of Friesland in 1605.)

[3] Febvre, *Philippe II et la Franche-Comté*, p. 748, with further evidence from AD Doubs, *B* 1767 (Account of the *gabelle* of Grey for 1582, with reductions for the cost of the bridge) and AGS *CMC* 2a/25, unfol., account of the expedition of Nov. 1577 in the Comté.

not lightly incurred. The government had to determine an exact route to be followed by the troops, and this was not easy. There was a surprising freedom of choice. Roman-style superhighways which connected distant capitals directly were neither constructed nor maintained during the middle ages; instead an intricate tracery of smaller roads developed, linking each village with its neighbours and with the nearest market centres. These formed the basic road-network of early modern Europe; the road-density was probably as great as it is today. A route which combined the maximum speed with the maximum safety could be chosen from the many alternatives available.[1]

The itineraries used by the king of Spain's troops were not special in any way. The Spanish Road, like all others, consisted of a string of obligatory fixed points – the essential bridges, fords and ferries which connected the communities large enough to accommodate travellers decently – and the local tracks between them. There was a wide choice of parallel or semi-parallel itineraries. Figure 10 shows several different 'roads' running from north to south through Franche-Comté, some over the pancake plain of Burgundy, others through the Jura foothills. The second Besançon map of 1573 (see Figure 11 on p. 104) shows the lowland 'roads' in more detail, with four separate itineraries of bridges, tracks and villages running roughly parallel. At some time Spanish expeditions used all of them.

Once the government had decided on the itinerary which its forces were to follow, detailed maps were called for. A map of the Franche-Comté was used by the duke of Alva on his pioneer march of 1567. It was prepared by Don Fernando de Lannoy, brother-in-law of Cardinal Granvelle, and Alva felt that the map was so accurate that he delayed its publication for a decade.[2] Unfortunately this map has not survived in original, but we have two maps drawn up for the expedition of 1573 (Figures 11 and 12 on pp. 102–5). They reveal everything which an army on the march would need to know: the route it should follow, the bridges available, the impassable obstacles (rivers and forests), the alternative itineraries and the position of the nearest towns. The maps are highly

[1] R.-H. Bautier, 'Recherches sur les routes d'Europe médiévale', *Bulletin philologique et historique du comité des travaux historiques et scientifiques* (1960), I, pp. 99–143 (on p. 101), an outstanding contribution in a most important volume of studies.

[2] For the history of Lannoy's map, which was eventually printed by Ortelius in 1579, cf. Febvre, *Philippe II*, p. 114 n. 1. It is clear that Lannoy had completed his map *before* he knew that the duke of Alva was coming: 'La carta de bourghoyne: je suis après pour en assever [sc. achever] une, bien saisie sur le patron que j'ay, et la envoyer à Myllan au maistre des postes, et *vient bien à point à cause de ce passage pour l'armée de Sa Majeste*.' (AM Besançon, *Ms. Granvelle* 24/247–8v, Lannoy to Granvelle, 19 Apr. 1567).

Figure 10. The Spanish Road–north

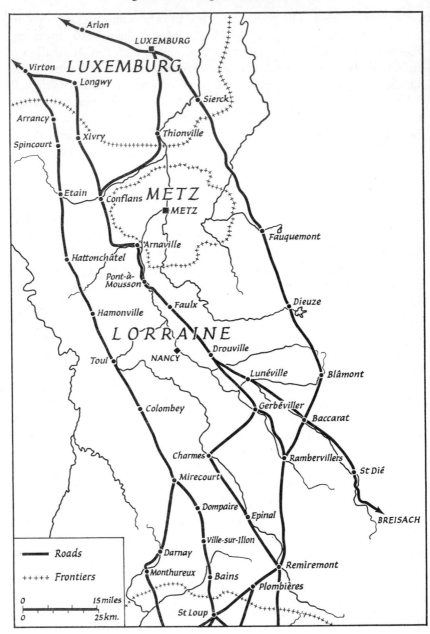

Figure 10. The Spanish Road–south

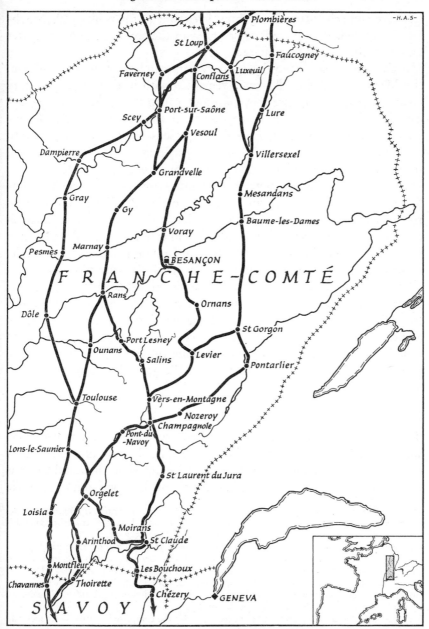

Once clear of the mountains, the Road separated into a number of parallel itineraries meeting only at certain road centres like St Loup near the northern frontier of Franche-Comté. The easterly route, both in the Comté and in Lorraine, ran over the Jura and Vosges highlands; the other routes went over the plains.

selective and schematic. Everything irrelevant to the military thorough-fare is omitted. It is difficult to see how, in the sixteenth century, better guides could have been prepared.

Maps were used widely by military commanders. A French veteran, the Marshal de Vieilleville, once remarked with justice that 'a military commander must no more move without a map than a pilot or a galley-captain unless he wants to court disaster'.[1] Even an indifferent if conscientious soldier like Don Luis de Requesens possessed 'compasses to make measurements on maps', while his predecessor as governor-general, the duke of Medina Celi, owned a large number of maps and descriptions of the Low Countries.[2] But maps and compasses were not enough. In unfamiliar country, especially in areas where the 'Road' was not easy to recognize, an expedition needed a guide and scouts. Most Spanish expeditions to the Netherlands were accompanied by local gentlemen who knew the terrain and the hazards well. Don Fernando de Lannoy, the cartographer, was able to guide the duke of Alva's army through almost all the Franche-Comté, but he was exceptional in his wide geographical knowledge. Normally each guide (the *conducteur*) only led the troops through his own country, two or three days' march at the most. In addition the armies were usually preceded by scouting parties who ensured that everything was prepared along the route; they 'marked the road' to be followed and kept their ear to the ground for any news of an ambush or danger.[3]

These problems of navigation and technology, considerable though they were, paled before those of lodging and feeding the marching armies. As one Spanish commander wrote ruefully: 'Feeding eight thousand men for two months is no joke'.[4] Indeed in the early modern period no one spoke

[1] Quoted F. De Dainville, *Les Jésuites et l'éducation de la société française. i. La géographie des humanistes* (Montpellier, 1940), p. 345. (My thanks go to Prof. J. H. Elliott for bringing this reference to my attention.) Vieilleville was governor of Metz 1553–71.

[2] Cf. the inventories of the estates of Requesens and Medina Celi printed by, respectively, J. M. March, *Don Luis de Requeséns* p. 28, and A. Paz y Melía, *Séries de los mas importantes documentos del Archivo y Biblioteca del excmo. Señor Duque de Medina Celi* (no date: Madrid, 1915?) I, pp. 162–5. We have three original campaign maps, with a description, drawn up for the duke of Alva in 1568 when he followed Orange's army into Limburg: AA 166/2, 'Relación de Juan Despuche y don Alonso de Vargas sobre el país y río.'

[3] The mounted posse which preceded the expedition of 1582 comprised 2 captains, 55 men and 33 horses. (AGRB *CPE* 1215, unfol., 'Rations de bouches de l'Armée venue presentement d'Ytalie'.)

[4] BNM *Ms.* 1031/54, marquis of La Hinojosa to Don Juan Vivas, 18 Feb. 1615: 'No es negocio de burla dar a comer dos meses a ocho mill hombres.'

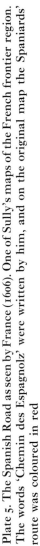

Plate 5. The Spanish Road as seen by France (1606). One of Sully's maps of the French frontier region. The words 'Chemin des Espagnolz' were written by him, and on the original map the Spaniards' route was coloured in red

or wrote about the number of *soldiers* on the march, only about the number of 'mouths' (*bouches* or *bocas*) which would have to be fed. This distinction was sensible because the difference between soldiers and 'mouths' in an army could be amazing. In 1567 the duke of Alva was expected to bring 8,646 Spanish infantry veterans and 965 cavalry troopers with him to the Netherlands, but the various communities along the way were told to cater for 16,000 'mouths' and 3,000 horses. A calculation of 1573 assumed that 3,000 Spanish infantrymen on the march, with their lackeys, women, children and horses, would be 5,000 'mouths' and 1,000 horses. This calculation was fairly typical, but it could be grossly inadequate – the Spanish veterans who left the Netherlands in 1577 numbered 5,300 soldiers and 2,000 lackeys but demanded food for 20,000 'mouths'.[1]

There were three ways of feeding an army on the march. If an itinerary was used by troops with great frequency, or if it was considered vital to have a route in a constant state of readiness for military movements, it was possible to maintain a chain of permanent food magazines. In the 1590s, during the war against France, a magazine was established in Milan to supply the necessitous Spanish troops in Lombardy with cheap food. A military corridor, however, did not represent a constant demand; even the Spanish Road was used only once every year or two. It was not thought to justify the cost of maintaining permanent military magazines. A proposal in 1577 to establish just one magazine, in Luxemburg, used by the German recruits as well as by Spanish, Italian and Burgundian troops, was dismissed as superfluous.[2]

The traditional method of provisioning European armies was primitive in the extreme: everything necessary for the soldiers was requisitioned on the spot, with or without compensation. The troops made for a village or group of villages (usually oblivious of their impending fate) and quartered themselves wherever they chose. When the houses were inhabited, the hosts were obliged to provide free food and room service; soldiers who found billets in empty houses were entitled to collect contributions from the neighbouring residents to pay for their bed and board. This was a terrible burden for a poor family to bear, especially in time of shortage.

[1] For Alva's army: BM *Addl. Ms.* 28,387/106–11, 'memorial', May 1567. In the event there were 1,200 light cavalrymen. For 1573: AGS *E* 1237/229, 'Per il passaggio delli 3,000 spagnuoli'. For 1577, C. Piot, *Correspondance...de Granvelle*, VI, p. 212, Morillon to Granvelle, 22 April 1577, and AGS *E* 573/218, G. de Roda to Zayas, 28 Mar. 1577.
[2] BNM *Ms.* 8695/605–11v, memorial of the treasury of Milan to the governor (*c.* 1605); AGRB *Audience* 1733/3 f. 227, Count Mansfelt, governor of Luxemburg, to Don John of Austria, 24 Sep. 1577.

Two or three extra mouths to feed weighed heavily on a subsistence economy. It was even alleged that it was not recruiting which ruined small communities but the movements of the troops after enlistment. A company quartered 'at discretion' on the march did 'more harm in a single night in the villages than a company raised by any captain in two or three months'.[1]

The increase in the size of armies and in the scale of military operations in the sixteenth century naturally intensified the burden of this casual arrangement. It became difficult to find communities large enough to quarter the larger armies on the move. Around 1550 a new institution made its appearance: the military *étape*. The idea was not new – 'staples' or *étapes* had long been in use for commercial purposes: a centre where merchants and their customers could be sure of meeting and where goods were collected for storage, sale and distribution – but in the sixteenth century the institution was adapted to military ends. In 1551, for example, to cope with the frequent passage of large bodies of French troops through the Maurienne valley to Italy, a chain of permanent *étapes* was established by the French occupation forces. They proved useful, and so they continued to function even after the French withdrew in 1559. *Etapes* also sprang up elsewhere. In 1567 the duke of Alva was able to use the *étapes* created by the French when he marched through the Maurienne, but he had to arrange a further chain of his own for the rest of his journey to Brussels. Later expeditions did the same. When in 1623 the first Spanish army marched through the Valtelline and Alsace to the Netherlands, a chain of *étapes* was created to feed it. Even Napoleon used *étapes* to provision his armies on certain occasions, although he preferred to arrange permanent magazines.[2]

Yet the *étape* was not accepted everywhere. Spain itself, ironically, rejected the idea. As late as 1632, when there was a storm of protest in the Cortes of Castile against the crushing burden of billeting, the Council of War in Madrid listened to a suggestion that it should organize *étapes* in Castile as if they had never been heard of before. Don Cristobal de

---

[1] AGS *GA* 188/19, *Corregidor* of Ciudad Rodrigo to the king, 17(?) Oct. 1586. Cf. the further remarks and texts cited by N. Salomon, *La campagne de Nouvelle Castille à la fin du XVIe siècle d'après les 'Relaciones Topográficas'* (Paris, 1964), pp. 236–8 and notes.

[2] AD Savoie G (*Maurienne*) 179/23. Proclamation of the French governor of Savoy, 18 Feb. 1551/2, reiterating an earlier edict of 22 Jan. 1550/1 which established *étapes* at Chambéry, Montmélian, Aiguebelle, St Jean de Maurienne, St Michel, Modane and Lanslebourg, and adding a further *étape* at La Chambre. AGS *E* 1926/210, governor of Lombardy to the king, 11 Sep. 1623: 'Despaché a Juan Pirovano, questor del Magistrado, a que hiciese las tapas en Grisones y Alsacia asta llegar a Lorena.' The *étapes* for the new route in Lorraine and Luxemburg were organized by the Brussels government.

Benavente, who had been inspector-general of the Army of Flanders, explained the advantages of a system where:

> Instead of giving money to every soldier to support himself on the march...it is given to the place where he has to spend the night, obliging it to provide all the necessary food, giving specific orders, as in an *étape* [*como en tapas*] about how much bread, wine, meat, cheese and other provisions should be given to each soldier, and sending in advance a commissioner who would arrange these obligations in the same place where the soldiers have to spend the night, just as has to be done for the same troops when they disembark at Genoa, making *étapes* for them in Lombardy and the Grisons, or in Savoy, Lorraine and Luxemburg.

It would be hard to find a more concise description of the *étape* system, and Don Cristobal's suggestion was warmly received by the council. The king, however, was less impressed. Indeed he affixed the kiss of death to the project by questioning whether the arrangement of *étapes* from the recruiting-grounds to the coast, a march of only three or four days at the most he claimed, was worth while. No doubt the impoverished communities saddled with finding food and lodgings for the levies would have been in favour, but for the government of Philip IV the challenge of implementing a new administrative arrangement was too great. The government was anxious to rid itself of as many responsibilities as possible, not to acquire more, and so in Spain the *étapes* were forgotten.[1]

The *étape* system was simple and sensible. One village was made the centre, the staple, at which the troops' food was collected and distributed. If the troops were to be given beds, the houses of the *étape* and of its surrounding villages could be used; those in charge of the *étape* together with the *furier* (the quartermaster responsible for the troops' lodgings) issued special chits, called *billets de logement*, which stipulated the number of persons and horses to be accommodated in each house. After the troops left, the householders could present the *billets* of the troops to the local tax-collectors and claim their outlay against future or past tax liability.[2]

The soldiers who marched up the Spanish Road were not always given a bed for the night. Shelter was the norm only in the mountains in winter, when a man could not survive without a roof over his head at night. At other times, the rank and file slept under hedgerows or impro-

---

[1] AGS *GA* 1052, unfol., *consulta* of the Council of War, 17 Dec. 1632. The levies whose march to the Catalan coast was under discussion eventually formed part of the cardinal-infante's army.

[2] A great deal of material concerning the quartering of the Spanish troops on their way to the Low Countries has survived. For one bulky and comprehensive example, cf. AD Savoie, *SA* 7461, 'Description des trouppes espaignolles' (St Jean de Maurienne, 1620). The *billet de logement* was also found in seventeenth-century England, called the 'lodging ticket'. Cf. C. A. Holmes, 'The Eastern Association', Cambridge Univ. Ph.D. thesis (1969), pp. 359–65.

vised huts in the fields, know as *barracas*, while their officers were entertained and lodged in the nearest town. Naturally this spartan arrangement for the troops had a vast appeal for all civilians. They did not relish the residence of a large contingent of brutish, penurious and probably rapacious soldiery within their walls. Some expeditions indeed managed to perpetrate an amazing number of crimes against the civilian population. A Spanish company lodged at Annecy in 1603 was accused of forty-three offences (the sergeant led the way: he was charged with six crimes of violence, more than anyone else), while at Aime-en-Tarantaise no less than fifty separate cases of robbery were reported against the men of another Spanish company which lodged in the town for just one night in 1597 – livestock, silks, kitchen ware and furniture as well as money were stolen in copious quantities. On other occasions the troops burnt down the entire village in which they stayed, while granaries and isolated dwellings were often callously destroyed by passing troops. Small wonder that most communities should do their utmost to keep the soldiers at arm's length.[1] At Epinal in Lorraine, as a Spanish expedition approached, the bailiff of the region advised the town to run no risks:

> When the Spaniards pass, which will be through the *faubourg* only, you should ensure...that your arquebusiers are in good order, and make all the merchants who want to sell their wares go out of the town to set up their stalls, so that they [the Spaniards] should not be anxious to get into the town...Do not fail to post forty or fifty arquebusiers in the market place...and tell my castellan to put some arquebusiers in the castle.

Even officers were suspect. At Gy in Franche-Comté in 1580 a house was set aside for the officers of the approaching Spanish *tercios*, but first all furniture was evacuated to another town and a cleaning-woman was given special responsibility to guard the temporary crockery which the magistrates installed during the officers' residence! In the sixteenth century, the motto of the Besançon Council, *Nulla fides viris qui castra sequuntur*, was widely endorsed.[2]

---

[1] AD Savoie, *SA* 6912, 'Informations prises par...occasion des foulles supportées...au logement des troupes espagnoles' (May 1603); AC Aime (Savoie) *EE* 2, 'Procès-verbal des dégâts et vols faits par les troupes à Aime' (June 1597). For one example of a village entirely destroyed cf. AD Meurthe-et-Moselle, *B*. 3313/9, petition of the villages of Chazelle in Lorraine, its houses 'entièrement bruslées et consommées, avec tous meubles y estant', in Jan. 1596 by the passing troops of the Archduke Albert. Further examples in Febvre, *Philippe II*, pp. 523–5 and 750–5.

[2] AD Vosges, AC Epinal *EE* 5 no. 6, Order of the Bailli, 8 Apr. (1580? no year given on the document). In 1580 (*ibid.*, *CC* 90) the town council paid £8. 5s. od. to the arquebusiers who did such 'grand debvior ès portes...pendant que les espaignolz retournans du Pays-Bas passent'. For the council which feared for its crockery: AD Haute Saône, 282 *E Supplément* 112 (AC Gy *CC* 7), town account of 1580 – cahier 2 ff. 30v–31.

There were two sorts of military *étape* used by the troops on the Spanish Road. The first type, found only in Savoy, was permanent and offered accommodation as well as food. Since the Alpine valleys of Savoy served as a commercial thoroughfare between France and Italy, there were always merchants in need of food, transport and a bed, and so the *étapes* served a constant need and were used by all travellers, including troops. The *étape* itself was fixed in a large town, all the communities contributed to the cost of providing the food and services, and each shared in the profits. The administration of each *étape* in Savoy was either entrusted to the magistrates (*sindiques*) of the chief town or, more democratically, to a general assembly of representatives from all the communities forming the *étape*. There was only a relatively loose control from the ducal government; the appointment of a ducal *commissaire générale des étapes* in 1607 made little difference to the independence of the local communities. The *étapes* of Savoy were permanent and, by and large, they were self-governing.[1]

The *étapes* of Franche-Comté, Lorraine and the Low Countries, although they shared the same name, were quite different. Since there was no constant circulation of merchants between Chambéry and Brussels, the *étapes* between these two points had to be created specially at the approach of each military expedition. The initiative, moreover, came not from the local communities but from the provincial governments either acting directly or through private contractors. The duke of Alva's passage through Franche-Comté, for example, was arranged very bureaucratically. A single officer was appointed to superintend preparations in each of the bailiwicks of the Comté through which the Spaniards would pass, and he calculated the total quantities of food and services which would be required, apportioning this total between the various villages, 'carts from some, meat from others...at a just price, leaving none without charge'. When the last Spaniard had passed, special commissioners were sent round the province to take a declaration of the food provided by each taxpayer to Alva's army. The claims, which covered 411 close-written folios, were then either paid off or else set against tax liability.[2]

[1] In Savoy each *étape* was subdivided into a number of *parcelles*, of two or three villages each; the charge was distributed between them according to the number of taxable hearths on the *taille* rolls. There are several references to the *Assemblée Generalle de l'Estappe* and its functions in AC Termignon (Savoie) *EE* 3. For a concise survey of the Savoy *étapes*, cf. G. Pérouse, *Les communes rurales et les institutions de l'ancienne Savoie d'après les archives communales* (Chambéry, 1911), pp. 95–9.

[2] The volume of claims is AD Doubs, 2 *B* 1512. (The title-page and first folio are missing.) On the work of Don Fernando de Lannoy, who was in charge of the preparations for Alva in the bailiwick of Amont, cf. AM Besançon, *Ms. Granvelle* 24/247–8v, Lannoy to Granvelle, 19 Apr. 1567 – a most interesting letter.

Naturally the provincial administration responded to the challenge of later expeditions with the same arrangements as those which had proved their value in 1567. Yet as the years went by there were strong protests against this procedure, known as 'cotisation', and the protests were justified. Although everyone involved in Alva's voyage seems to have received eventual satisfaction, those who supplied later expeditions were more often paid years later and sometimes not at all.[1] As the economic situation in eastern France deteriorated in the later years of the century with bad harvests, devaluation, the price-rise and finally war-devastation, governments became increasingly reluctant to organize military provisions directly.

Instead it was found that if the task of feeding armies along the Spanish Road was delegated to private contractors, efficiency was maintained and discontent minimized. It was not entirely free enterprise, because the contractors were forced to observe a price-tariff fixed in advance by the government. However, large profits (and losses) could still be made.[2]

Each expedition which used the Spanish Road was preceded by a special commissioner from Brussels or Milan who arranged with the governments of Luxemburg, Lorraine, Franche-Comté and Savoy the itinerary of the troops, the stopping-places, the quantity of food to be provided and the price. Normally each provincial government invited tenders for the provisioning of one or more *étapes* (offers very often came from a *robin* – a lawyer from one of the provincial tribunals of justice – or a local government official). The contractors whose offers were accepted would sign a *capitulation* which fixed the quantity of food they had to provide and the prices they could charge for it. The contract also stipulated the manner of repayment.

Sometimes the troops still had to pay for their every bite as they ate it, which meant that men who had squandered their meagre resources had to march long distances, perhaps in rain or frosts, on little or no food.

1 Some villages around Epinal in Lorraine which supplied an expedition of Spanish troops in 1587 were particularly unfortunate. They provided food on credit to the troops at a total cost of 8,557 francs. After repeated demands, the Spanish government sent this sum to the duke of Lorraine for repayment to the villagers. (In all 12,000 *escudos* – 30,000 francs – were sent because other villages were in the same plight as those around Epinal.) The duke, however, was at war when the money arrived; he therefore used it to pay his troops. The villages only received their due in September 1595, eight years after the food had been provided. (AGRB *Audience* 1832/4, unfol., duke of Lorraine to Parma, 11 Mar. 1591; AD Meurthe-et-Moselle, B 5971, duke of Lorraine to his receiver at Epinal, 30 Sep. 1595).

2 For the career and profits of a number of munitioners, cf. Febvre, *Philippe II*, pp. 751–5. Some munitioners in 1567, for example, managed to secure permission to charge 9½ *caroli* for a ration of food worth only 7, making a profit of 4,200 *escudos* (*ibid.*, p. 750 n. 1.) For examples of munitioners' losses, cf. pp. 94–5 below.

This could easily produce disorders or desertion. As one experienced official wrote in 1573: 'I am sure that when the soldier arrives wet, has to purchase and prepare his food...and is obliged to put his hand in his pocket every day, it makes for trouble.' It was also noticeable that the troops' temper worsened as the march proceeded. The same diligent commissioner later wrote that 'troops who have travelled three hundred leagues without a break' deserved and indeed demanded every consideration. His point was easily proved.[1] At the *étape* of Bastogne (in Luxemburg) in 1577 the victualler was forced to sell some 18,000 herrings at a loss because 'the soldiers refused to pay any more'. In the same year the munitioner at La Roche-en-Ardenne had to sell some of his bread at less than the official price because 'some of the officers of the troops found that the loaves weighed 23 ounces' instead of the regulation 24. That was the sort of sharp practice which could lead to real disorder. At Neuchâtel-en-Ardenne in 1582 the munitioner found that some of his loaves were underweight and so when the troops became unmanageable he agreed to give away eight loaves free for every hundred that he sold. At Thionville *étape* in 1578, however, the distribution of the bread was so badly organized that in the confusion the troops were able to steal 538 loaves off the victualler's cart while a further 53 loaves were carelessly trampled into the mud by the hungry multitude.[2]

Mishaps such as these (and worse) could be avoided when the troops were not obliged to pay in cash and when the victualler devoted a little more thought to the organization of his services. Normally he received an initial payment from the government which made it possible to purchase provisions in advance and in bulk. These could then be stored in a guarded house, or better still each commodity could be stored in a different house to forestall confusion. When the troops finally arrived, a single officer from each company presented himself at the store-house to collect all the rations due to his men. He would sign a receipt (a *police*) for the rations, which could be presented later to the representative of the military treasury of the Army of Flanders (usually the same commissioner who arranged the *étapes* and signed the *capitulation*). Either the munitioner would be paid on the spot or, if funds were short, he would receive a warrant on the

[1] AA 33/147, Hernando Delgadillo to the duke of Alva, 29 May 1573; AGRB *Audience* 1733/2 f. 131, Delgadillo to Count Mansfelt, 7 Jun. 1573.
[2] AGRB *CC* 25759, accounts of the Bastogne *étape*, 1577; *CC* 25776, account of Gilles de Neueforge, La Roche 1577; *CC* 25812, account of the *étape* at Neufchâtel in 1582; and *CC* 25785, account of Pierre Conders, Thionville 1578. The last account abounded in misfortunes: Conders, *échevin*, provost and burgomaster of Thionville, lost a further 2,831 loaves on a cart which broke down on its way to the troops and on a second which was ambushed and plundered by starving peasants.

treasury, payable in the Netherlands. In either case, in the gloom of the Army's accounts office some weeks later, a clerk would laboriously calculate the total cost of the food supplied to each soldier and officer and deduct it from his wages.[1]

The contract system was thus in the best interests of everyone. The government ensured that the troops were properly fed; the soldiers themselves received their rations without delay and usually on credit; and the peasants were paid immediately by the contractors for the food they provided. But of course in the sixteenth century no system of comparable complexity could function indefinitely without the occasional disaster. Thus in 1601 an important group of merchants and *robins* contracted to provide food to an approaching army of Spaniards and Italians at a large number of *étapes* in Franche-Comté and, as it happened, they overreached themselves and failed to get their provisions to the *étape* of Baume-les-Dames in time. They did not even warn the town that the troops were coming...

> At eight o'clock that morning, news arrived that the troops, Spanish, Milanese and Neapolitan, passing through this province, required lodging in our town, although there was no *étape* planned...Following this, at about nine o'clock, the Quartermaster of the first contingents arrived to prepare the lodging tickets and straight away the Spaniards arrived.

Since nothing had been prepared for the unforeseen multitude, the townspeople had to provide the testy soldiers, sixty-five companies of them, with food and shelter at their own expense. The magistrates compiled a special register to record all that the town spent on the troops and, naturally, when life returned to normal they sued the munitioners for the money they had spent.[2]

In 1603 the town of Pontarlier, also in Franche-Comté, was likewise all but beggared by the ineptitude of some military contractors. The town magistrates made an agreement to sell a quantity of food wholesale to the munitioners who had contracted to supply a nearby *étape* for an approaching army of Spaniards and Italians. After the food was delivered to the *étape*, a storm destroyed most of the provisions while the munitions which survived were disbursed 'mostly by illiterate labourers who knew

---

[1] These arrangements were all formalized in the lengthy *capitulations* which were made to regulate the provisioning of each expedition. There are a number in BNP *Lorraine Ms.* 598/ 2–4, 38, 47 etc. (for the years after 1605). For a wide sample of the administrative papers concerning the food supplied cf. AD Doubs, 2 *B* 1514. I have amassed a considerable volume of information on the quality and quantity of the food provided which I hope to present soon as a separate article.

[2] AC Baume-les-Dames (Doubs), *BB* 4/31v, Deliberation of the town council, 29 Jun. 1601, and *EE* 7, containing the *capitulation* and a host of other documents concerning the 1601 expedition. Alas, there is no trace of the separate register of costs.

neither how to write nor how to speak Spanish or Italian'. The soldiers (Italians and Spaniards) did not fail to profit from the ignorance of the contractors' clerks: knowing that their receipts could not be understood, they declared that they had received only a fraction of the victuals provided. Not surprisingly, the munitioners made a very large loss on their contract and they tried to share it with Pontarlier, claiming that they were not obliged to pay the full price for the food provided to them by the town. Here, however, yet another advantage of the contract-system emerged: the Supreme Court of Franche-Comté (the Parlement of Dôle) sided with the local community and ruled that the food had been provided in good faith. The contractors were forced to pay. As the magistrates of Pontarlier observed, citing the Golden Rule of Capitalism: 'Every one of the contractors only took on the venture in order to make a profit from it', and if they had failed to line their pockets like the other munitioners, that was simply bad luck.[1]

In addition to food, the *étapes* often had to provide the troops with baggage-transport. In the Alpine valleys carriage was by pack-mules, each animal carrying between 200 and 250 lb. for a small mule and between 300 and 400 lb. for a large one.[2] It was not always easy to concentrate enough animals at a single time and place since each company on the march might require between 20 and 40 mules. The 11,000 Spaniards and Italians who marched to the Netherlands in 1620 needed 673 mules – an astonishing total albeit somewhat inflated by the callousness or malevolence of the troops: of the 60 *bestes de voicture* supplied to the expedition between St Jean and Aiguebelle in the Maurienne valley, no less than 40 were killed or badly injured by the troops.[3] The Spanish Road left the sub-Alpine highlands shortly before Lons-le-Saunier, and from then onwards the troops' baggage was transported on long four-wheeled carts. Each company seems to have required between two and four carts, depending on the quantity of baggage. The 8,000 'mouths' of Don Lope de Acuña in 1573, only 25 companies, claimed to need 140 carts for their baggage.[4] Naturally it was not easy to collect so many carts, yet failure to

[1] AC Pontarlier (Doubs) *EE* 7 (Carton 144), no. 1. The legal defence of the town was dated 9 Oct. 1606 and the crucial phrase ran: 'Qu'ung chacung d'eulx desiroit telle entremise particulierement pour seul en tirer le profit.'
[2] A.-M. Piuz, *Recherches sur le commerce de Genève au XVIIe siècle* (Geneva, 1964), p. 165.
[3] AS Torino, *Sezioni Reuniti*, Art. 256 n. 7, accord of Claudio Sachetti, 26 Nov. 1620; AD Savoie, *SA* 7431, 7461 and 7470 – 7472, various accounts concerning the expedition of 1620 as it passed through Savoy.
[4] AD Doubs, *B* 1955, 'Compte de l'estappe de Marnay', 1573.

do so invariably resulted in chaos since the troops commandeered for their baggage the carts intended to carry victuals or their sick and wounded comrades. It was to avoid this waste and disorder that the government took to negotiating a special contract with the carters of Bresse (in Savoy) or Lorraine to guarantee a continuous supply of transport along the whole length of the Road.

The preparation of roads, food and transport in advance naturally increased the speed with which troops could be brought to the front. It was possible, if everything was in order, for a regiment to cover the journey from Milan to Namur, some 700 miles, in about seven weeks. One expedition in February 1578 took only 32 days (incredibly); one in 1582 took 34 days, another 40. The average duration of direct marches was 48 days (cf. Appendix D, p. 280).

One factor which affected the overall speed of an expedition was the number of contingents into which it was divided. It would seem that the largest single unit of marching soldiers which could be comfortably handled at one time was about 3,000 men; larger forces travelled better in sections. The most common arrangement was the traditional three divisions, van, battle and rearguard, but when provisioning was particularly difficult the expedition might be broken up into sub-divisions only 500-strong. The possibilities of accommodation also limited the size of the contingents. St Jean de Maurienne, the largest town in its valley, could lodge 700 soldiers at a time – but only if they slept three to a bed.[1] As far as possible each contingent was given a cavalry escort for its defence, and the different divisions of the army followed each other at intervals of one day's march, the second detachment reaching the *étape* used by the first the previous night, and so on. Only if there was any likelihood of attack, as there was in 1567, did a large expedition close ranks and march as a single unit.[2]

Obviously the duration of the march to the Netherlands was ultimately controlled by the speed at which the men were marched. The normal speed of armies using the 'Road' seems to have been about twelve miles a day. In 1577 the Spanish veterans who left the Netherlands in May were

[1] Abbé Truchet, *St Jean de Maurienne au XVIe siècle* (Chambéry, 1887), p. 433.
[2] The advantages of the various formations were set out by Don Luis de Requesens and Gabrio Serbelloni in their letters to the king in April 1573 (AGS *E* 1236/97 and 233). They recommended that on grounds of security up to 5,000 men might have to travel as a single unit, and it was Philip II himself who pointed out that far smaller contingents would still be safe if each had a cavalry escort.

said to be marching at 'double-speed, that is five leagues a day [sc. fifteen miles], to avoid the summer heat'. On the other hand the expedition of 1578 which took only 32 days to complete the march must have averaged 23 miles a day, including crossing the Mt Cenis in February! A speed like this could only be achieved by making the *étapes* as far apart as possible, and by allowing the troops no rest. Certainly on some occasions, mainly in summer, commissioners sent to arrange for the passage of some troops were specifically instructed to make the *étapes* further apart than normal because the days were longer, but it was normally recognized that the men had to be allowed to rest for a day or two before they crossed the Mt Cenis, for another couple of days when they reached the plains again at Lons-le-Saunier, and again at Givet or Namur when they reached the Low Countries. These rest-periods, called *gistes*, were time-consuming, but they were necessary if the troops were not to straggle or collapse from weariness.[1]

Yet even the most elaborate preparations could be invalidated overnight. The voyage of the troops commanded by Don Lope de Acuña in 1573 fully illustrates what could go wrong with even the best-planned expedition. The troops left Italy in mid-May and were quickly overwhelmed by torrential rain.

> The weather has been, and is still, so unfavourable to our march that ever since we left Italy it has rained every day without stopping, and at the frontier of Franche-Comté it rained for 48 hours with such force that when the time came for us to leave the last *étape* of Bresse [Savoy] and cross the bridge built at His Majesty's expense to take us into the Comté, everything was flooded by the swollen water.

Men fell into the floods, the rearguard was stranded at one *étape* without any food while the vanguard, which managed to reach the next *étape* at Montfleur in the Comté, arrived with hardly any men. The commissioner with the expedition was resourceful:

> The weather continued as before and so, because a bridge was down, we were forced to make new passages and roads besides those already constructed...I reconnoitred the road to Lons-le-Saunier, abandoning the one which was prepared (which was full of hollows and had become impassable) and I decided to clear a

---

[1] AM Besançon, *Ms. Granvelle* 24/247-8v, Lannoy to Granvelle, 19 Apr. 1567, advocating 'four leagues' daily for the entire army: 'as much for the duke of Alva's person as for the infantry and cavalry'. For the '*double chemin*', cf. Piot, *Correspondance...de Granvelle*, VI, pp. 214-15, Morillon to Granvelle, 13 May 1577. For two examples of reducing the number of *étapes*: AGRB *SEG* 7/28v-29v, Parma's Instruction to Juan Lopez de Ugarte, 1 Jun. 1582, and *SEG* 20/42-3v. Archduke Albert's Instruction to Antonio Davila, 12 May 1601.

way for the troops over the slopes of the mountain, which is very high. The route ran alongside an extremely dense forest, more than a very long league and a half which we covered that evening and the next morning.

By this improvised track the army of Acuña reached Lons-le-Saunier and there it had a well-earned rest: 'And since it did not rain those two days, the troops cleaned their weapons and rested...and they were given a general issue of cheese and eggs, fresh lard and fifty large carps per company.'[1]

The expedition's troubles were not over at Lons-le-Saunier. The itinerary arranged by Delgadillo worked well in Franche-Comté (cf. Figure 11) but it had to be abandoned in Lorraine. For no apparent reason the duke of Lorraine cancelled the *étapes* which were prepared and ordered the Spaniards to march by a more circuitous route. In consequence the troops entered the province of Luxemburg from an unexpected quarter and emergency arrangements had to be made to feed them. Small wonder that the veterans took their revenge by refusing to march more than a gentlemanly six miles a day.[2]

Some surprises like this were inevitable on a military route used as often as the Spanish Road. They were tiresome, but they happened relatively rarely. Prepared itineraries represented a considerable investment of time and money and they were only abandoned or altered in an emergency or as a last resort. The *étape* organization which underpinned the movement of troops to Spanish Flanders thus went a long way towards humanizing and softening the burden of billeting and feeding large bodies of troops. The local communities were paid and protected; the troops were fed and were able to move fast. Yet even the most perfect preparations and exemplary order among the troops could not neutralize one final potential hazard in all military movements.

In April 1580 some 6,000 Spanish veterans returning from the Netherlands to Italy neared Besançon. The city magistrates resolved: 'That no one coming from the Low Countries should be admitted to the town, as much to avoid contagious illnesses as for other good reasons.' In common with many other civilians along the Spanish Road, the burghers of Besançon feared that the troops might bring plague. The attempt to sow

---

[1] AA 33/147, Hernando Delgadillo to the duke of Alva, 29 May 1573. It is somewhat difficult to reconcile Delgadillo's description with the geography of the Suran valley along which he travelled. Presumably the troops crossed into the Comté from Poncin, making for Montfleur (the first *étape* in Franche-Comté). From Montfleur to Lons-le-Saunier is 26 miles. Two *étapes* had been prepared (at Gigny and Montaigu-lès-Lons – cf. Figure 11). If the route was really abandoned at Montfleur and the men made straight for Lons, Delgadillo's 'league and a half' was very long indeed!

[2] AGRB *Audience* 1733/2, ff. 130–5, Mansfelt to Alva, 9 and 10 Jun. 1573.

plague in the path of Alva's army in 1566–7 may have failed, but the duke's itinerary had to be directed away from Dôle and Grey in the Comté where the plague, as at Geneva, was already hot. In Salins-les-Bains the contagion broke out just after the Spaniards left. At Toul ten years later the city feared the return of the same Spanish veterans (April 1577) at a time when plague was already widespread in the area. In the event the Spaniards passed through on 16 May and contagion compelled the cathedral chapter to evacuate the town seven days later. As the veterans neared Italy, which was only just recovering from a terrible plague, one of the officers with the expedition warned the governor of Lombardy to send the troops off to sea as quickly as possible if he wanted 'to spare that province a second plague which is on the way, because I can assure Your Excellency that it will be no less', In 1586, finally, the governor-general of the Spanish Netherlands reported an alarming proliferation of plague in Franche-Comté. It reached such a pitch there that he even advised the king not to send him any reinforcements from Italy, much as they were needed for the Armada preparations, until the following year or at least 'until the frosts' which might reduce the pestilence. The plea was ignored. A Spanish *tercio* marched right through the infected areas in November. Philip II's imperial designs could not be shelved simply on account of a little plague.[1]

Of course the passage of troops alone did not spread the plague, but it did play a sinister role in its diffusion. In the sixteenth century plague seems to have been endemic in several parts of Europe including the borderlands between France and the empire. The area was densely populated and it was a great commercial and military axis: traffic and troops passing between Italy and the Netherlands crossed those passing between Germany or Switzerland and France. Further, in the sixteenth century plague seems to have come in cycles; at certain periods lasting two or three years the pestilence became general, spreading rapidly. The years 1563–7, 1575–7 and 1586–8 were all periods of peak infection, and therefore concern at the approach of the Spanish troops was natural: all movements between one region and another at such troubled times were potentially dangerous. But whereas merchants were stopped and their wares impounded and quarantined if there was a risk of infection, armies were a law to themselves. No civil authority had the power to stop them. Troops on the march ate the food provided for them by the civilian

[1] AM Besançon, *BB* 37/308v, deliberation of 7 Apr. 1580; AC Salins (Jura) *BB* 19, deliberation of 30 Apr. 1567; AD Meurthe-et-Moselle, *G.* 79 'Acta capitularia ecclesiae tullensis' (for 1577–9) f. 14; AGS *E* 452, unfol., *Contador* Alameda to the governor of Lombardy, 5 Jun. 1577 (copy); AGS *E* 590/103, Parma to the king, 30 Oct. 1586.

population, and they carried any surplus food on with them; they lodged in local houses, their baggage was carried on local carts. If there was plague in any area through which they passed, the soldiers ran a high risk of contracting it. If they became infected, they could hardly avoid contaminating the local communities further along their route. The moving army could become a vast incubator of plague; one can hardly imagine a more effective agent of diffusion.[1]

On balance, however, despite its plague-spreading proclivity (which was of course never proved), the organization of the Spanish Road and the other similar military corridors of the Army of Flanders marked a vast improvement on any previous mechanism for moving troops through neutral territory. The *étapes* cushioned the civilian population from the higher forms of violence, destruction and destitution normally associated with the passage of troops. Where they occurred, compensation was paid.[2] The cost of each expedition was amazingly small. It cost an average of 20 *escudos* (50 florins) over and above his pay to send each Spanish and Italian solider to the Netherlands from Lombardy in 1582 and 1585, an average of 24 *escudos* (60 florins) in 1602, and even some of this modest outlay was later recouped. If food was provided on credit, the rations of each man was deducted from his pay: thus rations worth 70,802 *escudos* were provided to the veteran troops who returned to Italy in April and May 1577, but a total of 51,801 *escudos* was deducted from their wages. The true cost of the expedition to the government was thus the 19,001 *escudos* outstanding, plus 21,267 *escudos* spent on guides, bridges, roadworks and so on; a total cost of 40,268 *escudos* or under 8 *escudos* per man in addition to pay (since there were only 5,334 soldiers).[3]

[1] Three examples of contagion definitely brought by military movements: (1) the *Peste di Milano* of 1630–1 which was brought to Italy by the German troops sent through the Valtelline to fight in the war of Mantua; (2) the plague which spread through south Germany in 1631–4 in the wake of the Swedish army, still remembered in Oberammergau where the famous Passion Play records the village's deliverance from the pestiferous Swedes; (3) the evidence that the Ottoman army of Hungary sowed plague all along the line of march used by its reinforcements, the Danube valley – the 'Turkish Road' perhaps? (Cf. B. Hrabak, 'Kuga u Balkanskim zemljama pod Turcima od 1450 do 1600 godine', *Istoriski Glasnik*, I–II (1957), pp. 19–37, with a French résumé, from which my information is taken.)
[2] When the troops committed damage for which compensation had to be paid by the government, the cost was divided up amongst the units responsible and each soldier forfeited a proportion of his wages.
[3] For 1582, AGS *E* 1256/123, governor of Lombardy to the king, 28 Jul. 1582, claiming 20 *escudos* per man as the average cost of the expedition of that year *and of previous ones*. For 1585, AS Milano, *Cancelleria spagnola* XXII, 33, f. 79: 40,000 *escudos* for Bobadilla's *tercio* (2,195 men). For 1602, AGS *CMC* 2a/875, part iii, account of the paymaster of the expedition, Pedro Ximenez: 205,164 *escudos* spent on 8,759 men. The figures for 1577 come from the superbly detailed AGS *E* 1246/161, 'Relación de lo que montan las vituallas.' The cost of sending troops from Spain to the Netherlands was roughly comparable: the two expeditions

By her ingenuity and tenacity, therefore, Spain managed to make her military expatriation system work – and at surprisingly little cost. Despite the problems of distance a large army was assembled as if by remote control hundreds of miles from the political centre of the Monarchy. Yet here was a final challenge to be overcome. An army of 60,000 men and upwards in the Low Countries could *not* be controlled from Spain. An independent high command had to be created. However, the central government had no intention of losing political control of its armies, however far away they might have to operate. And it never did.

of 1631, for example cost 16 *escudos* and 22 *escudos* per man, the difference arising from the greater number of vessels hired for the second voyage. (AGS *GA* 1,038, unfol., 'Tanteo de la costa que podra tener el pasage a Flandes'; *GA* 1042, unfol., marquis of Manzera to the Council of War, 14 Oct. 1631; *consulta* of the council, 21 Oct.)

Figure 11. The Spanish Road in Franche-Comté (1573), 1

This map, one of two prepared for the passage of the Army of Don Lope de Acuña through the Franche-Comté, showed the eleven *étapes* which had been prepared for the troops. Most of them were reached after crossing a bridge over one of the main rivers of the Comté (the Ain, Loue, Doubs, Ognon and Saone). South is at the top of the map, with the troops crossing the Ain to Chavannes and Montfleur and coming down the map through Lons-le-Saunier, Marnay, Gy and Faverney to St Loup on the border with Lorraine, the eleventh *étape*. These places are also shown on Figure 10.

Figure 12. The Spanish Road in Franche-Comté (1573), II

La Riviere de Soone

Buicy

Maznoy

La Riviere de longuay

La Riviere du doub,

La Riviere de Loue

The facing map, also prepared for Acuña's army of 1573, has north at the top. It shows the part of Franche-Comté lying between the Jura foothills (the arbitrary line at the bottom) and the River Saône (at the top), with the various alternative itineraries which linked them. Many of the places on this map also appear in Figures 10 and 11. The unknown cartographer limited himself to those things which a marching army would need to know: where to expect rivers and forests, and where the bridges and larger communities were to be found. The map showed four main itineraries for the troops. Reading from left to right of the map these were:

(i) 'Ban' [Bans, 13 km SE of Dôle] to Belmont across the Loue, then through the great forest of Chaux to 'Faletās' [Falletans], across the Doubs to Rochefort, then through the forest of La Serre to a bridge over the River Ognon between Vitreux and Pagney, leading to Bay, Cult and the Saône;

(ii) from 'Mōtsoulbauldrey' [Mont-sous-Vauldrey, SE of Dôle], over the Loue to Montbarrey, through the forest to 'Esclās' [Eclans] and 'Or' [Our], then over the Doubs to Orchamps and La Barre, on to the Ognon and over to Marnay;

(iii) from La Ferté or Vaudrey to Ounans on the Loue, over to Germigney or Santans and through the forest of Chaux to Rans and Ranchot commanding the Doubs; on to Marnay and so to Gy, Bucey, Fretigney and Grandvelle (the present R.N. 474). This was the route actually used by the 1573 expedition – cf. *étapes* 4 to 8 on Figure 11;

(iv) from 'Thoulouse' [Toulouse-le-Château, 17 km N of Lons-le-Saunier] to Chamblay on the Loue, across to Châtelay or Chissey, then to Fraisans or Dampierre across the Doubs. Then, presumably, to Marnay.

Every place and feature shown on this map can be readily identified on the latest 1/100,000 *'carte de France'*, sheets O–12, O–13 and P–12: no mean achievement for an amateur map-maker of 1573!

CHAPTER 4

THE HIGH COMMAND

The arrival of the duke of Alva and his 10,000 Spaniards in Brussels in August 1567 transformed the government of the Netherlands. A new political and military organization, based on Spanish precedents and manned by Spanish personnel, superseded the existing structures, and it lasted with few changes until the collapse of Spanish authority in the Low Countries in 1706. How remarkable, then, that this long-lived 'Spanish regime' was only intended to be temporary!

In despatching the duke of Alva to the Netherlands, Philip II seems to have aimed only at immediate repression of the rebellion. Alva's political role was to be limited to informal adviser to the regent, Margaret of Parma, perhaps after the style of Granvelle before 1564. The duke's patent specifically restricted his powers to military affairs. He and his troops were to pacify the Low Countries so that the king could go there himself, purge the administration, enforce existing policies and restore financial solvency.[1]

The king prepared for his voyage throughout 1567. His fleet was made ready, the state archives were combed for documents concerning the Netherlands, escort troops were even embarked in readiness at Corunna. Then there was a hitch. From Luxemburg the duke of Alva warned the king that since the prince of Orange and many other rebels were still at large, the royal safety could not be guaranteed. Accordingly, in mid-September Philip II (who hated long journeys anyway, especially by sea) decided to postpone his departure until 1568 when, he hoped, the Low Countries would be pacified. Alva did his work well. Despite a triple invasion by the 'rebels', by December 1568 the Netherlands were at last safe for the king.

Meanwhile the regent, Margaret of Parma, insisted on resigning; she refused to work with the duke of Alva and presided over the Council of

---

[1] Alva's patent as captain-general (1 Apr. 1567, printed in *Co.Do.In.* IV, pp. 388–96) went to great lengths to distinguish civil from military authority. Clearly the king's intention was to uphold Margaret's dignity and authority and thus to retain her services. Alva protested long and loud about the narrow powers accorded in his patent.

State in Brussels for the last time on 16 December 1567. Even though the king fully intended to go to the Netherlands, Margaret's unforeseen departure created a political vacuum. Someone had to be vested with executive civil power until the king arrived. The obvious if not the only candidate available was Alva. The duke was therefore appointed civil governor-general as well as captain-general of the Army – a formidable accretion of power, though of course it was only a makeshift, an improvised solution until the king could come... but the king never came. First, there was a succession crisis. Philip II lost his only son, Don Carlos, in July 1568; three months later he lost his wife. The widowed king was left with two daughters, the eldest just two years old. It was clearly essential that Philip II should take no risks, that he should avoid obvious hazards like the sea-crossing to the Netherlands. These reasons were reinforced by the outbreak of a revolt in Spain itself. On Christmas Night 1568 the moriscos of Granada began a dangerous rebellion which was not brought under control until autumn 1570. In that same year the Turkish navy attacked and overran the Venetian island of Cyprus while the pirates of Algiers captured Tunis from Spain's allies. Philip II, panic-stricken, ordered the evacuation of the Balearic islands; his continued presence in Spain became more essential than ever. The Netherlands would have to wait.

The duke of Alva, who had left Spain in the belief that his work would be over in eighteen months at the most, continued perforce to exercise his autocratic powers in Brussels. His position would have dismayed a lesser man. He had brought no political advisers or diplomats with him, only soldiers, and he was firmly convinced that all the native ministers who had experience of governing the Netherlands were tarred with the brush of heresy and treason, yet he had to govern a country of three million people. In this dilemma, the duke decided to leave the routine administration in the hands of the suspect but competent native departments and to reserve all matters of state and war for himself. All political control came to rest in the captain-general and the small, informal circle of advisers chosen by him. At first these were all Spaniards and Italians and if after 1579 Alva's more flexible successors placed more confidence in Nether-landers, real power still remained confined to the entourage of the captain- and governor-general. Men like Richardot or Roose were powerful in the Spanish regime not because they held office in the Netherlands administration but because they were admitted to the general's inner councils. In institutional terms the political system created by the duke of Alva and preserved for 140 years was a return to 'household government'.

The captain-general of the Army of Flanders was paid a salary of 36,000 *escudos* a year, the income of a very large estate in Spain. With this sum, he maintained a household in the aristocratic manner: secretary, treasurer, majordomo, gentlemen of the bedchamber and all the rest. In addition, the general was allowed to distribute special grants from government funds to maintain a certain number of his friends, obliging them to reside in his household. These were the *entretenidos cerca la persona* ('men maintained about the person of the general'), equivalent to staff officers. In 1567, after protracted haggling, Philip II agreed to allow Alva to grant a maximum of 500 *escudos* monthly in *entretenimientos* (maintenance grants). The duke did not feel that this was enough, so he disobeyed: on 4 June 1567 he signed a warrant which awarded *entretenimientos* to 35 gentlemen in his entourage at a cost to the king of 900 *escudos* each month. Disobedience succeeded and the duke got his way. The number of *entretenidos cerca la persona* increased even further after 1572: there were 52 in 1596 and no less than 138 of them in 1608.[1]

The officers of the general's household and the *entretenidos* about his person were almost always soldiers. They served the general personally, gaining experience of war and proving their suitability for a post of command. Many combined a household office with a senior post in the Army. The post of *mayordomo mayor* to the Archdukes Albert and Isabella (the most important officer in their household) was occupied by the Admiral of Aragon, *maestre de campo general* of the Army (1598–1602), then by Don Geronimo Walter Zapata, inspector-general of the forces (1602–6), and finally by Ambrosia Spinola, *maestre de campo general* and superintendent of the military treasury (1606–28). In this way the archdukes kept abreast of every development in the Army.

The only regular council in this 'household' system of government was a Council of War. Again most of its members were drawn from the household and the *entretenidos*, but some Netherlandish field-commanders might also be included. The competence of this body varied considerably according to the military situation. There was no council at all between 1609 and 1618: everything was dealt with by the Archduke Albert, Spinola and the secretary of state and war, Juan de Mancicidor. After Mancicidor's death a *junta de guerra* (war committee) was created, but it

---

[1] Alva complained about the small sum allocated for *entretenimientos* in his letter to the king of 27 Apr. 1567 (*Co.Do.In.*IV, pp. 354–7); the king refused to increase the sum on 4 May (AGS *E* 149/185); Alva's defiant warrant to the military treasury is in AGS *CMC* 2a/49, unfol., 'Copia del mandato primero que dio el duque de Alva...', 4 de junio, 1567.' For the later inflation of offices cf. AGS *E* 611/109, 'Relación' of 15 Aug. 1596 and *E* 2290/100, H. de Ugarte to the king, 6 Apr. 1608.

was only allowed to discuss trivia such as whether or not to issue a leave pass or award a wage-bonus to a supplicant. Later on, under the cardinal-infante (1634-41) the war committee met regularly and discussed basic questions of strategy and army size, but its members were still drawn overwhelmingly from the general's household.[1]

Not only did the captain-general monopolize executive authority in the Netherlands, he also exercised considerable influence over the Army's judicial tribunals, financial departments and patronage. Until 1595 the captain-general acted as the supreme court for all criminal and civil suits involving military personnel. There was no appeal, not even to the king. The captain-general's power over the Army's finances was less obvious, but it was equally effective. There were two vital financial departments in the Army of Flanders, and both were autonomous: the *pagaduría* or military treasury, and the *contaduría del sueldo*, the audit office which checked the paymaster's activities. Although both departments were quite separate from the household, their principals appointed by the king, neither could operate without warrants signed by the captain-general and neither could refuse to pay one of his warrants. For most of the 'Spanish regime', it was the captain-general who decided how and when the king's money in the military treasury should be spent.

This power to initiate payments from the *pagaduría* was the foundation of the captain-general's extensive patronage. We have already noted the *entretenidos cerca la persona* who owed their salary and their prestigious position to the favour of the general; there were many more. The 52 *entretenidos* about the general's person in 1596 formed part of a total of 373 *entretenidos* paid by the military treasury. They served in various departments of the Army – in the secretariat, in the household, in the field – but all were personally appointed by the captain-general. Their total salaries came to almost 550,000 florins yearly.[2] The general could also reward the common soldiers on his own authority. Good or long service in the Spanish army was rewarded by a wage-bonus known as a *ventaja*; it was a monthly addition of between 1 and 10 *escudos* to the soldier's basic wage, and it was conferred by a special warrant of the captain-general. Between 1604 and 1607, for example, the paymaster-general

---

[1] AGS *E* 2032, unfol., Spinola to the king, 3 Apr. 1618, announcing that a *junta* of five members would meet twice weekly. Its limited authority was regretted by a disgruntled member of the *junta*: AGS *E* 2308/83, Don Luis de Velasco to the king, 3 Feb. 1620.

[2] AGS *E* 611/109, 'Relación' of the Army of Flanders, 15 Aug. 1596: the 373 *entretenidos* cost each month 18,292 *escudos* of 50 pattards. In 1588 there were 668 *entretenidos* in the Netherlands, costing 23,204 *escudos* of 57 pattards each month – probably the record. (AGS *E* 594/192, 'Relación' of 29 Apr. 1588.)

received warrants authorizing the payment of new *ventajas* to a total value of 1,740,000 florins a year. Of these, 185 warrants came from the king and no less than 4,323 from the captain-general.[1] Besides purely monetary rewards the captain-general could bestow many military offices – all colonels, *maestres de campo* and captains of units raised by direct commission were appointed and replaced by him, as were the governors of citadels and captured towns. Finally the general could recommend a soldier or *entretenido* to the king for further reward or promotion. To be 'mentioned in dispatches' meant the possibility of a pension or an estate in Spain, Italy or the Low Countries, of a knighthood (*hábito*) or even a lucrative commandery (*encomienda*) in one of Spain's military orders.[2]

The authority of the captain-general of the Army of Flanders was thus indeed impressive. His word controlled (in as much as a general ever 'controls' an army) the actions of up to 100,000 men. A simple gentleman of very modest means like Don Luis de Requesens held command over probably the largest army of sixteenth-century Christendom (over 86,000 men in March 1574), allocated almost as he pleased six million florins a year (more than the revenue of the Queen of England) and borrowed on his own credit four millions more (certainly more than Elizabeth of England could do). The captain-general decided, after consulting only those whom he chose, the exact way in which the Army should be deployed, its strength, its composition, its geographical distribution. His subordinates might criticize and intrigue at court for his recall, but they had to obey his arbitrary commands for as long as he held the king's commission. The only power which was withheld was the right to make peace or to declare war, and even this could be usurped. In 1577 Don John of Austria declared war on the States General by himself; in 1579 the prince of Parma secured the reconciliation of the Walloon provinces without the king's prior permission; and in 1607 the Archduke Albert anticipated royal approval in order to open truce-talks with the Dutch.

The king of Spain was far from happy with the autocratic power accumu-

---

[1] AGS *E* 2289/248, 'Relación' about the cost of *ventajas* by the paymaster-general, Martin de Unceta. The captain-general could also allocate a restricted number of 'avantaiges' and 'entreteniments' to the troops paid directly from the revenues of the Netherlands and administered by 'ceux des Finances'.

[2] These requests could be quite blunt. In 1568 the duke of Alva told the king that Don Lope Zapata had served so well that 'I cannot refrain from pointing it out to Your Majesty nor from requesting you to do him the honour of giving him an *encomienda* in one of the Orders.' (*Epistolario*, II, p. 12, Alva to the king, 19 Jan. 1568).

lated by his chief executive in the Netherlands. The chief cause for alarm was the absence of any permanent institution to counterbalance and check the captain-general's power. In Spain, every army commander was closely supervised by the Council of War; in the Indies the authority of the viceroys (who were also captains-general) was circumscribed by the *audiencias*, permanent tribunals with wide judicial and administrative powers directly responsible to the king. Neither of these controls was appropriate for the Netherlands. The crown was unable to introduce an *audiencia* because of the implacable hostility of the Netherlands to any foreign institution, while the native tribunals were not considered loyal, responsible or impartial enough to be trusted to control the Army. At the Spanish court, the 'Council of Flanders' included Netherlanders (automatically suspect) and was restricted to matters of civil patronage and administration in the Low Countries; the Council of State, which was responsible for matters of state and war in all regions of the Spanish Monarchy, had to fit consideration of Netherlands affairs into its already overcrowded timetable. In any case, each letter exchanged between the court and the Low Countries took a minimum of twelve days to reach its destination, and often a month. It was obvious that effective everyday supervision of the Spanish army could not come from Madrid.

The Spanish crown in fact possessed a number of standard instruments which maintained an ultimate check upon ministers and armies abroad. In the first place, the Army of Flanders received the greater part of its money from the crown of Castile; it was a universal rule that all who received funds from the Castilian treasury had to render account to the audit office of the Spanish exchequer, the *contaduría mayor de cuentas*. The *contaduría mayor* was meticulous, incorruptible and seemingly infallible. In time it uncovered every sharp practice and malversation of public funds, and its punishment was a fine of three times the value of the fraud. But the time required to close an account might run to decades! The accounts of Pedro de Olave, paymaster-general of the Army of Flanders 1580–5, were not even presented until 1598; those of one of his successors, Don Juan de Lira (1634–41) were not finally closed until 1660 (and Lira was himself trained in the *contaduría mayor*). There were even two accounts which were never satisfactorily closed because the audit took so long that it became impossible to establish the truth. Francisco de Lixalde, paymaster-general from 1567 until 1577, died in office and thirty-five years of almost continuous investigation could not penetrate the gloom which surrounded some of his transactions. In the end, in 1612, Lixalde's heirs paid a fine of 13,000 ducats and in return the paymaster's account was closed. Similarly the accounts of Thomas López de Ulloa for his second and third terms as paymaster-general of the Army of Flanders (1642–51) were never closed. In 1701 the *contaduría mayor*, after fifty years of auditing, declared that Ulloa's heirs owed 309,325 florins to the treasury, and the family's estates in Spain were put under an embargo. The heirs, however, lived in the Netherlands and it seems unlikely that the debt was paid before effective Spanish rule in the Low Countries collapsed in 1706.[1]

The trouble with the *contaduría mayor* was that it had too much work to do, and that it was not allowed to handle important matters – the really major accounts like Lixalde's – before the rest. Habsburg imperialism produced an enormous outflow of Castilian treasure, and the *contaduría mayor* proved unable to track down every item of expenditure abroad as well as at home. It was therefore an important step towards discovering and thereby reducing fraud when in January 1609 a special cell of the *contaduría mayor* was established in Brussels, with authority to audit and close the accounts of all in the Netherlands who handled Castilian treasure except the paymasters-general – they continued to render account at the Spanish court. Although it was suppressed briefly during the truce (1615–19) this *sala de cuentas* continued to function, patiently checking all minor public accounts in the Netherlands which involved money from Spain, until the end of the Spanish regime. In 1641 it was joined by a second department, the *sala de los pagadores generales*, also formed of officials from the Spanish exchequer and committed to take the accounts of the paymasters-general. This body was also active, with a few inter- missions, for the rest of the century. Although they were unequal to the wiles of Thomas López de Ulloa, these new institutions went a long way towards establishing a more immediate control over the finances of the Army of Flanders and over the men who administered them.

The interminable processes of the *contaduría mayor de cuentas* meant in effect that the normal day-to-day check on fraud and abuse in the Army of Flanders devolved upon a single officer, the inspector-general (*veedor general*). The office, created by the Catholic kings in 1503, was directly responsible to the crown and independent of the captain-general. The *veedor* was supposed to preside at every muster where money was issued, examine every warrant sent to the treasury for payment, and attend at the treasury every time the paymaster received money. With an army of

---

[1] On Lixalde: A. W. Lovett, 'Francisco de Lixalde: a Spanish Paymaster in the Netherlands (1567–77)', *Tijdschrift voor Geschiedenis*, LXXXIV (1971), pp. 14–23. On Ulloa: C. de Vos, 'Limal, ses seigneurs et seigneuries. Don Thomas Lopéz de Ulloa, 1er baron de Limal, 1621–55', *Wavriensia*, XIII (1964), pp. 33–87.

70,000 men distributed in up to two hundred garrisons, and a turnover at the treasury of around ten million florins annually, it is not surprising that the inspector-general found it impossible to fulfil all his responsibilities. At one stage Philip II even debated whether the office served any useful purpose, but the mushroom growth of abuses in the Army whenever a *veedor* was not present in the Netherlands soon convinced him.[1] The trouble was that the inspector-general was not allowed to do anything by proxy. The high command bitterly resented the interference of a *veedor* and although they could not exclude him in person, they could and did refuse to give any information or assistance to his officials. In this, incredibly, the crown acquiesced.[2] Perhaps the king feared that an overmighty inspector might create more problems than he solved; perhaps also there was an anxiety not to offend a victorious commander – a reluctance to demand the proverbial 'Accounts of the Grand Captain', to ask a general who conquered kingdoms how he had spent his master's money. This sentiment was certainly expressed by one *veedor* who felt uncomfortable when told to investigate the conduct of the duke of Parma, captain-general of the Army of Flanders and at the height of his triumphs, in 1587:

> I know and am fully aware [wrote the *veedor*] that since the Duke is the person he is, and having served as he has, it would be very reasonable to leave everything involving money completely to his discretion and pleasure, because when it comes to winning Kingdoms that is not the most important thing.

There was certainly a view in Spanish court circles that a general who was capable of winning victories ought to be left alone. The poking and prying of many *veedores* therefore often failed to find support in Madrid.[3]

This curious paradox quickly disappeared when the general failed to

---

[1] When Inspector-General Valdes was killed in action in 1572 Philip II wrote to the duke of Alva: 'You should see whether we need to appoint a *Veedor* for the Army in the place of the late Jordan de Valdes, or whether we can do without one since there are two *Contadores*.' (AA 8/23, the king to Alva, 29 Oct. 1572.)

[2] The dispute between the *veedores* and the other clerical officers of the Army was a perennial one. There are many documents concerning the trials of *Veedor General* Juan Bautista de Tassis in 1587 in AGS *E* 593, and some of them are printed in *Co.Do.In.* LXXV.

[3] AGS *E* 593/7, Juan Bautista de Tassis to the king, 19 Jan. 1587. The story goes that in 1499 Ferdinand the Catholic greeted the return of the grand captain from his triumphant conquest of Naples with a demand to render account of how he had spent the state treasure. The conqueror replied the very next day, and read out a statement to the Catholic kings and their council. It began '200,736 ducats and 9 *reales* to friars, monks and the poor to ask God's blessing upon Spanish arms' and ended 'and a hundred millions for my patience as I listened yesterday to the King asking for accounts from the man who had won him a kingdom!' (Marqués de Velada, *Noticias y documentos de algunos Dávila...*, pp. 38–40; the original *Cuentas del Gran Capitán* were in the marquis' archive when he wrote.) Today the proverb has been debased: it means simply 'to overcharge'.

win his battles. The Spanish Monarchy regularly subjected its government departments to a thorough investigation by a royal commission of enquiry, and the Spanish regime in the Netherlands was by no means exempt. These inquests invariably coincided with periods of military failure. The first official scrutiny of the conduct of the high command took place in March 1574, just as the duke of Alva and his closest advisers were nearing Spain after the duke's somewhat inglorious recall. Two special committees in Madrid considered a paper prepared by the king's private secretary, Mateo Vazquez, concerning the abuses which were said to have marred the duke's government of the Netherlands. There was certainly some sort of trial of Juan de Albornoz, Alva's secretary whose voice had been important in distributing the army's money, but he was acquitted.[1] At the same time serious proposals were made for a special tribunal to be formed in the Netherlands to investigate the dealings of the Army's financial departments. Despite enthusiasm for this project in many quarters, its implementation was delayed from month to month until the collapse of Spanish authority in the Netherlands in August 1576 prevented any further retrospective enquiries for the time being.

The departure of the foreign troops from the Low Countries in April 1580 provided an opportunity for resurrecting the scheme. In November 1581 a full commission of enquiry, the 'Tribunal de las cuentas de Flandes', began to collect evidence in Madrid concerning the administration of the king's treasure in the Netherlands since 1559.[2] Yet although it had been so long meditated and although it lasted for four years, the enquiry was a disappointment. It proved to be hamstrung on three counts: many papers were destroyed or fell into enemy hands during the disorders of 1576; the inspectors did not reside in the Netherlands; and they were not drawn from the *contaduría mayor de cuentas*. Consequently the commissioners experienced great difficulty in collecting the material necessary to verify accounts, and such accounts as they managed to audit were not accepted as final by the *contaduría mayor*. The enterprise, although sound in intention, was thus a complete failure in practice.

[1] IVdeDJ 36/40, 'Lo que a Su Magestad ha parecido advertir sobre la relación de los excessos que se dize se han hecho en los estados de Flandes'. (A paper prepared by the king and Vazquez to determine the scope of the enquiries of the two committees: they met on 9 and 10 Mar. 1574.) Albornoz's trial is mentioned in AA 67/49, Don Fadrique de Toledo to Albornoz, 1 Apr. 1574 (copy).

[2] The Spanish Council of Finance proposed a tribunal to the king in a *consulta* of 12 Jan. 1574 (IVdeDJ 68/287); Don Luis de Requesens harped upon the need for one in several letters to the king (e.g. those of 27 Jun. 1574 and 7 Jan. 1575, AGS *E* 558/81 and BM *Addl. Ms.* 28,359/114). Letters concerning the formation of the tribunal of 1581 may be found in IVdeDJ 24/231,240,318,332, and 358, and AGS *CMC* 2a/28.

In April 1593, following the death of the duke of Parma, a new attempt was made. Two senior officials of the *contaduría mayor* were sent to the Netherlands to collect information about the conduct and competence of the Army's personnel since 1580. In May 1594 they were superseded by a full commission of enquiry, consisting of five judges appointed by the king and sitting permanently in Brussels: the 'Tribunal de la Visita'. The 'Visita' spent eight years patiently auditing the accounts and examining the conduct of all who had handled the Army's money or who were accused of fraud. A total of 117 people were tried. The 'Visita' levied fines and suspended from office all whose administration was suspect. Most of those who had served the duke of Parma were deprived of their offices.[1] Even so the 'Visita' was only a partial success. First it was expensive: between 1598 and 1600 the commissioners collected fines worth 14,056 *escudos* but their activities cost 44,000. Further, many of those it dismissed from office or disgraced were later rehabilitated, and many of the fines it imposed were later pardoned.[2]

The kings of Spain were uncomfortably aware of the imperfections and general ineffectiveness of the tribunals and commissions of enquiry with which they hoped to control the sins of their subordinates. Since they all took a long time to prepare, cost too much to run and registered only short-term gains it was occasionally necessary for the king to intervene directly in cases which were either too urgent or too minor to merit a fully-fledged 'Visita'. The king could easily make his authority felt in a dramatic way through his ultimate control of the Army's patronage and the Army's money.

Junior personnel were easy to deal with. They depended on a salary from the military treasury; if they fell foul of the king their salary could be 'reformed' (*reformado*, sc. stopped.) On a number of occasions all, or almost all *entretenimientos* and *ventajas* were 'reformed' at once. This process, known as a *reformación general*, was designed to prune government expenditure as well as dismiss undesirable persons. After the *reformación* ministers examined the credentials and service of all the officials before deciding who might be reinstated. The treatment of unwanted military personnel without an *entretenimiento* was yet simpler:

---

[1] The commission of the two inspectors (*visitadores* – Juan Lopez de Aliri and Domingo de Ypeñarrieta) dated 5 Apr. 1593, together with a number of their papers, is in AGS *CMC* 3a/947 (this *legajo* was kindly shown to me by Doña Ascención de la Plaza). On the 'Visita', cf. the article of J. Lefèvre, 'Le Tribunal de la Visite, 1594–1602...', *Archives, Bibliothèques et Musées de Belgique* IX (1932), pp. 65–85. Unfortunately M. Lefèvre did not use the papers of the 'Visita' itself, preserved in Simancas.

[2] On the 'Visita's' cost: *AHE* III pp. 176–9 (*consulta* of the Council of State, 7 Feb. 1602).

their names were removed from the wage-sheets and their pay automatically ceased.

More senior personnel were handled with equal firmness but greater tact. In order to uphold the dignity of their office, they were ordered to ask for permission to resign when the government no longer required their services. Members of the high command were rarely disgraced openly, but it could even happen to an inspector-general. In 1629 Don Gaspar Ruiz de Pereda, *veedor general*, was ordered to resign at once; he was thereupon thrown into prison for over a year while his professional conduct was investigated.[1] Such heavy-handedness is surprising when one discovers the disorders and rank disobedience which were tolerated from some of the field-officers. In 1622 two Italian *maestres de campo* abandoned their *tercios* in the face of the enemy just because their troops were not put in the vanguard of the army, the position which custom and the 'honour of their nation' demanded. This grave misdemeanour, and others like it, went unpunished although in other armies the offenders would have been shot. Indeed throughout the 1620s senior Spanish and Italian officers refused to obey the orders of their superior, Count Henry van den Berg, because he was a Netherlander – even though Berg had served with credit and courage since 1589. Incredibly, the disobedient officers found support in the Council of State in Madrid. At least three councillors, two of them veterans of the Low Countries' Wars, held the view that:

> Ever since His Highness [Don John of Austria, d. 1578] died until the present all we have seen has been attempts to abase the Spanish nation; this was the case under the duke of Parma, under the Archduke Albert, and now the Infanta [Isabella] wants to do the same.

The three councillors recommended that the king should never permit a foreigner to hold command over Spanish troops.[2] With such encouragement from above it is small wonder that disobedience among the senior officers continued to spread. By 1632 the exasperated commander-in-chief could report to the king that nobody took orders from anyone! It took

---

1 Pereda's conduct was investigated by the superintendent of military justice in the Netherlands, Juan Díaz de Letona. Enquiries were hampered, however, by Pereda's wife, who mobilized the ladies of the Infanta Isabella's bedchamber to protect her husband's reputation: cf. AGS *E* 2044/118, *consulta* of the Council of State, 18 Jun. 1630.

2 AGS *E* 2321, unfol., Infanta Isabella to the king, 10 Mar. 1628, about the refusal of the marquis of Campo Latero, another Italian *maestre de campo*, to take orders from Count Henry van den Berg, mentioning the incident of 1622. Campo Latero was in fact tried by a military tribunal for insubordination, but at the king's special request he was acquitted. The support of a part of the Council of State appears in: BM *Addl. Ms.* 14,007/379 and 382, *consultas* on Isabella's letters of 16 Mar. and 7 Apr. 1624. Eventually, of course, driven by desperation, insults and ingratitude, Berg deserted to the Dutch in 1632.

the arrival of the king's brother, the cardinal-infante, in 1634 to restore a semblance of order and obedience to the Army of Flanders.[1]

No such misconduct was tolerated from the commander-in-chief, however. Nor was failure. The king recalled the duke of Alva and Don Francisco de Melo from the Netherlands because they had failed. Don Luis de Requesens spared himself this indignity only by dying first. His successors Don John of Austria and the prince of Parma disobeyed their master and it was resolved to recall them, but again they died first.

The disobedience of a general was, of course, a very serious matter: it smacked of treason. Drastic measures might be necessary to prevent disobedience from turning into armed rebellion. The king had to be ready to use desperate expedients in order to impose his will on the Army. Every general needed massive financial support to keep his troops together. Contributions raised locally were not enough. Even Wallenstein needed 'a few million every year' from the imperial treasury in order to maintain his army in the field, and no commander in the Netherlands, a small country devastated by continual fighting, equalled Wallenstein's financial freedom.[2] Their dependence on the resources of the king who employed them was thus greater. Consequently, by stopping all remittances to a wayward general, the king could immediately neutralize the threat posed by disobedience. The classic use of this technique occurred in 1592. The issue was simple: Philip II ordered his nephew the duke of Parma, captain-general of the Army of Flanders, to invade France in 1591. The king sent large sums of money to the Netherlands to finance the operation, but they were used partly to pay off mutineers, partly to campaign against the Dutch. There was only one answer to this open defiance. Orders were issued to recall Parma, but they were not made public until his successor could reach the Low Countries – which took over a year. During this interlunary period, the king kept his nephew 'on a very short rein': the receipts of the military treasury plunged from 14 million florins in 1591 to 4.4 million in 1592. In anticipation of the arrival of Philip II's more dutiful nephew, the Archduke Ernest, the military treasury received 15.3 million florins in 1593. By then, Parma was dead.[3]

[1] AGS *E* 2046/17–18, *consulta* of the Council of State, 14 Jun. 1632.

[2] 'So mache man ein par Million alle Jahr fertig, diesen langwierigen Krieg zu führen', letter of Wallenstein to the imperial finance minister, 28 Jan. 1626, quoted A. Ernstberger, *Hans de Witte: Finanzmann Wallensteins* (Wiesbaden, 1954), p. 166.

[3] For further information on this incident cf. p. 246. Parma was of course painfully aware that funds were being withheld from him and he complained bitterly to the government about his penury. The ministers in Madrid could only agree: 'por los respectos que se saben, es assi que se le ha tenido muy corta la rienda'. (AGS *E* 2855, unfol., 'Lo que paresce sobre las cartas del duque de Parma de 28 de oct. y 10 de nov. 1592.')

Although between them these methods maintained the principle of royal control over the Army of Flanders, all were somewhat blunt instruments with which to correct the problem of ministerial irresponsibility. There was no attempt to introduce regular individual investigations of the conduct of each official before he left office – the *residencia* or secret professional enquiry which helped to ensure administrative probity in the New World. Nor did the crown seek to improve the processes by which the personnel of the high command were selected; the high standards which already prevailed in Spain's judicial hierarchy were not applied to other branches of the administration.[1]

In the sixteenth century at least, however, there was little to criticize in the training of the senior military personnel, most of whom had spent a number of years serving in the ranks to gain experience of the realities of war. The traditional cadres which provided Spain's military and naval commanders were the younger sons of the nobility (the *segundones*) and the gentry (the *hidalgos*). These men, who had neither wealth nor following of their own, treated service in the armed forces as their career; they were professionals, beginning life as gentleman-rankers (*particulares*) and working their way up by long and good service. A certain number of *ventajas* (wage-bonuses) in the infantry were set aside for the *particulares*, although many served with only the soldier's basic wage. The 'great lords who aspire to higher military office' thus learned 'how sensible it is to rise to them in this way and not to wish to begin as a soldier and as a General in a single day'.[2] From gentleman-ranker, the path to preferment led through *alferez* (lieutenant) and captain to *maestre de campo* or perhaps *entretenido cerca la persona*. This was the highest rank attained by the *hidalgos*, career-soldiers from the gentry class like Julián Romero, Cristobal de Mondragón or Francisco Verdugo; it was unusual to find such men rising to independent operational commands.[3] Generally speaking, in the sixteenth century, the highest posts in the Army were reserved for those who came from a titled family, *segundones* (younger

---

[1] On the *residencia* and *visita* as the standard instruments of administrative control in the Indies, cf. the admirably clear article of G. Céspedes de Castillo, 'La visita como institución indiana', *Anuario de Estudios Americanos*, III (1946), pp. 984–1,025; on the advanced legal bureaucracy of metropolitan Spain, cf. the fascinating information in R. L. Kagan, 'Education and the State in Habsburg Spain', Cambridge Univ. Ph.D. thesis (1968), Chaps. III–IV.

[2] Carlos Coloma, *Las Guerras de los Estados Bajos*, bk II (*BAE* edn, Madrid, 1948), p. 19. On the *particulares* and their significance, cf. pp. 40–1 above.

There are admirable biographical studies of these three men: A. Marichalar, marqués de Montesa, *Julián Romero* (Madrid, 1952); A Salcedo Ruíz, *El Coronel Cristobal de Mondragón: apuntos para su biografía* (Madrid, 1905); A. Rumeu de Armas, 'Nuevos datos para la biografía de don Francisco Verdugo...', *Hispania*, X (1950), pp. 85–103.

sons of noblemen) like Don Carlos Coloma or Don Hernando de Toledo, although they too served their apprenticeship in the ranks.[1]

After the 1590s, however, posts of command were bestowed increasingly upon men who had seen more service in the court than in the field. The change was caused basically by the crown's urgent need for commanders who could pay for their troops as well as command them, who could supplement the king's ailing credit with their own. Perhaps the first example of the new criteria in action occurred in 1588 with the duke of Medina Sidonia who was chosen to command the Invincible Armada not so much because he was uniquely qualified to govern a large enterprise or win a war but because he was able to finance it.[2] Likewise the appointment of Ambrosia Spinola as *maestre de campo general* of the Army of Flanders in 1603 and 1605 was primarily motivated by his ability to pay for the Army, not because he had displayed outstanding military skill. Wealth had become a prime military asset. Only the rich could afford to lead a Spanish army and the cost of command was enough to beggar even a banker: in 1603–4 Spinola advanced 5 million florins to the Spanish army besieging Ostend and he was not repaid in full until 1619.[3] Few generals could offer the king credit like that; fewer still were repaid the little they did lend. The duke of Alva, like many other grandees, pawned his estates in order to serve his king in war. During his government of the Netherlands (1567–73) and in other commissions executed for Philip II, the 'Iron Duke' saddled his inheritance with debts totalling 500,000 ducats (about 1,250,000 florins) and involving annual interest payments of 35,000 ducats. These debts were still giving his heirs trouble in the 1660s.[4] Service in the less responsible post of *maestre de campo* could be no less disastrous to the finances of a poorer man. The widow of Julián

---

[1] Coloma – soldier, viceroy, ambassador and historian – was the subject of a thesis by the late Miss Olga Turner, 'Some aspects of the Life and Works of don Carlos Coloma, 1566–1637', London Univ. Ph.D. thesis (1950). On Don Hernando de Toledo, Alva's bastard son, general of light cavalry in the Netherlands (1567–71), energetic viceroy of Catalonia and hero of Lope de Vega's play *El Aldegüela*, there is a study by A. Salcedo Ruíz, *Un bastardo insigne del Gran Duque de Alba: el prior don Hernando de Toledo* (Madrid, 1903). Unfortunately Sr Ruíz confused the prior with the *maestre de campo* Don Hernando de Toledo, this time from the family of Alba de Liste, who commanded a *tercio* in the Netherlands (1568–80) and afterwards in Portugal (1580–2).

[2] I.A.A. Thompson, 'The appointment of the Duke of Medina Sidonia to the command of the Spanish Armada', *The Historical Journal*, XII (1969), pp. 197–216, especially pp. 208–10.

[3] AGRB *SEG* 27/8 and 26v–7. Orders of 2 Oct. and 9 Dec. 1619 to reimburse Spinola.

[4] AHN *Consejos* 7228/26, *consulta* of the Council of Castile, 10 Feb. 1668. The debts of the 'Iron Duke' on his campaigns were claimed to be largely responsible for the endless financial troubles of his descendants during the seventeenth century. This *consulta* gives full details; I am extremely grateful to Dr C. J. Jago of McMaster University for drawing my attention to it.

Romero, who was renowned as an honest as well as skilful captain, asked the king to restore the 8,000 ducats of her dowry and estates which the late *maestre de campo* (d. 1577) had sold 'in order to campaign in the Netherlands'. In the event the widow was remunerated, but many others were not.[1] Kings, as the duke of Alva once observed, use men like oranges: they squeeze out the juice and then throw away the peel.

In the seventeenth century men of limited means like Romero tended to keep away from the wars. As armies became the preserve of the 'lackeys and labourers' despised by their generals, the posts of command went to those who made military contracting their profession, to those who were rich and vainglorious, or to those who could not shirk their traditional personal responsibility to fight for their king – the higher nobility. The professionals were there to make war pay; the vainglorious were there to enhance their prestige; the grandees regarded their military service, however exalted, as a necessary and unwelcome stage in their path to royal preferment. All of them expected to start, as royal cadets like Don John had always done, at the top.

Of course, not everyone came out of the war poorer than they began. There were common soldiers who acquired vast plunder at the capture of a town, unscrupulous captains who cheated at the muster, and ruthless contractors who made a fortune. Above all, there were those who did not fight at all: the clerks who staffed the military secretariat, the military treasury and the other clerical departments. These men received high wages (15, 20 or 30 *escudos* a month were the rule, compared to the soldier's basic wage of 3) and if any of them received wounds in the course of duty it was thought memorable. The clerks had few qualifications to justify such high pay. They were literate of course, but few of them had a university degree; they rose in the Army's hierarchy through undisguised nepotism, favouritism and patronage.

The promotion structure within the Army's clerical service was fairly simple. The king appointed all the heads of departments, the paymaster, the inspector-general and so on, and each of these ministers appointed his own subordinates, a certain number of whom received government salaries (cf. Appendix B, p. 276). On three occasions the king appointed

[1] Marqués de Saltillo, 'Servidores del Rey don Felipe II', *Hispania*, IV (1941), pp. 116–22. Cf. the parallel remarks of L. Stone, *The Crisis of the Aristocracy, 1558–1641* (Oxford, 1965), pp. 454–8, with sundry examples of English gentlemen and aristocrats ruined by their military service for the crown. Cf. also the contemporary judgement of Emeric Crucé (*Le Nouveau Cynée*, Paris, 1623, p. 13): 'pour deux soldats qui s'y enrichiront [in war] on en trouvera cinquante qui n'y gaigneront que des coups ou des maladies incurables. Pour le regard des Princes, ils y espuisent leurs finances'.

new heads for all the clerical departments at once: in 1567, 1603 and 1632 a special appointments committee was convened to find suitable candidates, and on the whole they did their job well.[1] At other times, appointments to the major positions in the Army of Flanders were made piecemeal as vacancies occurred. There were, basically, two types of candidate from which the king could choose. There were those who, although perhaps lacking experience of military administration, had the support of someone in the king's favour; on the other hand there were the professional administrators already in the Netherlands.

Few candidates were entirely satisfactory. Habsburg Spain had no proper system of apprenticeship or training for its administrators, only for its judges. Instead, every minister of the crown was expected to build up a private secretariat at his own expense to help him to transact the king's business. These officials were the private servants of the minister who fed and paid them, and it was to him that they owed their primary loyalty. Sometimes, however, the king appropriated one of these private officials for his own service, taking him on to the government pay-roll. Philip II in particular used his ministers' secretariats as a 'seminary'.[2] There were certainly advantages in this practice: a pool of administrators familiar with the methods of royal government was created at no expense to the king – Spain got her civil service on the cheap; and although a minister might lose some of his best men to the king, there were obvious compensations in placing a loyal servant in a department of state. Against these mutual benefits, there was a serious drawback: the practice tended to breed factions and partisanship in every branch of government. The candidates presented to the king from the Netherlands were normally the relatives or dependants of the outgoing minister (especially the *oficial mayor* or chief deputy who was almost always the minister's nephew, son or cousin and was often the only man who understood how the department worked); those recommended by someone at court were normally the 'creatures' (in the contemporary phrase) of one of the king's advisers, often already established in another government department. As Appendix E shows (pp. 281–6 below) most of the leading clerical ministers of the Army of Flanders fell into these two categories.

Unfortunately, the selection process which failed to instil a sense of loyalty to the state coupled with the lack of any machinery which regularly

---

[1] On the appointments of 1566–7 cf. BM *Addl. Ms.* 28,386/11–12, report on the candidates by Juan de Escobedo to Espinosa, 27 Dec. 1566; on those of 1603, cf. *AHE* III, p. 305 and AGS *E* 622/234, reports of the appointments committee and of the Council of State, Feb. 1603; for those of 1632, AGS *E* 2047/66, *consulta* of the Council of State, 14 Dec. 1632.
[2] Cf. L. Cabrera de Córdoba, *Historia de Felipe II*, part I, bk XII 3.

called ministers to account immediately they left office (if not before) permitted and at times promoted the spread of corruption. There was little to choose between those who grew up in the Netherlands and those brought in by the king from outside. Even in 1567 the crown appointed some officials of very dubious integrity. Juan de Navarrete, for example, selected to be paymaster of the artillery in 1567, could not take up his appointment for some time because he was serving a sentence of one year's suspension from holding all treasury office as a punishment for fraud. Once in the Netherlands, Navarrete profited from the absence of crown control to exploit the office entrusted to him. When he died in office in 1580, a rich man, the government's investigators had still not caught up with him.[1] They never caught up with Cosme Masi, the personal private secretary of the duke of Parma from 1568 until 1592. In 1580 he became secretary of state and war to Parma and virtual dictator of the military treasury. Throughout his term of office he was denounced and reviled as an unscrupulous villain by almost everyone and in 1594 he was interrogated by the 'Visita', but he was acquitted. In 1596 he turned financier, using his ill-gotten gains as secretary to lend money – no less than 443,750 florins – to the Netherlands government at extortionate interest. Indeed, his charges were so high that the Council of Finance initiated proceedings against him for usury. He survived this threat, however, and in 1627 he decided to ask for some reward for his 'long and valuable services' in the Low Countries. The same council which had previously condemned his usury accepted the lies he told about his past record and they recommended the king to award him a knighthood in one of the military orders in Spain and two dukedoms in Italy![2]

Yet despite these failures, the fact remained that the king of Spain never lost control of his army. The political direction of Spain's armed forces never left civilian hands; there was never a Spanish Wallenstein. This considerable success meant that the policies and the resources deployed by Spain against the revolt of the Netherlands were determined, throughout the war, at the Spanish court. Having created a vast army 800 miles

---

[1] BM *Addl. Ms.* 28,387/196, note from the count of Olivares to Espinosa about Navarrete's suspension for a year from 14 Nov. 1566. For Navarrete's later frauds, cf. the investigation of his dealings and his private fortune, AGS *CMC* 2a/28.

[2] AGS *CJH* (Ant.), unfol., 'Relación de los memoriales de Cosme Masi' 10 Jan. 1627. The inspector-general complained in 1587 that 'quiere su secretario [Masi] quedar director y dueño absoluto de la dispusición de la hazienda de V. Md.' (AGS *E* 593/7, Juan Baptista de Tassis to the king, 19 Jan. 1587.)

away (by the most direct route!) the central government of the Spanish empire had to supply, reinforce and maintain the new leviathan. This centralization was a mixed blessing. It enabled the crown to evaluate and balance the need to fight in the Netherlands against the need to intervene elsewhere, and it permitted a rational allocation of the empire's resources between the needs of the various member-states. This, however, did not necessarily increase the chances of a Spanish victory in the Netherlands...

Part II

Maintaining an army:
the problem of resources

War is waged not so much with arms as with money which is
the sinews of war.

Thucydides

The matter of greatest difficulty in the...maintenance of this
action is in proportioning the charge of the warres and the nombers
of souldiors to be maynteyned with the contribucions and meanes
of the countreys.

'Mr Wylkes' Declaration' on the state of the Low Countries' wars, 22 July 1587, printed by H. Brugmans,
Correspondentie van Robert Dudley..., II (Utrecht, 1931),
p. 402

CHAPTER 5

THE ARMY OF FLANDERS
AND LOGISTICS

I owne that let any War be ever so successful if persons will set down and weigh the Expences they will find...that it has impoverished the State, enriched individuals, and perhaps raised the Name only of the Conquerors, but this is only weighing such events in the Scale of a Tradesman behind his Counter; it is necessary for those in the Station it has pleased Divine Providence to place me to weigh whether expences though very great are not sometimes necessary to prevent what might be more ruinous to a Country than the loss of money.

Faced with a political situation abroad which gravely challenged his authority, George III of England, like Philip II of Spain two centuries before and many statesmen of varying ability since, refused to cut his coat according to his cloth. King George and King Philip both felt that the consequences of national dishonour abroad could not be measured in simple terms of profit and loss, that the risk of a foreign failure had to be assessed in terms of their general 'imperial' position and their international prestige.[1]

Habsburg Spain was perhaps the first European power of modern times to justify a war abroad with the sophisticated 'arguments' of global strategy which have since become the stock-in-trade of ailing empires everywhere. The basic justification advanced by Spain for the prolonged attempt to suppress the Dutch Revolt by force was the belief that the structure of Habsburg power resembled a house of cards: if one 'card' tottered or fell, the whole house would inevitably come crashing down. This argument, a super-domino theory which has been called the 'argument from the escalation of potential disasters', took many forms. Perhaps the most straightforward version was the earliest. In 1566–7 and for some years afterwards it was argued in Spanish court circles that weakness or ineptitude in handling the Netherlands rebellion would provoke

---

[1] Sir John Fortescue, *The Correspondence of King George the Third*, IV (London, 1928), pp. 350–1, the king to Lord North, 11 Jun. 1779. The rest of the letter, in which George III advanced his own 'domino theory' to justify the use of force against the rebellion of North America, is also of interest.

similar risings in Italy, especially in the two provinces won by conquest: Naples and Milan. Both in 1566–7 and in 1577, when the question of 'peace or war in the Netherlands' was exhaustively discussed by Philip II and his advisers, careful consideration was given to the deleterious effects which conciliation or concessions might have upon Spain's other imperial holdings. Force was used in 'Flanders' partly to safeguard Spain's position in Italy.[1]

Naturally this argument began to lose its point when after many years of inconclusive fighting punctuated by periodic disaster in the Low Countries there was still no sign of unrest in Italy, but a new 'domino theory' was soon found to replace the old. As the Low Countries' Wars became less a civil war and more an international confrontation, so Spain's continued commitment there came to be justified by the argument that as long as Spain's enemies could be made to fight in the Netherlands, they could not attack Spain herself. 'Flanders' came to be seen as the punch-ball of the Spanish empire. In 1600:

> The Council [of State] said that, as it has represented to Your Majesty on other occasions, the conservation of the Low Countries ought to be undertaken with the same care and earnestness as has been done in the past, because they are the bridle which restrains and curbs the French, the English and the rebels, whose forces, should that shield fail, would fall on Your Majesty and his Kingdoms in several parts, giving rise to greater expenses and dangers.[2]

Even those 'projectors' (*arbitristas*) who searched for a way to save Spain from crisis could not consider abandoning the Netherlands:

> Those who do not realize that the domestic peace which Spain enjoys derives from the long wars in the Low Countries know little of public affairs; they are only defensive and they further the tranquillity of these kingdoms because the day that Spain removes her armies from those provinces, we would inevitably see theirs in Spain.

These words of Pedro Fernández de Navarrete were echoed with striking similarity by the king in a letter of the same year (1626):

> Although the war which we have fought with the Dutch has exhausted my

---

[1] This 'argument' was first discerned and christened by Professor H. G. Koenigsberger. The discussion which follows owes much to conversations with Professor Koenigsberger. For specific examples cf. the views of Cardinal Granvelle in 1566: 'Claramente dice toda Italia que si el alboroto de Flandes pasa adelante, seguirá Milán y Nápoles.' Poullet, *Correspondance...de Granvelle*, I (Brussels, 1877), pp. 314–8, Granvelle to the king, 19 Jun. 1566; those of Cardinal Quiroga in 1577: royal weakness in the Netherlands would be 'poner en aventura su honor y estimación y aun la obedencia para con otros vasallos que es mucho de temer lo tomarían por ejemplo para se levantar, a lo menos los de conquista como Nápoles y Milán.' (AGS *E* 2843/7, Discussion of the Council of State, 5 Sep. 1577 – second copy: *E* 571/103*bis*; and the same opinion voiced in June 1578 by the duke of Sesa, AGS *E* 578/121).
[2] *AHE*, III, p. 7, *consulta* of the Council of State, 21 Mar. 1600.

Treasury and forced us into the debts we have incurred, it has also diverted our enemies in those parts so that, had we not done so, it is certain that we would have had war in Spain or somewhere nearer, as happened during the time of the [Twelve Years'] Truce in those provinces when the war moved to Italy: the cost was no less and the danger was greater because the armies of our enemies were nearer the heart [of the Empire].

The king pressed his argument even further, almost suggesting that if the Low Countries' Wars had not existed, it would have been necessary to invent them:

And it is true (and experience and past example prove it) that with as many kingdoms and lordships as have been linked to this crown, it is impossible to be without war in some area either to defend what we have acquired to divert my enemies.[1]

Advocates of this theory usually fell back on two examples which 'proved' (to their own satisfaction) that the war in the Netherlands safeguarded Spanish interests elsewhere. It was claimed that at all costs the Low Countries had to be saved for Spain in order to keep France in check, experience having shown that the best way to divert a French attack upon Spain was to invade France from the Netherlands. 'I am well aware that it is from the Netherlands that the King of France can best be attacked and forced into peace', observed Philip II; 'The surest means we have of keeping the French in check is to maintain strong forces in Flanders', echoed Cardinal Granvelle. Somewhat later the Council of State reminded Philip III that 'one can see in the history books how Spain has been superior to France since the day she was able to make a diversion in the Netherlands, and everyone has always realized that the conservation of this Monarchy depends on the possession of those provinces.'[2] It was also alleged that the Low Countries' Wars restricted Dutch piracy in the Indies. This view first gained prominence during the Twelve Years' Truce, when it appeared to the Spanish court that the prodigious increase in Dutch trade to the Caribbean and the East Indies was directly due to the suspension of hostilities at home. The decision not to renew the truce, taken by the council of Philip III at Christmas 1619, was dictated overwhelmingly by Spain's fears that unless war was re-

[1] P. Fernández de Navarrete, *La Conservación de Monarquías* (Madrid, 1626), p. 123; AGRB *SEG* 195/64, Philip IV to the Infanta Isabella, 9 Aug. 1626. The king's remarks formed a preamble to his proposal to extend the 'Union of Arms' project to the Netherlands.
[2] Philip II's instruction to B. Carranza, 5 Jun. 1558, quoted L. P. Gachard, *Retraite et mort de Charles-Quint* (Brussels, 1855), II, p. 431; BM *Addl. Ms.* 28,702/96–100, Granvelle to Idiaquez, 3 Mar. 1582; *consulta* of the Council of State, 16 Jan. 1614, quoted J. Alcalá-Zamora, 'La Monarquía Hispana de los Felipes', *Revista de la Universidad de Madrid*, LXXIII (1970), pp. 57–106, on p. 60, n. 8.

newed in the Netherlands she would lose her hold over the Indies.[1] Ultimately, this pessimistic view was extended to cover the rest of the Spanish Monarchy: once Spain showed her weakness by failing to defend the Netherlands, it was argued, her enemies would be encouraged to concentrate their efforts not only on the Indies, but on the domination of Italy and finally on the dismemberment of Spain herself.[2] Even those Spaniards whose vision or imagination was not equal to such a broad view probably felt (with Fernández de Navarrete) that waging some major war far from Spain was very sound public policy. And where better than in the Netherlands?

The logical strength of this 'escalation of potential disasters' argument, then as now, was impressive. Couched exclusively in defensive terms, it always assumed that the opponent was the aggressor, yet at the same time it justified one's own aggression. The fallacy underlying such general reasoning appeared as soon as it was applied to practical examples. The assertions that the war in the Low Countries actively prevented the French and others from fighting in Italy was easily refuted: Louis XIII invaded Italy in 1628 in alliance with the Dutch but without openly declaring war on Spain. After 1635 France managed to campaign with success on four fronts at once: in Lombardy, Catalonia and Alsace as well as in the Netherlands. Even the more limited claim that the Army of Flanders could remove the sting from any French attack on Spain was disproved by the failure of the cardinal-infante's thrust towards Paris in 1636 (the Corbie campaign) to ease the pressure on Catalonia. In any case if the Netherlands were to serve as an effective counterweight to French aggression, clearly the best policy for Spain was to compromise with the Dutch. Instead, Spain persistently fought on two fronts, which seriously undermined the effectiveness of the Army of Flanders' intervention in France. The conviction that war in the Netherlands would automatically save the New World likewise crumbled as the mushroom growth of Dutch trade continued unabated after 1621. Spain had forgotten that the resumption

---

[1] Cf. AGS *E* 634/328, *consulta* of the Council of State, 25 Dec. 1619 (minute), recommending the king not to renew the truce at any price.

[2] Three examples: AGS *E* 634/73, *Aviso* of Juan Andrea Doria, 1605: 'El conservar los estados de Flandes, tengolo por tan necesario que si se pierden, mucho temo que durará poco la Monarquía de España'; BRB *Ms.* 16147–48/139–40, Aytona to Olivares, 29 Dec. 1633: 'si esto [the Netherlands] se pierde, ni las Indias, ni España, ni Italia se podran defender'. AHN *E libro* 714, unfol., *consulta* of the Council of State, 19 Oct 1629 (on hearing of the loss of 's Hertogenbosch): 'perdido Flandes, se perderan tambien luego las Indias y otros Reynos de V. Magestad'. The argument was even capable of expansion. After 1621 the government in Brussels could argue that unless Spain helped the emperor to win his war in Germany, the Netherlands would be lost, and if the Netherlands were lost, then...(cf. text quoted by Alcalá-Zamora, in 'La Monarquía Hispana de los Felipes', p. 60, n.7).

of the Low Countries' Wars would divert Spanish resources from the defence of the Indies, especially from the distant Portuguese colonies in south-east Asia and Brazil, far more than it restricted the activity of the Holland capitalists. In 1628 the Dutch West Indies Company even captured an entire treasure fleet as it prepared to sail from the Caribbean to Spain.

The collapse of these strategic arguments did not make conciliation any more attractive to the Spanish court. A further obstacle in the way of starting peace-talks with the Dutch was Spain's desire to 'negotiate from strength'. This, of course, meant that Spain did not want to 'negotiate' (in the true sense of the word) at all; she wanted to dictate her own terms to her 'rebels', clothing the dictation in the form of negotiations for the sake of appearances. Spain only wanted to talk after total victory. The duke of Alva put the point crudely but characteristically in 1573: 'These troubles must be ended by force of arms without any use of pardon, mildness, negotiations or talks until everything has been flattened; that will be the right time for clemency.' Spain never offered to negotiate unless she was in serious trouble; even her greatest victories (the capture of Antwerp in 1585 or of Breda and Bahía in 1625, for example) were never followed up by determined efforts to reach a negotiated settlement 'from strength'. As the count-duke of Olivares observed in December 1635:

> The occasions on which Your Majesty gave orders to negotiate a Truce were quite inappropriate, a most remarkable thing, since one was as soon as we knew of the loss of the fleet of Don Juan de Benavides [the treasure fleet of 1628, captured by the Dutch] and the other was when the provinces of Flanders were more harassed and threatened than they have ever been with traitors within, enemies without, the States-General assembled at Brussels and the Infanta Isabella dead [i.e. 1632–3].

Typically, this speech prefaced a government proposal for new truce-talks with the Dutch at an equally 'inappropriate' occasion: this time Spain's desire for an agreement with the Dutch stemmed only from the embarrassment caused by France's declaration of war earlier in the year.[1] At other times, attempts at compromise (for instance the talks arranged under imperial aegis at Cologne in 1579) came to nothing because Spain was never prepared to concede anything substantial unless she needed peace at any price.

This consistent refusal to make concessions brings us closer to the real reasons which underlay Spain's persistent use of force in the Netherlands.

---

[1] The duke of Alva's view reported in AGS *E* 554/146, Don Luis de Requesens to the king, 30 Dec. 1573; the *voto* of Olivares in *E* 2050/115, *consulta* of the Council of State, 7 Dec. 1635.

It was felt that peace would be more damaging than war, and in the sixteenth century a peace which involved religious as well as political concessions was especially suspect. On four specific occasions, in 1566–7, in 1575, in 1577 and again in 1589, Philip II deliberately refused to come to terms with his rebels solely because he could not bring himself to become the ruler of heretics. Although there was agreement on almost all other issues, during the reign of the Prudent King negotiations always foundered on the rock of religious toleration.

Philip II stated his policy on the religious question even before he heard of the Iconoclastic Fury. In August 1566 he assured the pope:

> If possible, I will settle the religious problem in those states [i.e. the Netherlands] without taking up arms, for I know that to do so would result in their total destruction; but if things cannot be remedied as I desire without recourse to arms, I am determined to take them up and to go myself to carry out everything; and neither danger [to myself] nor the ruin of these states, nor of all the others which are left to me, will prevent me from doing what a Christian prince fearing God ought to do in his service, [and for] the preservation of the Catholic faith and the honour of the apostolic see.[1]

Philip II proved as good as his word, and in 1575 at Breda and in 1577 after the Perpetual Edict it was religion which sabotaged the talks with the Dutch. In 1589 too the same insistence that the 'rebels' would have to return to Catholicism as a precondition of reconciliation ruined the duke of Parma's promising peace-initiative. Parma only proposed that Calvinist worship should be allowed in certain areas in private, but to tolerate such an iniquity, argued Philip II's closest advisers, would automatically forfeit 'the claim His Majesty has made and the reputation he has won at the cost of so much treasure and so many lives not to concede one jot or tittle in matters of religion'.[2]

After the death of Philip II, this determination faltered. In 1609 a truce was concluded with the Dutch which omitted all mention of religion; even the Catholic inhabitants of the United Provinces were left in the lurch by Spain. In February 1621, Philip III declared his willingness to renew the truce if only the Dutch would withdraw their ships from the Indies; again the united Provinces were to be allowed to regulate their religious affairs as they pleased.[3] Unfortunately for Spain, by this stage such concessions were too late. The Dutch had no wish to abandon their

---

[1] Philip II to his ambassador in Rome, 12 Aug. 1566, quoted in the perceptive article of H. G. Koenigsberger, 'The statecraft of Philip II', *European Studies Review*, 1 (1971), pp. 1–21, on p. 11–12.

[2] AGS *E* 2855, unfol., 'Sumario de los 4 papeles principales que dio el Presidente Richardot', 11 Nov. 1589, with holograph remarks by Philip II, Idiaquez and Moura.

[3] AGRB *SEG* 185/24, Philip III to the Archduke Albert, 4 Feb. 1621.

lucrative trade with the Indies, and in any case the moderate Philip III died in March 1621. His son and successor, Philip IV, lost no time in rejecting all reasonable compromise: as in 1589 it was argued that Spain had committed so much of her capital and staked so much of her 'reputation' on the outcome of the war that withdrawal was simply unthinkable. Anything short of total victory would constitute an intolerable humiliation. This was an argument which gained strength with every year of fighting; each campaign consumed more of Spain's resources and thereby increased her commitment to the policy of force.

The need to keep on fighting simply to avoid humiliation was first used as a serious justification for the war against the Dutch as early as 1577. In a major discussion on the right policy to adopt in the Netherlands, the duke of Alva argued that the resumption of war was the only policy compatible with 'the glory of God's Holy Name and with the honour and reputation of Your Majesty, which is your greatest asset [*la honra y reputación de V. Md. que es la mayor pieça de su arnés*]'. Cardinal Quiroga, a minister of long experience, agreed with the duke: failure to use force against the rebels would 'strain Your Majesty's conscience and hazard your honour and prestige [*honor y estimación*]'. The President of the Council of Castile, also a cleric, completed the harmony: at all costs the 'authority' and 'reputation' of the king had to be preserved and this could only be done by using force, however expensive this might prove.[1]

Such a view was by no means restricted to the Spanish clergy, although it naturally enjoyed their whole-hearted support. There were many veteran commanders of the Low Countries' Wars ('hawks' as they would be known today) besides the duke of Alva who, despite their unpleasant memories of the financial shortage, mutinies and military collapse which characterized the Army of Flanders in wartime, protested loud and long against any move towards compromise. The vehement opposition in Spain to the conclusion of a truce with the Dutch in 1607–9, for example, was led by the count of Fuentes and Don Diego de Ibarra, who had been (respectively) captain-general and inspector-general of the Army of Flanders in the 1590s, a decade of almost unrelieved defeat. They concentrated their attack, as 'hawks' have always done, upon the innate reluctance of any government to be humiliated. A truce with the Dutch involved the recognition of rebellion as successful, concessions to an alien creed, the admission of defeat – three things that were hateful to a proud and self-confident imperial power.

I cannot refrain from pointing out to Your Majesty that it will appear good

---

[1] AGS *E* 2843/7, discussion of the Council of State, 5 Sep. 1577.

neither to God nor to the World if Your Majesty goes about begg'ng for peace with his rebels...If we lose our credit [reputación] only God by a miracle would be able to remedy the damage.[1]

'God and our honour' – despite the more sophisticated language this was little different from the 'justifications' advanced for the wars of the middle ages. But it was at the heart of Spain's determination to keep on fighting in the Netherlands. Wars in the early modern period continued to be fought primarily for 'honour', to avoid humiliation (as they still are, inexcusably, today), and to 'impose one's will' on an adversary. War remained the sport of kings. The trouble was that the 'sport' had undergone a profound change since the middle ages. The scale of warfare in the sixteenth century, as we have seen, was utterly transformed. The duration of wars and the number of troops involved steadily increased; the means of destruction and above all the cost of using them exceeded all expectations. Looking back in 1596, the Spanish secretary of state for war observed:

> If comparison were made between the present cost to His Majesty of the troops who serve in his armies and navies, and the cost of those of the Emperor Charles V, it will be found that, for an equal number of men, three times as much money is necessary today as used to be spent then.

If anything, this was an underestimate.[2] Because of this increased cost, the new warfare demanded far greater respect from governments as well as from combatants. A more responsible philosophy and new political assumptions were called for. It was dangerous to play the game of war with all the expensive new toys under the out-dated, time-honoured rules.

An early sign that the Spanish Habsburgs had not fully adjusted to the harsh realities of the new warfare was their uncertainty over how 'total' the war in the Netherlands was to be. For most of the Eighty Years' War, and particularly during its first phase, Spain could have used an ultimate weapon against the 'rebels'. Since the centres of revolt, Holland and Zealand, were low-lying, much of them below sea-level, it would have been possible to end their resistance by breaking the sea-dikes and flooding them into subjection. This possibility, as a general solution to the revolt, was seriously considered in 1574–5 by the Spanish leaders, but it was

[1] AGS *E* 1297/42, count of Fuentes to the king, 5 Nov. 1608.
[2] BM *Addl. Ms.* 28,373/129–30, memorial of Esteban de Ibarra to the king, 15 Dec. 1596. The cost to Spain of the Schmalkaldic war, Feb. 1547–Mar. 1548, was just under two million florins and the war with France in 1552–9 cost Spain at least four million florins every year (AGS *CMC* 1a/1231, 1467 and 1491, accounts of Paymaster-General Portillo); the war in the Netherlands in the 1590s cost Spain about nine million florins every year (cf. Appendix K below). The numbers in all three armies were roughly the same.

eventually rejected on the grounds that once effected it could never be reversed, that flooding Holland and Zealand would put some areas loyal to the king in jeopardy, and that the deed would earn for Spain an unenviable reputation for cruelty.[1]

Having rejected this 'ultimate solution' to the Dutch problem, however, Spain had to resign herself to the systematic reduction by conventional means of all the towns in rebellion. Given the nature of warfare at the time and the geography of the rebel provinces, this was indeed a daunting prospect. As early as 1574 the captain-general lamented to the king:

> There would not be time or money enough in the world to reduce by force the twenty-four towns which have rebelled in Holland, if we are to spend as long in reducing each one of them as we have taken over similar ones so far.

The war would take fifty years, another minister prophesied in 1577; 'To conquer [the rebellious provinces] by force is to talk of a war without end' claimed Philip II's chief advisers in 1589 (as they rejected all talk of peace).[2]

These isolated voices of doom had little impact. On the whole there were few in Spain prepared to admit the possibility that the war in the Netherlands could go on indefinitely and that its cost could prove too great for the treasury to bear. As Mr Wylkes observed (p. 125 above) the problem of 'proportioning' the expenses of a war with the resources available was one which challenged and defeated almost every government in the sixteenth century: policies in those days were seldom weighed in the 'Scale of a Tradesman'. So the Army of Flanders was under orders to maintain maximum military pressure on the Dutch until all resistance collapsed, whatever the cost. The invasions of Orange and his supporters in 1568 and 1572 therefore provoked massive recruiting intended to overawe the opposition and reduce all rebellion. The cost of the exercise was ruinous of course, but provided resistance collapsed within a year or so the expense could be absorbed. In 1568 this strategy worked well. The invaders failed to capture any major towns and they were therefore forced to withdraw from the Netherlands, broken and defeated, in

---

[1] AGS E 561/122, Philip II to Requesens, 22 Oct. 1574. The king favoured instead the systematic burning of certain rebel lands, notably the Waterland, a rich agricultural area north of Amsterdam. The execution of this plan was only delayed by the mutinies of the Spanish troops in 1574 and by the bankruptcy of 1575. The 'rebels' were less scrupulous. To defend Walcheren (1572), Leiden (1574) and Antwerp (1584–5), for example, they broke the dikes and flooded the land in the path of the Spaniards.

[2] *Nueva Co.Do.In.*, v, p. 368, Don Luis de Requesens to the king, 6 Oct. 1574; BNM *Ms.* 1749/361–79, memorial of Alonso Gutierrez to the king, 23 Oct. 1577 (cf. p. 5 above); AGS E 2855, unfol., 'Sumario de los 4 papeles principales que dio el Presidente Richardot', 11 Nov. 1589.

December. The invasions of 1572 were far more serious: upwards of forty towns were involved and although the rebellion was localized by the end of the year, confined to Holland and Zealand, it was far from over. Yet instead of demobilizing his forces over the winter, Alva continued to recruit more. A shrewd French observer in the Spanish camp correctly predicted: 'They will only end up with too many men for the money they have; I do not see them ordering any muster or payment.'[1]

Alva's troops were left unpaid for a very good reason: there was no money available. It was estimated by the Army's high command that their forces cost around 1,200,000 florins a month to maintain; in 1572 and 1573 the Army of Flanders received 7,200,000 florins from Spain, an average of 300,000 a month, with perhaps as much again from the Netherlands. The Army could thus only satisfy half its needs. In this situation no troops could be paid regularly: still less could accumulated arrears be settled and superfluous units discharged. All troops were thus perforce retained, unpaid, over the winter. By August 1573 the cumulative debt to the soldiers for their wages stood at 7.5 million florins.[2]

Spain could find no escape from this deadlock. Peace without total victory was ideologically unacceptable; total victory was militarily impossible. The Army of Flanders therefore struggled on, distracted from time to time while exasperated units mutinied in order to force the government to pay them their due. There were, of course, isolated successes but the general military position was impossible. In July 1576 it was estimated that the government owed its troops a total of 17,500,000 florins (far more than Spain's annual revenues) in wage-arrears. In August 1576 the entire military machine, a theoretical 60,000 men, dissolved in mutiny and mass desertion. Some of the troops had been fighting without

---

[1] L. Didier, *Lettres et Négociations de Claude de Mondoucet* (Paris, 1891), p. 53, Mondoucet to Charles IX, 25 Sep. 1572. It has been argued that it was actually *cheaper* to retain troops through the winter instead of paying them off in the autumn. Professor Michael Roberts has written: 'If then a mercenary force were not disbanded in the autumn, but continued from year to year, the calls upon the Exchequer were likely to be considerably lessened and the general nuisance of mutinous soldiery would be abated.' (Roberts, *Essays in Swedish History*, p. 201.) While this was true in the short-term (the final reckoning was deferred; this is partly why the practice developed) it was obviously not true in the long run (the troops had to be paid a far larger sum before long) and it certainly did *not* reduce the incidence of mutinies – cf. Chapter 8.

[2] Estimated cost from BNM *Ms.* 783/469–71, Granvelle to Don John of Austria, 28 Aug. 1573; in March 1574 Requesens put the monthly cost of the Army at 702,727 *escudos* or 1.4 million florins (AGS *CMC* 2a/14, unfol.), 'Relación' sent to the king. The provisions from Spain were declared by F. de Lixalde, AGS *CMC* 2a/55; the total arrears were stated by Lixalde in AA 41/171, 'Relación sumaria de lo que Su Magd. deve al exercito' (Aug. 1573 – 3,806,548 *escudos* of 39 pattards).

a single break (and in some cases without a single pay) since May 1572.[1]

This was not the only collapse engendered by the strategic impasse in the Netherlands. If the provisions sent by Spain were too small by half for the Army of Flanders, they were more than double what the Castilian treasury could afford. Between 1572 and 1576 the crown of Castile's expenditure reached a total of at least 80 million florins, yet its total revenues for these five years cannot have exceeded 60 million. The deficit of 20 million florins corresponds exactly to Spanish expenditure in the Low Countries: between 1572 and 1576 the paymaster-general of the Army of Flanders received 20,904,850 florins from Spain. It may therefore be claimed with justice that the crisis of the Castilian treasury in the 1570s was caused by the Low Countries' Wars.[2] Philip II's budget for 1574, the year of maximum expenditure in the five-year cycle, is both instructive and typical:

Philip II's budget for 1574 (all in florins of 20 pattards)

Castile		Army of Flanders	
		Receipt from	Estimated
Revenues	Expenditure	Castile	cost
11,060,289	*c*.20,215,237	7,357,730	*c*.16,380,000
Shortfall = *c*.9,154,948		Shortfall = *c*.9,022,270	

Source: Appendix F.

There was, no doubt, a degree of exaggeration in the high command's estimate of the Army's cost (certain economies were always possible), but even so it seems that Spain would have needed to send twice as much money in the Netherlands in 1574 in order to maintain the momentum of the reconquest. To increase the provision, itself a record, could only have been achieved by sacrificing Spain's warfleet in the Mediterranean, which cost 4 million florins in 1574, or by increasing the deficit of the Castilian treasury. Both were impossible. In September 1575 Philip II declared himself bankrupt and suspended all payments from the treasury.

Habsburg Spain, and many other European governments of the day, failed to adjust its medieval political assumptions to the changed conditions of war in a number of other ways. As in the middle ages there was

---

[1] AGS *E* 567/4, abstract of a letter of *Contador* Alameda, 1 Jul. 1576. In 1574–5, the paymaster-general received 12.3 million florins from Spain (AGS *CMC* 2a/55) against a presumed cost, over the two years, of 33 million florins (calculating at 700,000 *escudos* a month).
[2] Figures from Appendixes F and G.

considerable resistance in official circles to the idea that war was a permanent state, requiring durable institutions and effective long-range planning, even to the idea that armies were no longer disbanded over the winter. The failure to organize a system of regular leave for the troops in the firing-line or to introduce short-term military service, noted below, was symptomatic of the survival of medieval conventions of warfare: despite the transformation in the duration and intensity of conflicts, soldiers were still engaged to fight until demobilization. Similarly, the exchange of prisoners after each campaign, the tolerance of direct trade with the enemy and the organization of an official protection system which enabled individuals and communities to buy themselves out of the fighting may be seen as outdated survivals of the medieval, chivalric concept of war.

Of course these minor maladjustments, by themselves, did not spell defeat. They were common to most of the states of sixteenth-century Europe, even the Dutch. Principally, it was the insufficiency of resources, or the insufficient exploitation of resources, which undermined Spain's war-effort in the Netherlands. The correlation was not a direct one: the effects of financial inadequacy made themselves felt through the chief instrument of Spain's 'tough' policy in the Netherlands, the Army of Flanders. The Army was by no means a neutral agent. If thwarted by their commanders or starved of their wages, the troops, especially the expatriate units, could take the law into their own hands. The Flanders veterans lived their days so close to subsistence that even the slightest deterioration in their position, caused usually by the failure of the Army to provide them with food or money, provoked a mutiny. Without constant financial support, the expensive Army mobilized to repress the rebellion was liable to fall into revolt itself. In this lay the chief guarantee of Dutch independence.

CHAPTER 6

FINANCIAL RESOURCES

One of Philip II's principal objectives in sending the duke of Alva to the Netherlands in 1567 was to make the provinces pay for themselves. Because the provincial estates refused to shoulder the full financial burden of defending and governing the Low Countries after 1559, Spain was obliged to send money to balance the Netherlands budget which, throughout the regency of Margaret of Parma, registered an annual deficit of 500,000 florins. Between 1561 and 1567, Philip sent his sister Margaret of Parma over 5½ million florins; in 1567 he supplied the duke of Alva with a further 1.65 million. By 1568 the king was naturally anxious for this drain to stop. Alva was commanded to use his wits and his troops to secure a 'fixed, certain and permanent revenue from those provinces for their own maintenance and defence'. Spain, warned the king, could not send money to the Netherlands for ever.[1]

THE NETHERLANDS

Alva shared all his master's fears and convictions. In March 1569, aided by threats from the Spanish troops, the duke persuaded the provincial estates of the Netherlands to vote three important new taxes: a tax of 1 per cent on all income (the 'Hundredth Penny'), a tax of 5 per cent on the sale of real estate (the 'Twentieth Penny') and, the most controversial item, a sort of value-added tax of 10 per cent on the sale price of all moveables and all exports (the 'Tenth Penny'). The Hundredth Penny was soon in operation but the Tenth and Twentieth Pennies excited such passionate opposition that Alva decided to accept an *aide* (the traditional form of taxation) of 4 million florins payable over two years instead; in return the collection of the two unpopular new taxes was deferred.

The yield from the new taxes exceeded all expectations, but because of the cost of combating the invasion of William of Orange and his

[1] AA 6/12, Philip II to the duke of Alva, 13 May 1568; on the amount sent to the Netherlands from Spain, IVdeDJ 68/309 n. 6, 'Cuenta con J. de Curiel y F. de Lixalde'.

brothers in 1568 it was still not enough to achieve the king's aim of financial self-sufficiency for the Netherlands. Between 1568 and 1571 it was necessary to send a further 8.25 million florins from Spain to the Netherlands (cf. Figure 13). Castile could ill afford this extra expense. With a major war in the Mediterranean demanding all his resources, Philip II reminded his lieutenant: 'With so many other things to support from here it is impossible to provide for the needs of the Low Countries in future as we have done up to now.' Alva was urged to waste no time and to accept no excuses. The Tenth Penny was to be put into immediate execution.[1]

The duke's ready compliance with the king's command provoked a disaster. The new taxes were heavy and they alienated many of the Netherlanders; the threat of another tax, heavier still, created a vast pool of sympathizers for the Sea Beggars and the prince of Orange when they invaded the Low Countries in the spring of 1572. The people who had stood by and watched during the invasion of 1568 rose to aid the government's enemies in 1572. Their chief grievance, there can be no doubt, was the Tenth Penny – 'the cause of all our ills' as one despairing royalist put it some years later.[2]

Despite the king's impatient complaints and the disaster which they engendered, Alva had performed a near-miracle for the Netherlands treasury. In spite of a major campaign in 1568, he managed (as Figure 13 shows) to make the Low Countries almost self-supporting in 1570 and 1571.

Unfortunately for Spain the achievement was short-lived. The invasions of 1572 precipitated the government into massive recruiting. Alva's mobilization spawned troops in every corner of the Netherlands. The king, who refused to allocate more funds for 'Flanders' in February 1572, found himself obliged to send $3\frac{1}{2}$ million florins before the year was out. Simultaneously the provinces were bled by the soldiers who, distributed between 200 or more garrisons, greedily exacted what they could from the local inhabitants. No more tax-revenue came into the central treasury. Although in theory the pillaging of the troops was controlled and recorded by the

---

[1] Piot, *Correspondance de...Granvelle*, IV, pp. 594–5, minute by Hopperus of a letter from Philip II to Alva, Feb. 1572.

[2] 'Le xme denier, cause de tous noz maulx' – Piot, *ibid.*, VI, p. 205, Morillon to Granvelle, 22 Apr. 1577. On the history of the Tenth Penny, cf. C. Hirschauer, 'L'Artois et le Xe denier, 1569–1572', *Revue du Nord*, II (1911), pp. 215–35, and J. Craeybeckx, 'Alva's Tiende Penning – een Mythe?', *Bijdragen en Mededelingen van het Historisch Genootschap*, LXXVI (1962), pp. 10–42; on the Hundredth Penny, J. Craeybeckx, 'La portée fiscale et politique du centième denier du duc d'Alve', in *Recherches sur l'histoire des finances publiques en Belgique*, I (Brussels, 1967), pp. 343–74.

local revenue officers and set against the liability of each area for the Hundredth, Twentieth and Tenth Penny, in most areas decentralizaton of the Netherlands revenue system resulted only in chaos.[1] Often the troops refused to give receipts for the money they took and the Army's accounts department (the *contaduría del sueldo*) failed to keep abreast of the local contributions received by each unit. Worst of all, while some contingents with billets in the rich and secluded provinces prospered and multiplied, the troops actually fighting the enemy were left destitute and desperate. The situation was already unbearable when in March 1574 news arrived that the rebels had opened a second front in the east. Count Louis of Nassau's invasion with a large army compelled the government to raise yet more troops. A better method of supporting the troops and of keeping track of the money they received was urgently required, otherwise it was

Figure 13. The financing of Spanish imperialism in the Netherlands, 1566–76

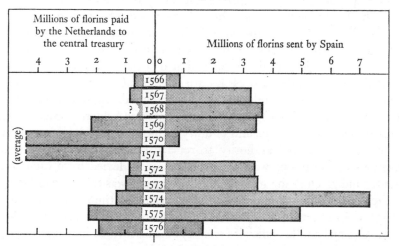

The duke of Alva's achievement in 'making the Netherlands pay for themselves' in 1570 and 1571 speaks for itself. It enabled Philip II to concentrate his resources on suppressing the revolt of the *moriscos* and on the defence of the Mediterranean. The effect of the invasions of 1572 was immediate: the receipts of the Brussels government from Spain soared as those from the Netherlands plunged. Source Appendix G.

---

[1] However, even in Utrecht (a province in the thick of the war at this stage) the contributions (*leeningen*) between 1572 and 1577 were all noted and counted as part of the provincial *aides*: 'Dese leeninge is gebracht in offslach van de twee hondert duysent gulden de Co. Ma'. geconsenteert bij de Staten van Utrecht in plaetse van den hondertsten, 20^{en} ende thienden penninck', said the Estates. (K. Heeringa, 'Utrechts Oorlogslasten, 1572–1577', *Bijdragen en Mededelingen van het Historisch Genootschap*, XLIV (1923), pp. 125–86, on p. 129, n. 1.)

crystal clear that the Spanish regime in the Netherlands could not long survive.

In July 1574 Don Luis de Requesens, the new captain-general, established a regular, permanent and rational contributions system in the Spanish Netherlands, perhaps the first of its kind in Europe. The system was not universally applied. Areas in which regular taxes could still be collected (Artois and Hainaut, for example) were left alone; so were the areas too poor to contribute anything. But in the other provinces, and especially in the richest and largest, Flanders and Brabant, special commissioners were appointed to fix a monthly contribution to be paid by each community and to distribute the money thus collected to the troops in the area. The system was under the general supervision of the Netherlands Council of Finance, but there was a 'superintendent of the contributions': Chiappino Vitelli until 1575, Juan Andrea Cigogna, a former servant of Margaret of Parma, thereafter.[1]

The upheavals of 1576 deprived the Army of Flanders of all receipts from the Low Countries and when after 1578 the Spanish forces began their reconquest, fighting for every inch of territory, means of supporting them had to be devised anew. There were not even provincial taxes against which local exactions could be set and at first the troops were allowed to raise what they could (a process known as *brandschatting*: exacting money from a farm or a village under threat of burning it down) but on 1 September 1579 Juan Andrea Cigogna was reinstated as 'superintendent of the contributions of the towns and country reduced to the obedience of His Majesty'. He received authority to replace the arbitrary and irregular exactions of the troops with a permanent quota levied from each community and given to the soldiers legally. Cigogna was to fix the obligation of each 'with the moderation which, according to the resources of each village and in view of the present conjuncture, your conscience feels is just'.[2] Cigogna and his officials (*commis*) first discovered how many troops

---

[1] Requesens claimed that Alva had not *dared* to impose contributions; he himself admitted to scruples of conscience over their legality: IVdeDJ 67/285 n. 5, minute of Requesens to Don Juan de Zuñiga, 9 Jul. 1575 ('no se osaron en su [Alva's] tiempo intentar ni executar lo de las contribuçiones, que muy contra mi voluntad y no sin gran escrupulo de conciencia me ha forzado la hambre a permitir'.) On the working of the system: AGS E 560/150, Requesens to the king, 25 Jul. 1574 and *ibid.*, f. 126, his Instruction to the receiver of Brabant to apportion the charge; cf. also *Nueva Co.Do.In.* IV, pp. 230–7, an instruction on how the regiment of Mondragón was to be paid from contributions (Aug. 1574). The system was nearly sabotaged by the lawyers of the council of Brabant, who ruled that contributions should be made a personal not a property tax, but Requesens reversed their judgement. 'The expenses of this war concern the conservation of property as much as of persons' he said. (AGRB *Audience* 1727/1, unfol., Requesens to Cigogna, 26 May 1575, minute.)
[2] AGRB *Audience* 1811/3, unfol., minute of Parma's instruction to 'le chevalier Cigogna', 1

the government wished to quarter in each area and how much they would cost; then the magistrates of the region were assembled to declare what each community had paid in the past. By dividing the cost of the troops by the number and size of the communities the commissioners arrived at the sum to be contributed by each. The villages paid a fixed amount to the *commis* and in return they received formal letters of protection sparing them from paying anything further to any other troops in royal service. They were also given receipts to present to the civil revenue collectors.[1]

As the prince of Parma's master-strategy gradually reduced Brabant and Flanders to Spanish rule the contributions system assumed a position of increasing importance in the Army's finances. By 1586 Cigogna handled 700,000 florins annually. The government became concerned about the methods employed in collection. A special investigator was appointed by Parma, but he offered no reassurance:

> I was unable to find anyone who could tell me for certain the method or manner by which the Chevalier Cigogna raised the contributions, but it is generally believed that as Superintendent of the said contributions he fixes their amount on his own, according to his pleasure, in every village or town.

The report ended with the pointed observation that 'in former times' the collection of all 'tailles, aides and contributions' was preceded by the consent of the provincial estates.[2]

The complaint was just. The burden of the contributions was unnecessarily heavy, especially on the rural communities. The devastation caused by the fighting which dragged on across the southern provinces from 1578 until 1588 crippled their economy, while plague and famine decimated the population. The prince of Parma was deeply sympathetic to the problems of the reconquered provinces, and he was anxious to conciliate them. He therefore favoured the gradual return of taxation in the Netherlands to the control of the provincial estates. In August 1588 he agreed to the re-establishment of the 'Four Members' (effectively the

Sep. 1579, commanding him to replace the 'irregular' contributions which had sprung up with a coordinated system.

[1] AGRB *Audience* 1686/1, unfol., 'Relación para asentar las contributiones asy en la villa de Diste y villajes que son debajo de su jurisdicción', and AD Nord *B* 6835-6, two accounts of Lieven Snouck, Cigogna's *commis* in West-Vlaanderen, 1579-81. For further information, cf. the correspondence of the government with Cigogna (AGRB *Audience* 1727/1, 1811/3 and 1869/3) and with Snouck (*Audience* 192/2 and 1788/4 – I am grateful to Dr H. de Schepper for bringing these two bundles to my notice.)

Contributions came in at 58,710 florins per month: AGRB *Audience* 2769, unfol., 'Estad de charge que porte presentement le plat pays', 9 Jan. 1586. The investigation for Parma is in the same bundle: 'Pour informer V. Excellence de ce que je peulx avoir entendu touchant les contributions.' On contributions in general, cf. the informative article of F. Redlich, 'Contributions in the Thirty Years' War', *Economic History Review*, XII (1959-60), pp. 247-54.

provincial estates) in Flanders; they immediately organized the collection of new excise taxes to produce money to support the province's garrisons. In return the contributions there were suspended. In 1591 the 'Four Members' offered to provide 50,000 florins each month, while the estates of Brabant agreed to raise 45,000 florins. Each provincial assembly was to administer the proceeds of the taxes it raised and the grant was to be applied exclusively to the upkeep of the troops within the province.[1] Contributions continued for some time to be collected in the frontier areas (Gelderland and Limburg, for instance) but even there the provincial estates eventually assembled and voted taxes of their own. After that only the troops' *servicio de casa* (their right to free lodgings, a bed, linen and candles with free oil, salt, vinegar, dishes and a fire for cooking) was provided directly by householders; their expenses were deducted from tax liability. In the seventeenth century even this residual obligation was normally commuted to a money payment of twelve *reales* a month, provided from the provincial *aides* directly to the troops.

The economic recovery of the southern provinces was naturally expedited by these moves to spread the burden of supporting the Army more equitably, although voices of complaint were raised in Madrid that the soldiers derived greater benefit from guaranteed lodgings than from a lump payment.[2] The amounts provided by the Netherlands treasury to the Army of Flanders rose rapidly. For most of the period 1600–40 the 'obedient provinces' appear to have paid for about 12,000 men (about one-fifth of the Army) and spent around four million florins every year on war. Unfortunately it is not possible to be more precise.[3]

---

[1] J. Dhondt, 'Bijdrage tot de kennis van het financiewezen der Staten van Vlaanderen (16e en 17e eeuw)', *Nederlandse Historiebladen*, III (1940), pp. 149–81; AGS E 600/149, Parma to the king, 18 Dec. 1591 (the restoration of the *aides* was part of Parma's arrangements for his absence on campaign in France; in fact he doubted whether the provinces would be able to meet their new obligations).

[2] For two objections to commuting lodgings-and-service for 12 *reales* a month, cf. AGS E 2037/11, *consulta* of the Council of State, 14 Apr. 1623 (*voto* of the 'Flanders' veteran Don Fernando Giron) and E 2238, unfol., Philip IV to the Infanta Isabella, 17 Apr. 1631.

[3] Two documents at least (AHN E *libro* 714, unfol., 'Relación de lo que monta el sueldo del exercito', 1631, and AGS E 2247, unfol., 'Relación de lo que importa en un año el pagamento', 1639–40) state that the Netherlands (*el país*) was paying some four million florins annually towards the cost of the war. It is not possible to be more exact because (i) the papers of the *conseil des finances* and of the *trésoriers des guerres* have been almost entirely destroyed; (ii) the receivers-general, whose papers have survived on the whole, received only about 50 per cent of the revenue actually collected by the local receivers (the rest was spent locally, some of it on the troops); (iii) the majority of the money raised for the troops was controlled directly by the provincial estates, largely independent of the *conseil des finances* and (often) of the *chambres des comptes*. The decentralized structure of the Netherlands revenue system has defeated all attempts so far to establish the global cost of the Eighty Year's War to the Low Countries.

The administration of the provincial *aides*, vested in the estates of each province, was under the general supervision of the *conseil des finances*. The troops maintained by the *aides* were mustered by commissioners (*commissaires des monstres*) appointed and paid by the council; the treasurer of war or the local receiver of taxes had to render account to one of the audit departments (*chambres des comptes*) of the Netherlands; and the wage-sheets and other accounts of the troops were retained in a special department of the council, the *contadorie des finances* (the military accounts office of the Council of Finance). The system was autonomous, orderly and efficient, and it became increasingly important. But it was not enough.

Both in quantity and in their manner of payment the taxes raised in the Netherlands were inadequate to finance a major campaign by the Army of Flanders. Even in 1574, before the war completed the ruin of the southern provinces, it was estimated that the Low Countries paid less than one-third of the total cost of the Army; even under the archdukes the provinces could only provide about a quarter.[1] Moreover, the majority of these payments by the Netherlands were disbursed locally; little reached the central treasury. For an offensive in the Netherlands money was required in larger amounts and it was required in a lump sum. It therefore had to come from Spain. 'To perform a miracle and pay the army without money from Your Majesty is impossible', wrote the prince of Parma in 1584.[2] Even then the miracle was only complete when the provisions arrived in bulk. Although the king sent the unprecedented total of 7.36 million florins to the Low Countries in 1574 the captain-general lamented that no campaign could be undertaken 'because we never had a lot of money at one time'. This remained true throughout the Eighty Years' War: only vast amounts of cash could set the Army in motion. The Netherlands supplied a certain minimum which kept the troops together, paid a few garrisons and secured their basic defence, but far larger sums were necessary to mount a campaign and win the war, and they had to come from Spain.[3]

SPAIN

Habsburg Spain, however, already had many fish to fry. We have already

---

[1] *Nueva Co.Do.In.*, II, pp. 136–9, Requesens to the king, 9 Apr. 1574 (copy; original = AGS E 557/135); cf. also preceding note.

[2] AGRB *Audience* 188/22–5, Parma to the king, 20 Apr. 1584.

[3] *Nueva Co.Do.In.*, IV, p. 107, Requesens to the king, 25 Jul. 1574: 'Nunca se ha tenido golpe de dinero junto'. It is interesting to note that the same broad fiscal division characterized the English army in Normandy after 1415: the garrisons were financed locally but the money for the field army and the campaigns had to come from England. (R. A. Newhall, *The English Conquest of Normandy, 1416–1424* (London, 1924), p. 156.)

seen that Philip II's principal motive in pressing the 'Tenth Penny' on the Netherlands in 1572 was to free resources in Castile for his other imperial commitments. They too had to be financed from Spain. Likewise, after the war against the rebels began in earnest, Spain always fought in the Netherlands with only one hand; at the same time she sought to defend the Mediterranean (until 1578), conquer Portugal (1579–83), invade England (1587–8), set a Habsburg on the French throne (1589–98) or secure the duchy of Mantua for a Spanish claimant (1627–31). The support given by Spain to the Army of Flanders depended absolutely upon the place which the Netherlands occupied at any moment in Spain's general imperial policy. If a campaign in the Mediterranean, against France or in Lombardy was deemed more urgent to the interests of Castile (the overriding consideration) than the offensive against the Dutch, then Castilian treasure was exported to the Netherlands in smaller quantities. With so many enterprises to support, the resources of Castile had to be expended where they were most useful.

Castile had long been the financial heart of the Habsburg empire. As early as 1540 – only twenty years after the revolt of the *Comuneros* against overtaxation for foreign war – Charles V observed that 'I cannot be sustained except by my kingdoms of Spain'. It was not long before Castile was exporting money to pay for Habsburg imperialism all over Europe. How was it done?

'The surest and swiftest method of sending you money is by letters of exchange', wrote the king to his captain-general in 1576.[1] It was indeed impossible, at most times, to send money from Spain to the Netherlands other than by paper credit, in the first place because of the delays and dangers inherent in the despatch of 6 million florins and more every year in specie, and second because the crown never had that much money on hand and available for export at one time. The Spanish government therefore needed short-term loans to anticipate the slow trickle of collected taxes, and it also required a means of making the loans payable in the Low Countries. The answer to both needs was the bill of exchange, the *asiento*.

Normally the king, represented by his Council of Finance, concluded a contract (*asiento*) with a merchant, binding him to supply a fixed sum of money to the paymaster-general of the Army of Flanders or his agent. The merchant was invariably resident and based in Spain and he acted through his partners or perhaps correspondents in the north. Alternatively, an *asiento* could be negotiated by the captain-general of the Army of Flanders who might solicit a loan from a merchant resident in the Netherlands,

---

[1] AGS E 569/68, Philip II to Don Luis de Requesens, 26 Feb. 1576, minute.

giving him in return a bill of exchange payable by the Council of Finance in Spain on a specified future date. The first method was known as an *asiento de España* (Spanish exchange contract), the second as an *asiento de Flandes* (Netherlands exchange contract – it was little used after 1609); the banker who made the contract with the crown was termed an *asentista*.

The bill of exchange was devised by private businessmen, not by the crown. The crown therefore, at least in the sixteenth century, had to enter the world of merchants in order to make use of their instruments of credit. Each *asiento*, public or private, was made, paid and repaid in one of the select gatherings of bankers and traders known as 'Fairs of Exchange' – every major commercial centre (Antwerp, Lyon, Frankfort...) held two, three or four such Fairs every year at which all commercial payments were regulated. Vast amounts of money were brought to the Fairs by individual merchants either to pay their debts or to invest: as much as 12 million *escudos* might change hands at a single Fair.[1] The crown therefore sent its agents to the great Fairs to solicit loans, offering competitive rates of interest to raise the money it needed, promising repayment at the next Fair or the next but one. Often loans were prolonged from one Fair to another. In the sixteenth century most *asientos* of the Spanish crown were raised and reimbursed in the Fairs of Medina del Campo, and those payable in the Netherlands were usually paid at the Fairs of Antwerp, although when Antwerp was in hostile hands (1577–85) or when it was impossible to collect enough ready money together there (which happened a number of times between 1585 and 1600) arrangements had to be made to pay the *asientos* in some other neighbouring commercial centre.

This state of affairs could not last. The delicate mechanism of Fairs and merchant credit was not made for the enormous loans which the crown demanded: the government asked too much for too long. In the end so much money was tied up in outstanding state loans that business came to a standstill through cash shortage. Towards the end of the sixteenth century, therefore, changes were made. The *asientos* of the Spanish crown came to be made and repaid outside the Fairs: they were concluded at the court instead of at Medina, and they were made directly repayable from a specific source of revenue instead of in a future Fair The *asiento* system of the Spanish Habsburgs had fallen into the hands of specialists. Men like Ottavio and Vizente Centurione who on 31 December 1602 arranged to provide 7½ million *escudos* (18.75 million florins) in the

[1] The 'Fairs of Besançon', held at Piacenza after 1579, involved a maximum of only 200 people, of whom 60 effectively controlled all transactions, but a single Fair might see 12 million *escudos* change hands. (F. Braudel, *La Méditerranée et le monde méditerranéen à l'époque de Philippe II* (2nd edn, Paris, 1966), I, pp. 460–1.)

Netherlands had no need of a Fair to maintain their liquidity. Merchants who could not lend 'in bulk' (*en grueso*) were rapidly excluded from the club of professional *asentistas*. The 'specialists' who monopolized the financing of Spanish imperialism were overwhelmingly Genoese from 1577 until 1627. After 1625 Portuguese financiers gained a foothold, encouraged by Olivares, and from 1627 until 1647 they cornered roughly half of the *asientos* made in Spain for the Netherlands.

The *asiento* was thus essentially a short-term loan repayable from a specific revenue: it was only an 'anticipation', it was not deficit borrowing. Each contract presupposed that the state possessed secure and proximate sources of income to pledge to borrowers. The *asiento* could not raise floating credit for ever. If expenditure, financed by short-term borrowing, exceeded revenues by too much for too long, then infallibly the crown would have no revenues left to offer potential creditors. There came a point when all the available revenues for years ahead were already assigned to repay creditors whose loans had already been absorbed in war or administration, a point at which bankers would not regard a revenue five or more years ahead as a safe investment and would therefore refuse any further loan. Spain reached this crisis-point for the first time in 1557.

It has been clearly shown that between 1551, when Charles V was again forced into war on several fronts, and the end of 1556 the Castilian regency government raised almost twice as much by *asientos*, that is by 'anticipations', as it could expect to receive in revenue. By July 1556 all revenues until 1561 were alienated to creditors; no new loans could be found. It was the same story or worse in the other states of the Habsburg Monarchy. The cause of this financial prodigality is not in doubt: between 1551 and July 1556 the crown of Castile accumulated debts worth $25\frac{1}{2}$ million florins; no less than 22 million florins were sent in these years to the Netherlands.[1] Overawed by the impossible financial situation which his wars had created, Charles V wisely abdicated. He had hardly exaggerated when, as early as 1543, he confided to his son and heir that 'matters of finances will be in such a state that you'll have a lot of trouble'![2]

The problem which faced Philip II at his accession was clearly urgent and it demanded a radical solution. After considerable thought, the king

---

[1] These figures come from R. Carande, *Carlos V y sus banqueros*, III (Madrid, 1968), pp. 16–21; AGS *CJH* 19 (Ant., unfol.,) 'La carta del Consejo de Hacienda que llevo don Fadrique...' 13 Jun. 1556 (minute) and the lucid and detailed exposition of the financial state of the empire by Philip II himself: AGS *E* 513/174, undated but surely autumn 1556 and apparently the king's reply to the *Remonstrance* of Emanuel-Philibert.

[2] 'Lo de la hazienda quedará tal que pasareys gran trabajo' – the emperor's instruction of 1543, quoted J. M. March, *Niñez y Juventud de Felipe II* (Madrid, 1941), II, p. 24.

and his advisers hit upon an ingenious scheme. They took advantage of the fact that the revenues of the crown of Castile, like those of most other European governments, were of two distinct sorts: 'ordinary' and 'extraordinary'. The 'extraordinary' receipts were those collected by the government only after securing the consent of the taxpayers' representatives (the Cortes in the case of the laity; the pope or the Spanish Church Council for the clergy). Because of the element of consent, these taxes were in general more predictable and their yield was known in advance. They were surer as well as larger than the various 'ordinary' revenues like the domain income or the customs which were the king's by right. It was therefore natural for the *asentistas* to insist that their loans should be secured on the yield of an 'extraordinary' revenue, and especially on the crown's receipts from the Indies, the most 'extraordinary' revenue of all. The 'ordinary' revenues of Castile, by contrast, were used to finance another variety of crown borrowing: the *juro*. There were three main types of *juro* (government bond: *juro* literally means 'bond'): *juros perpetuos*, which were bonds ceded by the government for ever and bearing a low but guaranteed interest (always under 5 per cent); *juros de por vida*, virtually life annuities which expired on the death of the holder and bore interest of 10 or $12\frac{1}{2}$ per cent; and, by far the commonest variety, *juros al quitar*, yielding interest of 5 to $7\frac{1}{2}$ per cent until the government redeemed them.[1] All *juros* were 'situated on' (sc. tied to the yield of) the various 'ordinary' revenues of the crown. Thus a man would hold, say, 10,000 ducats of *juros al quitar* at 5 per cent charged against the yield of the customs dues paid at the frontier between Castile and Portugal. He would receive, upon presentation of his certificate of entitlement to the local collector of taxes, 500 ducats of interest every year until the government chose to redeem the bonds – not a bad investment. The *juro* was thus a form of consolidated debt; a long-term investment bearing moderate interest payable from less valuable sources of revenue. It therefore seemed to Philip II's advisers that the best way out of their financial dilemma was to convert the high-interest, short-term *asientos* secured on 'extraordinary' revenues into low-interest, long-term *juros* payable from 'ordinary' taxes.

[1] In 1573, for example, the king estimated that he owed about 35,000,000 ducats of *juros al quitar*, but only 296,000 ducats of *perpetuos* and 186,666 of *de por vida*. (*Actas de las Cortes*, IV, p. 91, treasury statement of 7 Aug. 1573.) Interest on the *juros* was expressed in a somewhat unusual way. The formula might be 'juros de a 20,000 al millar' (bonds at 20,000 to 1,000) which meant that for every 1,000 units of interest one needed to invest 20,000 units of capital, a yield of 1 to 20 or 5 per cent. 'Juros de a 14,000 al millar' yielded 1 to 14, or 7.14 per cent, 'juros de a 10,000 al millar' yielded 10 per cent and so on. The smaller the number of units of capital 'al millar' the higher the rate of interest. The same method was used with the French government bonds: '*rentes au denier 20*' meant bonds at 1 to 20 or 5 per cent.

Accordingly, on 1 January 1557 the king decreed that no *asiento* promising repayment from a future revenue would be repaid until further notice. Instead he offered his creditors a choice: either they could stick to their contracts and wait for the crown to resume payments (clearly not a likely prospect with France again rattling the sabre) or they could surrender their *asientos* in return for compensation in *juros* to the value of their original loan plus a little interest. Most bankers, with regret, accepted the latter and the king thereby succeeded in turning his floating debt into consolidated stock. He had to surrender the yield of certain 'ordinary' taxes in order to pay the interest on the *juros*, but in return he recovered his alienated 'extraordinary' revenues for the coming years. Thanks to this dishonest manœuvre Castile again held some acceptable securities to offer bankers in return for further loans when in February 1557 France once more declared war. The whole quadrille could begin again.

The success of the king's strategem, known as the 'decree of bankruptcy', led to its repetition whenever the Spanish crown found itself in the same position of having alienated all its revenues so that it could neither pay for its needs nor obtain new loans: in 1560, 1575, 1596, 1607, 1627, 1647 and 1653. Later decrees were in fact somewhat harsher since the king initially declared the principal and interest of all loans forfeit. It was only some time after the decree (often a year and sometimes more), in a compromise known as the *medio general* (general agreement), that the crown consented to repay the bankers a portion of their credits in royal lands and lordships and the rest in *juros* situated on the 'ordinary' revenues. This stern treatment brought the crown a further dividend: the *medio general* obliged the bankers whose loans had been frozen by the decree (called *los decretados*) to provide a new *asiento* (7 million *escudos* – 20 million florins – from the victims of the decree of 1596).[1]

The decree of bankruptcy may have been the right solution for Castile's internal finances, but it spelt disaster for all enterprises abroad which depended on Spanish funds (as well as for the bankers whose liquid assets were suddenly frozen). By 'breaking credit' with the bankers, by repudiating and then freezing the capital of their loans, the king automatically deprived himself of the merchants' credit organization. Without letters of exchange, the crown could not send enough money to the Army of

[1] At the moment, the best descriptions of the credit system of the Spanish Habsburgs are: A. Castillo, 'Dette flottante et dette consolidée en Espagne, 1557–1600', *Annales E.S.C.*, XVIII (1963), pp. 745–59, and *idem*, 'Los juros de Castilla: apogeo y fin de un instrumento de crédito', *Hispania*, XXIII (1963), pp. 43–70. Professor Castillo and Professor F. Ruíz Martín are both preparing major studies on Castilian finance under the Habsburgs which will no doubt modify the simple sketch I have given here.

Flanders. This emerged most clearly from the bankruptcy of 1575, which took two years to settle in a *medio general*. As soon as he heard of the decree the captain-general in the Netherlands realized that defeat was now inevitable:

> Even if the King found himself with ten millions in gold and wanted to send it all here, he has no way of doing so with this Bankruptcy Decree...because if the money were sent by sea in specie it would be lost, and it is impossible to send it by letters of exchange as hitherto because there is no merchant there [in Spain] who can issue them, nor anyone here who can accept and pay them.

It was not long before the king himself recognized this truth. 'I have not escaped from my necessity [he wrote to his secretary], rather am I in greater need since I have no credit and cannot avail myself of anything except hard cash which cannot be collected quickly enough'.[1] There was nothing for the king and his captain-general to do but be patient and see what effect the termination of the remittances from Spain would have. They did not have long to wait. In July and August 1576 the foreign troops in the Army of Flanders mutinied; the rest soon deserted. At the same time the smaller business firms which had participated in the *asiento* system were obliged, one by one, to close their doors and admit their bankruptcy. The Spanish *asentistas* were almost all ruined.

One may well wonder, after all this, what possible incentive there could have been for any banker to lend money to the king of Spain. The answer is not obvious, but in the early modern period it was convincing. First we must remember that although there were risks, grave risks, involved in lending to the crown, they were not necessarily greater than those which surrounded any other form of investment. A ship carrying precious spices might sink; a consignment of cloth might arrive at a time of glut and have to be sold at a loss; a private borrower (even a nobleman) might go bankrupt – and he had no *juros* to offer his creditors in compensation. Second, the crown offered good prospects of profit. The greater the government's need for money, the higher the interest it was prepared to pay. At times when the crown's requirements were modest and capital plentiful, *asientos* could be concluded at only 7 or 8 per cent; when the intensity and frequency of borrowing increased, interest-rates naturally rose – 16 and even 20 per cent annually became common. The amounts involved in merely paying interest became a crippling burden: in 1627 it was estimated that the interest on the crown's floating debt alone (the *asientos*, not the *juros*) cost around 12,000 florins a day.[2]

---

[1] IVdeDJ 67/121, Don Luis de Requesens to Don Juan de Zuñiga, 30 Oct. 1575; IVdeDJ 60/138–43, Philip II billet to Antonio Perez, 23 Mar. 1576.
[2] AGS *CJH* 632 (Ant. unfol.), *consulta* of the Council of Finance, 11 Mar. 1627. They estimated

Interest, however, was only one of the rewards. The banker also had his *juros*. As part of his contract each *asentista* received a number of special bonds, known as *juros de resguardo* ('security bonds'), to the market value of his loan. These began to yield interest on the day when the king was obliged to repay the *asiento* and failed to do so, and most of them were promptly sold for cash by the *asentista* to his friends, colleagues and others in Spain or Italy. After all, government stock at 5 per cent was a reasonably attractive opening for investment. The *juros* received by bankers after a decree were also passed on or sold to the *asentista's* own creditors. The financiers thus preserved their own liquidity by paying their debts 'in the same coin used by the king to pay them' – in *juros*.[1]

Besides interest and *juros*, the crown had other favours to bestow: lands, titles and other honours could be used to reward or cajole the faithful financier – the king could make his bankers respectable as well as rich. Finally, the king could give the *asentistas* a valuable commercial advantage over their competitors by allowing them to export silver currency from Spain. Because of its high silver content, Spanish *reales* (the basic silver coin) were worth 4–5 per cent more than their face value outside Castile. This final remuneration for lending money to the king of Spain brought the effective rate of interest up to an estimated 25 per cent and more.[2]

At most periods it was illegal to take bullion out of Spain (although, of course, smugglers found ways) but for the arrangement of an *asiento* it was essential:

> Because the *asientos* involve so much money the financiers do not have the capital to undertake it without making use of the ready cash which they are given [by the king]; this has to come from the specie which arrives on the fleets from the New World.[3]

The Spanish credit system, complex as it was, depended absolutely on

the interest due from 31 Jan to 4 Feb. 1627 (inclusive) at between 24 and 30,000 ducats. For interest charges on individual *asientos*, cf. AGS *CMC* 2a/1056, unfol., with *asientos* at 7 per cent in 1567, 8 per cent in 1568–9 (even on a large contract like the 600,000 ducats lent by G. de Salamanca on 30 Oct. 1569), but rising to 12 per cent in 1572–3 and to 14 or 16 per cent in 1574–5.

1 Braudel, *La Méditerranée*, I, p. 467. According to F. Ruíz Martín, *Lettres marchandes échangées entre Florence et Medina del Campo* (Paris, 1965), p. xxxi, *juros de resguardo* were first given in 1561. As he says, the face-value of the *juros* often exceeded the amount of the loan: the reason was simple – *juros* normally circulated below par, but the bankers demanded guarantees calculated on the market value, not the face value of the securities (cf. IVdeDJ 24/16, Pero Luis Torregrosa to Juan de Ovando, 6 Feb. 1574).

2 Cf. the example of an *asiento* of 400,000 *escudos* for the Netherlands which cost the king 35 per cent: Braudel, *La Méditerranée*, I, p. 466.

3 AGS *E* 2853, unfol., *consulta* of a *junta* summoned by Olivares, 4 Feb. 1625 (*voto* of the marquis of Montesclaros, president of the Spanish Council of Finance).

specie and principally on the treasure of the Indies landed at Seville for the king. The *asientos* payable in the Netherlands were particularly dependent on the transport of bullion from Spain. After 1572 the faltering commerce of the southern provinces simply could not provide the enormous monetary stock, the sheer number of coins, required to turn the merchants' paper obligations into hard cash. Specie had to be brought in specially, sometimes by the king directly (especially in the decade 1577–87) but most often by the individual *asentistas* who thereby gained an additional profit. The bullion allotted to the banker when he made his loan acted as the indispensable 'float' for the whole operations, releasing other credits and paper bonds all over Europe. It did not pay for the entire process (the *asiento* was, after all, a bridging loan) but a certain amount of new liquid capital was required to lubricate the wheels of credit and to maintain some point of contact between paper bonds and the coins which they were taken to represent.[1]

The direction taken by the bullion exported legally from Spain to float the *asientos* destined for the Army of Flanders was decided by the financiers themselves, within the limits imposed by the political geography of Europe at that time. Specie in the service of Spain was almost as vulnerable to attack as the *tercios*. It is therefore not surprising that the convoys of currency which found their way from Spain to the Netherlands tended to follow the itineraries of the troops: the closing of the Channel to Habsburg shipping in 1568 was almost as serious for the supply of Spanish treasure as for the transport of Spanish troops and both tended to travel overland thereafter (cf. pp. 56–9 above). At first the bankers were able to send a certain amount of bullion through France, either entirely by land from Hendaye or else by sea to Bordeaux or Nantes and thence by land. This route was closed after 1578. The civil war and the cupidity of the duke of Alençon made France almost as unsafe as the Channel for Spanish treasure. Instead the bankers, and particularly the Genoese, transported specie in ever-increasing quantities from Seville to Lombardy, changing it into gold (which was abundant at the Fairs of northern Italy) before taking it on, either along the Spanish Road or through the Swiss cantons to Basle and down the Rhine to the Low Countries. This conversion of silver into gold, of *reales* into *escudos*, had a triple importance. First, gold was far easier to carry: a single horseman could carry 8,000 *escudos* in gold but only 800 in silver; even a slow, fully-loaded pack-mule

---

[1] Cf. the perceptive remarks of F. Braudel and F. Spooner, in *Cambridge Economic History* IV (Cambridge, 1967), pp. 447–8. On the immediate impact of the arrival of Seville silver on money markets outside Spain, cf. J. Gentil da Silva, *Stratégie des affaires à Lisbonne entre 1595 et 1607* (Paris, 1962), pp. 31–92.

could only carry 4,000 *escudos* in silver *reales*. Second, between 1578 and 1590 the Army of Flanders demanded their wages exclusively in gold. Third, the high-quality Spanish silver coins were urgently needed by the Italian merchants for their Levant trade. Spanish 'pieces of eight' (8 *reales*) were the preferred currency of the Middle East and 'after 1580 the real distribution centres of silver, as much or even more than Spain, were the Italian towns'.[1] A steady stream of gold therefore reached the Army of Flanders by way of Genoa throughout the Eighty Years' War.

Nevertheless, after about 1585 it was not physically possible to run the Spanish Netherlands exclusively on the specie brought from Italy. The amounts involved became too great and the journey took too long. From Seville to the Low Countries via Barcelona and Genoa took a minimum of four months, and further delays were always possible: the galleys might be held up in port by the threat of pirates, there could be time wasted in converting silver coins to gold, and at the end of it all the Mt Cenis pass or the St Gotthard might be blocked by snow for months. (By contrast a bill of exchange took two to four weeks to reach the Low Countries and usually matured for payment thirty days after its arrival.)

By one of those double-standards which are the despair of modern historians, it was the Dutch who came to the rescue of the Army of Flanders and supplied their own enemies with the sinews of war. Although all trade with Spain was prohibited in the Republic between April 1586 and August 1588, Dutch merchants subsequently found it highly profitable to ship silver down to Antwerp where it was always scarce. Ironically, much of the silver in Holland was Spanish in origin, removed illicitly from the Indies fleets either at sea, in the Azores or off Lisbon.[2] The dependence of Antwerp and her *asientos* upon Dutch supplies of currency was pointed out by an English officer in Holland in 1603. Spinola arrived at Antwerp from Spain bearing letters of exchange but no specie.

Itt is imagined that if our marchants in these partes will hold their purses too,

---

[1] Braudel, *La Méditerranée*, I, p. 450, an assertion backed by an astonishing range of information. F. C. Spooner, 'Venice and the Levant: an aspect of monetary history (1610–14)' in *Studi in onore di Amintore Fanfani*, V (Milan, 1962), pp. 645–67, showed that 84 per cent of the large amount of silver exported by Venice to the Levant between 1610 and 1614 was sent in Spanish *reales*. I intend to examine the reasons for the soldiers' insistence on payment in gold in these (and only these) years and the logistics of transporting bullion to the Netherlands in a separate article.

[2] V. Ma ghalãesGodinho, *L'économie de l'Empire portugais aux XVe et XVIe siècles* (Paris, 1969), pp. 472–95, explains how this commerce took place. Amsterdam and Middelburg cornered so many Spanish *reales* that they were able to become principal suppliers of the 'rials' indispensable for the trade of the English East India Company during the reign of James I. (K. N. Chaudhuri, 'The East India Company and the export of treasure in the early seventeenth century', *Economic History Review*, XVI (1963), pp. 23–38.)

that there will be no mony found in Anwerp to pay his bills of exchaunge; butt as the last year, so questionles this year, the gaynes by making of mony over to Anwerp will be so great as that the marchants will one way or another convey monyes thither.[1]

Since the 'marchants' possessed the dominant voice in the government of the Republic, there was no way of preventing them from engaging in their profitable trade with the enemy.

This monetary lubrication from the burgeoning north Netherlands continued throughout the seventeenth century, aided by the growth of a large and prosperous community of exiled Portuguese Sephardic Jews in Amsterdam after 1598 (there were about 1,000 Jews there by 1630). With firm bases in both Lisbon and the Low Countries these Portuguese exiles were uniquely qualified to participate in the *asientos* of the Army of Flanders. The first major *asiento* involving Portuguese financiers was concluded in 1625. From that time forward the bankers who 'helped the King of Spain with the wealth they possessed in Amsterdam in the power of his own enemies' became the butt of satirists and the shame of patriotic statesmen.[2] But there was no alternative. Although a number of consignments of specie managed to reach Flanders by sea during the 1630s (some sent via England after the treaty of 1630, some transported direct on the fleets which carried Spanish recruits to the Army of Flanders) the destruction of Oquendo's fleet in 1639, which carried a large consignment of silver, discouraged further attempts to run the gauntlet of the Dutch.[3] Instead, after 1644 the Dutch agreed to insure the bullion ferried by *asentistas* from Spain to Dunkirk and Antwerp; after 1647, indeed, detachments of the Indies fleet were routed direct to the Netherlands in order to preserve the liquidity of the Antwerp exchange where the *asientos* were paid. At all costs the Army of Flanders had to be sustained with

[1] *HMC De L'Isle and Dudley*, III, pp. 274–5, Sir William Browne, acting governor of Flushing, to Lord Lisle, 23 May 1606.

[2] The phrase is Quevedo's, quoted by A. Domínguez Ortiz, 'El proceso inquisitorial de Juan Nuñez Saravia, banquero de Felipe IV', *Hispania*, xv (1955), pp. 559–81, on p. 561, n. 3. On the place of the Portuguese financiers in Philip IV's imperialism, cf. A. Castillo, 'Dans la Monarchie espagnole du XVIIe siècle: les banquiers portugais et le circuit d'Amsterdam', *Annales E.S.C.*, xix (1964), pp. 311–16.

[3] AGRB *SEG* 223/239, Don Antonio de Oquendo to the cardinal-infante, 24 Sep. 1639: 'yo traia dos millones de plata para V.A.' The first major convoy of specie by sea sent directly by Philip IV was sanctioned in Oct. 1632 after the *asentistas* complained to Olivares that 'the occupation of the corridors to the Netherlands via Italy and Germany has created a great shortage of specie at Antwerp, because merchants cannot send bullion there'. Therefore they could not pay the provisions. A year later 500,000 ducats arrived in silver aboard the royal fleet at Dunkirk. (AHN *E libro* 714, billet of Olivares to Philip IV on behalf of the merchants, 5 Oct. 1632; BRB *Ms.* 16147–48/134–5v, Aytona to Olivares, 5 Nov. 1633, announcing the money's arrival.) Cf. also the article of H. W. Taylor, 'Trade, Neutrality and the English Road, 1630–48', *Economic History Review*, 1971–2 (in printing).

credit and specie as long as Castile had funds to send and could find bankers to send them.

However, the credit system only worked when the king had revenues to spare and the desire to spend them in the Netherlands. Royal mistrust of the commander-in-chief (notably of Parma in 1592), a sudden emergency in another sector of the empire, a revolt in Spain – all these deterred the king from sinking his valuable resources in the Netherlands. More sinister, serious plague or famine in Spain could reduce the yield of taxes and thus complicate the repayment of *asientos* and damage the indispensable base of heavy taxation in Castile which underpinned the entire structure of imperial finance. After 1627–8 there is no doubt that the economy of Castile entered a prolonged and serious crisis, and that royal revenues suffered a serious decline. All these contingencies, personal and economic, had the same ultimate effect: the Army of Flanders received less money from Spain.

OTHER RESOURCES

There were few escapes from this situation. The military treasury (*pagaduría*) could open its doors in the 1640s as a deposit bank (interest 8 per cent per annum) to attract capital which might finance a campaign, but there were always safer investments to be found.[1] The Army could also try to billet some of its troops on neighbouring neutral countries. During the war of Cologne (1583–9) Spanish troops were allowed to winter in the bishopric of Liège in return for aid against the Protestants of Cologne (the elector of Cologne was also bishop of Liège). However, when the Army of Flanders quartered itself in Westphalia during the winter of 1598–9 there was a major international crisis. The German princes of the Westphalian Circle mobilized their own army (with Dutch assistance) to drive out the Spaniards.[2]

Attempts to make other areas of the Spanish empire contribute directly towards the cost of the war in the Netherlands also met with only mixed success. In 1625 a sophisticated plan to apportion the overall expense of defending the empire among the various provinces was submitted to Philip IV by his chief adviser, the count-duke of Olivares; it was known as

---

[1] BRB *Ms.* 12428–29/318, copy of an order of the captain-general to the paymaster-general, 13 Jun. 1642, authorizing him to accept private deposits. In the years 1642–5 the *pagaduría* received a mere 20,413 *escudos* (under 13,000 florins a year) 'por vía de depósito a 8 por ciento'. (AGS *CMC* 3a/993, 'Relación Jurada' of T. Lopez de Ulloa.)

[2] Cf. F. Boersma, 'De diplomatieke reis van Daniel van der Meulen en Nicolaes Bruyninck naar het Duitse Leger bij Emmerik, Augustus 1599', *Bijdragen en Mededelingen betreffende de Geschiedenis van de Nederlanden*, LXXXIV (1969), pp. 24–66.

the 'Union of Arms'. In 1626 Aragon and Valencia agreed, under protest, to shoulder part of the burden of paying their own garrisons (Catalonia refused even this) and some of the cost of defending Castile's American dependencies was off-loaded on to the colonies themselves. In 1627–8 the Netherlands and Spanish Italy were persuaded to accept the scheme.[1] In fact the Low Countries had long paid their quota (12,000 men) and much more; for them the 'union' was merely old wine in new bottles. Olivares' idea that all parts of the empire should contribute to the defence of any province under attack bore fruit only in Italy. In 1621–5 the kingdom of Naples sent small sums to the Army of Flanders; thereafter the amounts increased dramatically. From 1628 until 1631 Naples and Sicily both helped to finance the war in Lombardy, but after 1631 more was sent to the Netherlands. Between 1631 and 1643, the kingdom of Naples exported 9.2 million ducats, some to Lombardy, the rest to the Low Countries.[2]

These efforts were considerable, and they caused bitter resentment among those required to provide them, but they brought little relief to the Army of Flanders. The new resources of Spanish Italy could not compensate for the fall in the financial power of Castile. The Army of Flanders continued to rest upon the twin pillars of the *asientos* of Spain and the *aides* of the Netherlands. The failure of either of these supports was therefore catastrophic. A fall in receipts produced a marked effect on the troops in the Army; their behaviour followed a familiar but fatal pattern, through misery and prolonged suffering to mutiny, massive desertion and military collapse.

[1] Cf. J. H. Elliott, *The Revolt of the Catalans* (Cambridge, 1963), pp. 204–6 and 514–15, and J. Lynch, *Spain under the Habsburgs*, II (Oxford, 1969), pp. 94–101; neither author discusses the application of the 'Union' to Spain's European empire. Further study of the implementation of the project is called for.

[2] G. Coniglio, *Il Viceregno di Napoli nel secolo XVII* (Rome, 1955), p. 272; for Sicily, I am indebted to M. Maurice Aymard (who is preparing a study of the island under Habsburg rule) for confirming that large payments were sent to the Netherlands after 1631.

CHAPTER 7

LIFE IN THE ARMY OF FLANDERS

The trouble with the Netherlands, complained a harassed captain-general, was that:

> Everything is so expensive that even if wages could be paid in full every month, [the soldiers] could not live on three times as much because even the most efficient and most frugal soldier needs just for food 10 pattards a day and his wages are 4; and the light cavalry trooper, who causes the greatest resentment here, needs almost 30 pattards daily to feed himself, his horse and his lackey, and his wage amounts to no more than 9.[1]

Such was the acute and eternal practical problem of the Army of Flanders: how to adjust the soldiers' wages to the violent fluctuations and general rise in the cost of living. A number of attempts were made to solve it.

The obvious remedy, of course, was to increase wages until prices should fall. That was the reaction of the English Parliament to the grave subsistence crisis of 1649: the soldiers of the New Model Army received a wage supplement while grain prices were high.[2] But Spain found the cost of wages at even the grossly inadequate rates of the 1570s an impossible burden. The soldiers' pay fell further and further into arrears; an increase was out of the question. Despite a four-fold rise in food-prices, the basic wage of the Spanish foot-soldier remained at 3 *escudos* from 1534 until 1634 (when it was raised to 4).

However, this apparently immutable remuneration in fact masked a considerable increase in real terms. In the first place the *escudo* in which payments were calculated rose steadily in value from 39 pattards in the 1560s to 50 pattards (or 10 *reales*) after 1590, an increase from 117 to 150 pattards per month or 28 per cent. In addition a large number of individual soldiers were awarded a bonus for long or valorous service, a *ventaja* or wage-supplement from the military treasury of between 1 and 6 *escudos*

---

[1] *Nueva Co.Do.In.*, v, p. 233, Requesens to the king, 19 Sep. 1574. Many other letters from members of the high command in 1574 expressed the same view: cf. AA 31/83, Alonso Carnero to J. de Albornoz, 16 Sep. 1574 – 'The men cannot live on their wages; foodstuffs are so expensive that no man can afford to live in the Netherlands.'

[2] C. H. Firth, *Cromwell's Army* (new edn, London, 1962), p. 184–5.

monthly. These *ventajas*, some awarded by the captain-general (the *ventajas particulares*) others by the company captain (the *ventajas ordinarias*), raised the 'average wage' of the soldiers (a concept employed by the Army's accountants for their calculations) from 156 to 300 pattards monthly between 1567 and 1590. Finally, as we have seen, the troops received considerable payments from the Netherlands as well as from the *pagaduría*. Basically, every man in the Army was entitled either to a free bed and room service, or to a payment of 12 *reales* (60 pattards) in cash every 30 days (the *servitiegeld* or *servicio*) in addition to his wages. Between them these increments raised the basic monthly wage of the Spanish soldier in the Netherlands from a mere 117 pattards in 1567 to 210 pattards (including wages and service-money, but without *ventajas*) in 1590, an increase of 80 per cent in 23 years.

Many of these increases were the result of aggressive corporate action by the troops. The abolition of the *escudo* of 39 pattards in favour of the *escudo* of 50 pattards (*de a 10 reales*) as the Army's money of account, for example, was forced upon an unwilling government by the Spanish mutineers of Kortrijk in 1590.[1] It was therefore understandable that the king should have attempted a 'clawback' operation from time to time designed to reduce the cost to his treasury of the Army's wages. Quite legitimately the entire Army was stopped ten days' pay in February 1583 to compensate for the days lost when the Gregorian calendar was introduced in the Spanish Netherlands. With far less justification, in 1632 Philip IV urged his officials to let 'four or five days pass unnoticed' before each month's wages were paid, in the hope that the 12 pays due each year could be 'insensibly reduced' to 10.[2] This was preposterous! A 'clawback' system can only operate when something has actually been paid: had the soldiers of the Army of Flanders received even ten pays during the year they would have been jubilant. Their complaint was not that the remuneration was inadequate, but that it was so seldom paid. There were indeed troops in the Army, as one commander pointed out,

---

[1] Cf. the first-hand account of the *contador* of the day, Antonio Carnero, *Historia* (Brussel s 1625), pp. 241–2.

[2] AGS *CMC* 2a/4, has the papers of the *tercio* of Iñiquez which lost its pay for the '10 días del Calendario'. For the unworthy and unrealistic suggestion of Philip IV, cf. AGS *E* 2239, unfol., Philip IV to the marquis of Santa Cruz, 24 Jun. 1632. The king may even have introduced a special 'month' of 42 days for calculating the wages of his armies in Spain (J. Deleito y Piñuela, *El Declinar de la Monarquía española* (2nd ed., Madrid, 1947), p. 184) but this *Heeremaand* was never introduced in the Army of Flanders although it was known to be the basis of Dutch military finance. Cf. the sarcasm of Don Carlos Coloma (*Guerras*, bk VII – *BAE* edn, p. 100) about the States General 'who are accustomed to pay their troops with lard and beer, and, against all good astrology, to divide their months into forty days'. Of course the Dutch were right...

'who don't know what pay is'.[1] Given Spain's permanent inability to mobilize sufficient resources to finance all its undertakings, any attempt by the high command to pay the soldiers entirely or mainly in cash was bound to leave the men destitute and to deliver them into the tyranny of the only people with credit to sustain them – their captains.

Every captain in an early modern army held enormous power over the rank and file of his company. In absolute charge of discipline he could flog, fine or otherwise humiliate his men whenever he chose; because he alone decided who should perform sentry guard and other onerous duties, the captain was free to victimize the men he disliked and excuse his friends; without interference from above the captain chose the two sergeants and eight corporals of his company (the *cabos de escuadra* or corporals were in charge of twenty-five men and received a wage-bonus of 3 *escudos* each per month), and he distributed at his pleasure 30 *escudos* of treasury bonus-pay among his men.[2] As if this were not enough, the insolvency of the military treasury made the company captains into money-lenders and welfare-officers as well. Every company had a chest (*caja*) kept by the captain and used by him to advance subsistence wages (the *socorro*) to necessitous men when no money arrived from the treasury. The captains were also responsible for ransoming, re-arming or re-horsing any of their men who had the misfortune to lose their liberty, their weapons or their mounts. Naturally when the treasury did contrive to pay an instalment of wages the captains expected to receive it first in order to deduct the sums already advanced 'on account'. The scheme was excellent in principle, but it assumed that all captains were honest and scrupulous men. Of course they were not. As Dr Cruickshank has written of the similar system which prevailed in the Elizabethan army: 'The arrangements for paying the troops played right into the eager hands of the captains, who took full advantage of the generous opportunities afforded them.'[3]

Although the government made a number of attempts, often at times of mutiny, to arrange for the troops to be paid 'on the table and in their own hand' (*en tabla y mano propria*), these always broke down because it was never possible to pay wages in cash for long. The men were soon begging

---

[1] AGS *E* 554/154, Pedro de Paz to Requesens, 15 Nov. 1573: 'no saben que cosa es paga'. This was a slight exaggeration: all troops received one full pay upon enlistment – although that was often all they saw for years! The German regiment of Baron Polwiller, for example, received one full pay upon enlistment in 1572 but no more until 1579 (AGS *E* 580/23, Polwiller to Philip II, 10 Feb. 1579; cf. also p. 223 below).

[2] The arbitrary flogging of soldiers by their officers was a frequent complaint of the mutineers – cf. p. 199 below; for concern at the victimization of a few men by the captains, cf. AGS *E* 571/1, minute of Philip II's instruction to his inspector-general, 1567 and 1577.

[3] C. G. Cruickshank, *Elizabeth's Army* (2nd ed., Oxford, 1966), p. 143.

their captain to lend them money again in order to save them from starvation. The way was again open for illicit profit. Time and again officers of impeccable lineage, as well as the base-born, were found guilty of cheating their men and defrauding the treasury. At every muster they presented new recruits and claimed they were veterans (and therefore entitled to higher pay), they put their lackeys and even sturdy peasants into the ranks and swore that they were soldiers (these impostors, known as *santelmos* – will o' the wisps – because they were come and gone in a moment, were bribed with a token payment). The captains pocketed the wages due to all who passed false muster.[1] There was no direct remedy to this corrupt system: control of the captains by the central government proved to be no more effective than its control of the army's clerical staff. Everyone was guilty, but 'one cannot cut off everybody's head', as one outraged captain-general lamented.[2]

The true answer both to the miserable standard of the soldiers' existence and to the problem of official irresponsibility was to supply the troops' needs directly and in kind. It was easier, more humane and far safer to run up debts to the merchants who supplied food and other munitions to the army than to leave the soldiers unpaid and unprovided, and it was not difficult to supervise a small clique of entrepreneurs dealing in bulk and subject to contract. Bread, clothes, arms and shelter came to be provided directly by the Army; eventually medical and spiritual care, a trustee service for wills, even marriage allowances were regularly supplied. By 1630, about half the soldier's wages were paid in kind, and the rest was made over to the men themselves, not to their captains.

This system not only protected the troops against rapacious captains and penniless paymasters; it also saved them from themselves. War, as Cervantes wrote, made the miser generous and the generous man profligate: the soldier had to be prevented from squandering his wages the moment they were paid. Time and again the payment of a large arrears of wages provoked a massive wave of conspicuous spending among the troops

---

[1] Two examples: (1) Don Gaston Spinola, *maestre de campo*, later count of Bruay and trusted councillor of the archdukes, was found in 1598 to have embezzled 18,000 florins in wages for men who were not soldiers (AGS *E* 621, unfol., 'Relación de las resultas que contra diferentes personas se han sacado', a *catalogue raisonnée* of cases of fraud and corruption uncovered by the Royal Commission of Enquiry in the Netherlands – the 'Visita' – 1598–1601); (2) Don Sancho Martínez de Leyva, brother of the Armada hero, Don Alonso, was imprisoned for pocketing 10,000 florins intended for his men (AGS *E* 607/71–2 and 212, interrogation of some of Leyva's soldiers, and AGRB *SEG* 15/172v, Order of 19 Nov. 1594).
[2] *Nueva Co.Do.In.*, I, p. 371, Requesens to the king, 16 Mar. 1574.

– gambling, fine clothes, women – resulting all too soon in a new era of destitution. If instead the soldiers were given their subsistence and little more, discipline, order and military effectiveness might be preserved. 'It is good to keep [troops] short of money sometimes in order to make them more obedient and to feed them with hope', wrote the perceptive military commentator Blaise de Vigenère. 'In short, the soldier must be not too poor and not too rich.'[1]

The first and most important item to be supplied to the troops in kind was their daily bread – the *pan de munición* of mixed wheat and rye baked into a single loaf of 1, 2 or 3 lb.[2] *Pan de munición* (government bread) was

Figure 14. Annual expenditure of the *pagaduría* on victuals for the troops

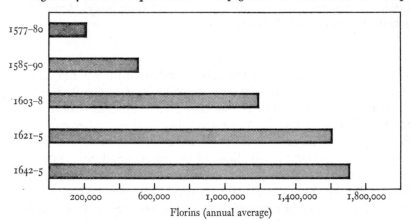

Florins (annual average)

The eight-fold increase in government spending on victuals included an increase of perhaps 50 per cent in basic food prices, but since other factors (the number of troops in the Army and the composition of their basic ration) remained constant, at least five times as many troops were receiving government bread in the 1640s as in the 1570s. Source: Appendix.

[1] Blaise de Vigenère, *L'Art militaire d'Onosender* (Paris, 1605), pp. 272 and 272v. Cf. the identical statements by the German military writer Reinhard of Solms (quoted Redlich, *The German Military Enterpriser*, 1, pp. 132–3) and by Michel le Tellier, French secretary of state for war: 'Les soldats, qui bien loin de ménager aucune chose, consomment souvent en un jour ce qui leur est donné pour dix, n'auroient jamais de quoi se pourvoir d'habits ni de chaussures' (quoted by L. André, *Michel le Tellier et l'organization de l'armée monarchique* (Paris, 1906), p. 341).

[2] The bread was to be one-third rye and two-thirds wheat, but at certain periods 'when the Spanish and Italian troops are divided from the other 'nations'...they may be given bread of pure wheat without any other mixture'. (AGRB *SEG* 20/144v–8, Order of 10 Jan. 1602). For a philosophical justification of feeding troops on mixed bread, cf. Vigenère, *L'Art Militaire*, pp. 636v–7v: mixed bread was cheaper than loaves of pure wheatmeal and it lasted longer, in addition rye was more appropriate [*plus propre*] to working men.

the fuel which really moved armies in the modern period: 1½ lb. of bread was recognized to constitute the minimum daily ration without which no soldier could survive. From the 1590s onwards, most of the men in the Army of Flanders began to receive their daily bread (often a 3 lb loaf every two days) from the government and their wages were stopped 15 florins per year – whatever the real price of the bread. The rapid rise in government spending on victuals for the troops is shown in Figure 14. After 1601 the provision of victuals to the entire army was centralized. It was entrusted to a single official, the *proveedor de viveres*, who was in fact the contractor who offered to supply a year's bread to the troops at the cheapest price. Despite highly competitive bids, the cost of feeding the troops rose steadily, following the upward trend of market prices. Eventually it was decided to charge the troops 30 florins a year for their daily bread, deducted from their wages. It was still cheap at the price: the soldiers were insulated against the brutal fluctuations and scarcity of the local markets, and the government had less to fear from men freed from the sting of starvation. The high command did not need Sancho Panza to remind them that 'bread makes good every grief'.[1]

Of course in the early modern period no government initiative was proof against misfortune. The victuallers sometimes went bankrupt, leaving the troops without bread – a circumstance which never failed to strike terror into the high command since it was supposed (melodramatically?) that, left without bread for three or four days, 4,000 men would inevitably die of starvation.[2] Sometimes, on the other hand, the bread which the contractors provided was worse than no bread at all. On a number of occasions the loaves issued to the troops caused illness, even epidemics in the army.[3] One such lethal preparation of 'bread' was found to contain offal, unmilled flour, broken biscuits and lumps of

---

[1] *Don Quixote*, II, chap. 55. In the 1590s, a year's supply of bread cost each man 6 *escudos* (15 florins – AGRB *SEG* 15/112v) and in the 1630s 12 *escudos* (30 florins – *SEG* 217/461). The soldier's daily ration of 1½ lbs was larger than that of the Antwerp poor who, throughout the sixteenth century, were expected to subsist on 1 lb. per day (E. Scholliers, *De Levensstandaard in de XVe en XVIe eeuw te Antwerpen* (Antwerp, 1960), pp. 60–1).

[2] AGRB *SEG* 236/73–7, marquis of Castel Rodrigo (the captain-general) to the king, 18 Jul. 1646.

[3] The 'coarse, black, bad bread' supplied to the Army in 1631, for instance, was widely considered to have caused the 'pestilence' which crippled the Army throughout the summer (AGRB *CPE* 1500/40, paper of the *veedor general*, 29 Feb. 1633, and f. 198, P. Roose to the king, minute, 3 Dec. 1637). In 1574 the Spanish mutineers claimed that their bread-ration 'ha sido y es tal, y hecho de tales pastas, que ha causado pestilencia grande' (AGS *E* 560/13, letter of the mutineers of Holland to Requesens, 7 Nov. 1574). Since the '*pan de munición*' contained rye, the pestilence may well have been ergotism ('St Anthony's Fire'), a disease caused by eating infected ears of rye.

plaster...many of those who ate it died; many of those who refused it starved.[1]

The clothing of the troops, which was also undertaken by the government after the 1580s, was less regular but less prone to disaster. After 1585 and the reactivation of the Antwerp *bourse*, most *asientos* payable in the atrophied metropolis of the Netherlands were paid partly in cloth. This solved two problems. It eased the difficulties of bankers who could not raise enough specie in Antwerp and it ensured that the troops were clothed. After 1594 some *asientos* were made solely in order to provide suits of clothes for the Army. The *asentista* was shown a suit of clothes and had to produce a thousand or more suits of the same design and measurements – a top-coat, breeches, jacket, shirt, underwear and stockings.[2] There were only two sizes ('large' and 'small') and, perhaps surprisingly, there was no pressure upon the contractors to produce suits of a standard colour. It was considered that the distinguishing marks traditionally carried by the different sides – the cross of St Andrew and a red scarf, sash or feather in the hat for Spain – were enough.[3] Indeed the idea of a standardized uniform was rather frowned upon, at least until the 1630s. Military men considered that a soldier who was allowed freedom of sartorial expression would fight more ferociously:

> There has never been a regulation for dress and weapons in the Spanish infantry because that would remove the spirit and fire which is necessary in a soldier.
> It is the finery, the plumes and the bright colours which give spirit and strength to a soldier so that he can with furious resolution overcome any difficulty or accomplish any valorous exploit.

The adornments and finery of soldiers were expressly excluded from the Spanish Sumptuary Laws of 1623 and after.[4]

We know little about the dress worn by the soldiers in the Netherlands.

[1] AGS *GA* 1017, unfol., duke of Feria to the king, 17 Sep. 1630.
[2] The first *asiento* for '*vestidos enteros*' was concluded on 6 Feb. 1594 (AGRB *SEG* 15/31v–2v, further details in subsequent contracts registered in *SEG* 15/33–4, 17/223–4, 20/36–7 and so on). In the course of 1607, merchants provided the army with no less than 9,000 complete sets of clothes, as well as cloth (all English) to the value of 559,000 florins (AGS *E* 2290/15, 'Relación del Paño').
[3] The 'croix rouge' of St Andrew and Burgundy was the 'marque et devise' of Philip II's troops in the 1550s and after 1567 (AE Geneva, *PH* 1825, unfol., bailiff of Gex to the Council of Geneva, 12 Apr. 1567). The ordinances of the Army of Flanders in 1596 decreed that all soldiers should wear 'L'escharpe rouge dessus ses armes ou cassaque, et celluy qui n'aura point d'escharpe rouge portera une croix rouge à descouvert, et qui n'aura cette marque sera tenu pour ennemy et traité comme tel.' (BRB *Ms.* 12622–31/177–200v, Edict of 27 May 1596, clause 41.) Cf. the red cross and the red sash on all Spanish troops portrayed by the military painters of Antwerp, Vranckx and Snaeyers.
[4] These two quotations, one from a manuscript of 1610, the other from *El Guzmán de Alfarache*, appear in Deleito y Piñuela, *El Declinar*, pp. 177–8.

One Spanish *tercio* in the 1580s dressed in black, earning itself the nickname '*tercio* of the sextons', while the men of its sister regiment so adorned themselves with 'plumes, finery and bright colours' that they were known as the '*tercio* of the dandies'.[1] Such sartorial vanity and variety could not last. Alva's Spanish veterans, too, resembled princes and captains as they marched from Italy to the Netherlands in 1567 (according to Brantôme), but they soon became the 'old ragged rogues' who terrified their commanders as much as the enemy. A man on active service needed a new suit of clothes and a pair of shoes every year; since the government could rarely supply either enough money or the new clothes, the troops rapidly degenerated into the pitiful band of frost-bitten scarecrows painted by Snaeyers in 1641 (cf. Plate 6).

Arms and armour were also provided on credit to the troops by contractors engaged by the government. This was essential since few men could afford to purchase their own firearms (a musket cost 10 florins in the 1590s, more than a musketeer's wage for a month), but it was perhaps shortsighted to charge the powder and shot used by each man against his account – it was hardly an encouragement for a marksman to use his weapon! In their defence the government argued that the musketeers and arquebusiers already drew a slightly higher wage to cover the cost of using their guns, but of course this was only effective when wages were actually paid... The light cavalry was hamstrung by a similar assumption by the government: the troopers were entitled to a high wage designed to offset the cost of purchasing, equipping and feeding their horses, but for months they never saw a penny. A considerable number of cavalrymen were therefore permanently grounded, their horses dead either from neglect or combat, while those who remained mounted were often scarcely mobile. In 1576, for example, the horses in the stable of the late captain-general, Don Luis de Requesens, were put up for auction. Two unfortunate animals were so 'maimed and mutilated' that no purchaser could be found for them either in Antwerp or Brussels; they were therefore sold to the light cavalry...[2] The only solution, once again, was to provide horses to the troops on credit and deduct the cost from their wages. After 1590 this began to be done.

[1] For the story of how 'los sacristanes' and 'los almidonados' got their names, cf. Alonso Vazquez, *Los Sucesos* (*Co.Do.In.* LXXIII), p. 323. There is an interesting parallel here with the two predominant styles of dress in Spain itself at the time, cf. B. Bennassar, *Valladolid au Siècle d'Or* (Paris, 1967), p. 463.

[2] March, *Don Luis de Requeséns*, p. 141 n. Cf. AGS *E* 2289/56–7, muster of the Army, 18 Mar. 1607: the light cavalry numbered 4,164 men, of whom 795 were 'a pie' (on foot) and 195 'mal a cavallo' (badly mounted).

Even with the soldiers armed, fed and clothed, accommodation still had to be found for them. This was virtually no problem during the campaign season. The normal improvised campaign shelter of the early modern soldier was the 'barrack' or hut, usually constructed of materials taken from deserted houses rather than from virgin timber. After the siege of Haarlem in 1572–3, for example, one eye-witness recalled that 'the soldiers suffered in the great frosts and went up to three or four leagues in search of firewood to burn and tables and beams for shelter, tearing down houses and making "*barracas*"'. Ready-made timber was clearly preferable to tree-trunks which required hewing and shaping. The shelter was thus simply made, and it was equally simply destroyed: when the soldiers moved on, their huts were burnt.[1]

It was in winter-quarters and in garrison-towns that serious billeting problems arose. The traditional method, lodging the troops free of charge in private houses, was certainly an advantageous arrangement for the soldiers, but it imposed a crippling burden on the householders. Until 1598, civilian protests went unheeded by the government, but Philip II's decision to make the archdukes into independent rulers of the Netherlands led to some changes. The Archduke Albert was a sovereign prince as well as captain-general of the Army of Flanders; he had to balance the interests of his subjects against those of his soldiers. It soon became clear that the archdukes favoured the civilians: the traditional obligation to lodge troops was often commuted to a money payment (despite protests from Madrid) and in the key strongholds of the Spanish Netherlands a number of more durable shelters, also known (somewhat confusingly) as 'barracks', were constructed. The standard 'barrack' contained accommodation for 4 persons sleeping in 2 beds: 4 single or 2 married soldiers. There was also the 'double barrack' with 4 beds, sleeping 8. Stone-and-timber constructions sprang up at 's Hertogenbosch (1609), Dunkirk (1611), Maastricht and Damme (1616) and thereafter in most other centres.[2] In the citadels

---

[1] AGS *CMC* 2a/883, unfol., Alonso de Alameda to F. Lopez del Campo, head of the 'Tribunal de las Quentas de Flandes', 11 Jun. 1582. Cf. the same practices recorded for the English Army by C. G. Cruickshank, *Army Royal* (Oxford, 1969), pp. 41–2, and R. E. Scouller, *The Armies of Queen Anne* (Oxford, 1966), p. 166. There are rare illustrations of these primitive 'barracks' in C. Ó. Danacháir, 'Representations of Houses on some Irish maps of c. 1600', in G. Jenkins (ed.), *Studies in Folk Life* (London, 1969), plate facing p. 63 and on pp. 93–4.

[2] AGRB *Conseil des Finances* 323, unfol., contains correspondence about the construction and repair of 'baracques' in many towns of the South Netherlands. At 's Hertogenbosch, the 'barracken binnen de Stad' are described by C. J. Gudde, *Vier eeuwen geschiedenis van het garnizoen 's Hertogenbosch* ('s Hertogenbosch, 1958), p. 31. There is extensive information about the 'barracks' built at Breda after its capture by Spinola in 1625 in Gemeente Archief, Breda, nr. 406 pp. a, b and c. The 'double barraque' for 8 persons was incorporated into the larger military installations of the eighteenth century. One of the first of these, Ravensdowne

of the Spanish Netherlands (Ghent, Antwerp, Cambrai) the barracks were somewhat larger and stood within the castle walls. The beds, furniture and so on were reluctantly furnished by the local magistrates.[1] However, it was never possible to lodge a large garrison entirely in barracks. Some troops always had to be quartered on the townspeople, or at least on those not protected by special exemption from billeting. The garrison of Nieuwpoort in 1631, for example, consisted of 727 men, of whom only 194 were lodged in the 83 'baraques du Roy' inside the town. Nieuwpoort in 1631 consisted of 580 houses, 150 with two stories, the rest *petites maisons ou maisonnettes* of one storey, many of them no more than hovels; 86 of the best houses were exempt from billeting so the rest of the garrison – 533 men and 278 wives – were quartered in 269 of the remaining dwellings. Up to 5 soldiers could be billeted in even a small house.[2]

Whatever its failures in other directions, the Army of Flanders managed to provide admirable free medical care for a large number of its troops. Although the soldiers raised locally were expected to make use of the charitable institutions of the Netherlands (a somewhat harsh rule which was applied even to the German and Burgundian troops) those brought from the British Isles, Spain and Italy demanded special treatment. These troops, like all Spanish troops in Italy, received free medical care in a permanent military hospital; in return the government deducted 1 *real* per month from their wages.[3] The principle military hospital of the Spanish Netherlands was located, after 1585, at Mechelen; in 1637 it had 330 beds, which was adequate for the expatriate troops in most

Barracks in Berwick-on-Tweed (built 1717–21) had two ranges accommodating 600 men each and divided into rooms for 8 men.

[1] Cf. the illustration of the military installations in the citadel of Ghent in A. Sanderus, *Flandria Illustrata*, I (Cologne, 1641), p. 148. For the furniture supplied by the Antwerp magistrates to the new citadel after 1569, cf. E. Rooms, 'Politieke, sociale en economische studie van het garnizoen van Antwerpen...', 1567–77' (Gent licenciaatsverhandeling, 1969) pp. 184–6.

[2] AGRB *Audience* 1995/2, unfol., *Visite* of the Nieuwpoort garrison, 5–7 Jan 1631. Cf. also AD Savoie, *SA* 7551, an account of the lodgings given to Spanish troops in Modane (in the Maurienne) in 1620: 10,560 persons were lodged in 2,054 houses (spread over a number of weeks), an average of over 5 per house.

[3] This practice appears to have begun among the Spanish troops in Italy, cf. AGS *CMC* 1a/1491, unfol., order of the duke of Alva, 1 Nov. 1552, setting up a hospital at the siege of Metz, to be financed by a *limosna* of one *real* per man per month 'as has been done in armies and campaigns in the past, and as has been the custom in Italy, Germany and the Netherlands'. Rather like the 'National Health Stamp' of Britain's present welfare system, the *real de limosna* only paid for about one-third of the total cost of the medical service. The rest was provided directly by the government: in fact the military hospital cost each year about 100,000 florins to maintain (AGS *CMC* 2a/2, Paymaster-General Unceta paid 172,010 *escudos* of 50 pattards to the hospital 1603–8; *CMC* 3a/975, Paymaster Lira paid 346,802 *escudos* 1634–41, about 1 per cent of the *pagaduría's* total expenditure).

years. When a long siege or a particularly bloody campaign increased the numbers requiring medical treatment, special field hospitals were set up at strategic points, or else a civil hospital was taken over by the Army. In such emergencies, all troops, expatriate and local, received free treatment.[1]

The military hospital had to deal mainly with surgery cases – limbs injured by sword, pike or gunshot. Of the three, bullet-wounds were by far the most serious. On one occasion when many of his men were wounded, Don Luis de Requesens reflected that: 'Most of the wounds come from pikes or blows, and they will soon heal, although there are also many with gunshot wounds [*arcabuzazos*] and they will die.'[2] All the medical textbooks of the time confirm this judgement: a bullet was more likely to cause internal bleeding, induce blood-poisoning or shatter a bone – three conditions which sixteenth-century medicine was powerless to cure. Yet within these limitations, the Army's doctors and surgeons registered some remarkable successes. Of 41 badly injured Spanish veterans in 1574, for example, 1 had lost both legs and 3 both arms, 5 more had lost the use of one leg and 13 lacked a hand or an arm (left and right limbs suffered equally); 11 more were recorded as having bad gunshot wounds (in their mouth, their eye or disabling a limb) and 4 more had lost a limb by a cannon ball. The roll-call is gruesome but it gives a remarkable testimony to the skill of the army's surgeons: all these unfortunates had survived their injury.[3] For such mutilated survivors a special home was established in the seventeenth century: the 'Garrison of Our Lady of Hal'. In January 1640 there were 2 officers, 236 soldiers and 108 *entretenidos* in the garrison, all of them injured veterans too maimed for service in the field.[4]

On top of the routine of mending or amputating broken limbs the

[1] The hospital of Mechelen is being studied by Mlle L. Van Meerbeeck; cf. her preliminary articles: 'L'Hôpital royale de l'armée espagnole à Malines en l'an 1637', *Bulletin du Cercle archéologique de Malines*, LIV (1950), pp. 81–125, and 'Le service sanitaire de l'armée espagnole des Pays-Bas à la fin du XVIe et au XVIIe siècles', *Revue Internationale d'Histoire Militaire*, XX (1959), pp. 479–93.

[2] AGS *E* 564/134, Requesens to the king, 4 Nov. 1575.

[3] BPU Geneva, *Ms. Favre* 60/104–10, *Visita* of injured troops, May 1574. All the victims were either repatriated or given a place in some safe garrison. AGRB *SEG* 17 and 18 record 386 soldiers discharged from the Army in 1596–9 for various reasons (not all connected with ill-health). Of these 142 (36 per cent) had scars or wounds on the face which served as a permanent distinguishing mark and some had 'la frente llena de heridas' (a face full of wounds) or were 'muy fea de heridas' (very ugly with wounds). A further 5 per cent lacked the sight of one or both eyes, 7 per cent had a severely damaged or amputated leg, and 17 per cent had lost – or lost the use of – their arm. Once again, the Army's surgeons had saved the lives of the badly injured.

[4] AGRB *CPE* 1574/81–99, memorial of P. Roose, 28 Jan. 1640.

hospital encountered many cases of infectious disease and even of psychological illness. Of the 386 Spanish and Italian soldiers who were permanently discharged from the Army between 1596 and 1599 no less than 76 (20 per cent) were recorded as incapacitated by an 'incurable illness'.[1] Perhaps this was tuberculosis or malaria, but more probably it was a venereal disease, scourge of all armies on foreign service. Venereal diseases were certainly rife enough in the Army of Flanders for a regular annual payment to be made by the military treasury enabling the hospital of Mechelen to treat all sufferers from 'el mal galico' languishing there.[2] The possible scale of the disease may be inferred from the British Army in India where 'In the 14 years ending 1883, the average [hospital] admission rate...for venereal disease was 225 cases per 1000 men. In 1895 these admissions reached the enormous proportion of 537 per 1000 men.'[3]

In the seventeenth century another more puzzling ailment appeared – or began to be diagnosed – among the troops. A considerable number of men were discharged because they suffered from *el mal de corazón* (literally, heart-trouble): most probably their trouble was a sort of shell-shock or deep despair which made them unfit for service. After all, the soldiers had no leave to look forward to, and in the reign of Philip IV many of them were conscripts. Another expression in the Army which probably referred to the same condition was 'to be broken' (*estar roto*) and therefore useless and fit only to be sent home.[4]

In the seventeenth century, most soldiers received humane treatment when they fell into enemy hands: the injured and sick were placed under a special safeguard and were repatriated with a minimum of formality.[5] From 1599, if not before, there was a formal agreement between Spain and the States General to give quarter and to ransom all prisoners taken by the other side. The *cuartel general* obliged every captain to ransom those of his men captured by the enemy within twenty-five days, paying a charge appropriate to the man's rank for his ransom and his 'entertain-

[1] AGRB *SEG* 17 and 18; analysis of 386 '*licencias*' (discharges) registered 1596-9.
[2] The standing charge of 1,275 *escudos* of 50 pattards every April appears in the accounts of Paymaster Ulloa, 1645-8 (AGS *CMC* 3a/937), reduced to 1,200 *escudos* in those of Paymaster Diego Enríquez de Castro, 1668-71 (*CMC* 3a/1760). The treatment appears to have been a combination of steam-baths, cauterization and sterilization which, although unable to cure the victims, at least kept them serviceable for another campaign.
[3] V. L. Kellogg, *Military Selection and Race Deterioration* (Oxford, 1916), p. 194.
[4] AGRB *SEG* 43 (Register of Orders, 1643-4) records at least six soldiers discharged from the Army on account of the '*mal de corazón*'. SEG 37/148 records a *licencia* discharging a man of 42 from the Army who 'Por hallarse roto y con otros achaques esta inhutil'. Psychological complaints were no doubt commonest amongst the soldiers conscripted or impressed against their will and then sent off to the Netherlands (cf. pp. 46-7).
[5] Van Meerbeeck, 'Le service sanitaire', p. 493.

ment' while in captivity. A detailed scale of charges was established.[1] The soldiers were rarely required to pay anything towards their own ransoms – insistence on this would have led all prisoners of war to enlist with the enemy. Instead another heavy and steadily increasing charge was laid upon the central treasury. Every survivor of the Invincible Armada of 1588 cost 100 florins to ransom. They were cheap at the price. Around 1600 it cost between 800 and 1500 florins to ransom a man caught by the privateers of Dunkirk. In 1641 it was estimated that it would cost 400,000 florins to ransom all the prisoners of war held by the Dutch.[2] This was an enormous burden on the military treasury, although a certain amount was recouped in the ransoms paid by the Dutch to redeem their men held by Spain. In all cases the prisoners of war continued to earn their wages for the duration of their captivity (less the cost of their 'entertainment' by their captors) while their wives received the daily bread and *servicio* money to which the soldiers would have been entitled.[3]

The Army performed another humane service for its soldiers: it guaranteed the honest execution of their wills. The king always claimed the unpaid wages of soldiers who died intestate, and until 1574 even soldiers who made a will but died in service forfeited their due. In August 1573 the government promised that the pay-arrears due to the

[1] The first *cuartel general* was negotiated on 29 Oct. 1599 by the Spanish field commander, the Admiral of Aragon. The *cuartel* was re-issued on 14 May 1602 and 18 Oct. 1622 (ARA *Staten van Holland* 2604 no. g, and BRB *Ms.* 12622-31/273-5v, Copy). In the sixteenth century the ransom and exchange of prisoners was negotiated piecemeal between rival town governors, but in 1567-76 and in 1593 no quarter was given in the war. The duke of Alva, for example, hanged all the Dutch troops who came into his hands (AGS *E* 561/167, Alva to the king, 7 Jul. 1573). He even executed the German garrison of Haarlem when the town surrendered on terms (thus stiffening the resistance of all 'rebel' garrisons elsewhere). This never seems to have happened in the Eighty Years' War after 1600 (although it did in Germany, cf. Redlich, *The German Military Enterpriser*, I, p. 479). The most that could be done was to release prisoners of war 'from the most remote parts, as usual, so that they will not find it easy to return home' (AGS *E* 2251, unfol., Philip IV to Don Francisco de Melo, 17 May 1644, minute).

[2] Cf. AGRB *SEG* 11/150 and 163v-4, orders of 2 and 17 Mar. 1589 about the ransom of 500 Armada prisoners held by the Dutch and English. AGRB *Amirauté* 61, unfol., containing four lists of ransoms collected: 'Relación' of 10 Feb 1601 (139 prisoners ransomed for 161,572 f.); 'Los prisioneros que los baxeles de guerra...han tomado' 18 Mar. 1601 (95 prisoners at 80,949 f. – actually, these men were exchanged for Spanish prisoners captured by the Dutch at the battle of the Dunes); 'Dese naervolghen persoonen zijn op huyden...' 10 Nov. 1600 (87 persons for 135,400 f.); and 'Lyste van al de ghevanghenen uuyt zee opgebrocht', 1597-9 (104 persons for 138,200 f.). Finally, AHN *E libro* 969, unfol., Don Miguel de Salamanca to Olivares, 25 Jun. 1641, minute.

[3] AGRB *SEG* 175bis/46, order of the Archduke Albert, 10 Jun. 1609 to pay the wage-arrears of soldiers in captivity (re-issued 10 Jul. 1610, *SEG* 24/411v); *SEG* 43/186v, order of F. de Melo, 19 Nov. 1643, to issue bread to prisoners' wives. In addition to bread and *servicio*, the wives of men in enemy hands as well as soldiers' widows and orphans received alms from the government from time to time, usually distributed by the chaplains (cf. AGRB *Jésuites*, *Collège de Bruxelles* 1968, containing many papers on alms-giving).

dead Spanish soldiers who had left a will would be paid to their legatees but in fact nothing was done. In May 1574 a special commission was set up to investigate and execute all wills, but such a large number of frauds were uncovered – tricksters who masqueraded as legatees, testators who turned out to be still alive and so on – that the payment of all arrears due to the dead was suspended awaiting a full enquiry. In consequence the 1,428 soldiers of the *tercio* of Naples whose arrears were paid in May 1574 received on average 119 *escudos* (232 florins) each, while the legatees of their 396 dead comrades received only 19 *escudos* (37 florins) each. The neglect of the dead was still marked, but at least it was an improvement on the situation before 1574, when nothing was paid at all.[1]

For the rest of the sixteenth century the administration of the testaments of dead soldiers was in the hands of the chaplains. The professional standards prevailing among the field chaplains of the Army of Flanders were, at least until the 1590s, abysmal. The duke of Alva, typically, wrote off all army padres as 'either vicious or stupid'; equally characteristically, he offered no positive suggestions for improvement.[2] Even in the 1590s we find engaging chaplains like Fra Marcello Marsa from Rome and Fra Antonio Granata. The first conducted a lively traffic in forged relics (saints' heads were his speciality) and at his trial he was found to have a fine stable of horses, a twelve-year-old son and heretical leanings. Small wonder that in their defence he drew his sword against the court official sent to arrest him. Fra Antonio was yet more colourful. He dressed in furs and wore a gold chain, entertained the bishop of Antwerp with bawdy ballads sung to the lute, and masqueraded (successfully) as a papal commissioner in order to enter and 'reform' a nunnery.[3]

[1] AGS *CMC* 2a/1, unfol., the *pliegos de asiento* of the *tercio* of Naples: 169,780 *escudos* of 39 pattards paid to 1,428 live men, 7,897 *escudos* for the 396 dead. Cf. also *CMC* 2a/79, unfol., order of Requesens, 28 Aug. 1574, forbidding the paymaster-general to pay any more claims made by legatees of dead soldiers unless approved by the *auditor* (judge-advocate), Pareja; and *CMC* 2a/9, unfol., contract of Requesens with L. Spinola and T. Fieschi, 8 Nov. 1574, to pay the testaments of the dead which had been approved. The general position of soldiers who died in service was made clear by Captain-General Fuentes in a curt note to the mutineers of Zichem on 26 Aug. 1595: the arrears of those who left heirs and testaments would be paid, but '*de lo demas es heredero el Rey*' (the king inherits the rest – AGS *CMC* 2a/6, unfol., third set of articles exchanged between the government and the mutineers).

[2] AGS *E* 553/89, Philip II to Alva, minute, 17 Mar. 1572. At the time the chaplain's pay was 3 *escudos*, like the common soldier's, and Don Sancho de Londoño urged that the rate should be increased (in fact Parma doubled it in 1583) to avoid entrusting the sacraments and the cure of souls to 'a load of idiots and part-timers who seem to form the majority of those who enter the service for 3 *escudos* a month' (Londoño, *Discurso*, p. 8v).

[3] *Cahier Van Der Essen*, xxv, pp. 5 and 25–7 contains copies of documents concerning these gentlemen from the now-destroyed Naples Archive, *Carte Farnesiane, fascio* 1631A. Cf. also J. Schoonjans, 'Castra Dei', in *Miscellanea Historica in Honorem Leonis Van Der Essen* (Louvain, 1947), I, pp. 523–40.

These men were exceptional, however: there was little panache about most Flanders field-chaplains. Most of them, in fact, supplemented their wages (which after 1583 amounted to twice the soldier's basic pay) by forcing dying soldiers to leave them money in their wills. It was all too simple: the chaplain refused to confess the soldier or copy down his will (chaplains were literate and many soldiers were not) unless a considerable legacy was ear-marked for the chaplain's benefit.[1] It would seem that improvements in the type of man who undertook the spiritual care of the soldiers in the Spanish Netherlands only came with the arrival of the Jesuit Thomas Sailly, a veteran of Possevino's mission to Poland, and his companions in 1587. There were about 30 Jesuits permanently attached to the Army in the seventeenth century, men of courage and integrity, closely supervised by the local provincial of the company. They created a dedicated, humane and lasting mission in the Army, the *missio castrensis*.[2]

Ironically, at the same time as this improvement in the calibre of the chaplains, the administration of wills and testaments was taken away from them and entrusted to a new officer appointed by the captain-general, the *depositario general*. From 1596 onwards all clerics were expressly excluded from taking possession of a dead soldier's goods; everything was to be given to the *depositario*.[3] He was responsible for realizing the estate of any man in the Army who died. This was done by public auction, often in Brussels. The *depositario* acted with the executors of the will (if any) and paid all the debts and legacies of the deceased, subtracting 2 per cent of the estate for his own services and 5 per cent for those of the auctioneer.[4] The complete eradication of the malignant practices of the chaplains is demonstrated by the fact that of 226 wills proved before the auditor-general of the Army between May 1604 and April 1606, only eight left any money to a chaplain![5]

1 BNM *Ms.* 5785/86–96, Don Francisco de Bobadilla (*maestre de campo*) to Garcia de Loaysa, the king's confessor, 9 Jul. 1586. Alas there is no obvious way of measuring literacy in the Army: most wills have survived only in copy, usually without a note of whether the soldier signed or only marked his approval. One can only state the obvious and say that clearly a number of common soldiers *could* write their names and even compose a letter, but that a probably greater number could do neither.

2 There were 24 Jesuits paid by Army funds after 1585 (more with the fleet) and 12 Franciscans after 1599 (AGRB *Jésuites, Bruxelles* 1969 and *SEG* 19/139v). There is an interesting study of the activity of the chaplains attached to the fleet of the Spanish Netherlands: E. Hambye, *L'aumônerie de la flotte de Flandre au XVIIᵉ siècle* (Louvain, 1967).

3 BRB *Ms.* 12622–31/201–8, ordinance of the Archduke Albert on military organization, 28 Oct. 1596, clause 4: 'Que ninguna persona ecclesiastica a titulo de capellan, confessor o testamentario se apodere de los bienes de la tal persona militar defunta.'

4 Information from AGRB *Tribunaux Militaires*, 24, 279 and 280.

5 AGRB *Tribunaux Militaires* 22, 'Registro donde se notan y escriven los testamentos que en

The surviving wills of the soldiers of the Army of Flanders reveal a great deal about the quality of the life they led. Among other things, they measure the effect of the government's change of policy from payment in cash to payment largely in kind: of the 226 wills, only six men had anything to leave except the arrears of pay which the government owed them. This was precisely the intention. 'To keep the troops together it is a good thing to owe them something' wrote Ambrosio Spinola; 'It is good to keep them short of money sometimes, in order to make them more obedient and to feed them with hope', echoed a military commentator.[1] By providing the basic necessities of life – bread, clothes and shelter – and by cushioning the men against the accidents of ill-health and capture, the government won a breathing-space in which to assemble enough money to pay an instalment of wages. Subsistence was guaranteed, discontent reduced, obedience preserved. With their bread and a little money from time to time, wrote an inspector-general, the soldiers 'know how to live'.[2]

Yet subsistence alone could not turn a dispirited rabble into an effective

Figure 15. The legatees of soldiers of the Army of Flanders

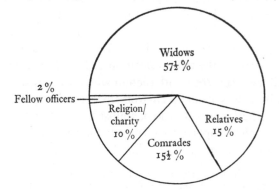

From a register of wills proved in the *auditoría general* of the Army of Flanders, May 1604–April 1606 (AGRB *Tribunaux Militaires* 22). In all, 226 wills were proved; all but six testators had nothing to bequeath except their wage-arrears, and in most cases there was only one beneficiary.

esta Auditoria General se aprovaron y las personas que fueron legitimadas para cobrar sueldo de difunctos' (15 May 1604–Apr. 1606).
[1] AGS *E* 634/74, proposals of Spinola for the reform of the Army of Flanders, 1 Jan. 1605 (p. 2, n. 4): 'para mantener la gente es bien que alcanzen un poco'; cf. p. 162, n. 1 above.
[2] AGS *E* 2028, unfol., *Veedor General* Benavente to the king, 29 May 1614.

fighting force. The 'broken men' who were sent home in the seventeenth century were symptomatic of a grave problem of morale in the Army: life had to be made not only bearable but attractive. The testaments of the soldiers suggest three areas in which they found solace. An analysis of the 226 legatees who claimed the inheritance of a dead soldier between 1604 and 1606 reveals 130 widows, 34 other relatives of the deceased, 39 'comrades' or fellow-soldiers and 39 religious houses, charities or chaplains: the representatives of the soldier's family, his friends and his religion (see Figure 15).

In Lope de Vega's play *Don Juan de Austria en Flandes* the Netherlander Mons. de Prate ordered his daughter to be branded and sold as a slave for having loved a Spanish soldier. Although good for dramatic effect, by the time Lope wrote (1606) relations between the Spaniards and the Netherlanders were in fact less inimical. Many Spanish commanders made an effort to learn French or to refurbish their recollections of the language retained from school.[1] The rank-and-file of the Army rapidly became domesticated, acquiring 'more affection for the Low Countries than for their own homeland'; even the Spaniards were soon calling the Netherlands '*su casa*', their home.[2] After the reconquest of the southern provinces in the 1580s there was an increasing 'compenetration' between Spaniards and Netherlanders: the expatriate troops acquired lands and securities in their new homeland and they adopted Flemish customs and titles. The Netherlanders, for their part, began to learn Spanish and many Spanish words passed into Flemish and Walloon.[3] There was also some intermarriage between the two populations. Of 54 Spaniards and Italians who left a will between 1604 and 1606 in which their widow or 'guardian of their children' was named, 18 women were clearly Spanish, but 34 were clearly Netherlanders, a ratio of almost 1 to 2.[4] Later on in the seventeenth century, the proportions changed. Of 527 marriages of Spanish soldiers celebrated at the garrison church in Antwerp between 1625 and

---

[1] Even an arch-chauvinist like Esteban de Ibarra, who had not found it necessary to learn French in 1568–73 when he was secretary of Don Fadrique de Toledo, struggled to master the language after 1594 (and succeeded): cf. several examples of his improving French style written to Count Hermann van den Bergh, RA Arnhem, *Archief...Berg* 528–30.

[2] Coloma, *Las Guerras* bk XII (*BAE* edn, p. 186) refers to the Spaniards' 'cariño de aquellos estados, a quien tenían mas amor que a sus proprias patrias'; AGS *E* 598/125, Parma to the king, 21 Oct. 1590, noted 'que todas las naciones y en particular la española llama su casa' the Low Countries – Philip II, clearly disturbed by this development, underlined the passage.

[3] Cf. J. Lefèvre, 'La compénétration hispano-belge aux Pays-Bas catholiques pendant le 17e siècle', *RBPH*, XVI (1937), pp. 599–621; on the linguistic question, cf. J. Herbillon, *Éléments espagnols en Wallon et dans le Français des anciens Pays-Bas* (Liège, 1961).

[4] From AGRB *Tribunaux Militaires* 22.

1647, 216 of the brides had Spanish or Italian surnames and 258 had Netherlands surnames, but in fact the figures are somewhat deceptive. We find from the church's marriage register that by far the majority of the Spanish brides were already resident in the Netherlands, many of them born there, while many of the Netherlands brides were actually the daughters of Spanish mothers. A large number of the brides were described as *huius castri filia* (brought up in Antwerp citadel) and several (12 per cent) were widows of some other soldier. These figures testify to the growth, by the mid-seventeenth century, of a self-contained, inward-looking, almost inbred military society in the Spanish Netherlands, independent of the local population.[1]

Marriage was very common in the Army (cf. the data in Appendix I below) despite several government attempts to prohibit or limit the growing number of married men in service (they were thought to be more expensive, more likely to mutiny and more fearful in action).[2] There is a moving passage in Von Grimmelshausen's *Simplicissimus* which describes the uses of a soldier's wife: seamstress, scullion, cook..., anything to turn an honest penny which might augment the soldier's meagre and overdue receipts.[3] On the other hand soldiers begot children, and those born in wedlock had to be supported. The priest of the garrison church of Antwerp baptized 571 children in the decade 1628–37; the garrison numbered only 600, probably under half of them married.[4]

Small wonder then that many soldiers preferred not to marry. For them, and indeed for the rest, the Army regulated the supply and salubrity of the prostitutes who accompanied the troops. Opinions varied, but most commanders agreed that each company of 200 men required between 4 and 8 whores.[5] The comprehensive military orders of 1596 which regu-

---

[1] Stadsarchief Antwerpen, *Parochieregister* 167, 'Registro de los que se baptizan, casan y entierran en esta iglesia parochial de San Phelippe del castillo de Anveres' (1599–1658), ff. 88–145 and 222–46v.

[2] Cf., for example, the disapproval of Cardinal Granvelle (Piot, *Correspondance de...Granvelle*, IV, pp. 581–2, letter to the king, 11 Oct. 1573). The military ordinances of 1632 decreed that only 1 man in 6 was to be allowed to marry (AM Besançon, *Ms. Chifflet* 63/1–26, *Ordenanzas Militares*, 28 Jun. 1632). At a meeting of the Council of State in 1623 Don Fernando Girón, a 'Flanders' veteran, complained that most soldiers there were 'married and burdened with children, and with such troops one can achieve nothing because the women promote mutinies, inciting their husbands to disobedience on account of the necessities they suffer and see their children suffering'. (AGS E 2037/11, *consulta* of the Council of State, 14 Apr. 1623.)

[3] H. J. C. von Grimmelshausen, *Simplicius Simplicissimus*, IV. 7 (Eng. edn, tr. A. T. S. Goodrick (London, 1924), pp. 254–7).

[4] Stadsarchief Antwerpen, *Parochieregister* 167, ff. 4–87v. It would be impossible to apply the 'family reconstitution' method to this parish register because of the frequent moves of the soldiers of the garrison.

[5] There were 5 per company in the Netherlands in the 1550s (AGS E 502/137, Spaniards billeted in Cambrai); 6 per company in 1574 (AGS *CMC* 2a/21, order of Requesens, 12 Jul.

lated the minutest details of the soldier's life were less liberal. With a puritanism perhaps related to his clerical calling, the Cardinal-Archduke Albert decreed that only 3 '*femmes publiques*' per company would be tolerated. They were to be under constant scrutiny both for their means of support and for their 'health and *bodily disposition*' (a sensible precaution with such small numbers). Even then the whores had to ply their trade 'under the disguise of being washerwomen, or something similar, performing a servile task', and they had to be 'of a *competent* age' [*d'age competent*]![1]

Wives and whores formed only part of the enormous host of camp followers who trailed behind the Army of Flanders. And 'such a long tail on such a small body never was seen' remarked three virtuous pastors of Bergen-op-Zoom: 'Such a small army with so many carts, baggage horses, nags, sutlers, lackeys, women, children and a rabble which numbered far more than the Army itself.'[2] This was a pardonable exaggeration, but we have already seen that on the march from Italy to the Netherlands the *bouches* to be fed could be almost double the number of actual soldiers. Likewise in the Netherlands, the garrison of 's Hertogenbosch in 1603 numbered 5,519 persons of whom only 3,000 were soldiers. Even in Lombardy, where military life was more closely regimented, between 35 and 40 camp-followers were considered appropriate for 200 men.[3] Many of these appendages to the Army were the *mozos* – lackeys or batmen who served the soldiers. A captain would have 4 or 5 *mozos* and perhaps 20 or 30 would be attached to individual soldiers of the company, sometimes more: the 5,300 Spanish veterans who left the Netherlands in 1577 were said to be accompanied by 2,000 lackeys.[4]

At most times the Army was also accompanied by a number of sutlers (*vivandiers*) who provided food, equipment or credit to the troops. Army regulations stipulated that there should be only three sutlers per company, but this was often exceeded: the *vivandier* could make large profits. Often

---

1574); 8 in the Army of Lombardy (AS Alessandria, *Alloggiamenti* 4/133, order of the captain-general, 18 Sept. 1559). For literary sources also recommending 8 whores per 100 soldiers, cf. J. Almirante, *Bibliografía militar de España* (Madrid, 1876), p. 446.
[1] BRB *Ms.* 12622-31/177-200v, ordinance of the Archduke Albert on military discipline, 27 May 1596, clause 30.
[2] C. A. Campan (ed.), *Bergues sur le Soom assiégée* (1622; edn Brussels, 1867), p. 247.
[3] Gudde, *Vier eeuwen geschiedenis van het garnizoen 's Hertogenbosch*, p. 29; for a sample of the camp followers who accompanied the marches of the Spaniards, cf. Appendix I, pp. 288-9 below; for Lombardy, AS Alessandria, *Alloggiamenti* 4/133-5v, order of 18 Sep. 1559, and 10/622-3v, Order of (?) Jan. 1584.
[4] Piot, *Correspondance de...Granvelle*, VI, p. 212, Morillon to Granvelle, 22 Apr. 1577. For further information on the *mozos*, cf. M. de Isaba, *Cuerpo enfermo de la Milicia española...* (Madrid, 1594), p. 29v-31, and Londoño, *Discurso*, f. 18v.

the troops acquired booty which they could not carry and they were therefore compelled to sell it cheap to the sutlers for cash; often the personal belongings of soldiers and officers killed in action were auctioned in the camp immediately and the sutler could pick up bargains because officers in the early modern period usually carried their gold and silver, their wardrobes and their other trappings around with them on campaign. Some sutlers indeed did not provide food at all: they followed the Army solely to buy booty and the auctioned goods of the dead.[1]

Many troops, of course, served without wife or servant, without booty or private wealth. For them the informal fellowships or *camaradas* which sprang up between the men of each company were important. There were two distinct types of *camarada* in every Spanish Army, one between the captain and five or six companions, the other between a similar number of the rank-and-file. The comrades lived together (in the same *camara* or chamber), sharing profits and possessions, dangers and misfortunes. These comradeships, as one might expect, were most common amongst the expatriate troops, especially amongst the Spanish infantry. Most of these military exiles appointed their comrades to be executors of their will and in a number of cases they left money to them.[2]

---

[1] Cf. F. Redlich, 'Der Marketender', *Vierteljahrschrift für Sozial- und Wirtschaftlich Geschichte*, XLI (1954), pp. 227–52, and *idem, De Praeda Militari: Looting and booty, 1500–1815* (Wiesbaden, 1956), pp. 48–50, describes the sutler's role in general terms. In Struzzi's toy replica of the Army of Flanders, 'The huts and offices of the sutlers who sell victuals are also much in evidence, with their signs and notice-boards [*insignias y tablillas*] at the doors and with their tables laid out at the disposition of the multitude' (A. Struzzus, *Imago militiae auspiciis Ambrosii Spinolae* (Brussels, 1614), unpaginated). For one example of what a captain took with him to the front, cf. AGRB *Tribunaux Militaires* 24 (2), auction of the goods of Captain Hieronimo de Ysla, 25–6 Apr. 1596, at the camp before Calais. His clothes alone fetched 60 *escudos*, his horse and cart 112 (bought by a *vivandier*), his two horses 75 *escudos*; the captain's 38 ounces of silver went for 34 *escudos*, his gold chain for 277. He had 227 *escudos* with him in cash. In addition the captain had property worth 33 *escudos* in Brussels and 300 more in a bank; he was entitled to considerable wage-arrears but he 'pardoned' the king 500 *escudos* of this 'for a similar sum which I owe him' (acquired falsely by cheating at the musters?). The total estate of the captain, who came from a well-known but poor *hidalgo* family, was almost 1,200 *escudos* plus pay-arrears!

[2] The best descriptions of the *camarada* are by two French writers: De Vigenère, *L'Art militaire*, p. 149v–150, and F. de la Noue, *Discourses politiques et militaires*, discours 16. 'Comradeships' were also found in the English Army (Cruickshank, *Elizabeth's Army*, pp. 142 and 194). In Sweden the crew of the wrecked warship *Vasa* appear to have had comradeships too: small casks were found on the wreck containing two wooden bowls, a wooden jug (for beer) and seven spoons. The idea was developed furthest in the Spanish Army, however. Although in 1574 a new captain-general found that the Spaniards in the Netherlands 'no tienen la orden de camaradas que en otras tierras solían' (AGS *E* 560/142, Requesens to the king, 8 Jul. 1574), we find that the 18 Spaniards of the Dunkirk garrison who died around 1590 appointed between them 39 executors, of whom 22 were comrades (AGS *CMC* 2a/76, second bundle, containing 18 original testaments). Likewise of the 133 Spaniards and Italians whose wills were proved in 1604–6, 28 (21 per cent) left money to their comrade

The idea of comradeships also helped to foster a sense of unit awareness. The nicknames given to the Spanish *tercios* in the Netherlands – the '*tercio* of the dandies', 'of the sextons' and so on – reflect a sense of pride and of corporate solidarity. When the *tercio viejo de Lombardia*, a unit which had served for twenty years in 'Flanders', was broken up in 1589 as a punishment for insubordination, it caused genuine regret throughout the Army because of the unit's high morale, professional skill and seasoned courage.[1] Beyond a feeling of pride in their regiment, many of the troops in the Army had a loyalty to their 'nation'. This was particularly true of the Spaniards: they were often referred to by the Netherlanders as 'ceux de la Nation'. Foreign service, and in particular service among the 'heretics and rebels' of the Low Countries, brought out the Spaniards' feeling of innate national superiority. They were the elite troops, the *übermensch*, the chosen people. In April 1574, the captain-general himself pandered to this latent chauvinism in one of his grovelling appeals for a return to obedience during the mutiny of the Spanish infantry at Antwerp:

> Remember, gentlemen, that you are Spaniards, and that your King and natural lord is today the sole defender of the Catholic religion which, for our sins, is persecuted and molested throughout most of the world, and you should esteem it highly that God has chosen you to be His instrument to remedy this situation....[2]

Patriotism linked with a sense of religious mission: it was a potent formula. The fact that this particular appeal did little to bring the Spanish mutineers back to their duty should not be taken to mean that neither emotion counted among the troops.

The crabbed nun who chronicled the Spaniards' residence in 's Hertogenbosch after 1568 listed every crime which could reasonably be imputed to the soldiers, but she had to admit that 'they had great respect for the Holy Sacrament and they were devout in the churches and they favoured the clergy and did them no harm'.[3] The Army of Flanders was always referred to as 'the Catholic Army'; it was the army of the 'Catholic King'. In 1589 a 'Confraternity of the Holy Sacrament' was established among the soldiers by papal bull, and other religious gilds for the troops soon developed, particularly in the garrison towns.[4] Enemies were always

(AGRB *Tribunaux Militaires* 22). Cf. finally the remarks and quotations of F. Picatoste y Rodríguez, *Estudios sobre la grandeza y decadencia de España: los españoles en Italia* (Madrid, 1887), II, pp. 24–5.

[1] Cf. the lament of Coloma, *Las Guerras*, bk II (*BAE* edn, p. 20) and also pp. 220–1 below. On the names of the *tercios*, cf. the fascinating details narrated by Alonso Vazquez, *Los Sucesos* (*Co.Do.In.* LXXIII), pp. 322–4.

[2] *Nueva Co.Do.In*, II, pp. 197–9, copy of Requesens' address of 24 April 1574.

[3] Quoted Gudde, *Vier Eeuwen*, pp. 21–3.

[4] The original bull of Sixtus V establishing the *Confraternitas Santissimi Sacramenti inter milites*

surprised when they saw the number of religious effigies, crucifixes, *Agnus Dei* and other charms carried by the Spaniards who died in action; the legacies of many soldiers to the fraternities and monasteries which they patronized and the money they left to be spent on good works and distributed in alms testifies to at least a death-bed piety.[1] The soldier had to live with the daily risk of a violent, sudden death; it is no surprise that he kept an anxious eye on his chances of gaining the comfortable after-life which his Church taught him to expect. Charity and piety among the troops were in fact associated overwhelmingly with the fear of death. At other times they behaved like brutes.

From the moment the Spaniards first entered the Netherlands in August 1567 they acted 'as if they were in enemy territory, beginning to live at discretion', and they continued on their way 'confiscating everything, rightly, wrongly, saying that everyone is a heretic, that they have wealth and ought to lose it'.[2] Even in the seventeenth century, when the foreign troops were more domesticated, countless cases of rape, murder, robbery and arson were committed by the soldiers. The brutality of the Spanish troops in 'Flanders' became so legendary that it even gave rise to a proverb in Spain: '¿ Estamos aquí o en Flandes?' (Are we here or in the Netherlands?) – meaning 'Is that a proper way to behave'. The

is in AGRB *Jésuites, Bruxelles* 1966; on the *Confrérie de la Sainte-Barbe* for the artillery in Mechelen, cf. *Jésuites, Bruxelles* 1965. There was a *Confradía de Nuestra Señora del Rosario* in most garrison towns with Spanish troops; the chief chapel of the Confraternity, at Brussels, received a grant of 250 florins per month from the *pagaduría* from 1627 onwards (AGRB *SEG* 53/58-vo, order of 25 Mar. 1656).

[1] The Protestant pastors who chronicled the Spanish siege of Bergen-op-Zoom remarked on the number of icons carried by the besiegers (Campan, *Bergues sur le Soom*, p. 215–16). For the legacies, cf. 18 Spanish soldiers who died in Dunkirk between 1588 and 1596, leaving total wage arrears of 5,862 florins; of this total, 316 f. were left to the Confraternity of the Rosary in Dunkirk, 588 f. to a Franciscan monastery in the town, and 1,447 f. in alms to the poor or for good works – a total charitable donation of 2,351 florins or 41 per cent of the total (AGS *CMC* 2a/76, second bundle). Cf. also the legacies to charity and the church in Figure 15 on p. 173 above. But there were exceptions, even as doom approached, to this picture of death-bed generosity and pious resignation. The unrepentant soldier Bartolomé Cedrellas had few regrets for his past life; his last will and testament of 21 Sep. 1593 included the clause: 'Item, I state and declare that I have had in my power a woman called Maria, with whom I had sexual relations, and she says she is pregnant by me. If it turns out to be as she says, it is my wish that the child which may be born [*lo que ansi pariere*] should have and inherit all my goods...but it must be clear that the first time I had carnal knowledge of her was St Peter's day last year, and when she gives birth account is to be taken of whether the time is consistent with the aforesaid.' If it was, the child of Cedrellas was to inherit; if not, the money (192 florins) was to go not to Maria but to the Franciscan monastery and the Confraternity of the Rosary in Dunkirk (AGS *CMC* 2a/76).

[2] AGS *E K* 1508/46, archbishop of Cambrai to Don Frances de Alava, 16 Aug. 1567 (copy); L. P. Gachard, *Correspondance de Philippe II*, 1 (Brussels, 1848), p. 565, Jean de Hornes to Arnold Munten, 25 Aug. 1567; and *Co.Do.In.* XXXVII, pp. 17–21, Alva to the king, 8 Aug. 1567.

garrisons of the Spanish Netherlands, concentrations of bored, impoverished but well-armed young men, inevitably formed a pool of lawlessness, of gambling and vice, crime and cruelty, lechery and licence in the centre of every community. The increasing resort to criminals as a source of recruits can only have accentuated the innate unruliness of the troops, especially when the men were lodged in overcrowded private houses away from the supervision of their officers. The soldiers soon came to exhibit the same *picaresque* values which invaded Spanish society in the late sixteenth century: idleness, brutality and bravado, the thirst for gambling, the urge for falsification. The remarkable diffusion of the cult of the *pícaro* in seventeenth-century Spain no doubt owed something to the deserters and mutineers who returned from the wars in increasing numbers after 1590, their pockets filled with gold, their minds full of the dissolute ideas they had imbibed in the Army. Although not to be compared with the *Indianos* and *Peruleros*, those entrepreneurs who returned to spend in Spain the fortune they had made in the New World, many 'Flanders' veterans came back to Spain far richer than they had left. They certainly returned with a distinctive ideology, and they returned to a Spain which was already questioning its values, doubting its standards, losing its purpose. It was hard for a society in flux to absorb large numbers of men who had become habituated to lawlessness and easy living. The soldiers paraded their parasitic way of life with impunity and thereby encouraged others to emulate them. The domestic *pícaro* of Spain's 'Golden Century' was step-son to the military *pícaro* of the last years of Philip II.[1]

Both in military and civil life the development of the *pícaro* was stimulated by the basic injustice of life. Existence seemed to oscillate interminably between great riches and destitution. Poverty one day, plunder or pay the next: the choice was dictated by events far beyond the individual's control.[2] In the Army of Flanders, for all the humanitarian reforms of the high command, life was all too often 'nasty, brutish and short'. Take the case of the *tercio* of Don Antonio Manrique, 2,000 Castilian recruits raised in the spring of 1586 and sent direct to the Netherlands overland along the Spanish Road. After a long galley voyage

[1] On the *pícaro* phenomenon, cf. the lucid pages of Bennassar, *Valladolid au Siècle d'Or*, pp. 548–55.
[2] The famous manifesto of reform by M. González de Cellorigo, *Memorial de la politica necessaria y util restauración a la Republica de España* (Valladolid, 1600), also highlighted the polarization of Castilian society into very rich and very poor, with the consequent loss of the 'middle people' (f. 56–56v). It is my argument that both in the Army of Flanders and in Castile this development encouraged the rise of the *pícaro*.

from Catalonia to Genoa (which proved to be the death of many) the survivors arrived in Luxemburg in December and at once unslung the guitars they had brought with them. They danced and sang throughout the winter, to the disgust of the veteran troops who never 'danced and whirled, an indecent thing in war, except with Flemish ladies'. The recruits were therefore christened 'Tercio de la Zarabanda' (Regiment of the Saraband), living 'as if they were in Spain. But they very soon forgot the tunes and dances because the trials and miseries which befell them in the Low Countries gave them no more time for such diversion'.[1] The harvests of 1587 and 1588 were disastrous all over northern Europe. The new recruits who had enlisted in the hope of invading England either starved in the worst famine of the century or else learned to '*garbear*', to scrounge and to plunder, in order to survive. The pattern was typical: these troops were paid scarcely anything until 1590–1. Another band of *picaros*, of disillusioned, amoral scavengers, was born.

On the one hand life in the Army of Flanders offered destitution; but on the other there was the chance of vast riches. Against the possibility of losing life, limb or liberty, the soldier might capture a rich prisoner or take some fine booty. Any successful siege profited the soldier: if the town was taken by assault it was sacked and he got plunder; if it surrendered on terms the troops of the siege-army normally received 'storm-money' in lieu of plunder.[2] Such windfalls were rare, however. Most of the time the soldier lived on credit. He and his friends were usually strong enough to coerce shopkeepers to provide food and drink on credit: if the military treasury failed to pay him, he too refused to pay his bills. When he did receive his wages he might escape to another garrison, even flee the country, before his creditors realized what had happened.[3]

---

[1] Vazquez, *Los Sucesos* (*Co.Do.In.* LXXIII), p. 323. I believe the passage refers to male dancing (still current in Greece and parts of southern Spain). Worse still than the experience of Manrique's volunteers was that of the *tercio* of Don Antonio de Zúñiga, also recruited expressly for the invasion of England, which marched along the Spanish Road in 1587. The duke of Parma told the king: 'They came not only without arms but also without clothes and they were badly treated. It is a shame to see them. So bad are they that I don't believe that such misery has ever been seen in the Spanish nation, which makes me ashamed, not just on compassionate grounds but that soldiers of Your Majesty and 'of the nation' should have been seen by people along their route so broken and ill-treated...' (AGS *E* 592/141, Parma to the king, 14 Nov. 1587.)

[2] On booty, cf. F. Redlich, *De Praeda Militari: looting and booty 1500–1815* (Wiesbaden, 1956). On the conditions under which a town could and could not be legitimately plundered in the sixteenth century, cf. the series of articles by L. Van Der Essen, 'Kritische studie over de oologsvoering van het Spaanse leger in de Nederlanden tijdens de XVIe eeuw, nl. de bestraffing van opstandige steden, *Mededelingen van de Koninklijke Vlaamse Academie...Letteren*, XII (1950), XIV (1954), XV (1955), XVII–XXII (1955–60) – nine instalments. Of course when the Army of Flanders was on the defensive there could be no plunder.

[3] Cf. Gemeente Archief, Breda, nr. 239/35 and 43, 'Schulden van de Spaengnaerden' (31,119

However, it was the settlement of accounts which was always the major event in the soldier's budget. The shorter the rein on which the men were kept over the years, the larger the final sum (the *alcance* or *remate*) due to them. There were only 4,305 Spanish veterans in the Netherlands by September 1585, but they were paid a total of 810,511 florins after the surrender of Antwerp – their arrears in full. This represented an average of 200 florins per man for three years' service.[1] At the next major settlements of accounts, in the 1590s, payments sometimes averaged double this sum: 125 cavalry troopers at La Chapelle were paid 27,668 *escudos* of 50 pattards in 1596, an average of 532 florins per man; 126 Spanish infantrymen at St Pol in 1594 received arrears of 27,363 *escudos*, or 542 florins per man; 8 men paid at Diest in 1601 received individual letters of exchange (payable in Spain) for their arrears worth a total of 4,609 *escudos*, an average of 1,240 florins per man. Staggering as this aggregate total was, it conceals even greater individual *alcances*: of the 8 soldiers at Diest, 1 received 2,375 florins, a second 2,500 florins, another 2,990 florins...These men became rich overnight, and their fortune was transferred (by letter of exchange) directly to Spain.[2]

Naturally the maximum profit from military service was achieved by combining these three sources of enrichment: plunder, pay-arrears and broken credit. The classic case occurred in 1577. The Spanish veterans had suffered appallingly in the Low Countries' Wars since 1572, but there had been good plunder now and again, notably the sack of Mechelen (1572) and Antwerp (1576). Then came the revolution of the southern provinces after August 1576 which forced the Spaniards to escape from their billets – and from their debts. When they were finally paid in Maastricht in April 1577 all their obligations to the Netherlanders, who were in overt rebellion, were forgotten. The settlement of the veterans' arrears came to 1,234,293 florins which, shared between the 5,334 survivors of the wars, averaged 231 florins per man. In fact most of this was transferred to Italy and Spain by letters of exchange; it was therefore just baggage and plunder which bowed the backs of the 15 asses, 118 small mules and 365 large mules hired to carry the troops' effects across the Alps into Lombardy. The expedition's combined baggage weighed 2,600 tons, or

florins owed to various townsmen of Breda by the Spanish garrison 1567–77 and never repaid) and nr. 409/A2 and C1 (original certificates of the Spanish muster commissioners for services and fodder provided to the light cavalry, deducted from the troopers' pay and repayable – but never actually repaid – by the government: 6,369 thalers of 32 pattards, or 10,190 florins).

[1] AGS *CMC* 1a/1726, 'Datta' of Juan de Lastur to the Spanish infantry; AGS *E* 590/7 and 47, muster of the veterans.

[2] Figures from AGS *CMC* 2a/3 (Mutiny of La Chapelle), 2a/47 (Mutiny of St Pol); and AGS *E* 619/7. For a wider sample of *remates*, cf. Appendix J.

half-a-ton per man. Every soldier was on horseback. It did indeed re-semble, as a somewhat pretentious clerk put it, 'Israel's exodus from Egypt'.[1]

It is important to see military life in perspective. The soldier was cer-tainly in constant danger and almost constant discomfort. He was 'pushed on like a sheep to the slaughter, driven with blows to charge under cannon fire and to labour at siege-works with no other wage than a measly ration of bread'.[2] But at least that daily bread was guaranteed, and at least his wage was assured by the month, not by the day. It was moreover, free of seigneurial dues, tithes and taxes.[3] No day-labourer, whether artisan or agricultural worker, enjoyed advantages like those! Finally, if the soldier survived to collect his plunder and pay he was rich. Many ordinary volunteers, poor men when they enlisted, left the Army with 1,000 ducats in their purse and, in rural Castile at least, a man with 1,000 ducats to his name was rich, one of the *villanos ricos* (rich peasants) who ruled their village.[4] Sudden wealth followed years of miserable subsis-tence; the paradox of the picaresque life of the Army of Flanders was complete.

There was, however, a catch. The soldier's claim to his arrears of pay was incontrovertible: his problem was to collect it. The only legitimate way of collecting his just reward was to secure a discharge from the king's service. Unfortunately the Army had no short-term enlistment: a man agreed to serve until he was demobilized, which meant either until he was hopelessly injured or until the war ended – which, in the Nether-lands, might take thirty years. Of course men could always desert, especially after the sack of an enemy town which yielded booty. After the sack of Mechelen in 1572, for example, 'most of the troops in the camp

---

[1] For the *fenecimiento de cuentas* of 1577 – 632,971 *escudos* of 39 pattards – cf. p. 225. On the baggage, AS Milano, *Militare* PA 165bis, unfol., 'Rotullo delli mulli venuti da Chiamberi' (1577 – this document was generously put at my disposal by Prof. D. Sella). The actual weight of baggage was 9,017 *rubbi* of 640 lb. The Biblical reference is from AGS *E* 573/218, Geronimo de Roda to Gabriel de Zayas, 28 Mar. 1577. In fact the Antwerp magistrates tried unsuccessfully to stop anyone giving the Spaniards exchange facilities 'in order to avoid the transportation of looted and pillaged goods and merchandise from the city' but the measure had to be dropped. (Gachard, *Correspondance de Philippe II*, v (Brussels, 1879), p. 551 and note.)

[2] Campan, *Bergues sur le Soom*, pp. 321–2, complaint of some Spanish deserters.

[3] For the significance of this, cf. Salomon, *La Campagne de Nouvelle Castille*, pp. 213–51, estimating that 50 per cent of each peasant's income 'went to enrich the non-peasant classes' (p. 250).

[4] Salomon, *ibid.*, p. 276.

went home, fully realizing that the plunder was their pay.[1] Men could desert with their booty, but they forfeited their wages. In fact the only way by which the soldiers could force the government to pay outstanding wage-arrears before the end of the war was by coordinated, purposeful strike-action – by mutiny. With wars lasting thirty years and upwards the troops had ample opportunity to perfect techniques of collective bargaining.

Mutiny, desertion, demobilization: thanks to the inadequate resources of the Spanish Monarchy it was only in these circumstances that the troops could procure their just deserts, only thus that they could become rich. The rest of the time they suffered in silence, serving on bread and patience, *pan y paciencia*. But the balance was fragile, the tolerance narrow. When either of these vital commodities failed, the constant fatigues, tensions and hardships of life in the Army of Flanders were bound to produce a violent reaction.

[1] Didier, *Lettres et Négociations de Claude de Mondoucet*, pp. 87–90, letter to Charles IX, 8 Nov. 1572.

CHAPTER 8

MUTINY

I was forgetting to tell you a dreadful and most unworthy thing that His Excellency [Requesens] said to me: he insisted that it was not the prince of Orange who had lost the Low Countries, but the soldiers born in Valladolid and Toledo, because the mutineers had driven money out of Antwerp and destroyed all credit and reputation, and he believed that within eight days His Majesty would not have anything left here...It was a speech of almost three hours.[1]

Don Luis de Requesens, who had a habit of crying over his spilt milk and had many occasions for doing so, was absolutely right. The mutinies of the Army of Flanders spelt financial and military disaster for Spain. Time and again the outbreak of a major military revolt paralysed the Army for a whole campaign, sabotaging any offensive, jeopardizing the security of loyal but vulnerable towns. The mutiny which provoked Requesens to speak ill of his nation, the mutiny of Antwerp in 1574, was no unique or isolated event. Between 1572 and 1607 there were over 45 mutinies in the Army of Flanders; at least 21 of them occurred after 1596, many of them lasted a year or more (cf. Appendix J). This frequency of organized disobedience, unparalleled in other armies, requires explanation. Why did the mutinies break out so often? Why did they last so long?

In the first place there were the unpleasant facts of military life: 'The cold of the sentry-go, the danger of the assaults, the horror of the battles, the hunger of the sieges, the destruction of the mines.' Even if he was lucky enough not to be involved in action, the soldier of the Army of Flanders was never far from necessity. Many commanders were astounded at the endurance of their men who 'resisted the enemy's attacks with an empty belly'. The great mutiny of Hoogstraten, the longest of the war, broke out in 1602 at a time of acute shortage. 'It is still incredible how our soldiers survived,' wrote one of their officers many years later.[2] Indeed both the main cycles of mutiny, 1573–6 and

[1] AA 33/156, Hernando Delgadillo to Juan de Albornoz, 9 Jul. 1574.
[2] Cervantes, *Novelas Ejemplares – el Licenciado Vidriera* (Clásicos Castellanos edn, pp. 14–16); RA Arnhem, *Archief...Berg* 530, unfol., Count Herman van den Berg to Count Fuentes, 24 Jun. 1595; C.-A. de Croy, *Mémoires guerriers* (Antwerp, 1642), p. 70.

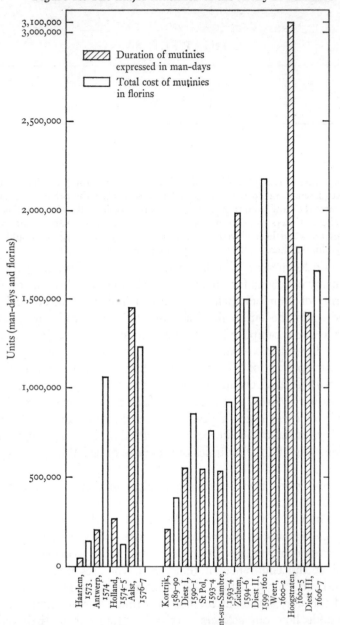

Figure 16. The major mutinies of the Army of Flanders

The gravity of a number of Flanders mutinies measured by the cost of settling them and by the number of 'fighting days' lost to the Army. The 'man-days' are simply the product of the number of men involved multiplied by the number of days taken up by the mutiny. The inexorable increase in both the cost and duration of the mutinies is apparent.

Source: Appendix J.

1589–1607, coincided with prolonged *crises des subsistances* in the Low Countries; the effects of the famine prices on the army were intensified by the serious delays in the payment of the troops' wages. Conditions were particularly serious for the expatriate troops, for the soldiers brought to the Netherlands from the British Isles, from Burgundy, the empire, Spain and Italy. Far from their homes, it was harder for them to escape the hardships of their profession; cantonned amid a hostile population they had almost as much to fear from the civilians as from the enemy. Throughout the sixteenth century the rigours of military expatriation spurred the troops on foreign service, and particularly the Germans and the Spaniards, to collective disobedience in order to improve their lot.

The military revolts which became so familiar in the early modern period were unique. They were not simply *émeutes sans lendemain* nor were they just strikes, although they shared certain characteristics with both. Like the *émeutes* they were essentially the product of misery, born of the constant danger, discomfort and destitution of everyday life; like the *émeutes*, the actual provocation of the mutiny might be trivial – rumours of a new campaign without pay, an insult from an unpopular officer, the accidental break-down of the food supply. It might even be the soldiers' wives who incited their husbands to disobedience.[1] Once disillusion set in, little was needed to turn passive discontent into active revolt: 'Upon men who are depressed by the ruin of the hopes they had founded on the last offensive, exhausted by...years of war, small incidents have large effects.'[2] Here, however, the military revolt departed from the pattern of the spontaneous peasant uprising. Once resolved on disobedience, the mutineers organized themselves with considerable sophistication in order to achieve their objectives. They elected leaders to govern them, followed a rational and orderly plan, and concentrated their efforts on limited and attainable goals. When the Germans mutinied, the *gemeinde* (community) of all the soldiers elected an *ambosat* (representative) to negotiate with the high command; with the Spanish troops (emulated in due course by the other 'nations' in the Army) the rank-and-file (*el escuadrón*) delegated absolute authority to an elected leader (the *electo*) with an elective council to advise him. The mutinies of the Army of Flanders, which became virtually an institution of military life, form

[1] Cf. p. 175, n. 2.
[2] The words of an observer of the French Army in April 1917, on the eve of a series of important mutinies. These have been studied meticulously by G. Pedroncini, *Les mutineries de 1917* (Paris, 1967) – cf. p. 94 for the quotation – and they present an interesting parallel to the mutinies of the Army of Flanders.

one of the earliest chapters in the history of collective bargaining in Europe.

* * *

Often unrest came into the open among one section of a regiment before the rest – the lowest-paid men, the *picas secas* (pike-men without body-armour) and the arquebusiers, formed a sort of military proletariat which was especially prone to disorder – but success depended on unity. Once a group had decided to mutiny they had to convince all their comrades to join in. This was the crucial stage of any mutiny. In his description of the mutiny of the *tercio viejo* in 1589, which began with the pike-men, Don Carlos Coloma put the crisis of the movement at the point where 'With every minute arquebusiers and musketeers were passing over to the side of the seditious troops, so the matter was on the point of becoming very serious.' The *maestre de campo* and his officers arrived at this moment and with their bravery and sound sense they managed to isolate the leaders of the unrest and then persuaded everyone to give up their attempt.[1]

Few mutinies were quelled so easily. In most cases the majority of the troops in a regiment or garrison rallied to the standard of sedition, and then the mutineers could expel all officers and any others who would not join them on an equal footing. If chaplains, drummers and even lieutenants wished to participate in a mutiny they did so on the same level as the poorest pike-man. The whole community of the mutineers then assembled and elected democratically their *electo* (leader), a council to advise him (anything between three and eight soldiers) and a secretary to write his commands and handle his correspondence. The *electo* ruled his troops with absolute authority. There was no appeal from his orders; discipline was maintained with an iron hand; all disobedience was

---

[1] C. Coloma, *Las Guerras de los Estados Bajos*, bk II (*BAE* edn, p. 19); A. Vazquez, *Los sucesos de Flandes y Francia* (*Co.Do.In.* LXXIII, 414–19). In the mutiny of the *tercio* of Italy in 1574–5 the 'shot' were for precipitate action and the pike-men and halbardiers resisted for a time (AGS E 560/39, '*Copia de cartas*', letter of P. de Paz, 24 Nov. 1574). These divisions between the various groups might reappear at any time during a mutiny. For instance the mutiny of Kortrijk in 1590 was ended by a violent split between pike-men and 'shot' over whether or not to accept the terms offered by the government. 'The arquebusiers and musketeers replied that they should accept and the pike-men said no, and on the question of whether to take it or leave it they divided into rival camps in the town square and battle commenced between them.' Hostilities were only averted when an enterprising and courageous chaplain appeared bearing the Holy Sacrament and slowly moved between them. The troops fell on their knees and the pike-men swallowed their pride and accepted the offer. (AGS E 598/82, Parma to the king, 26 Jun. 1590; A. Carnero, *Historia*, pp. 241–2).

punished with instant death. As Bentivoglio wrote in his famous description of the 'Flanders mutinies': 'Never has disobedience been seen which produced greater obedience.'[1]

After electing their leaders the mutineers made haste to defend themselves. Garrisons which revolted were, of course, already safe behind the walls they were supposed to defend, but when detachments of the field army mutinied they had to capture a fortified town themselves, often by persuading its garrison to mutiny and let them in. If this went well, the mutineers set about securing an income and formulating their grievances. For armed, mounted veterans with a strong walled town to defend them, it was easy enough to raise a living from the defenceless villages of the neighbourhood. The mutineers of Zichem in 1594 raised contributions over a radius of 50 miles, even from villages under the walls of Brussels, the seat of government. Those of Hoogstraten in 1602–5 levied contributions from as far afield as Trier, Aachen, Luxemburg and Lorraine; in May 1604 they passed through Hainaut on a prolonged *chevauchée* with their own artillery train in order to collect contributions more effectively and to impress the government with their strength.[2] Resistance to determined men like these was hopeless. When the depredations of the mutineers of Diest in 1591 provoked the townsmen of St Truiden to raise a sort of Home Guard for their defence, the mutinied veterans did not rest until they had hunted down and annihilated the makeshift militia in pitched battle.[3]

The fury of the mutineers could be directed against their elected leaders as well as against outsiders. The *escuadrón*, the corporate body of

[1] Guido Bentivoglio, *The history of the wars of Flanders*, I, viii (Eng. edn, London, 1678, pp. 109–10), an excellent description of the structure of the Flanders mutinies. The account which follows is based on the Army's own records concerning the mutinies; these are, happily, particularly rich for the major military revolts of Antwerp (1574), Holland (1575), Zichem (1594–6) and Hoogstraten (1602–5).

[2] AGRB *MD* 206/46 and 50, Archduke Albert to Count Mansfelt, Feb. 1603; M.-A. Arnould, 'Une requête inédite des habitants de Gosselies aux Archiducs', in *Etudes d'Histoire et d'Archéologie Namuroises dediées à F. Courtoy* (Gembloux, 1952), pp. 705–10. The small village of Gosselies was compelled to pay 600 florins *brandschatting* at once and 100 florins in contributions every month. For further first-hand information on this mutiny, cf. Croy, *Mémoires guerriers*. Croy served as the mutineers' hostage for eleven months; and A. Louant, *Correspondance d'Ottavio Mirto Frangipani, premier nonce de Flandre (1596–1606)*, III (Wetteren, 1942), pp. 797–856, Frangipani's correspondence with the mutineers in 1602–3 (28 letters).

[3] Carnero, *Historia*, pp. 253–4. The mutineers of Weert in 1601 threatened to attack even regular troops who approached 'their territory' – the villages from which they raised contributions. They warned a government commander: 'Our intention is to ensure with all our power that neither the troops of His Majesty, nor of the Archdukes nor of the enemy shall enter our territory.' (RA Arnhem, *Archief. . .Berg*, 536, unfol., *Eletto et Consiglio* of Weert to Count Herman van den Berg, 7 and 9 Aug. 1601.)

the mutineers, always retained ultimate control over at least their 'foreign policy'. No overture or offer could be made to the government without the consent of all. An *electo*, or any other mutineer, who negotiated with the government or the enemy on his own initiative was shot.[1] Normally individual mutineers made their wishes known to the *electo* and his council by posting up a fly-sheet or *cartel* in some public place. The *carteles* of the mutineers of Antwerp in 1574 were read out in public by the sergeant of the guard, posted for a day on the guardhouse door, and only at sunset taken to the *electo*; in the mutiny of the *tercio* of Italy also in 1574 all the soldiers' fly-sheets were nailed to a certain 'Tree of Justice' before going to the *electo*.[2]

Once the mutineers reached a consensus of opinion about the conditions under which they were prepared to return to obedience, 'talks about talks' could be initiated. Sometimes a personage respected by both sides (a gentleman-ranker was ideal) would hold a conference (*parlamento*) with the *electo* (or with the whole body of the mutineers, depending on the relative power of each) and then report back to the government. Alternatively the *electo* or *escuadrón* might negotiate directly with the government by letter.[3] In either case, the aim of both sides was to set the mutineers' grievances down on paper in an articulate form, normally a sort of Magna Carta of petitions to be answered by the captain-general.

The requests were fairly predictable. First, inevitably, came the demand for payment in full of all wage-arrears due to the mutineers and to their dead comrades.[4] Next came security: the mutineers demanded a full pardon (with guarantees) for their actions and passports for their leaders

---

[1] The first *electo* of the mutiny of the *tercio* of Italy in 1574, Diego Sanchez de Bahamonde, was shot for his pro-government stand (AGS *E* 562/14, 'Lo que en substancia resulta de todas las cartas'), while the mutineers of Antwerp earlier in the same year threatened to shoot their *electo* and council unless a settlement with the government were quickly made (IVdeDJ 67/311a, copy of the mutineers' *billete* to their *electo*, 6 May 1574).

[2] Copies of a number of *carteles* of the Antwerp mutiny of 1574 – fascinating documents – are in AGS *E* 558/41, 42, 44, 45, 48 and 50 and IVdeDJ 67/311–12 and 315–17. The 'arbol de la justicia' is mentioned in the letters of *Electo* Diego Sanchez to F. de Valdes, 18 and 23 Nov. 1574 (AGS *E* 560/39, 'Copia de cartas del Maestre de Campo Valdes').

[3] The mutineers of Antwerp citadel in 1598–9 began all their correspondence: 'El esquadrón ha determinado que...' (The community of the soldiers has decided that...) and signed 'Nos los soldados'. (Cf. AGS *CMC* 2a/73, Settlement of the Mutiny of Antwerp.) Most mutineers delegated more power to their leader and letters were normally signed by the *electo* alone – 'Yo el Electo' (I the *Electo*), an incredibly pompous formula since it was, at other times, the exclusive style of the Spanish royal family ('Yo el Rey' etc.). The mutineers of the *tercio* of Italy in 1574 even imitated the style of the king's secretaries: the secretary of the mutiny – who possessed a very fine italic hand – countersigned all letters 'Por mandado de los señores soldados, electo y consejo, Alonso Velasquez, secretario'.

[4] 'All, all, all' was the terse slogan adopted by the Spanish veterans who mutinied at Mook immediately after their victory over Louis of Nassau. It was expanded in a *cartel* of the soldier

and anyone else who wished to leave the Low Countries after payment. A third invariable petition was for a 'general muster' at which every soldier could choose the unit in which he wished to serve, whether infantry or cavalry. This concession enabled a man to escape from the tyranny of a malevolent officer or sergeant. Finally there might be specific grievances. In the two mutinies of 1574 the Spanish veterans demanded a military hospital to care for the wounded, a magazine to supply them with food at a price they could afford, and a surgeon and a chaplain for each company. They asked that no soldier should be given corporal punishment without due trial and that any officer who drew his dagger and stabbed a soldier in anger should stand trial for assault.[1] These and other similar petitions were sent to the captain-general for consideration. If he was able to offer satisfaction on all the major points the settlement of the mutiny became a merely practical matter: how and when the troops could be paid. With a small revolt, involving arrears of 200,000 florins or less, payment could usually be made without much delay, but larger mutinies were more difficult. Often a special provision was required from Spain and, since this might take some months to arrive, an interim settlement was advisable. In these cases the government accepted the mutineers' petitions, promised them redress and payment in full, and meanwhile guaranteed them a regular monthly payment (called the *sustento*) from the military treasury with an inland town of little strategic importance to serve as a refuge. In return the mutineers were required to cease collecting their own contributions from the countryside; they were to evacuate the town they had taken; and they had to act as the official garrison of the new town granted them by the government. Above all the *sustento* obliged the mutineers to participate in the regular campaigns of the Army if urgent need arose. Although the cumulative cost of the monthly *sustento* was enormous – in a long mutiny it could amount to as much again as the total of the arrears themselves – the mutineers were often the Army's most experienced veterans and their intervention in a campaign could tilt the balance between success and failure.[2]

'Pie de palo' (Peg-leg?) who reminded his comrades: 'I beg you, gentlemen, not to forget those four letters which we made our own at Mook the day we defeated Count Louis: *Todo, todo, todo y muertos y servicios*' [All, all, all and pay for the dead and our contribution-money]. Another anonymous *cartel* of the same mutiny also concluded with the rousing catch-phrase of Mook: 'Let us say with a loud voice that four-letter word which sounds so sweet in the ears of poor soldiers who have served so well: *Todo, todo, todo*' [all, all, all] – AGS *E* 558/41, and 45, copies of the *carteles*.

[1] AGS *E* 558/51, articles agreed with the mutineers of Antwerp, 23 May 1574, arts 4, 10, 12 and 14.

[2] The mutineers of La Chapelle in 1596 led the relief force which raised the French siege of

The mutineers were skilful professionals – that was their greatest asset. In the end the government always needed to buy back their allegiance. After the petition of grievances had been accepted, the officials of the accounts department (*contaduría del sueldo*) were admitted to the mutineers' stronghold. First they identified the men present and the companies to which they belonged, then they returned to their offices to labour over the wage-sheets (*pliegos de asiento*) of each company until they established the government's debt to each man. The total wages owing to each mutineer was calculated and set against the clothes, food and money already supplied. Normally every company with some of its soldiers in the mutiny was paid in full, loyal troops and mutineers alike, to keep the unit on the same footing and to avoid giving the impression that only the disobedient were rewarded.

When an account-sheet had been prepared for each man the mutineers were notified of the result and asked for their comments. Two or three of the oldest soldiers in each company would be deputed by the rest to declare on oath their recollections concerning the money paid and the length of service of individual soldiers. The exchange of information between the *contador* and these deputies (*diputados*) of the companies was written on the account-sheet of the soldier concerned, covering minor and specific problems such as the date of a man's enlistment, the date he had received a *ventaja*, the number of days he had been absent and so on. More general questions – how much of the dead men's arrears should be paid and to whom; how much should be deducted for food supplied by the government – were hammered out directly by letter between the *electo* and the captain-general.[1]

It would be a mistake to see this haggling as a formality. Real obstacles stood in the way of ascertaining the true arrears of a veteran. The basic problem was the length of time which had elapsed between compiling the company lists and the settlement of accounts. At the mutiny of Antwerp in 1574, for example, the company records from which the *contaduría* (the accounts department) had to work were those compiled seven years before in 1567. Men who were 'young' in 1567 were prematurely aged seven years later, those designated 'healthy' on the lists were now covered with scars and sores. Besides these problems of identification it was hard for the government to discover how much the troops had taken or received

La Fère; the mutineers of Diest fought well for the government at the battle of the Dunes in 1600, and so on. Both were in receipt of a *sustento*. For an idea of the cost of mutinies, cf. Figure 16 and Appendix J.

[1] Cf. the large number of documents concerning the settlement with the mutineers of Zichem, AGS *CMC* 2a/6.

from the Netherlands since their arrival, while the confusion was compounded by the presence in the mutiny of a number of Spanish newcomers and of some 'Hispanized Walloons' who masqueraded as veterans of the *tercios* although they were not. Finally a number of true veterans reappeared unexpectedly either from hiding or from hospital in order to claim their arrears.[1] To this situation there was only one solution: the mutineers – 4,562 men – were all accepted at the final muster, and the government agreed to pay them exactly half their total claim and to overlook the money or goods they had received 'on account'.[2] Some similar compromise had to be made with all later mutinies which involved the unpaid arrears of many years; ironically, certitude was only possible with troops who were mutinying for the second time since their accounts had been fully verified the time before!

After each detail of every man's due was agreed, the treasury organized a heavy escort to take a convoy of bullion into the stronghold of the mutineers. In one of the local churches the men were formally pardoned and paid. Each man's due, his *remate*, was paid down in cash upon his hat (as in the Royal Navy today) and as the troops emerged from the church, their hats brimming with gold and silver, their creditors were waiting. Supervised by the sergeant of the mutiny, the troops had to pay all their debts in full and in cash; mutineers who owed more than the total of their arrears were condemned to the galleys without more ado.[3] Next there was a 'muster general' at which all those who wished to join another company did so. Those who wished to leave the Army were given a safe-conduct, although even here military expatriation worked in the government's favour: it was as difficult to return legally to Spain, Italy or Germany from the Low Countries as it was to desert. The peasants waylaid, robbed and killed passing soldiers without troubling overmuch to find out whether they had a passport or not, and a mutineer, his pockets bulging with silver, was an obvious target. Generally speaking, it was only those with a special cause to fear vengeance who chose to escape from the Netherlands after a mutiny.[4] The leaders of the mutiny were usually marked men: the *electo*

---

[1] IVdeDJ 67/215, Don Luis de Requesens to Don Juan de Zuñiga, 28 Apr. 1574 (copy = AGS *E* 557/123); AGS *E* 557/156, 'Relación de las dificultades para el fenecimiento de cuentas con los soldados amotinados', 15 May 1574 (copies = IVdeDJ 67/313 and 109/87).

[2] AGS *CMC* 2a/1, unfol., memorandum of *Contador* A. de Alameda, 1574: 'En el motín de Amberes se concerto con los soldados que se diese la mitad de lo que pretendian por sus servicios y que no se les descontase nada de lo que a quenta dellos huviesen recibido.'

[3] Cf. Croy, *Mémoires guerriers*, p. 179.

[4] Roger Williams, *The Actions of the Low Countries* (Cornell 1964 edn), p. 94, noted that after the mutiny of the Spanish infantry at Haarlem (1573) every man gave one *escudo* of his due to the *electo* to facilitate his escape.

and council were often required to leave the Army as a condition of the settlement of the mutiny. In addition, regular officers and gentleman-rankers who had mutinied often felt it was prudent to retire with their gains. Of the 41 mutineers of Pont-sur-Sambre who asked for and received a permanent discharge in 1595, 14 were *entretenidos*.[1]

Such precautions were not entirely idle. The high command was prepared to use fair means or foul in order to be rid of those who had shown a capacity for stirring up trouble and organizing disobedience. After the troubles were over many mutiny leaders were killed for their misdeeds. Often a list of pardoned mutineers was sent back to the Spanish court so that if ever the men crossed the path of the law in Spain or Italy they could be given the maximum penalty. Sometimes the mutineers were pardoned for their disobedience but punished in some other way – for instance by banishment. Thus in 1599 the mutineers of Antwerp citadel were paid in full and pardoned, but then they were peremptorily ordered to leave the Netherlands within twelve days. The same happened to the mutineers of Ghent citadel and those of Lier later in the same year. Some of these troops, mostly Spaniards, defied the ban and re-enlisted in one of the *tercios*, but many were massacred by the German peasants as they tried to escape to Italy. In desperation many more deserted to the Dutch.[2] In 1607 the same strategy was employed against the mutineers of Diest: they were pardoned and paid on 27 November but on 4 December they were declared outlaws with a price of 25 *escudos* on every head unless they left the Netherlands within 24 hours. In December 1609 the government went further: all soldiers who had participated in three mutinies and all officers and *entretenidos* involved in one were outlawed. Even ex-mutineers who had retired from the Army and remained in the Netherlands as civilians were expelled. With peace on all fronts the high command could at last give full vent to its exasperation with the mutineers who had absorbed so much money and aborted so many campaigns.[3]

---

[1] AGRB *SEG* 15/71, pardons issued 24 Jul. 1594. Don Carlos Coloma, *Guerras*, bk IX (BAE edn, p. 146) says that more than half the Italian mutineers of Zichem-Tienen went home after their arrears were paid. The rest, as in other mutinies, almost all profited from the 'muster general' to transfer their services to a cavalry unit.

[2] Coloma, *Las Guerras*, bk XII (*BAE* edn, p. 186); L. P. Gachard, *Actes des Etats Généraux de 1600* (Brussels, 1849), pp. lvi–lx; the decree of banishment (4 Apr. 1599) was registered in AGRB *SEG* 19/59v. For the story of one Spanish ex-mutineer who took refuge in the Dutch Army for many years and then at last returned to Spain, cf. AHN *Inquisición* (*espontáneos*) *libro* 1150/24–6v. (My thanks for this reference go to Prof. M. Van Durme.) It was two Spanish renegades in the Dutch army who recognized and captured the Spanish commander-in-chief, the Admiral of Aragon, at the battle of the Dunes in 1600.

[3] The ban on the mutineers of Diest is printed in V. Brants, *Receuil des Ordonnances des Pays-Bas : Règne d'Albert et d'Isabelle, 1597–1621*, I (Brussels, 1909), p. 371 and p. 374 (a re-issue

Yet not all the troops mutinied. Despite the government's constant fear of a 'general mutiny' which would set the entire army in ferment for its arrears, this never materialized. To a large extent the chaotic character of the Army's finances was itself instrumental in preventing a universal revolt. Because the Army lived always from hand to mouth some units were left destitute for long periods while others were relatively prosperous. Neglect of the troops was selective, not universal. It was also unpredictable. Thus the 600 Spaniards who garrisoned the new citadel at Antwerp after July 1587 received 106 months' wages for their service up to May 1596, a period of just 107 months. No Army could do better than that. But after May 1596 the military treasury seems to have lost all recollection of the Antwerp garrison; virtually nothing arrived for fifteen months and on 8 August 1598 the garrison mutinied. Their arrears totalled 159,285 florins which, shared between 600 men, was well worth a mutiny.[1] Likewise the Italian troops who served in the Netherlands after 1582 were relatively well-paid until 1591 because the prince of Parma was especially solicitous for their welfare. However, the drastic cut-back in the provisions from Spain in 1592 and the hostility of the new regime to all Italians thereafter soon provoked the mutiny of most Italians in the Army (at Pont-sur-Sambre in 1593 and at Zichem in 1594). The Italians' arrears stretched back to 1582, but the greater part dated from 1590. The *electo* of the mutiny of Zichem, Esteban Milanese, was typical in this respect: he earned wages of 944 florins between 1582 and June 1590, and received 628 florins, or 66 per cent; but between June 1590 and July 1594 (the mutiny) he earned 1,112 florins and received only 490, or 44 per cent.[2]

Even within a 'neglected' unit some wage-earners were affected more than others. The *socorro* system (flat-rate subsistence payments made to every man) which was so popular with the high command in the sixteenth century, was particularly unfair to the troops with a wage-bonus (a *ventaja* or *entretenimiento*): they only received their bonus when a proper muster-pay was held. The *entretenidos* therefore accumulated arrears at an alarming rate. At the mutiny of the Antwerp garrison in 1598–9 one

of the ban with some amendments). The ban was defended in a letter of Spinola to the king, 5 Dec. 1607, and discussed by the Council of State in a *consulta* on Spinola's letter, 5 Jan. 1608 (AGS *E* 2289/273 and *E* 2025/66 resp.) The ban of 12 Dec. 1609 is published by Brants, *Receuil*, II (Brussels, 1912), p. 25. At least 92 ex-mutineers were expelled under the terms of this edict, and they received only one-third of their arrears: AGS *E* 2290/114–15, 'Relación de los soldados que fueron comprendidos en el vando que S.A. mando publicar', 45 cavalry and 47 infantrymen.

[1] AGS *CMC* 2a/73, *Fenecimiento de Cuentas* with the Antwerp mutineers, 1598–9: total paid, 63,714 *escudos de a 50 placas*.
[2] AGS *CMC* 2a/6, *Fenecimiento* with the *tercio* of Don Gaston Spinola, 1596; *pliego de asiento* of Esteban Milanese.

veteran, Diego de la Torre, 'an old man with very white hair', had 25 *escudos* of *entretenimiento* and arrears stretching back to 1584; he was paid 5,248 florins. The light cavalry too amassed arrears rapidly: 71 troopers of one company at the same mutiny received 51,627 florins for only two years' service (May 1596–August 1598), an average of 727 florins per man.[1] Even more striking was the case of two Albanian cavalry troopers who joined the mutiny of Lier in July 1598. They were paid their full arrears on 7 February 1599. On 13 October 1599 their company mutinied again, having received nothing at all since they returned to obedience: the two soldiers, who had no bonus-pay, were owed 205 florins apiece for their brief service of eight months and four days.[2] With arrears mounting at this rate it was clearly in the interests of every soldier to mutiny each year. Many did. Mutiny became the 'domestic remedy' of the discontented veterans of the Army of Flanders.[3]

Here was another fundamental reason for the increasing incidence of mutiny in the Army of Flanders – success. The high command was trapped: if the mutineers were not paid they ravaged the countryside and paralysed the government's military efforts; if on the other hand their claims were met, other troops, seeing their comrades emerge with a full purse, were encouraged to emulate them. This dilemma often led to provocative decisions. Time and again money was promised to a necessitous regiment in the front line only to be appropriated at the last minute to settle accounts with a group of mutineers. The chain of events which ignited the important mutiny of Zichem was all too typical. The Italian *tercio* of Don Gaston Spinola, having served since 1582 without a break, was withdrawn from Frisia to Brabant in June 1594 in preparation for a new campaign in France. The ragged veterans were promised two pays – out of all their arrears! – at the end of July and meanwhile they were given the village of Aarschot in the Campine for their quarters. Upon arrival they discovered the walls in ruins, few inhabitants and fewer beds. Shortly afterwards they were casually informed that the two pays intended for them had been used instead to pay off their Italian comrades at the mutiny of Pont. What else was there to do but mutiny?[4]

---

[1] AGS *CMC* 2a/52, bundle 'Compania de don Bernardino de Ayala' for D. de la Torre – 2,099 *escudos* of 50 pattards; bundle 'Compania de don Juan Gamarra' for the rest – 20,651 *escudos*. Both companies were lancers.

[2] AGS *CMC* 2a/882, *Fenecimiento* with the company of Nicolai Basta, mutiny of Herenthals.

[3] AGS *E* 607/50–1, Archduke Ernest (the captain-general) to the king, 22 Aug. 1594: 'Llega ya esto de los motines a tomarse por...doméstico remedio.'

[4] On the great mutiny of Zichem, cf. Carnero, *Historia*, pp. 343–5, and Coloma, *Guerras*, bks VII and IX (*BAE* edn, pp. 96–7 and 146).

A cynical observer in 1605 asked himself the difference between the mutineer and the loyal soldier in the Army of Flanders. The mutineer, he reflected, was comfortably quartered in a large town, far away from the fighting, in receipt of liberal contributions either from the countryside or from the government, and confident of payment in full. In contrast the loyal troops were unpaid, unfed and unprotected against enemy attack.[1] Small wonder then that the habits and techniques of mutiny perfected by the Spaniards (and to a lesser extent by the Germans) should have been copied and adapted by the other 'nations' of the Army. In October 1576 the States General of the Netherlands lamented that 'the soldiers of this country, who until now did not know what a mutiny was, have learnt the trick so well that we see nothing but perpetual rebellions and uprisings of the troops ahead'.[2] Their fears were well-founded. The town of Zierickzee in Zealand surrendered to a joint army of Spaniards, Germans and Walloons on 2 July 1576. At once the Spaniards mutinied and headed for Brabant and their wages. The Walloon contingent in Zealand was not long in following suit. On 4 August the Walloons addressed a letter to the Spaniards, who by then had reached Aalst, recalling the 'good friendship and understanding which have existed between us' and suggesting a

Figure 17. The international composition of two later mutinies of the Army of Flanders

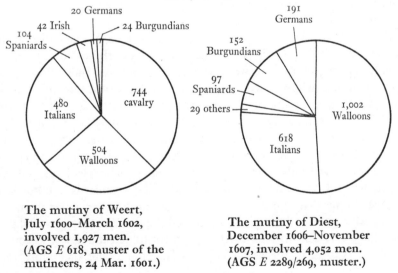

The mutiny of Weert, July 1600–March 1602, involved 1,927 men. (AGS *E* 618, muster of the mutineers, 24 Mar. 1601.)

The mutiny of Diest, December 1606–November 1607, involved 4,052 men. (AGS *E* 2289/269, muster.)

---

[1] BNM *Ms.* 8695/127–32v, Anonymous 'Discurso y acuerdo' of 1605 belonging to the count of Fuentes.

[2] L. P. Gachard, *La Bibliothèque Nationale à Paris*, I (Brussels, 1877), pp. 151–6, States General to the king, 27 Oct. 1576.

closer union to achieve their common goal. Another letter of the same tenor followed on 8 September and the chances of a multi-national entente among the discontented soldiery seemed likely. A 'general mutiny' was only prevented by the wave of violent revulsion against the Spaniards which swept across the Netherlands in the autumn of 1576, aided by the States General's offer to pay the Netherlands troops of the Army of Flanders themselves.[1]

In the 1590s, encouraged no doubt by the high command's tendency to use the troops of the various 'nations' in combination to form an *escuadrón*, multi-national mutinies became more common. If a mutiny broke out among one 'nation' in a garrison, the troops of the other 'nations' in the same town could usually be persuaded to join – after all, they had nothing to lose. The Italians in the campaign army of 1593–4 who mutinied at Pont-sur-Sambre and Zichem, were soon joined by Irish, Walloon, Burgundian and other discontented comrades; at Zichem it was said that thirteen different languages were spoken in the camp. Figure 17 illustrates the cosmopolitan character of two later mutinies, Weert and Diest.

Yet it seems clear that money did not constitute the only motive for mutiny, otherwise all the troops would have revolted. Instead many units entitled to vast arrears remained loyal while others which were owed virtually nothing took advantage of the slightest excuse to revolt. Why? The *carteles* (fly-sheets) which circulated amongst the mutineers suggest a number of subsidiary grievances.

First there was a distinct element of war-weariness, of frustration at the duration and futility of the war which found its outlet in mutiny. In the bloody fighting of 1572–6, when this feeling emerged most clearly, the Spanish troops who formed the spearhead of the invasion of Holland were worn down by the rigours and cold of the winter-siege of Haarlem. Already in November 1572, when the siege was barely begun, the *tercios* were owed 20 months' wages and the duke of Alva was 'astounded that they can bear it'. When the town surrendered in July 1573 the veterans received only four pays as storm-money (Haarlem surrendered on terms and so could not be sacked). The Spaniards mutinied in disgust. Somewhat appeased by a payment of 30 *escudos* per man, the *tercios* were sent to besiege Alkmaar and Leiden (neither were taken); then they were sent without further payment to defeat a new invasion by Louis of Nassau in the east Netherlands. After doing their duty they

---

[1] The two letters are in AGS *E* 567/115 and BNP *Ms. Espagnol* 421/320–2 (both copies). The best account of the mutiny was given by the Council of State itself on 2 August 1576 in the pamphlet *Discours veritable sur ce qui est advenu touchant l'alborote et esmotion des Espaignols mutinez ès îles de Zelande*. On the payment of the Walloons' arrears, cf. p. 224 below.

mutinied again (April 1574). The mutineers begged that 'His Excellency should not keep the soldiers more than six months in the field unless there is great necessity on account of the great sufferings caused by the frosts and the cold which have caused many soldiers to die, frozen to death on the open road or keeping watch in the trenches'. Other units suffered the same privations. At the end of 1574 the Spaniards who had been left to fight in Holland since June 1573 without a single pay also mutinied rather than spend another winter unpaid amid the frozen wastes. They too pleaded that 'during the time when the enemy is not campaigning or is not besieging places, Your Excellency should order us to winter-quarters in walled and populous towns'.[1]

The veterans' weariness in the face of the enemy becomes more respectable when one considers that there was no regular system of leave in the Army of Flanders. Although a unit was eventually withdrawn from the front when it was so reduced in numbers as to be uneconomic, on the whole the expatriate, elite troops were expected to be in permanent combat with the enemy. In a way this unreasonable practice stemmed from the failure to adapt military organization from the medieval tempo of warfare which drew to a close every October, enabling the troops to spend the winter in billets as a garrison, to the new, more intensive wars which went on throughout the year. The expatriate troops were certainly not cowards – the fact that they mutinied *after* action, after the victory of Mook, after the capture of Haarlem and Zierickzee, proves it – but continuous active service, without even a day of relaxation, inevitably dismayed and dispirited even the most hardened veteran. The mutinies did afford a brief respite.[2]

The mutinies were also a protest of a deeper, more basic type. Often the mutineers complained about humiliation by their superiors. In 1574 the mutineers of Antwerp asked that no man should be given 'a dishonourable punishment, like strokes of the lash, if the offence does not

[1] AGS *E.* 558/51, articles agreed with the mutineers of Antwerp, 23 May 1574, article 18. (The captain-general's reply was suitably ironic: 'What they ask about this will be granted, and if it is not necessary there will not be a campaign *even for six months*'); *E* 559/118, articles agreed with the *tercio* of Italy, 4 Jan. 1575, article 7. The same sense of disillusion was an important influence in the mutinies of the French army during the Great War: Pedroncini, *Les mutineries de 1917*, chap. 2.

[2] There were a number of suggestions that units should be regularly sent from the garrisons to the field army and vice versa (e.g. AGRB *SEG* 211/157-8v, Philip IV to the cardinal-infante, 21 Nov. 1634), but as noted on pp. 34–5 above there were (for Spain) insurmountable difficulties. Pedroncini, *Les mutineries*, sees the lack or irregularity of leave for troops at the front as a prime cause of the French mutinies in 1917; he also records (p. 213) rejoicing among mutineers who were condemned to prison because thereby they escaped from the firing line. On leave in the Army of Flanders, cf. p. 209 below.

merit it, because often a man is dishonoured for little reason, leaving him and his friends outraged and perplexed with an excuse for indiscipline'.[1] The tyranny of the officers over their men, which extended to every aspect of military life, has already been described (pp. 160–1 above); in addition, the men were insulted daily by the contemptuous terms in which they were addressed. They were 'lackeys and labourers', '*canaille*', 'pay-grabbers', 'vagabonds', 'the vilest and most despicable people in the kingdom', 'low-born people who must be frightened and chastised for the sake of the future'. . . .[2]

The common soldier of early modern Europe was thus despised by his officers, hated by civilians and abused by both. But not when he mutinied! The mutineer was respected, feared, humoured; he was 'somebody'. It may well be that, as has been suggested for the popular revolts of seventeenth-century France, the mutinies of the Army of Flanders were in part a manifestation of the dignity of the underdog, a 'collective affirmation of existence' on the part of the humiliated soldiers.[3] In the first place their vanity was flattered by the eloquent appeals, harping upon their sense of honour and duty and their distinguished past service, with which their paternalistic commanders bombarded them: they became 'los *señores* soldados'. The duke of Alva always saluted his mutinous soldiers as affectionate and respected children – 'Magníficos señores hijos' (Magnificent and honoured sons) – signing himself disarmingly 'Vuestro buen padre' (your good father). Other commanders adopted the same tone (cf. Figure 18). These smooth insinuations were not without response among the soldiers: their epistolary style and pretensions soon matched the government's own. Mutiny secretaries began to keep an archive; they had a distinctive seal made to authenticate correspondence, often with a subtly symbolic emblem (cf. Figure 19). At one mutiny the participants commissioned two official banners displaying the Virgin Mary with Christ in her arms, together with the motto 'Pro Fide Catholica et Mercede Nostra.' These mutineers who were harried from Hamont to Hoogstraten, back to Grave and finally to Roermond between 1602 and 1605

[1] AGS *E* 558/51, articles agreed with the mutineers of Antwerp, 23 May 1574 (cl. 12).
[2] A random sample: AGS *E* 607/50–1, Archduke Ernest to the king, 22 Aug. 1594: 'La mayor parte vagamundos y chorrilleros'; Gachard, *Actes des Etats-Généraux de 1600*, p. lix–lx, Archduke André to Archduke Albert, 11 Feb. 1599: 'telle canaille'; BRB *Ms.* 16149/16–18, Aytona to the king, 26 Apr. 1630: 'No quedando en el servicio de V. M. sino la gente mas vil y ruín que ay en todos sus provincias y reinos'; AGS *E* 2025/66, *Voto* of Don Juan de Idiaquez at the Council of State, 5 Jan. 1608: 'Es gente comun para que sirva de terror y escarmiento para lo de adelante.'
[3] Cf. the short but perceptive article of R. Mandrou, 'Vingt ans après, ou une direction de recherches fécondes: Les révoltes populaires en France au XVIIe siècle', *Revue Historique*, CCXLII (1969), pp. 29–40.

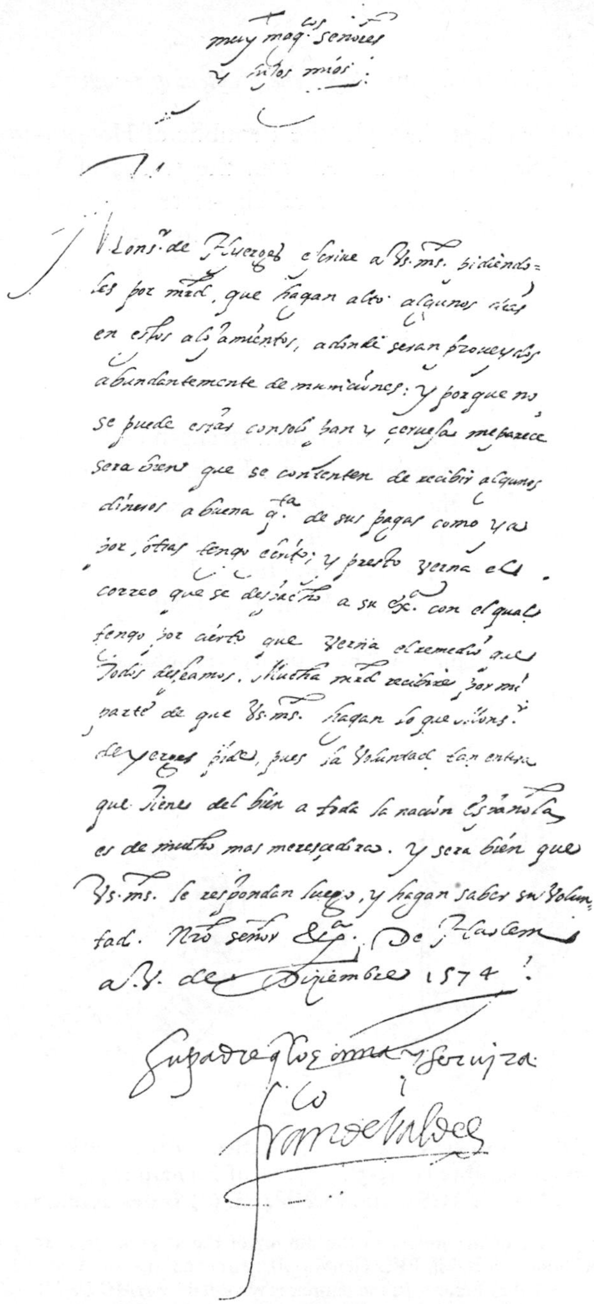

muy mag.cos señores
y hijos míos:

Alonso de Vergara escrive a Vs. ms. pidiéndo-
les por md. que hagan alto algunos días
en estos alojamientos, adonde serán proveydos
abundantemente de municiones; y porque no
se puede estar con solo pan y cerveza me parece
será bien que se contenten de recibir algunos
dineros a buena q.ta de sus pagas como ya
por otras tengo escrito; y presto verná el
correo que se despachó a su Ex.a con el qual
tengo por cierto que verná el remedio que
todos deseamos. Mucha md. recibiré por mi
parte de que Vs. ms. hagan lo que Alonso
de Vergara pide, pues la voluntad tan entera
que tiene del bien a toda la nación española
es de mucho mas merescedora. Y será bien que
Vs. ms. le respondan luego, y hagan saber su voluntad. Nro señor &c.a De Haslem
a V de Diziembre 1574.

Su padre que los ama y servirá.
Francisco de Valdes

Figure 18. The mutineers: deference

Maestre de Campo Francisco de Valdes begs the soldiers of his mutinous *tercio* (the *tercio de Italia*) to stay at their posts for a few more days and promises that with the return of the courier sent to 'His Excellency' (Requesens) 'I am sure that we shall see the remedy which we all desire' (sc. payment in full). Notice that the mutineers are addressed as 'My most magnificent gentlemen and children' (*Muy magnificos señores y hijos míos*) by their commander, who signs himself 'Your father who loves and serves you'. (*Su padre que los ama y servira*). Source: BPU Geneva, *MS. Favre* 60/215, Francisco de Valdes to the mutineers, 5 Dec. 1574, preserved in the mutineers' archive...

even presumed to adopt the style 'the Republic of Hoogstraten', dressed in green to distinguish themselves from the troops of both sides and claimed to be an independent, neutral city-state. They only abandoned their titular independence when Spanish loyalists proclaimed them outlaws and forced them to flee to the Dutch. The mutineers could not accept even this reverse gracefully: outraged, they issued a longish apology for their action which was published in several languages.[1]

In the face of corporate identity of such strength among its troops there was little that the government could do. In the first place the loyal troops often refused to fight their mutinied comrades. This was only natural, as even the government realized, 'Because, since they are all one, it is like someone saying: "What you do to me today, I'll do to you tomorrow." '[2] Second, an outright frontal attack on a particular group of mutineers,

Figure 19. The mutineers: sophistication

Seal of the mutineers
of Pont-sur-Sambre (1593–5).

Seal of the mutineers
of Zichem (1594–6).

Source: AGRB *Audience* 1841/1. (1½ times actual size.)

[1] There are fragments of the archive of the mutiny of the *tercio* of Italy (1574–5) in IVdeDJ 67/342–50 and 109/74–8 and in BPU Geneva, *Ms. Favre* 60/212–16. A couple of the mutineers' seals are printed as Figure 19; the banner is recorded by *HMC De L'Isle & Dudley*, III, p. 43, Browne to Sydney, 18 Jul. 1603. For the multi-lingual pamphlet: L. M. G. Kooperberg, 'Een muiterij in den Spaanischen tijd', *Bijdragen voor Vaderlandsche Greschiedenis en Oudheidkunde*, 5e reeks V(1918), pp. 113–72, on p. 142, n. 1. The mutineers of Zichem in 1594–5 also styled themselves the 'Republic of Zichem'.

[2] Quoted by Rodríguez Villa, 'Correspondencia de la Infanta...Isabella...con el duque de Lerma', *Boletín de la Real Academia de la Historia*, XLVII (1905), p. 356, letter of the infanta of 2 Nov. 1602.

although it might be successful in immediate terms, could produce a serious backlash later on. The aftermath of the mutiny of the Spanish veterans at Haarlem in 1573 is a case in point. The mutiny, which lasted 18 days, was settled with a payment of 30 *escudos* per man, but as soon as the mutineers dispersed the duke of Alva and his son Don Fadrique (the field commander) arrested the ringleaders and shot them a score at a time (despite the pardon they had granted to all) and then they refused to pay any money to the sick, the wounded and the legatees of the dead (despite their solemn undertaking to do so given during the mutiny). At first it seemed as though Alva had scored a great success and restored full authority over his men, but when the same troops mutinied again at Antwerp in April 1574 they wisely refused to trust anything the government told them. They demanded the pope and the king of France as guarantors of their pardon in one of their wilder moments, but they were perfectly serious when they demanded 'a safeguard signed by the King himself...and let us not be trusting as we trusted the duke of Alva and his son don Fadrique since they were so illustrious and since the same don Fadrique made his promises on oath, for words and promises were borne away by the wind'. The troops also swore 'not to accept any money until five pays in cloth have been given to the dead, and remember what happened at Haarlem, how they went out and killed men twenty by twenty, and how don Fadrique and Esteban de Ibarra [his secretary] said there was no money left for the sick and the wounded'. So it would seem that the intransigence and cynicism of the mutineers of Antwerp – which cost the government 1,000,000 florins and perhaps its only real chance of winning the war – was a direct consequence of Alva's 'tough' policy after Haarlem.[1] Likewise it seems certain that the successive edicts of outlawry pronounced by the Brussels government against the Spanish mutineers on 26 July, 2 August and 22 September 1576 provoked the lamentable sack of Antwerp later in the year. Hounded from pillar to post by loyal troops and outraged civilians, a price on their heads, the Spaniards were eventually surrounded, left without a safe refuge. On 4 November, early in the morning, they therefore made a surprise attack on Antwerp, carried the walls without any preliminary battery, and then sacked the city. There they found safety as well as the satisfaction of their wage-claim.

[1] At least two *carteles* of the mutineers of Antwerp referred to the happenings after Haarlem: IVdeDJ 67/312 (8 May 1574) and *Nueva Co.Do.In.*, II, p. 262 (17 May; copy AGS E 558/48). For Alva's justification of his harsh treatment of the mutineers, cf. *Epistolario*, III, pp. 491–6, letter to the king, 30 Aug. 1573. Conversely, Requesens, who was the man who had to face the mutineers at Antwerp, repeatedly assured them 'que no sera como lo de Harlem' ('It won't be like Haarlem' – *Nueva Co.Do.In.*, II, 212–15, two letters of 27 Apr. 1574).

It was a long time before the government tried to take a firm stand against mutineers again. However, in December 1594 suspicions mounted that the mutineers of Zichem were in contact with the Dutch; worse, the mutineers had refused to help the government to save Groningen earlier in the year and so Spain lost its last stronghold in the north. Loyal troops and artillery were therefore sent in to drive the 'traitors' from Zichem. The mutineers fought back (the only pitched battle between mutineers and loyal troops in the whole war) and shot down two assaults by government forces. However, their position soon became untenable and they asked for and received asylum in the territory of the States General (16–17 December). This shook the government's nerve. Less than a month later the mutineers were offered the town of Tienen (Tirlemont) as a security for their eventual payment in full.[1]

So even in the short run the use of force against the mutineers achieved nothing; moreover there could be long-term repercussions even more disastrous than those of Haarlem. At first all mutineers were relatively reasonable. They tried to keep their numbers small, knowing that only thus could the government raise enough money to settle their claim quickly. Any attack like the one on Zichem put an end to this moderation however. It became imperative for the mutineers to increase their numbers in order to defend themselves. All discontented veterans in the Army were therefore welcomed into the mutineers' stronghold and comrades who had left to fight in another war or who had gone home were urgently recalled. All had long arrears. The cost of settling the mutiny rose accordingly. Not surprisingly there was always a vociferous group within the high command which opposed any measure which might thwart or antagonize mutineers.[2]

In any case a 'tough' reaction was largely unnecessary. The mutineers were certainly not revolutionaries. Naturally a direct frontal attack by the government provoked them to take desperate measures: they became

[1] AGS *E* 607/95, Archduke Ernest to the king, 17 Dec. 1594, describes the attack; Carnero, *Historia*, pp. 343–5 and Coloma, *Guerras*, bk VII (*BAE* edn, pp. 100–1), provide further details. The government also used force against the mutineers of Hamont in 1602, forcing them to flee to Hoogstraten; in August 1603 the government even moved on Hoogstraten and the mutineers were only saved from ignominious surrender by the arrival of the Dutch army which escorted them to safety in Holland. There is an excellent account of the affair by Kooperberg, 'Een muiterij in den Spaanischen tijd'. Cf. also RA Arnhem, *Archief...Berg* 538*bis*, unfol., Count Frederick to Count Herman Van Den Berg, 15 Aug. 1603 – an eyewitness account of the Dutch rescue operation.

[2] For the fear that the use of force would make other mutineers more intransigent, cf. Gachard, *Actes des Etats-Généraux de 1600*, pp. lix–lx, letter of Cardinal André of Austria to his cousin Albert, 11 Feb. 1599; *AHE*, III, p. 124, *consulta* of the Council of State, 22 Apr. 1601; AGS *E* 2023/70, *idem*, 22 Oct. 1602.

cornered rats, their last refuge threatened – but if they were left alone, they made little trouble. Although they were remarkably articulate and could produce manifestos of surprising sophistication they had no political or social programme. There was no positive intention of sabotaging the war in order to secure peace; there was no Leveller-like drive to overturn the social order.[1] The military proletariat in ferment with its leader and council may bear a superficial resemblance to a Soviet with its revolutionary committee, but the mutineers had few leaders of foresight and fewer of political vision. All the seals, banners and self-styled 'Republics' were a means, not an end; the mutineers did not want to create a city-state, they just wanted to be paid. They asked for better conditions of service if they remained in the Army or for the freedom to go home with their just reward. In short, the mutiny was simply a collective protest, a sort of strike intended to persuade the state to treat its employees more honestly, more humanely, more respectfully.

This mechanistic, 'mercenary' interpretation is borne out by the disappearance of mutinies from the Army of Flanders after 1607. The long truce with the Dutch (1607–21) provided a cooling-off period with little fighting. In addition, harvests were good and adequate financial support came from Spain. In 1623, after only two years of war, Spinola managed to secure an undertaking from the prince of Orange that he would not support any mutineers from the Army of Flanders.[2] This was a valuable asset to the government, but it did not of itself prevent the resurgence of military revolts. Far more important were the actual improvements in the conditions of service – the hospital, the impartial and independent judiciary and so on, and above all the guaranteed supply of bread, clothes and shelter to every man (cf. Chapter 7 above). Even such money as the troops received was issued in proper 'pays', not in flat-rate *socorros*, and thus the higher-paid troops received their due. In this way the accumulation of enormous arrears by relatively neglected regiments or

[1] It is true that there are a few cases of mutineers selling their stronghold to the enemy: St André and Crèvecoeur forts (near 's Hertogenbosch) in 1600, Isendijk in 1604 and Sta Clara fort on the Scheldt in 1605, but these were exceptional cases. Treachery among mutineers was much more common on the Dutch side at the time, especially with the British troops. For a similar non-revolutionary interpretation of the mutinies of the French army in 1917, cf. Pedroncini, *Les mutineries*, Chap. IV.

[2] In 1622 some 26 soldiers of the Army of Flanders mutinied, received immediate protection from the Dutch and soon numbered 150 men. Spinola managed to provoke a similar revolt, also involving 26 men, in the Dutch army and he gave them a base in Spanish territory. In this stalemate the governments of Brussels and the Hague undertook not to support any mutiny on the other side. The two mutinies then afoot immediately collapsed. (AGS *E* 2313/27, Infanta Isabella to the king, 2 Jan. 1623, and *E* 2319, unfol., Spinola to the king, 23 Aug. 1627.)

groups was avoided and the sting of hunger and cold was largely removed.

There was another important change in the conditions of service in the Army of Flanders which favoured the disappearance of the mutinies. In the seventeenth century government control over movements across frontiers became less effective. It therefore became easier for the soldiers, even the expatriates, to desert. More important, as we shall see, the French and the Dutch, formerly so hostile to all Spaniards, began to realise the advantages of helping deserters from the Army of Flanders to escape. In this way they could promote the disintegration of the Spanish army. But it might have proved a shrewder counsel had they closed the frontiers and thus forced the discontented, war-weary troops to seek their solace in the accustomed military manner, by mutiny. This truth was firmly grasped by at least one adviser of Philip IV, Don Sancho de Zúñiga y Monroy, marquis of Castañeda. In 1632 Olivares proposed that desertion from the Army of Flanders could be significantly reduced if strong guards were mounted on the frontiers of Italy, Spain and the Netherlands. Castañeda thought little of the scheme.

> Even if it were possible [he told the Council of War] to put such a plan into action – which he doubted – and close all the exits from the Netherlands and all the entries into Spain and Italy, desertion springs principally from the ill-treatment and necessity which characterize the Army of Flanders. The oppression, and the impossibility of escaping from it, would therefore lead to a reappearance of the Flanders mutinies. Those would indeed provide [the soldiers] with the freedom to leave – and with the money to do so! Since experience had shown the great inconvenience of all that, surely it was better to permit the troops to enter the service of the rebels or of other princes suspect to His Majesty.[1]

In the last analysis mutiny and desertion were the two principal channels through which military discontent made itself felt; they were the two safety valves of the desperate soldiery. If resort to one was for any reason blocked, discontent flowed irresistibly into the other. Castañeda was right: anything was better than mutiny. In any case, even the expatriate troops seem to have preferred to desert rather than organize a mutiny. They lost their wages but they gained their freedom and they saved their skins; the government lost the services of its troops, but it retained their money. Easier desertion meant less mutinies, but it was not the perfect solution. Desertion itself, on a large scale, created a number of new embarrassments for the Army of Flanders.

[1] AGS *GA* 1052, unfol., *consulta* of the Council of War, 21 Jun. 1632, *voto* of Castañeda.

CHAPTER 9

WASTAGE AND 'REFORMATION'

'Your Majesty should see', Don John of Austria once wrote to Philip II, 'how the army of 60,000 men which you in Spain think we have is diminished.' The situation of the Army of Flanders when Don John arrived to take up his post as governor- and captain-general in November 1576 was indeed bleak. Death and disease had taken a savage toll of the troops still loyal to the king; desertion had decimated the rest. There were in fact only 11,000 men left under Spanish control, and they were isolated in a few strongpoints – Antwerp, Maastricht, Roermond...The Army had lost 80 per cent of its men in eight months.[1]

Disintegration on this scale seldom occurred. On the whole it is the stoic endurance of the troops of early modern Europe in both adversity and hunger which stands out; similar hardships would be tolerated by few armies today. Between October 1570 and May 1572 the Spanish infantry in the Netherlands received hardly any pay, and its numbers declined by 14 per cent, or 0.7 per cent per month (cf. Figure 20). This probably represents the absolute minimum wastage of any army at that time: the troops were well-disciplined, hardened by long service, and the period in question was one of peace.[2] The wastage of the same elite troops during the years of war which followed also constituted, in all probability, the minimum rate for the time: they lost on average 2 per cent per month until August 1573 and a further 1 per cent per month between March 1574 and May 1576 – a period which saw some of the bloodiest fighting of the war with entire companies lost in action.[3] The Spanish and Italian units which formed the spear-head of the reconquest of Brabant and Flanders

---

[1] AGS *E* 569/150*bis*, Don John of Austria to the king, 21 Nov. 1576.
[2] BM *Addl Ms.* 28,387/112 gives 6,148 men for the *tercios* of Sicily, Lombardy and Naples on 12 Oct. 1570; f. 165 gives 5,290 men for May 1572, a loss of 858 men.
[3] Cf. IVdeDJ 68/309*ter*, 'Relación de Bilanzo' (Mar. 1574, 8,016 Spaniards plus 430 more who arrived in 1575) and AGS *E* 566/23–4, 'Relación' of *contador* Juan de Navarrete, 22 May 1576 (6,125 men in the same units – a loss of 28 per cent). The wage-sheet of the company of Don Fernando de Saavedra (*tercio* of Naples) was closed in 1573 with the words: 'This company was lost in the Holland navy with Count Bossu in October 1573.' (AGS *CMC* 2a/1.)

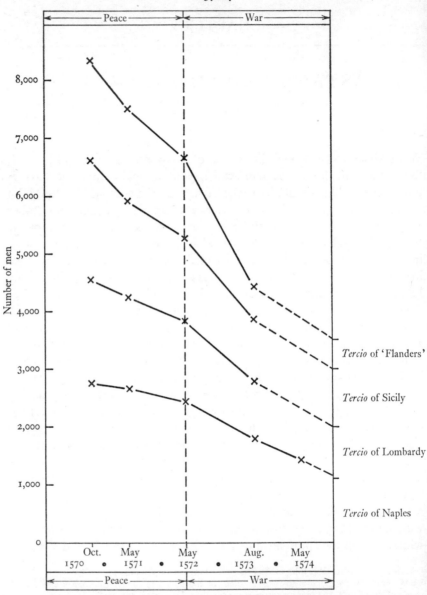

Figure 20. Losses among the Spanish veterans in the Low Countries 1570–4

The wastage rate increased after the fighting began in April 1572 but, except in the case of the *tercio de Flandes* (the unit with the least number of veterans), the increase was smaller than one might expect. In war, as in peace, desertion and not death or injury was responsible for most of the losses. Source: AGS *CMC* 2a/63.

between 1582 and 1586 had a similar record. Of 17,415 men sent to the Netherlands between September 1582 and 1586, only 5,845 were still in service at the muster of April 1586, a loss of 66 per cent or 1½ per cent per month.[1] The normal wastage among the troops of the other 'nations' of the Army in war-time varied between 2 per cent and 7 per cent per month.

Although these troops were continually engaged in front-line fighting, by modern standards the cumulative losses were fairly high. The French army in the eighteenth century (for which we have precise figures) lost around ½ per cent of its numbers every month in peace-time, and about 1 per cent per month in war-time.[2] What factors contributed to the notably higher wastage in the Army of Flanders?

Very few troops went absent on leave. As noted above, the Army of Flanders had no regular leave system; only the most pressing personal reasons – the death of a relative leaving an inheritance to be claimed, incurable illness or incapacitating wounds, the performance of a religious vow – could secure a permit to leave the Army and even then the permit was often only temporary. In any case, permits were usually accorded only to officers and gentleman-rankers. Between 1582 and 1586, for example, only 854 leave-passes were issued to the Spanish and Italian troops, while the total loss over the period was 11,570.[3] The rest of the soldiers either died or deserted. It is almost impossible to be more precise: data is extremely scarce. However, we know that between May 1572 and April 1574, the *tercio* of Naples served in the forefront of all action in the Low Countries and lost 41 per cent of its men: 17 per cent died and 24 per cent were unaccounted for, presumed deserted.[4] A rather different pattern was recorded for the German regiment of Count Sulz in the 1590s. Between 18 August 1593 and 28 May 1595 the regiment's strength fell from 2,264 to 1,199 men, a loss of 47 per cent; 32 per cent were reported dead and only 15 per cent deserted, but the losses among the three 'arms' differed noticeably. (See table on next page.)

Since the numbers of pike-men and 'shot' (arquebusiers and musketeers) were roughly equal in this regiment, the heavy mortality among the pike-men is as striking as the heavy desertion among the 'shot', especially

---

[1] Cf. Appendix C, pp. 278, for the number of troops sent; and AGS *E* 590/7 and 47, 'Relación' of the muster of Apr. 1586.

[2] A. Corvisier, *L'Armée française*, II, p. 682 (deaths) and p. 737 (desertions).

[3] *Licencias* registered in AGRB *SEG* 7, 8, 9 and 10 (*Registres aux Ordres* for 1582–6). There seems to have been a slight improvement in later years: 523 *licencias* were issued in the 16 months Jan. 1635 – May 1636 (*SEG* 215/212) but the number was still insignificant in terms of wastage.

[4] AGS *CMC* 2a/1, unfol., *pliegos de asiento* of the *tercio* of Naples: 1,428 men alive and 396 dead where there had been 2,415 men two years earlier.

	Total loss		Dead		Deserted	
Pike-men	585	(26%)	513	(22%)	72	(4%)
Arquebusiers	349	(15%)	120	(6%)	229	(9%)
Musketeers	140	(6%)	98	(4%)	42	2%)
	1,074	(47%)	731	(32%)	343	(15%)

the arquebusiers. No doubt the poor conditions in which the troops were obliged to serve had much to do with this. The musketeer received a considerable bonus-pay, while the system of double-pays which operated in the German infantry (cf. pp. 274–5 below) gave most pike-men a reasonable remuneration; the arquebusiers were therefore left as the worst-paid troops, and it was they who deserted.[1]

The distribution of *ventajas* (bonus-pays) had the same restraining effect on desertion as the double-pays. The Walloon company of Captain Pierre de Nervèse began life with 8 officers and 134 men on 4 August 1629. A total of 29 *ventajas* were awarded. On 17 June 1630 only 7 officers and 36 men appeared at the muster – a loss of 70 per cent or 7 per cent per month. Of the lost men only two had died, the rest had deserted. The deserters were overwhelmingly the men who did not have *ventajas*.

August 1629: 8 officers, 29 *aventajados*, 105 others
June 1630:   7 officers, 24 *aventajados*, 12 others

Since the soldier's life was normally such a grim struggle for survival, it is not surprising that the lower-paid men abandoned the colours first.[2]

The Army commanders constantly reiterated that it was the hardships and the miserable remuneration which made the troops desperate to escape from the Netherlands.

> The infantry which serves Your Majesty in this Army has been disintegrating: some men have gone because there are better wars and greater rewards in other countries, others because they have not been given their wages with the punctuality and at the times which are desirable, because we have not the means to do so...[3]

Thus ran the lament of the Infanta Isabella in 1627; her nephew and

[1] AGS *CMC* 2a/17, unfol., *pliegos de asiento* of Sulz's regiment.
[2] The 24 *ventajas* cost 35 *escudos* (87½ florins) per month above the troops' basic pay. Cf. AGRB *Conseil des Finances* 299, unfol., *liste* of the company of Captain Pierre de Nervèse. Sadly this is the only company list which I have found for any unit of the Army of Flanders during this period, whether paid by *exercito* or *finances*.
[3] AGS *E* 2318, unfol., the Infanta Isabella to the king, 28 Feb. 1627.

successor the cardinal-infante, who arrived to govern the Netherlands in 1634, was more specific:

> In many deserters despair plays a greater role than fear, so much so that these days many soldiers go over to the enemy solely in order to get a safe-conduct to Italy or Spain...Sire, the majority of the soldiers who serve in these provinces do so with much discontent and affliction; of four or five thousand applications for leave which are pending, the majority say that they will be happy with just their discharge in payment for all their services. This stems from the fact that the fighting here is very fierce, of long duration and great hardship. The lack of wages causes great miseries and those who come here think about this and about the state in which they see their compatriots; they soon regret that they ever came. But above all [they suffer from] the lack of rewards, because there is no way to reward services here.[1]

There are countless examples which support this thesis that despair not fear motivated most deserters. At the siege of Bergen-op-Zoom in 1622, for example, the Army of Flanders lost 36 per cent of its men in 3 months: the besiegers were 20,600 strong in July; by October they had dwindled to 13,200 (including 400 wounded). Of the missing men no less than 2,500 (one-third of the total lost) were so desperate that they fled to the very city they were besieging, Bergen, to beg for asylum and re-patriation! Even in the midst of an assault on the town, some of the attackers threw down their arms and defected to the other side in order to escape. At other times:

> From dawn till dusk one could see the soldiers jumping like rabbits from their holes, leaving the trenches, hedges, thickets and ditches where they had hidden, in order to run breathless to the town.

There they complained bitterly of their treatment in the trenches, how their officers drove them on with blows 'like sheep to the slaughter', how they served without pay; in Bergen they pleaded pitiably for 'A little bread and a little money' and, of course, for a passage home. Many other soldiers of the besieging army made their escape by some other route. From the walls of Bergen the guards regularly saw Spanish sentinels slyly leave their posts, pretending to cut grain, hay or wood, or to search for vegetables to dig up. They strayed further and further from the camp, finally making their break for freedom. One day towards the end of the siege of Bergen an Italian deserter staggered up to the town walls. 'Where have you come from?' asked the watch. 'D'infierno', he replied. 'From Hell'.[2]

[1] AGRB *SEG* 213/157–8, cardinal-infante to the king, 11 Oct. 1635.
[2] AGS *E* 2313/3–4, *Contador* Luis de Casuso Maeda to the king, 22 Oct. 1622, gives the Army's estimate of losses; C. A. Campan (ed.), *Bergues sur le Soom assiégée le 18 de juillet 1622 &*

Naturally a long and difficult siege like Bergen produced the greatest exodus from the ranks. At some sieges, especially those where provisions were scarce, groups of 30, 50, even 100 men at a time broke out of the siege-works fully armed and led by elected chiefs.[1] On other occasions the troops were gripped by sheer panic. The most celebrated example of this occurred at Leiden in 1574. After the mutiny of the Spanish veterans (15 April–30 May) the town was invested and the blockade tightened throughout the summer. Despite widespread desertion and threats of a new mutiny, by the end of September the surrender of Leiden seemed near, In desperation, the Dutch broke the dikes around the town in the hope of flooding the land deep enough to allow provisions to be sailed right up to the beleagured defenders. This action had an unexpected result. As the waters slowly rose around their siege-works on the night of 2–3 October the Spaniards, long restless, broke into a panic ('un tan grande y repentina miedo', 'un miedo y tremblor'). They fled. Leiden was relieved and Holland preserved by the desertion of the most experienced troops in the Army of Flanders.[2]

It was the soldiers driven by fear or despair who, as the marquis of Castañeda pointed out, were the most dangerous: if thwarted in their desire to escape, they would mutiny (p. 206 above). They were not, however, the only men prone to desert. Many soldiers simply grew tired of service in the Army of Flanders and wished for a temporary return to civilian life. Many of them later enlisted anew: it was well-known that the deserters of one year often responded to a new levy some years later. Some indeed alleged that the persistence of mutinies in the Army of Flanders owed something to the fact that 'a large number of the same soldiers who have served before return to serve again', the old infecting the new recruits with their dissolute habits.[3] Temporary desertion of this type, almost a form of prolonged unofficial leave, was particularly common after

---

desassiégée le 3 d'octobre ensuivant, selon la description faite par les trois pasteurs de l'église d'icelle (Brussels, 1867; original edn Middelburg, 1623), pp. 132, 133, 255, 321–2 and 407, describes the Spaniards through the eyes of the besieged.

[1] AGS *E* 560/103, Don Luis de Requesens to the king, 19 Aug. 1574: 'de 50 en 50 y de 100 en 100 se van con sus armas y con cabeza que eligen' (copy printed in *Nueva Co.Do.In.*, v, pp. 62–81).

[2] The Dutch side of the siege is beautifully narrated by R. Fruin, *The Siege and Relief of Leyden in 1574* (Eng. edn, Oxford, 1927); AA 28/3, Alonso de Laloo to Juan de Albornoz, 9 Oct. 1574, gives an interesting account from the Spanish side, taken from eye-witnesses. The Spaniards later tried to excuse their panic by claiming that the rising water threatened to engulf them, but as Laloo pointed out (a) the Hollanders loyal to the king (the *glippers*) who were with the Army swore that the water would not rise any higher; and (b) the waters were never deep enough to allow the Dutch relief fleet to sail outside the existing canal system.

[3] AGS *E* 2024/87, anonymous paper of 1605, 'Tocante a los motines'.

a successful siege in which the troops won notable plunder or after a major settlement of wage-arrears.[1]

Many soldiers wanted to leave the Netherlands in order to fight in some other army, perhaps for some other prince. These men were complete professionals, mobile soldiers (known as *rouleurs* or *billardeurs* in the eighteenth century), abandoning an army in one place in order to reappear in another elsewhere. They might be driven by fear of persecution (after a mutiny for instance) or by the victimization of a hostile sergeant or captain. Or they might simply, as one general claimed, be motivated by 'an inclination to change their surroundings'.[2] The Spanish troops in 'Flanders' often felt drawn to Italy. In particular those who had served in Naples before moving to the Netherlands had 'an unbelievable desire to return'. It was seriously suggested at one point that Spanish soldiers should no longer be sent to the Netherlands by way of Italy because they remembered 'the leisure and good lodgings of Italy' so vividly that they deserted in order to return. Even the prince of Parma, who commanded the Army of Flanders from 1578 until 1592, subscribed to this view, claiming that 'a Spanish soldier who had never breathed the air of Italy served better in the Netherlands than two who had, because they never lost the desire to return'.[3]

At least these men remained in Spanish service. Frequently, however, soldiers of the Army of Flanders deserted to the service of a neighbouring prince, even to the enemies of Spain. As early as 1575 three Spanish soldiers were found fighting for the rebels; in 1607 German troops in considerable numbers defected to the States General – a manœuvre which was particularly easy for men of a 'nation' which fought on both sides.[4]

---

[1] E.g. the mass defections from the Army of Flanders after the sack of Mechelen in 1572 reported by a French observer: L. Didier, *Lettres et Négociations de Claude de Mondoucet* (Paris, 1891-2), I, pp. 87-90, letter to Charles IX, 8 Nov. 1572; special measures were taken to prevent the Spaniards from deserting after their arrears were paid in full in September 1585 following the capture of Antwerp: AGRB *SEG* 10/94v-6, orders of Parma, 21 Sep. 1585.

[2] AGS *E* 560/103, Requesens to the king, 19 Aug. 1574. This urge could take Spaniards into forbidden waters: cf. the ten Spanish soldiers who deserted from the expedition to the Low Countries in June 1573 in order to visit Geneva (AE Geneva, *RC* 68/118, deliberation of the city council, 1 Jun. 1573).

[3] AGS *E* 1924/66, duke of Feria to the king, 20 Aug. 1620 ('no se puede creer el desseo que tienen de volver a Nápoles'); *E* 609/88, instruction of the Archduke Ernest to Don Diego Pimentel, 30 Jan. 1595; *E* 1924/121, Juan de Ayzaga to the king, 6 Sep. 1620, quoted the lament of Parma, his ancient master. Of course Parma still wanted *veteran* troops though (cf. p. 32 above). Cf. also Don Carlos Coloma, *Las Guerras* bk v (*BAE* edn, p. 52) who claimed that the rapid disintegration of the Spanish *tercio* of Don Luis de Velasco in 1591-2 was due to the troops' familiarity with the life and luxuries of Naples which made them unable to survive, like Coloma and the rest, in the man's world of 'Flanders'.

[4] AGS *EK* 1537-54, Don Diego de Zuñiga to the king, 29 May 1575; for later examples cf. p. 194 above. The desertion of German troops to the Dutch was denounced as a new and

Yet more common was the drift of soldiers from the Army of Flanders to other Catholic forces, the Habsburg army in Hungary or the army of the French Catholic League, for example. There were always soldiers moved by 'the attractions of a war...where they know the country is rich and plentiful and they know they will be under no restraints'. On many occasions, indeed, foreign powers offered positive financial inducements to encourage soldiers to 'change their surroundings'.[1]

It is, predictably, difficult to uncover the tortuous network by which troops were brought from the Army of one power into that of another, but now and again the clandestine activities of the *debauchers* (as these agents were known) were unearthed by the government and thus exposed for posterity. The proudly autobiographical account of one irrepressible *debaucher*, Thomas Finglas, reveals some operational techniques and hazards. Finglas was modest in his aims: he confined himself to his own compatriots, the Irish troops of Sir William Stanley in the Army of Flanders. Stanley and his regiment, 816 men, defected to Spain from the service of the States General at Deventer in 1587; with a few reinforcements of similar provenance, the regiment numbered 890 men by February 1589. Finglas started work. Based on Paris he first suborned two of Stanley's men to act as his agents, then through them he enticed men of the regiment to Paris by twos and threes until there were 300 of them at his headquarters. By December 1589 the regiment was down to 596 men. As there were English forces fighting in Normandy at this time, Finglas made his men enter the service of the French Catholic League (against which the English were fighting) in the hope of taking them into Normandy, there to desert to the English army. This complicated strategy was foiled when the duke of Parma demanded that the League (his ally) should send back all deserters from the Army of Flanders. Finglas and his men were duly handed over. Stanley's regiment was up to 739 men by January 1590. Finglas began again. With infinite patience he managed to 'debauch' afresh 100 men and he led them back towards the English positions in Normandy. Once more they were intercepted; this time the Catholic League commandeered them. A third time Finglas, nothing daunted,

pernicious evil in an ordinance of 3 Feb. 1607, cf. V. Brants, *Receuil des Ordinances des Pays-Bas, Règne d'Albert et d'Isabelle* (Brussels, 1909), I, pp. 319–20. Although it was mainly the Germans and British who served on both sides, during the war with France after 1635 Italian troops were in the pay of both powers. In 1646, for example, large bodies of Italians defected from the French Army of Picardy to the Spanish Army of Flanders (AGRB *SEG* 46/127 and 144v, orders of 15 Sep. and 20 Oct. 1646).

[1] AGS *E* 589/113, Parma to the king, 6 May 1585. It was often rumoured that the Guises offered rewards to any Spaniard who joined the Army of the French Catholics. Cf. for one example, AGS *E* 560/83, Requesens to the king, 24 Sep. 1574.

went back, but at last Colonel Stanley became suspicious of the 'oft going and coming' of his men: his regiment was down to 424 men by November 1591. One of Finglas' principal accomplices was arrested and, under torture, he confessed all. Finglas and his friends were put out of business.[1]

The problem did not end there of course. There were many other military 'head-hunters' at work in the Army of Flanders. Not long after the unmasking of Finglas the government in Brussels became concerned about the activities of another 'debaucher':

> We are informed [wrote the captain-general to the governor of Luxemburg] that in the duchy of Luxemburg there is a man named Massieure who is suborning and hiring secretly and covertly all the soldiers he can find of the King my Lord, in order to send them to the wars in Hungary...

The provincial governor was ordered to capture Massieure, who was reported to have a special interest in 'debauching' cavalry troopers.[2]

In theory the penalties for desertion, with or without encouragement from a foreign power, were severe. Although for at least part of the middle ages soldiers were allowed to return home 'without blame' if their wages fell more than six weeks in arrears, by the sixteenth century all European armies treated desertion as a felony punishable by death.[3] This penalty was often exacted in Habsburg armies. When in 1574 the captain-general received warning that a group of 52 Spanish soldiers had abandoned the siege of Leiden and were making for the French frontier 'armed and in good order', he commanded his staff officer Hernando de Sandoval to take all the troops he could find in the frontier garrisons in order to stop the deserters at all costs. The Walloon troops from the frontier hid themselves in ambush near Charlemont and completely surprised the deserters who believed (erroneously) that they had already crossed the frontier into France and were therefore safe from pursuit. The fighting was fierce: 13 Spaniards and 7 or 8 Walloons were killed, 13 or 14 more Spaniards were

---

[1] AGS *CMC* 2a/6, unfol., *pliegos de asiento* with Stanley's regiment 1587–94, and *Calendar of the State Papers relating to Ireland, 1592–6*, pp. 63–7, 'An account made of my life from my first going out of England into France.' Although he mentions almost everything else, Finglas does not state where his money came from. 'Debauching' troops was expensive. One suspects that the English government kept him in funds throughout this venture.

[2] Biblioteca Laurenziana, Florence, *Ashb. Ms.* 1766/33, the Archduke Albert to Count Mansfelt, 7 Jun. 1597. For a further example, this time of English troops raised for the Army of Flanders and 'debauched' as they disembarked at Calais by Dutch agents, cf. AGRB *Audience* 1465/1, bundle 2, unfol., Diego Ortiz to Juan de Mancicidor, 7 Jul. 1605.

[3] A. E. Prince, 'The Indenture System under Edward III', in *Historical Essays in Honour of James Tait* (Manchester, 1933), pp. 283–97: pp. 292–3 records legalized desertion, but as early as 1439 the English Parliament made desertion a felony (R. A. Newhall, *Muster and Review* (Cambridge, Mass., 1940), pp. 150–4).

seriously wounded. Eventually all the surviving deserters were captured and brought back to Brussels in chains to await their execution.[1]

In general, all deserters who resisted capture were shot, but in other cases execution at least of expatriate troops, was avoided whenever possible. So much time, trouble and money was expended on 'getting a pikeman to Flanders' that the extreme penalty seemed rather wasteful. In Spanish Italy and in the Low Countries, Spanish deserters might escape with three strokes of the lash.[2] Even so, an example sometimes had to be made. Desertion was particularly rife on the expedition of 40 companies of Italian recruits brought to the Army of Flanders by Ambrosio Spinola in 1602; in an effort to staunch the flow, Spinola organized a large posse to ride behind the expedition and pick up deserters. A reward of 10 *escudos* a head was offered for every one captured. In Lombardy, Savoy and Franche-Comté over 100 men were caught and they were brought back to the camp and hanged. Discipline was restored.[3]

Despite a short-term success of this sort it is unlikely that the severity of the penalties alone could have restrained the urge of the desperate soldiers to desert. Sooner or later, misery would force them to try. The Roman emperors ordered their soldiers to be branded on enlistment in order to facilitate recapture if they deserted, but desertion still took place if the soldiers' position became unbearable.[4] No more did the threat of execution in the sixteenth century stop a starving man. A far more powerful restraint was the attitude of civilians and of foreign governments towards individual deserters.

While the mutinies were essentially a collective response to the harsh realities of military life, desertion was largely an individual reaction.

[1] AGRB *Audience* 1691/2, unfol., billet of D. de Çabala to the *audiencier*, ordering him to give Sandoval a patent requiring all local troops and their commanders to obey him and to intercept the deserters; AGS *E* 560/83, Requesens to the king, 24 Sep. 1574 and AA 31/83, Alonso Carnero to Albornoz, 16 Sep. 1574. Cf. also the lip-smacking report of the incident by the French ambassador, Mondoucet, printed by L. P. Gachard, *La Bibliothèque Nationale à Paris*, II, pp. 553–5.

[2] BM *Addl. Ms.* 28,390/354, duke of Albuquerque (governor of Milan) to the king, 20 May 1569.

[3] AGS *CMC* 2a/875, third bundle, 'Cuenta de Pedro Ximenez', Paymaster of Spinola's expedition of 1602 who paid 10 *escudos* for every deserter's head brought in. This reward was offered in Spinola's edict against desertion issued 'in His Majesty's name for the conservation of his Army'. For further examples of the execution of deserters from expeditions along the Spanish Road cf. AGS *E* 1255/59, governor of Milan to the king, 21 Aug. 1582 (8 executed, 12 to the galleys); *E* 1272/226, *idem*, 22 Nov. 1593 (12 executed); *E* 3336/138, *idem*, 12 Apr. 1631 (5 executed).

[4] A. H. M. Jones, *The Later Roman Empire, 284–602. A Social, Economic and Administrative Survey* (Oxford, 1964), II, pp. 617–18. The whole of Chapter XVII gives a fascinating insight into life in the Roman imperial army.

Many deserted alone, some in twos and threes; parties of twenty and upwards, although spectacular, were very rare. Deserters were therefore extremely vulnerable. There are innumerable examples of the peasants falling upon isolated soldiers or bands of soldiers on the move and killing them. In 1576–7 even full cavalry companies were not proof against frontal assaults from hordes of armed civilians. In later years, unwary infantry companies might be murdered in their sleep, while mutineers who deserted in order to return home with their arrears were often murdered for their money along the way.[1]

Peasants in this frame of mind, to say nothing of the Zealand pirate who in 1573 ripped out a Spaniard's heart with his teeth, were not likely to smile on deserters. Around 1600, however, the climate changed. The Dutch saw the advantages of helping enemy deserters to escape. Long before the siege of 1622 (cf. p. 211) troops from the Army of Flanders fled to Bergen-op-Zoom and the other seaports of the States in order to purchase a passage home. In 1605 the English governor of Flushing was informed that the Italian troops in the front-line of the Army of Flanders were: 'Almost all run hither and so passed for France; they run away by scores and half-scores at a time. Ere it be long they say that all their fellows will be here...'[2] It was recognized to be in the Dutch interest to facilitate the escape of enemy troops in every possible way. France too soon saw the light. Barely three months after the peace of Vervins in 1598 the Brussels government became alarmed at the stream of troops who were deserting through France. Soon the stream became a flood.[3] Even after the resumption of war in 1635 the Paris government helped to repatriate as many Spanish troops from the Netherlands as possible. In 1648, for example, 600 of the Spaniards captured at the siege of Ieper were sent back to Irun by the French – although by then it had become standard policy that prisoners of war should be liberated wherever they would be least useful. It was in order to intercept and re-enlist the constant flow of deserters and ex-prisoners who returned from the Netherlands by way of

[1] In 1576 the entire peasantry of Hainaut united (successfully) to keep the Spanish light cavalry out of their province, and any isolated Spaniards on the roads was killed (AGS *E* 567/88, Sancho Davila to the *Conseil d'Etat*, 3 Aug. 1576). For examples of whole companies destroyed by the peasants, cf. AGS *E* 578/71 (17 Walloon cavalry troopers ambushed and killed near Gravelines); AGRB *Audience* 1809/3, unfol., Berlaymont to Parma, 2 Apr. 1583 and *Audience* 1857/1, unfol., Berlaymont to Mansfelt, 6 Apr. 1593 (on both occasions the count wrote to complain that full companies of his regiment had been annihilated by peasant bands). For the waylaying of ex-mutineers, cf. Coloma, *Las Guerras*, bk XII (*BAE* edn, p. 186), concerning the mutineers of Antwerp castle (1599).
[2] *HMC De L'Isle & Dudley*, III, pp. 205–6, Throckmorton to Viscount Lisle, 22 Sep. 1605.
[3] AGS *E* 615/146, Archduke Albert to the king, 26 Jul. 1958.

France that the Spanish Council of War kept a permanent member stationed in Navarre.[1]

The new sympathy for deserters was not confined to governments. As the proportion of volunteers decreased, compelling the various states of Europe to conscript and impress their soldiers – often at gunpoint – civilians tended to feel more pity for fugitives and were more inclined to shelter and assist them. The case of a Spanish soldier, almost certainly a deserter, who was found in a field near Epinal in Lorraine in 1596 is instructive. He was found with both legs broken, 'mutilated and beaten', having lain several nights in a field amid the heavy frosts. The magistrates of Epinal, whose previous experience of the Spaniards was far from happy, nevertheless decided to help the injured man. Probably regarding his survival as something of a miracle, they provided ointments, medicines, pocket money, a cart and an escort to help the crippled Spaniard to the next town.[2] In general, in the seventeenth century, deserters enjoyed the complicity not only of their comrades, but of the clergy, the local population and the magistrates as well.[3]

This humanitarian view was a luxury which the high command at least could not afford. The cumulative loss of men, which could only increase as popular sympathy for the deserter grew, posed an acute problem of cost-effectiveness. The Army simply could not afford to maintain companies which numbered 20 men instead of 200; it was not economical to do so, especially since, as we have seen, the troops who remained longest were normally those with the highest pay.

There were two solutions to the problem of the company which had wasted away to an uneconomical size: either the captain could be authorized to recruit more men and so bring his company up to strength, or else the unit could be broken up. The first procedure was, of course, only

[1] AGS *GA* 1680, unfol., *consulta* of the Council of War, 13 Aug. 1648, and the despatches of the member, Don Luis Ponce de Leon, in *GA* 1679 and 1680. Cf. also p. 170 n. 1 about the repatriation of prisoners of war.

[2] AC Epinal (Vosges), *CC* 106 ('Compte de la ville...1596'), f. 6v: 'Donné pour Dieu et en aulmosne à ung pauvre espagnol ayant heu les deux jambes coupées par accident à luy survenu, ayant esté mutilé et battu...et couché ainsy blessé plusieurs nuictes parmy les champs pendante les grandes froidures, luy fut donné £2. 8 gros. A Mre. Cosme Poulet, pour avoir medicamenté et fourny quelque boiste dungent audict pauvre affligé...15 gros. Donné à ung guidan darchette ayant conduict sur sa charette ledict Espagnol à Remiremont, 18 sols.' Cf. p. 92 n. 1 above for the unpaid provisioning of Epinal. It is interesting to note that the Spaniard was being sent south (to Italy) not north to the (closer) Netherlands.

[3] Corvisier, *L'Armée française*, II, pp. 693–747, especially 700–3.

possible with troops raised locally; the second, known as a 'reformation', was applied to most expatriate troops, especially in the sixteenth century. In 1574, for example, it was found after the mutiny of Antwerp that there were 68 companies of Spanish infantry in the Netherlands, each with a theoretical strength of 250 men, grouped into 5 *tercios*. In fact the 68 companies contained only 8,016 men, an average of under 120 men. The 68 companies were therefore 'reformed' into 30, the five *tercios* into 4. The officers who lost their commands were either given the same pay as before (*reformado* pay) although they had to serve in the ranks, or else they were allowed to return home.[1]

The 'reformation' was extremely unpopular with the Army, especially with the officers whose posts were suppressed. It could therefore be used as a punishment as well as an economy. The decision to 'reform' the Spanish units in 1574 was partly motivated by a desire to punish a number of officers who had been found guilty of defrauding their troops and to punish the troops for their mutiny by reducing the number of *ventajas* they enjoyed. Since all units of the Army of Flanders lost over 10 per cent of their strength every year, the threat of 'reformation' could easily be used to secure good behaviour.

The punitive value of the 'reformation' was illustrated by the breaking-up of the *tercio* of Sardinia, one of the four Spanish regiments which came to the Netherlands with the duke of Alva in 1567. The trouble began with Count Louis of Nassau's invasion of Friesland in May 1568. The incursion met with initial success and Count Louis defeated a strong government force under the count of Aremberg at Heiligerlee (just outside Winschoten), killing Aremberg and a large number of Spaniards from the *tercio* of Sardinia. The story became current that after the battle a number of the defeated Spaniards took refuge in the villages nearby and were either handed over to Count Louis and executed or else murdered by the peasants themselves. This alleged massacre was not forgotten when, later in 1568, a new Spanish army checked Count Louis' advance and drove him back. In due course the government forces passed through Heiligerlee. The *tercio* of Sardinia formed the rearguard. Incited by the ignominious death of their comrades, the Spaniards began to set fire to houses and even entire villages in the area proceeding 'with such insolence and disorder that had they received express orders to wreak similar

---

[1] On the 'reformación' of 1574, cf. the unfavourable but factual account of AA 31/83, Alonso Carnero to Albornoz, 16 Sep. 1574. The idea of reserve pay was taken over by other armies: cf. '*reformado* pay' in the English Army, P. Young, *Edgehill 1642: the campaign and the battle* (Kineton, 1967), p. 5.

destruction on enemy territory they could not have done it better'.[1] In fact the arson and havoc were being committed on the lands of Philip II, on the estates of the same count of Aremberg who had been killed at the head of the *tercio* of Sardinia in the defeat at Heiligerlee...The duke of Alva, marching in the wake of his forces, was puzzled by the smoke which billowed in such dense clouds across his path. The military police were sent to investigate. They executed on the spot anyone caught setting fire to property and in this way order was restored. Alva, however, was horrified by the indiscipline of his men. From the first moment he set eyes on his Spaniards at Asti in June 1567, the duke had poured forth lamentations upon their poor calibre and arrogant disobedience. The burning of the Frisian villages marked but the climax in a rising crescendo of defiant disrespect and restive insubordination. The duke took a particularly dim view of the indifference of the captains in the affair: none of them had made any attempt to restrain their men. Accordingly, on 28 July, two days after the disorder, Alva ordered the *tercio* of Sardinia to be broken up. All the captains were dismissed from the king's service forthwith; their men, who lost all their *ventajas*, were redistributed among the other Spanish units in the Army. This drastic action had a salutary effect. It at last achieved the duke's aim of imposing respect and obedience on his men.[2]

Another Spanish *tercio* which disobeyed orders and actually abandoned an enterprise in 1589 was also punished with total 'reformation'. The trouble originated in the campaign of 1585, in which three Spanish *tercios* were ordered to cross the Maas and winter on the Bommelerwaard, in the middle of the Great Rivers. The advance was badly prepared: no sooner had the Spaniards reached the island than they were surrounded by the Dutch fleet. Their retreat was thus blocked, and to their horror the troops found that all the crops and supplies on Bommel had been destroyed by the enemy. The end seemed near for the veterans, 'the flower and distillation of all the Spanish infantry remaining from the wars of forty years',

---

[1] B. de Mendoza, *Comentarios*, bk III, 14 (*BAE* edn, p. 427), gives a readable account of the affair, the accuracy of which is supported at every point by the Army's own records (e.g. AGS *CMC* 2a/5, *pliegos de asiento* of the *tercio* of Sardinia).

[2] Cf. Alva's grouses about the Spanish troops on 1 Jun. 1567 (to Espinosa, *Epistolario*, 1, pp. 646–7), of 29 Nov. 1567 (to the king, *ibid.*, pp. 705–7), and of 6 Jan. 1568 (to the king, *Co.Do.In.*, xxxvII, pp. 82–5). For Alva's solution: AA 165/9, 'Orden que se dio a Chiappin Vitelli para reformar el tercio de Cerdeña' (copy). Alva wrote: 'para castigar una insolencia y inhumanidad nunca vista...cassara y abholira el maestre de campo y los diez capitanes del dicho tercio, ordenandoles de parte de Su Magestad y de la mia que se tengan por despedidos.' Only Captain Armendariz was left with his rank because he happened to be absent with leave at the time of the outrage.

when a miraculous frost on 8 December froze the river Maas hard enough to allow the marooned and starving veterans to scramble to the mainland.[1] Three years later in 1589 the *tercio* of Lombardy, one of those involved in the Bommel fiasco and described by one commentator as 'the father of the other regiments and the seminary of the best soldiers who have been seen in Europe in our time', was ordered to winter on another island across the Maas, the Land van Altena. Mindful of the winter of 1585, the troops refused. The commotion was so great that the commanding officer (Count Charles de Mansfelt both in 1585 and 1589) ordered the retreat. This dangerous disobedience by the oldest and most trusted unit in the Army was punished by the captain-general with 'reformation'. The *alfereces* ceremonially broke their staffs and tore up their colours 'which, since they no longer represented His Majesty the King, no longer demanded the veneration and care in which they were held'. The sergeants destroyed their halbards, the captains their epaulettes. The *veedor general* supervised the distribution of the soldiers and their demoted officers among the other units of the Spanish infantry. The most famous regiment in Europe ceased to exist.[2]

Even where there was no punitive intent, the 'reformation' was always an unpopular process among the troops. Soldiers with long service were often deprived of their bonus-pays and separated from their comrades; officers who had acted honestly and with distinction might still be unavoidably downgraded. Eventually an alternative had to be found. Already the military entrepreneurs who took a larger share in raising German and British troops for the Army of Flanders were allowed to recruit their own reinforcements and gradually it became the custom to retain the existing *tercios* of veteran Spanish and Italian troops in permanent service too, keeping up their strength by 'reforming' any new units to arrive from Italy or Spain into the old. This solution was not ideal – knowledge that 'reformation' awaited them in the Netherlands discouraged many officers and men from going there at all – but it was a workable compromise between the desirability of humouring experienced soldiers and commanders and the need to save money and prevent the Army of Flanders from total disintegration before the end of the war.

[1] Carnero, *Historia*, p. 203, gives a fine account: such a hard frost in early December, he claimed, had never been known. Perhaps understandably, the Spaniards regarded it as a miracle.
[2] Cf. the eye-witness accounts of the 'reformation of the *tercio viejo* by Alonso Vazquez, *Los Sucesos de Flandes y Francia* (*Co.Do.In.*, LXXIII), pp. 433–6 and Coloma, *Las Guerras*, bk II (*BAE* edn, pp. 18–20). From Coloma's detailed description (p. 19) it is clear that after occupying the Bommelerwaard, the Spaniards were ordered to cross to Altena, taking the fort of Loevestein first. Vazquez (pp. 414–19) talks of the isle of 'Bura (for Betuwe?) and Carnero, *Historia*, p. 239 speaks of 'Tola , which I cannot explain.

CHAPTER 10

DEMOBILIZATION

In many ways the actual mechanics of demobilizing an army resembled the settlement of a mutiny: the principal concern of the government was to establish the arrears due to the troops. The military treasury had to ascertain the wages due, and then subtract the money, food, clothes and contributions provided already. In fact this task was impossible. The government was never able to determine in detail all the payments which local receivers of revenues, officials of the *pagaduría* and sundry contractors had issued to the troops – at least this could never be done quickly enough; mutinies only involved 4,000 men at the most, but there might be 60,000 troops due for demobilization and they all continued to earn their pay until they were formally disbanded.

Accordingly, the government always tried to reach some compromise with the troops in the interests of a speedy settlement. Normally the state agreed to ignore all the money provided other than by the *pagaduría* if the troops in return would relinquish a portion of their total arrears. This proportion varied according to the government's bargaining power. Thus in 1580, when the Spanish regime was particularly weak, the German troops who were to be disbanded would only forgo six months' arrears out of the eight years' back-pay due to them. Conversely in 1609, when Spain had secured a long truce with the Dutch, Ambrosio Spinola was able to bludgeon the German troops in the Army into accepting only one-third of their arrears as full payment, forgoing the rest in lieu of their receipts in kind from the civilian population. This was the most favourable agreement ever negotiated by the Spanish government with its troops over their pay-claim. The normal compromise payment was three-quarters, two-thirds, occasionally one-half of the arrears due.[1]

The government still possessed a certain room for manœuvre after the

[1] AGS *E* 582/4, copy of the accord between Parma and Count Berlaymont's regiment, 13 Mar. 1580; cf. *E* 2291, unfol., the *fenecimientos* with various German regiments in 1609; *CMC* 2a/10, settlement with the regiment of Berlaymont the younger, May 1596, conceding one-quarter; and *CMC* 2a/43, settlement with Munichhausen's regiment, Jun. 1597, conceding ('haze suelta y quita al beneficio de la real hazienda de Su Magestad') one-third.

compromise was agreed. Where a unit was deemed to have asked too much the government insisted on paying the agreed sum in instalments. The troops, suspecting nothing, consented to disband upon payment of the first instalment with guarantees (usually oral) of the proximate payment of the rest. The way was then open for the Spanish government to default on its debts: once they had disbanded, the troops had lost for ever their bargaining strength. In 1579, for example, after the fall of Maastricht, the prince of Parma dismissed a large contingent of German heavy cavalry which he had engaged some months before. He solemnly promised them payment in full (no less than 209,623 florins) at the next Frankfort Fair or, failing that (a suspicious proviso), within a year of their demobilization. The troops disbanded. They received a fraction of their due in 1579; a little more in 1580 and 1581; then nothing. Agitation by the contractors who had raised the cavalry, important princes like Duke Francis of Saxony among them, achieved little. At last, on 15 December 1588, Parma signed a warrant ordering the paymaster-general to honour the debt. Hopes were raised among the veterans but, as with so many warrants (*libranzas*) at that time, payment was delayed for several years. Not until February 1591, twelve years after the troops concerned had been demobilized, did they receive their due.[1]

At least these troops were paid, albeit tardily. The settlement of accounts with the rapacious German infantry in 1580 was even harsher. The men may have driven a hard bargain with the government (waiving only $6\frac{1}{4}$ per cent of their massive claim) but they had, alone of all the troops of the Army of Flanders, remained staunchly loyal to Spain since 1572: they had neither mutinied nor deserted. They deserved well of the crown. All the same, the price of loyalty was daunting. The regiment of Count Berlaymont alone had accumulated arrears of 827,000 florins for its eight years' service. In August 1580 the regiment conceded six months' of this arrears, received 55,000 florins in cash with promises to pay the rest within two years, and disbanded. In fact the veterans received a further 27,000 florins of their arrears in May 1589 and 22,000 florins more in June 1598. The rest of the debt was, it seems, never liquidated. The German regiment of Count Fronsberg, demobilized at the same time, was hardly more fortunate. Its total arrears for service 1572–81 were agreed at 160,683 florins. A token sum was paid at demobilization, then nothing. Fronsberg enlisted the support of the duke of Bavaria and, thanks to his

---

[1] AGS *CMC* 2a/27, unfol., containing the documents relating to the settlement of accounts with these troops (arrears agreed at 87,343 *escudos* of 48 pattards). The bundle contains Parma's solemn promise to pay the full arrears within one year of August 1579.

intervention, Parma issued a warrant ordering payment of the regiment's arrears (in 1588). Again only a pittance was paid: 21,000 florins to the veterans in 1590, 1,250 florins in 1591...[1]

These sordid examples only concern partial demobilizations. In fact the Army of Flanders was completely or almost completely disbanded on four separate occasions: in 1568, 1577, 1609 and after 1659. There was a considerable variation between the cost to the government of these different settlements: in 1568 and 1577 most troops were paid absolutely all, whereas in 1659–64 few troops appear to have received anything!

Disbanding the army raised by the duke of Alva in 1568 to throw back the invasions of Count Louis of Nassau and the prince of Orange was a costly operation, but at least the expense could be spread over three years. The demobilization of 1577 was a very different problem in theory, although the Army managed to wriggle out of many of its paper obligations.

In May 1575, after only three years of hostilities, the military treasury discovered that it had run up debts amounting to over 14 million florins, including 11 million to the troops for their wages. The debt continued to increase. By July 1576, when the troops mutinied for their wages, the total arrears due were estimated at 18 million florins, the total debt at 21 million.[2] It is highly improbable that Spain could have ever found this sum, or anything approaching it, but as it happened the events of 1576 simplified the problem considerably. In the first place the Netherlands troops in the Army of Flanders, both Walloon and 'Low German' (i.e. Flemish-speaking), were offered their arrears in full by the States General if they would only desert to the 'patriot' side. Most of the native troops appear to have accepted this offer, and some at least received their due.[3]

---

[1] AGS *CMC* 2a/29, unfol., *pliegos de asiento* with the regiment of Berlaymont; *CMC* 2a/43, unfol., *idem* with the regiments of Fronsperg and Fugger. The government's undertakings to pay are AGS *E* 582/4, 7 and 8.

[2] AGS *E* 568, unfol., 'Relación de lo que queda deviendo por cuenta del ejército en los Paises Bajos' (up to May 1575), and *E* 567/4, 'Relación' of a letter by *contador* Alonso de Alameda, 1 Jul. 1576.

[3] AGRB *Audience* 651/4, instruction of the States General to the commissioners appointed to 'attirer au service' the Netherlands troops in Spanish service, 17 Nov. 1576. Cf. also *Audience* 650/1, a *cahier* entitled 'Affrekeningen by den commissarien Van Wegen, de Generale Staten gedeputeert, gemaecht en gehouden mitten bevelhebber ende knechten van Johan van Barlaimont haeren hopman absent zynde.' In this register, and it must have been one of hundreds, the arrears of every man in the company was calculated on the basis of his length of service. Each province was then made responsible for part of the debt. Groningen and Friesland, for example, had to pay the arrears of the Walloon regiment of M. de Billy quartered in the provinces (Gemeente Archief, Groningen, *R.F. 1577* no. 62, 'Concept staatsresolutie om tot afbetaling van het genegotieerde geld voor de Waalsche soldaten' and J. J. Woltjer, *Friesland in hervormingstijd* (Leiden, 1962), pp. 246–52). The cost of paying all the defectors proved to

Spain was thus relieved of the obligation of paying these men.[1] It also proved possible to avoid paying the arrears of the German troops in the Army of Flanders until 1580 and even then the Army managed, as we have seen, to persuade the troops to disband with only a minute fraction of their pay. This left only the Spaniards. Upon examination, it was found that the Spanish infantry in the Army was owed 23 months' wages and the light cavalry no less than 73 months – over six years' backpay. The total arrears amounted to 1,234,293 florins (although the veterans numbered only 1,329 horsemen and 4,005 foot). Spain found it impossible to muster even this fraction of the total wage-bill due to the Army.

The Spaniards had already mutinied for their pay in July 1576. Since then they had taken by assault the city of Antwerp and they flatly refused to desert this stronghold unless their arrears were paid in full. For months Spain and the States General argued over who should pay this bill; in the negotiations the food and clothes taken by force and the munitions and contributions provided by the government 'on account' were entirely forgotten. Eventually, since the departure of the Spaniards was urgently desired by all Netherlanders, the States General provided 300,000 florins towards a settlement, and the captain-general raised a further 120,000 by letter of exchange. This represented one-third of the total debt, and the troops received this in May 1577. An ingenious formula was devised for payment of the residue by Juan de Escobedo, the captain-general's secretary and a former secretary of the Spanish Council of Finance. Individual letters of exchange were made out for the arrears of each company, payable by bankers in Chambéry within one month, or in Lombardy within two. The bankers would be repaid in Spain. With this the Spaniards were content. Amid public celebration and songs of execration the Spaniards left the Netherlands in May 1577 with money in their pocket, plunder and booty in their bags, and the firm promise of twice as much more to come.[2] Thus the Spanish troops, thanks to their superior

be beyond the means of the States. One of the field commanders of the States (himself a former general of Spain) wished in vain 'qu'on ne leurs eust tant promis, puisqu'on avoit sy peu de moyen d'y satisfaire' (G. Groen van Prinsterer, *Archives*, VI, p. 52, Hierges to Orange, 8 Apr. 1577).
Spain only paid the colonels and loyal captains of the Walloon regiments: cf. AGS *CMC* 2a/10 for the sums paid to Colonel Verdugo and *CMC* 2a/77 for payments to Colonel Mondragón and others.

[2] The total due to the troops is calculated from AGS *E* 1247/7, *Contador* Alameda to the governor of Milan, 16 May 1577, stating that the troops had been paid one-third of their arrears, and *E* 1246/72, a 'Relación' which put the arrears outstanding (viz. two-thirds) at 421,981 *escudos* of 39. The total must therefore have been 632,971 *escudos* or 1.2 million florins. AGS *CMC* 2a/26 contains 13 original *policias* together with the original *asiento de flandes* given by Pedro Rodrigues de Malvenda for 300,000 *escudos* on which the *policias* were issued.

corporate organization (the mutiny) received far more than their due at the demobilization of 1577 while everyone else received far less.

The demobilization which followed the conclusion of the Twelve Years' Truce was organized more competently. All government debts outstanding were calculated and it was found that the German troops in the Army, all of whom were to be disbanded, were entitled to arrears of 7,009,142 florins, and the rest of the Army to a further 7,064,525 florins, a total of 14 million, not far short of the daunting debt of 1575–6. This time the government argued (probably with justice) that the troops had already received the equivalent of two-thirds of their arrears in sundry receipts from contractors and civilians; the troops were offered immediate payment of the remaining one-third of their due in cash and without any deductions as a final settlement. These terms were accepted and the government began to assemble the funds needed to liquidate the arrears due to the entire army and to discharge the unnecessary troops – the Germans and the ex-mutineers. This was largely achieved by 1611: the Army of Flanders was reduced to 15,055 men.[1]

This pattern of demobilization could not be repeated after the Peace of the Pyrenees in 1659. In the first place, unlike 1609, peace on one front did not mean peace on all: the French suspended hostilities in May 1659, before the signing of a formal peace, but their armies were not demobilized for some time; in any case Republican England continued its war with Spain until May 1660. In addition to these political considerations demobilization was impeded by financial difficulties: Spain had no money with which to pay off her veterans. After the Peace of the Pyrenees, therefore, no troops of the Army of Flanders were actually disbanded. Instead the Army of Flanders was reduced to a peace-time footing after 1659 by re-deployment combined with 'reformation'. A number of German, Walloon and Irish regiments in the Netherlands were sent to Spain between 1660 and 1664 to strengthen the forces already engaged in the war against the 'rebels' of Portugal. The English troops in the Army went back to their homes with Charles II at the Restoration. This still left over 42,000 men in the Spanish Netherlands. Instead of paying off selected units, the government decided to 'reform' them: in the months

In fact all credits payable at Chambéry on 15 August 1577 were cancelled by Don John at the last minute and were made payable at Milan instead from 31 August onwards. News of this put the veterans in an ugly mood, 'Like children who are now in no mood to take jokes because of those already played on them.' (AGS E 452, unfol., 'Copia de una carta que el contador Alameda escrivio', 5 Jun. 1577.)

[1] AGS E 2138/7 and 10, *consulta* of the Council of State on a paper of Don Iñigo de Brizuela, envoy of the Archduke Albert, 1 Jun. 1609. On the advisability of discharging the persistent mutineers first: E 2025/234, *consulta* of 29 Oct. 1609.

after February 1660, 41 *tercios* and 120 companies of cavalry were broken up and their men redistributed among the remaining units. A parallel reduction was effected among the infantry. At this point, desertion and ordinary wastage took over. Without further planned reductions the Army of Flanders dwindled to 33,008 men in August 1661, and down to a mere 16,000 in June 1662. In March 1663 an order was issued that every company of German infantry which fell vacant was to be 'resumed' automatically into the rest. In this way the natural tendencies of the troops – desertion amongst the men, absenteeism among the officers – were harnessed to governmental policy. Without any of the crippling financial outlay which had complicated previous demobilizations, the Army of Flanders reached its permanent peace-time footing of 11,000 men by the end of the year 1664.[1]

[1] AGS *E* 2270, unfol., Philip IV to the marquis of Caracena, captain-general, 31 Dec. 1659, explaining why the methods of 1609 could not be re-applied. For the solution adopted, cf. AGRB *SEG* 57/208–18, orders 'reforming' units of the Army of Flanders issued 13–28 Feb. 1660. On the declining size of the Army: AGS *E* 2097, unfol., *consulta* of the Council of State, 1 Jul. 1660, *E* 2098, unfol., 'Relación de los oficiales y soldados...' at the musters of 13 Aug. and 7 Sep. 1661 and *E* 2100, unfol., Caracena to the king, 16 May 1662; AGRB *SEG* 59/105, Order of 1 Mar. 1663 and *SEG* 278/155, marquis of Castel Rodrigo, captain-general, to the king, 10 Dec. 1664.

Conclusion

Spain, her enemies and the revolt of the Netherlands

Asked to give his verdict on the foreign policy of Queen Elizabeth, Sir Walter Raleigh replied that: 'Her Majesty did all by halves.' It was a fair criticism, but it was one which could be levelled against every European ruler at the time: against the kings of France and Spain, the German Protestant princes, even against the States General. None of them would or could put all their eggs in one basket. All of them tried to win their wars by 'half-doing'. The casual character, the insouciance, of the Eighty Years' War in particular stands out as one of its most important and most persistent traits.[1]

Yet what alternative was there? Certainly the fate of the Netherlands was important to Spain, England, France and Germany, but was it more important than their commitments or ambitions elsewhere? Should England abandon her position in Ireland in order to support the Dutch; should Spain neglect the defence of the Mediterranean in order to suppress the revolt in the Low Countries? These were real choices, for no European state in the early modern period possessed sufficient resources to fight effectively in the Netherlands and also attain its political objectives elsewhere. The policies of the various major combatants in the Low Countries' Wars must therefore be considered within the context of their overall foreign ambitions and overseas commitments; changes in one were normally linked with changes in the other; the course of the war was often affected by events far outside the Netherlands. From the very first, as we shall see, the Dutch Revolt was a problem which no government could tackle in isolation.

1567-76

Just as an unfavourable international situation obliged Philip II to

[1] Charles Wilson, *Queen Elizabeth and the Revolt of the Netherlands* (London, 1970), gives full attention to this important point. Cf. his quotations from Raleigh and Walsingham on pp. 105 and 136.

temporize and offer concessions in the Netherlands between 1559 and 1566, so a reduction in the pressure of his foes enabled him to take the Low Countries 'troubles' in hand by sending an army in 1567. The Ottoman navy, whose campaigns had tied down Spanish resources since 1551, was outmanœuvred in 1565 and 1566 and it stayed at home in 1567. Only this permitted the duke of Alva to take with him to the Netherlands 8,000 of the Spanish veterans who had manned the Spanish Mediterranean fleet throughout the 1560s; even the Iconoclastic Fury could not have justified depriving Italy of their services had there been any danger of a descent by the Turkish navy on the scale of previous years. The Spaniards left for 'Flanders' only when it was known that the sultan would not be able to send out a fleet in 1567.[1]

Although it took longer and cost more than expected, the 'first revolt' of the Netherlands was fully suppressed before the Ottoman fleet assailed Christendom again. The last rebel army was destroyed by the end of 1568; the army of repression was paid off, albeit at inordinate cost, in 1569. The Netherlands actually began to 'pay their own way' in 1570 and 1571 (cf. Figures 13 and 21), to the delight of Philip II who was faced by the revolt of the moriscos in 1569–71 and was then obliged by a new phase of Turkish aggression to spend large sums on the defence of Italy and the

Figure 21. The receipts of the *pagaduría*, 1: 1567–76

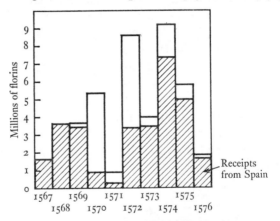

[1] Spain's policies during the 'prelude' to the Dutch Revolt are considered in my article: 'Spain, her enemies and the Revolt of the Netherlands, 1559–1648', *Past and Present*, XLIX (1970), pp. 72–95. The chronological account which follows here is merely intended to stress the various influences which affected the military performance of the Army of Flanders. I shall be giving my own account of the Dutch Revolt in a separate volume which I am preparing for The Penguin Press.

west Mediterranean. The main fleet which fought at Lepanto cost Spain 2½ million florins.[1]

Following the success of Lepanto, a new naval offensive was planned by Philip II for 1572. Preparations were already far advanced when disturbing rumours arrived that, following the peace of St Germain which ended the fighting between Catholics and Protestants in France (August 1570), Louis of Nassau, in the name of the Netherlands rebels, and Admiral Coligny, leader of the French Huguenots, had concluded a formal alliance with the intention of invading the Netherlands, possibly as the first blow in a new war between Habsburg and Valois. Philip II was fearful, but even when news of the rebels' invasion arrived he refused to abandon the Mediterranean. Too much had been staked on the outcome of the next campaign.[2]

The Prudent King was fortunate: on 24 August 1572 the massacre of St Bartholomew removed Coligny and many of his Huguenot followers from the scene. Orange and the Sea Beggars had to fight on without overt French aid. Confident that the troubles of the Netherlands would remain localized, Philip II spent heavily both in the Mediterranean and in the Netherlands, trying for a victory in both theatres at once: 3.6 million florins were sent to the Mediterranean fleet in 1572, 3.4 million to the Netherlands; 3.3 million and 3.5 million respectively in 1573. In 1574, 4 million florins reached the Mediterranean fleet, and an unprecedented 7.35 million went to the Army of Flanders.[3]

This sustained effort to fight two wars simultaneously was a crippling financial burden. In 1574 alone Castile spent around 22 million florins (over half of it abroad) although her revenues were under 12 million (cf. Appendix F). It was Philip II's tragedy that in the very year in which he beggared his treasury, his armies were paralysed by ill-luck, indecision or insubordination. In the Mediterranean, the Spanish fleet was powerless to save Tunis from the Turks; in the Netherlands Middelburg, the last Spanish outpost in Zealand, surrendered to Orange in February 1574 while the striking defeat of a new rebel invasion under Count Louis of Nassau at Mook (14 April) failed to prevent the Spanish victors from

---

[1] BPU Geneva, *Ms. Favre* 62/35, 'Relación' stating that 1,226,241 *escudos de oro de Italia* had been spent on the fleet of the League in 1571.

[2] Cf. the brilliant detective work of F. Braudel concerning Philip II's changing aims in the 1572 naval campaign (*La Méditerranée* (2nd ed., Paris, 1966), II, pp. 407–8).

[3] AGS *CMC* 2a/55, Account of F. de Lixalde, paymaster-general of the Army of Flanders (1567–77 – money received from merchants and by *asientos de flandes*); *CMC* 2a/814, account of J. Morales de Torre, Spanish paymaster of the *Armada de la Liga* (1571–8 – all from Spain). In 1572 the duke of Alva raised a further 4 million florins by anticipation from various bankers in the Netherlands, repaid later.

mutinying for their pay. Even before the war began the veteran *tercios* were owed 13 months; they had mutinied for some wages after the capture of Haarlem in July 1573 but they had received only 30 *escudos*; on the morrow of Mook the Spaniards were able to claim 37 months' back-pay. The victors of Mook proceeded to paralyse Spain's war-effort far more than Count Louis could have done: they marched on Antwerp, entered the city and held it to ransom. The 4,562 veterans of an army of 86,000 managed to corner over 1 million florins (15 per cent of the year's provision from Spain) for themselves. Only after payment in full did they consent to take up their arms for the king again (30 May).

The belated campaign of 1574, intended to capture Leiden, proved a fiasco. The fearless mutineers deserted their trenches in terror as the Dutch broke the dikes around the beleaguered town (2–3 October). Worse was to follow. On 1 November another Spanish *tercio*, left to garrison the government's forts and villages in Holland, issued a mutinous ultimatum: unless they received their pay within fifteen days, they would abandon their posts and take refuge in Brabant, safe from the fighting and the frosts. The government strained every sinew to find some money to prevent this disaster, but it failed. The Spaniards remained at their posts until 1 December, albeit in mutiny, then they abandoned everything, even their comrades who had fallen into the hands of the Dutch, and fled. When on 5 March 1575 the mutineers were finally paid, it was found that their arrears only amounted to 130,000 florins. For the lack of such a sum Spain had forfeited her hold on Holland and with it one of her best chances of winning the war.

Lack of money was at the root of all these military failures. Spain could not provide the Army of Flanders with enough funds unless the defence of the Mediterranean was abandoned, and that was unthinkable. Even in 1574, the year of greatest effort, the Army's receipts were inadequate: there was not enough to pay all the troops (even the Spaniards at the siege of Leiden never received any pay), to purchase vital munitions, to organize a proper supply of food to the troops, to repay pressing debts. The price of this financial inadequacy was military failure: by the end of the year of maximum effort the Orangists were in control of every town in Holland and Zealand except Haarlem and Amsterdam.

The following year was hardly better for the king's cause. Philip II did his best – almost 5 million florins reached the military treasury from Spain; over $1\frac{1}{2}$ million more went to the Fleet – but time was running out. Unknown to the combatants in the Netherlands, a secret advisory committee had already informed Philip II that the only way of restoring solvency to the Castilian treasury was to repudiate all debts. This solution, it was realized, would be disastrous for all enterprises abroad which depended upon Spanish provisions: breaking credit with the crown's bankers would inevitably deprive the crown of its sole means of sending large sums of money abroad, the letter of credit. Without the services of its bankers, the crown could not support the Army of Flanders. The king therefore refused to implement the recommendation of his financial advisers (made on 14 July 1574) until he found it totally impossible to raise any more loans. The Army of Flanders was therefore permitted one more campaign.

The campaign of 1575 was altogether more adventurous. There was to be a two-pronged advance which would drive a wedge between Holland and Zealand. It was believed, probably correctly, that 'if the islands are recaptured, the mainland will fall of itself'.[1] After some weeks had been wasted in abortive peace-talks with the 'rebels' at Breda, one Spanish force advanced south-west from Utrecht towards Rotterdam, taking Oudewater, Schoonhoven and Buren, while another crossed the 'drowned land' to the islands of St Filipsland, Duiveland and Schouwen. The new offensive was triumphantly successful: the islands of South Holland were overrun within a few weeks. Only the town of Zierikzee in Schouwen held out for Orange. The outlook for the rebels was extremely grave.

But success had come too late for Spain. Philip II, at last unable to find further credit, issued his decree of bankruptcy freezing the capital of all existing loans on 1 September 1575. From Antwerp, as the Dutch lit joyous bonfires and offered prayers of thanksgiving, Governor-General Requesens was in agony:

> This Decree of Bankruptcy has been such a blow to the Exchange here that no one in it has any credit...I cannot find a single penny. Nor can I see how the King could send money here, even if he had it in abundance. Short of a miracle, all this military machine will fall into ruins...and all this at a time when, if the King could have delayed for three months, I hold it certain that in that time we could have recaptured all the rest of Zealand and even the other provinces.

Neither Requesens with his lamentations nor the Dutch with their bonfires erred in their assessment of the consequences of the Decree: Spain could no longer send money to the Army of Flanders. The receipts of the *Pagaduría* slumped to under 2 million florins in 1576. A general mutiny of the Army became inevitable.[2]

[1] BPU Geneva, *Ms. Favre* 30/71–4, Philip II to Requesens, 20 Oct. 1573 (copy of royal holograph).

[2] AGS *E* 564/134, Requesens to the king, 4 Nov. 1575 and IVdeDJ 37/72, Requesens to Zuñiga, 12 Nov. 1575. For the machinery of bankruptcy cf. pp. 148–51 above; cf. also A. W. Lovett, 'Juan de Ovando and the Council of Finance', *The Historical Journal*, XV (1972), in printing.

As usual the Spanish troops were the first to organize a collective protest, and as usual they only did so when they had performed their arduous military duties. They remained at their posts until they had obliged the town of Zierikzee to surrender (2 July 1576); then they mutinied. The Spaniards immediately poured out of Zealand into Brabant and on 25 July made an unexpected assault on the town of Aalst (Alost) which they proceeded to sack. The Walloon troops were not slow to learn from their more experienced Spanish comrades and they too soon mutinied, maintaining an amicable correspondence with the Spaniards (cf. pp. 197–8 above).

The sack of Aalst, however, introduced an important new element into the situation. The brutality of the Spaniards, so signally demonstrated, provoked a wave of nausea and Hispanophobia in the Netherlands. Weariness with the inconclusive and ruinously expensive war, hatred of the troops' insolence, frustration with the hardships and severity of nine years of Spanish rule, all were brought to a head by the news of the sack of Aalst. Bowing to popular indignation, the Council of State declared the mutineers outlaws to a man the very next day; everyone was free to kill them (26 July). The edict was re-issued on 2 August and 22 September in even stronger terms: killing the mutineers was made obligatory. Events then moved quickly. As anarchy threatened, the political leaders of the southern provinces, muzzled since 1567, took the law into their own hands, levied troops in the name of the States General and began formal negotiations with Holland and Zealand. A ceasefire was arranged on 30 October and signed on 5 November (the 'Pacification of Ghent'), the final ratification precipitated by the brutal assault and sack of Antwerp by the Spanish mutineers on 4 November.

The 'great victory of Antwerp', as the Spaniards saw it, marked the formal demise of the Army of Flanders as a fighting force. It precluded any compromise between the king and the States General which failed to specify that all foreign troops should be withdrawn. In the event, bargaining about the terms of withdrawal went on for five months, but in April 1577 the Spaniards, burdened with plunder, families and vast baggage, departed. Spain's first concerted attempt to suppress the Dutch Revolt by force had failed.

1577–82

Throughout the five years which followed the Pacification of Ghent it was never clear whether Spain had decided upon conciliation or war in the

Netherlands. Formal peace, in fact, only lasted for six months (February–July 1577). The main obstacles to a settlement were the refusal of Holland and Zealand either to demobilize or to tolerate Roman Catholic worship, and the irascibility of the new governor-general, Don John of Austria. In July 1577, in a somewhat theatrical gesture, he defied the States General and seized the citadel of Namur; more significant, on his own authority he summoned the Spanish veterans to return to the Netherlands. This obliged Philip II to take a new decision on the policy to be followed in 'Flanders'.

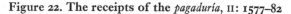

Figure 22. The receipts of the *pagaduría*, II: 1577–82

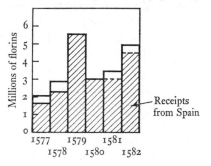

The king's initial reaction was to forbid the governor of Lombardy to send any troops to Don John; he was not going to be dragged into war again by a mere viceroy of thirty-two. The royal council, however, favoured a renewal of the war. The king changed his mind: on 31 August the Spanish veterans were ordered to stand by; on 11 September they were ordered to march.[1]

Philip II's change of heart was at first sight surprising. At the beginning of the year he had appeared unshakeable in his desire for peace in the Netherlands:

> At all costs [he wrote to Don John on 31 January] you must prevent negotiations breaking down – as I have written to you so many times and as you have heard from my own lips...I have to urge, brother, that you must avoid a break-down and that you should accommodate yourself to Time and Necessity, which are the best counsellors you can have...[2]

But Time had brought important changes in Spain's situation since January. Above all, and much to his surprise, the king managed to secure

[1] AGS *E* 1247/133, king to Ayamonte, governor of Lombardy, 28 Aug. 1577 (minute); BPU Geneva, *Ms. Favre* 28/195–6, king to duke of Sesa, general of the Mediterranean Fleet, 11 Sep. 1577 reiterating the order of 31 Aug.
[2] AGS *E* 2843/3, king to Don John of Austria, 31 Jan. 1577 (minute).

an informal agreement from the sultan to suspend hostilities in the Mediterranean for one year, beginning in March 1577. On 7 February 1578 a formal truce was concluded between Spain and the sultan and it was prolonged into the 1580s. Philip II was at last free of the great responsibility which had preoccupied him since 1559. As in 1566–7, it is unlikely that the king could have contemplated the use of force in the Netherlands after the Pacification of Ghent without some assurance that the Mediterranean would not thereby be endangered.[1]

The same year of 1577 brought improvement to the king's position in another direction. Since the bankruptcy of September 1575 Philip II had been able to secure loans only from bankers not involved in the decree (like the celebrated Simon Ruiz) or from those, like Lorenzo Spinola, who were expressly exempted from its terms. These men had not the resources to satisfy the Spanish crown for long. Since August 1577, Don John had depended for money on a solitary Spanish merchant residing in Paris, Jeronimo de Curiel, who raised loans from merchants friendly to Spain, promising them repayment in Spain. The proceeds were sent in gold by courier to Namur. Between August 1577 and December 1578, 1.7 million florins reached the military treasury in this way from Paris.[2] It was not enough to run a war. The Army of Flanders was steadily driven back.

Spanish success in the Netherlands really depended upon a reconciliation between Philip II and the great financiers whose loans he had confiscated in 1575. In voting in favour of war in September 1577 the duke of Alva, who had painful memories of his financial embarrassments in 1573, insisted that enormous provisions had to be arranged – and had to be seen to be arranged. He wrote to the king's private secretary:

> This Flanders question has become very difficult to settle by force. By 'difficult' I mean it will take a long time if we are to proceed by measuring His Majesty's forces against those of his rebels. And more than anything else a quick conclusion will be promoted by the authority of the provisions which His Majesty is now arranging and the foreknowledge of those which are in preparation. That is the spirit and soul of this matter. If the provisions are cut up into instalments and

[1] BPU Geneva, *Ms. Favre* 28/131, king to Sesa, 6 Apr. 1577, passing on news of the secret truce arranged for the year. Cf. also the original documents printed and discussed by S. A. Skilliter, 'The Hispano–Ottoman armistice of 1581', in *Iran and Islam* (Edinburgh, 1971), pp. 491–515.

[2] Curiel, royal factor in Antwerp 1561–70, was appointed to reside in Paris by Don John on 4 Aug. 1577. He received 392,719 *escudos* for the king before his death on 17 Feb. 1578. (AGS *CMC* 20/75, bundle iii, account of Curiel). Thereafter Curiel's nephew and partner Alonso continued to raise funds in Paris and he provided the military treasury with a further 465,352 *escudos* before the end of the year. (AGS *CMC* 2a/44, account of Paymaster-General M. de Unceta.)

reduced, all spirit and vigour [*brío*] will be removed – which is the exact opposite of what is required.[1]

The *medio general* of 5 December 1577 met the duke's demand: in return for compensation for their previous loans in the form of two-thirds in *juros al quitar* at the very low rate of 3 per cent and one-third in crown lands, the bankers affected by the decree (the *decretados*) agreed to lend the crown a further 5 million ducats (10 million florins), payable in Italy over two years.[2] On 10 June 1578, the first instalment of the new loan of the *decretados* reached the military treasury and by April 1579, 3.6 million florins had arrived.[3]

These years also brought the Catholic king new financial strength independent of his bankers. In 1577, probably for the first time, a fleet arrived from the New World carrying over 2 million ducats for the king. The 'royal cycle' of American treasure imports had begun. In 1583, over 3 million ducats arrived for the king; in 1587, just in time to finance the 'Invincible Armada', almost 5 million. The aggregate input was equally impressive: almost 12 million ducats of 'treasure' arrived for the king in the decade 1571–80, 18.7 million in 1581–90 and over 25 million in 1591–1600.[4] The significance of the Indies treasure in the *asiento*-system of the Spanish crown can scarcely be exaggerated: it provided the security as well as the new bullion necessary for most large-scale crown borrowing, and it influenced business confidence all over Europe. The dramatic and sustained increase in the king's revenues from the Indies, especially from the new silver mines of Peru, meant that twice as much could be borrowed on the security of the Indies fleet in the 1590s as in the 1570s.

Despite the arrangement of provisions *con brío* for 1578 and 1579, however, and despite the encouraging increase in the treasure arriving from the Indies, the impetus of the new Spanish offensive in the Netherlands was allowed to die away. There were two main reasons for this. In the first place, important divisions had appeared among the adherents of

---

[1] IVdeDJ 38/4, Alva to Mateo Vazquez, 11 Sep. 1577 (holograph). This statement, terse, lucid and authoritative, is a typical example of Alva's style.
[2] AGS *CMC* 2a/1056, unfol., *medio general* of 5 Dec. 1577.
[3] AGS *CMC* 2a/26 and 36, unfol., accounts of J. Judici, agent for the crown to collect the *asientos* 'a cobrar en la villa de Vizzacon'. Since Antwerp (the financial centre used by the crown's bankers until 1575) was in enemy hands, the new loans were paid in the 'Fairs of Besançon', held mainly in the city of Piacenza in Italy, until the northern metropolis was recaptured in August 1585.
[4] For the decennial totals, cf. J. H. Elliott, *Imperial Spain* (London, 1963), p. 175 – Hamilton's figures converted into ducats. For the annual receipts, cf. the audited declarations of the *Casa de Contratación* at Seville, AGS *Contadurías Generales* 3056, unfol.: 811,002,628 *maravedís* in 1577; 1,188,012,010 *mrs.* in 1583; 1,677,097,636 *mrs.* in 1587.

the States General; in particular, the provincial estates of Hainaut, Artois and French Flanders declared themselves ready to return to obedience. After a preliminary accord in May 1579, the 'Treaty of Arras' was formally signed on 13 September. One of the crucial conditions of the agreement, by which the three provinces were reconciled to Philip II, was that all foreign troops in the Army of Flanders should be dismissed. The same condition was imposed by the towns of Groningen and 's Hertogenbosch which also defected from the States General in 1579. The foreign troops were to leave within six months of the Treaty of Arras. As it happened, a lull in hostilities in the Netherlands and a reduction in the provisions was just what Philip II wanted. In August 1578 the childless king of Portugal, Dom Sebastian, died in battle. Apart from a senile and epileptic uncle in holy orders, Cardinal Henry, Philip II had the best claim to the Portuguese succession.

Throughout 1579 therefore, King Philip laid his plans for the conquest of Portugal as soon as Cardinal Henry should die. He welcomed the opportunity of reinforcing his army with the Spanish veterans from the Netherlands (they left Luxemburg in May 1580 and went straight to Lombardy and thence to Spain). The Netherlands were virtually abandoned in 1580–2 while Spain annexed Portugal and the Azores; very little money reached the military treasury (cf. Figure 22).

Despite the king's neglect, the reduced Army of Flanders won a number of victories. Even a French army under the duke of Anjou which fought for the States, could not prevent the royalists from capturing the towns of Kortrijk, Breda and Nivelles in 1580, Tournai in 1581, and Oudenaarde in 1582. It was not an undistinguished record, but the provinces and also the new governor-general, Parma, knew that they had not deserved their success. They knew that they could not achieve much more without a substantial and regular provision from Spain: on this they were for once agreed with their old enemy the duke of Alva. The 'reconciled' provinces, not long after their reconciliation, pressed the king to declare exactly how much he was prepared to send to the Netherlands. The king angrily refused. Rather more tactfully, Parma beseeched his uncle to send 'a fixed sum every month' to the Army of Flanders.[1] Again the king demurred. Even the return of the foreign troops in September 1582, which the 'obedient provinces' hoped would produce an increase in the money from Spain, failed to improve the regularity of the provisions. In desperation Parma sent his close collaborator, Jean Richardot, a man closely

[1] AGRB *Audience* 176/67–71, the king to Parma, 12 Sep. 1579, complaining of indecent financial probing by the States of Artois; *Audience* 192/238–41, Parma to the king, 30 Aug. 1580.

connected with the Walloon provinces, to lay before the king in person the advantages to be gained from augmenting the provisions and from sending them in regular instalments. The mission was triumphantly successful. In June 1583 Philip II wrote to his senior finance minister:

> The present necessity [in the Low Countries] is so great that it would be of the greatest importance to be able to provide at once some four or five hundred thousand ducats and for the future it would be very good to arrange a provision by months, from 150,000 to 200,000 ducats per month.[1]

Parma now had the guarantee of a regular supply of money with which to organize the reconquest of the Netherlands. He also had a master-plan. As early as 3 January 1581 he explained to the king that, thanks to the geographical configuration of the south Netherlands, a coordinated blockade of all the towns along the Scheldt (Mechelen, Antwerp, Ghent and so on) would automatically reduce the whole of the provinces of Brabant and Flanders to royal obedience. With the promise of regular support guaranteed in advance, even though the amounts were small, and a large number of rich towns to besiege and perhaps to plunder, in 1583 Parma was ready to undertake the reconquest of the south.

1583–97

From 1583 until the end of 1585, Philip II devoted all his attention and all his resources to the reconquest of the Netherlands. At his command the prince of Parma maintained a relentless military pressure against the towns of Flanders and Brabant while the king's gold was used to suborn all who faltered in their allegiance to the States. In particular the English troops in the Army of the States were offered considerable bribes to defect and many of them did so, betraying valuable towns to the Spaniards: Lier (1582), Aalst (1584 – for 128,250 florins), Deventer (1587) and St Geertruidenburg (1589). Many Netherlands noblemen too were enticed back to the royalist cause by the promise of a pension, property and pardon. As one frustrated commander serving the Republic wrote in 1586 as yet another town (Grave) surrendered readily to Spain: 'Everyone knows that the King's golden bullets made a greater breach in the heart of the traitor who commanded it than did the normal battery or any catholic virtue.' Parma, like Henry IV in France after 1594, perfected the com-

---

[1] IVdeDJ 68/306, *consulta* of Don Hernando de Vega, president of the Council of Finance, to the king, 8 Jun. 1583, with the important royal response.

bination of stick and carrot to effect a rapid reconquest.[1] Between the capture of Maastricht in July 1579 and the capture of Antwerp in August 1585, the Army of Flanders took over thirty major towns with hardly one concerted effort by the States General to relieve them. Moreover, this reconquest was achieved at remarkably little cost to Spain: about 22 million florins were received by the military treasury from Spain over these years. Success at such low cost was achieved by the efficient exploitation of the Netherlands through the contributions system organized by the Army, supplemented by the indemnities paid by the towns captured and

Figure 23. The receipts of the *pagaduría*, III: 1583–97

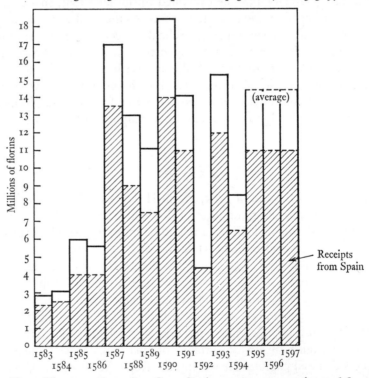

Note: The annual receipts from Spain are averages estimated from the totals in Appendix K.

---

[1] Lincoln Record Office, *Ancaster* X/7, Lord Willoughby to (?) C. de Mondragon, Castellan of Antwerp, Jun. 1586; cf. AGRB *SEG* 8/221v, order of Parma to pay 45,000 *escudos* of 57 pattards to the English garrison of Aalst, 15 Feb. 1584. The cost of Henry IV's *rachat du royaume* in 1594–6 was far greater: 922,000 *écus* to Lorraine, 629,600 to Guise, 533,000 to Mayenne...(all recorded in the lapidary entries of Sully's account-books: Archives Nationales, Paris,120 *AP* 9 and 11).

above all by the regularity with which the money from Spain arrived – 600,000 *escudos* in gold at a time.

Parma's victories were even more remarkable in view of the growing foreign support which arrived to stiffen Dutch resistance. The end of the seventh war of religion in France (with the Peace of Fleix, November 1580) inaugurated a period of domestic peace and in 1581 a Huguenot army made its appearance in the service of the States, led by the duke of Anjou, heir-apparent to the French throne and 'Defender of the Liberties of the Low Countries' since 1578. The French forces played a prominent part in the campaigns of 1581–3, but this assistance ended with the death of Anjou in June 1584 and the organization of a Catholic League to oppose the succession of the new heir-apparent, the Huguenot Henry of Navarre. The Guise leaders of the League could count on regular financial support from Spain (under the Treaty of Joinville, 31 December 1584) and, at a modest cost to Spain, they successfully intimidated the French Huguenots and prevented them from further intervention in the Netherlands for ten years.

It seemed as if the triumphant restoration of Spanish authority in the Netherlands might continue indefinitely. In 1586, master of Flanders and Brabant, Parma successfully besieged and captured a number of key-towns along the rivers Maas and Rhine (Grave, Megem, Venlo, Neuss, Mörs); the provisions sent by the king in 1585–6 were the highest since 1575. Yet the situation was swiftly transformed. On 20 August 1585 the States General signed an alliance with Queen Elizabeth of England, the Treaty of Nonsuch. Under the terms of this agreement, the Queen provided 7,350 men, a regular subsidy (to be $\frac{1}{4}$ of the total cost of the war) and political advisers. These arrived in December of the same year. Already Francis Drake was bound for the Spanish Indies with 20 sail on a major privateering mission openly sponsored by the Queen. England had, in effect, declared war on Spain.[1]

English intervention in the Netherlands was highly disturbing to Philip II. It had seemed as though the States General were prepared to discuss peace with Spain – there was certainly a peace-party within the Republic; this wavering was scotched by the Treaty of Nonsuch. The English *secours*, though militarily ineffectual, strengthened the flagging resolution of the States to resist. Philip II therefore decided to take steps to counter England's aggression. As early as 1583 the idea of a seaborne attack on England from Spain was proposed to him; now on 29 December

---

[1] The significance of these events is highlighted in the recent study of Charles Wilson, *Queen Elizabeth and the Revolt of the Netherlands*, pp. 81–90.

1585 he asked his advisers to collect plans, maps and information concerning the project. Preparations for a great fleet began in 1586. Reinforcements and larger provisions were sent to the Army of Flanders, which was to participate in the invasion project. In spring 1587 the Army moved to encampments close to the Flemish coast.

Here the momentum of the reconquest was lost. The organization of a food-supply to the areas newly captured by the Army had always been a problem, but it became a nightmare after 1586. The Dutch imposed a rigid blockade on the southern provinces, which prevented the arrival of any Baltic grain – the traditional stand-by of the great towns of Flanders and Brabant. This was desperately needed in the years 1587–9 because the harvests failed completely for three years in succession. The Netherlands fell prey to the worst famine of the century and there was no relief: there was no food to be had. The famine decimated the population of the provinces newly reconciled to Spain, and it carried off a large number of the troops collected for the 'enterprise of England'. The same ravages continued in 1588, while more troops and more money arrived for the Armada, and at the end of it all the Army of Flanders was never able to effect a junction with the great fleet before it was defeated.

Early in 1589 the outlook for the Army of Flanders appeared somewhat brighter. Open war broke out in France in May 1588 and the Dutch lifted their embargo in September; the defeat of the Armada at least meant that the war against the Dutch could be resumed. Early in 1589 the important town of St Geertruidenburg, commanding a crossing over the Maas, was betrayed to the Spaniards by its garrison, while the Army overran the island of Bommel in the course of the summer. Then the situation darkened again. The troops in the forefront of the Bommel campaign mutinied, and all the troops on the island had to be withdrawn. More significant for the future, on 2 August 1589 Henry III, the last of the Valois, died.

Spain was already deeply involved in French affairs. By the Treaty of Joinville Philip II had promised the French Catholic League that, if need arose, Spain would provide military support in order to prevent the succession of the Protestant leader, Henry of Navarre, to the French crown. Henry was unacceptable to Spain not just for his religion but for his policies: he was the heir and pupil of Admiral Coligny who in 1572 had so nearly involved France in the Netherlands' rebellion against Spain. Philip II was prepared to go to any lengths to prevent Navarre from becoming king. On 2 September 1589 the Spanish Council of State discussed the French situation after the death of Henry III. There was a unanimous recommendation in favour of full military intervention on the side of the *Ligue*. On 7 September Philip II signed the crucial order commanding his nephew to move all available forces in the Netherlands down to the French frontier to assist the *Ligue*. The war against the Dutch was to become merely a defensive holding-operation: strong garrisons in the key-towns with a small strike-force in reserve.[1]

Parma, who was to take command of the French expeditionary force, had no doubt that Spanish interests made it imperative to assist the *Ligue*. He was, however, profoundly uneasy about the king's decision not to make some sort of compromise with the rebels while the Army of Flanders was involved in France. In November 1589 he proposed a peace-plan to the king which, he felt, the rebels might accept. The main concession was that the king should agree to permit private Calvinist worship in the 'rebel' areas in exchange for a return to obedience. The king flatly refused to endorse such a proposal. Parma was ordered to fight on two fronts.[2]

The king had made a fatal mistake. For virtually the first time, the States General managed to sink their differences and organize a serious campaign of their own. While Parma was away in France in 1590 they captured the town of Breda – their first military success for twelve years! Worse still, the Army of Flanders fell a prey to mutiny. In the course of 1590 two Spanish *tercios*, virtually unpaid since 1585, mutinied for their arrears, effectively preventing the organization of an army to contain the Dutch. It was to become a classic pattern. In 1591, Parma was warned that the Dutch were preparing a major campaign, to recapture the Spanish positions in Frisia. Despite express orders from the king to return to France at once, Parma led his army north to beat off the Dutch attack. He only informed the king of this disobedience on 24 July. On 4 August the king repeated his urgent injunction that the war in France must come first. Still Parma hesitated. It was 21 December 1591 before he marched into France again.

Philip II was not used to disobedience. He had, as he informed his wayward nephew, 'opened his heart' to him and he expected to be obeyed; moreover, he had sent unprecedented sums from Spain in 1590 and 1591

---

[1] AGS *E* 2855, unfol., *consulta* of 2 Sep. 1589; *E* 2219/197, king to Parma, 7 Sep. 1589: '...con estas obligaçiones en que ponen las cosas de Francia (a que no se puede faltar por yr tanto en ellas como va) pareçe que pues no se puede atender a muchas cosas juntas sin que lo padezcan todas, demas de que la hazienda no sufre, conviene neçessariamente tomar forma en la de la guerra dessos estados, reduziendola a defensiva...'

[2] The Parma peace-plan was unfolded to the king and his ministers by Richardot: AGS *E* 2855, unfol., 'Sumario de los 4 papeles principales que dio el presidente Richardot', 11 Nov. 1589, with the royal rejection appended.

expressly for the support of the League. Parma had spent the king's money on other things. These considerations convinced the king that it was time for Parma's recall. On 31 December 1591, therefore, the marquis of Cerralvo was appointed governor and captain-general of the Netherlands but unfortunately for Philip II's plans the marquis died *en route*. Next the king chose the count of Fuentes (June 1592) but he only arrived in Brussels on 23 November 1592. He never met Parma, who died at Arras on 6 December.

These delays and changes had a disastrous effect on the Army of Flanders. The king's mistrust of Parma led the king to withhold funds until a suitable successor could take command. Since this took an entire year, during 1592 the military treasury received only 4.4 million florins in place of the 18 million of 1590 and the 14 million of 1591.[1] Already the mutinies of 1590–1 had shown that the Army was in need of more money, not less, but in 1592 there was hardly enough money to pay any wages. In 1593, collective disobedience by the troops began in earnest. In July and August mutinies broke out amongst the Spanish army in France at St Pol and Pont-Sur-Sambre involving about 1,500 men each. In July 1594, just as the government mustered the money required to settle these mutinies, another yet more serious one broke out amongst the troops left to defend the Netherlands, the mutiny of Zichem, involving almost 3,000 veterans.

These events were critical since the resources of the Army of Flanders were already strained to the limit. There were so few troops available for operations that the immobilization of even 3,000 men in a mutiny aborted every enterprise. In four brilliant campaigns (1591–4) Maurice of Nassau captured all the Spanish outposts north of the Maas, meeting with little effective resistance because the only Spanish forces which might have driven him back were locked in mutiny. The corner-stone of the Dutch reconquest, Groningen, fell to the small siege-army of Count Maurice in July 1594 largely because the mutineers of Zichem refused to march to its relief. Spain was as incapable of resisting the advance of the States in the 1590s as the Republic had been of driving back Parma's forces during the previous decade. In France too the disobedience of the elite troops of the Army of Flanders in 1593–4

---

[1] For the positive reasoning behind the reduction in the provisions cf. p. 117 above. Nevertheless Parma was expected to send three-quarters of all the money which *did* arrive to France: AGRB *SEG* 14/20, order of 15 Apr. 1592: 400,000 *escudos* expected, 'a saver los 300,000 escudos dellos para este dicho exercito [in France] y los 100,000 escudos restantes para el de Flandes'. No doubt Philip II used any spare resources to suppress the 'troubles' of Aragon in 1591–2.

shipwrecked Philip II's plans. For lack of loyal soldiers the Brussels government was compelled to conclude a six-months' truce with Henry of Navarre in July 1593, which afforded him precious time to buy over the supporters of Mayenne and to destroy the power-bases of the Catholic League in eastern France. By trying for victory on two fronts at once, Philip II failed in both. The turning-point in the Low Countries' Wars, as in the struggle for the French crown, came in the years 1593–4.[1]

Although there was some withdrawal of Spanish forces from France after 1595, as late as October 1597 the governors of loyal towns in Gelderland invested by the Dutch were ordered to surrender when they were summoned to do so, since no relief force could possibly be organized.[2] The 'France-first' policy, pursued unwaveringly since 1589, was not abandoned by Spain until the Peace of Vervins in 1598. Philip II's desperate bid to stop Navarre had cost Spain immense sums – 88 million florins were sent to the Netherlands alone in the 1590s, mostly for use in France – and also her last real chance of victory over the Dutch.[3]

1598–1608

The position of the Army of Flanders in 1598 was far worse than it had been in 1589, on the eve of the intervention in France. Above all, France had a strong king again. Henry IV's good sense, his gold and his military victories managed to unite his country; Spain and her ally the Catholic League were decisively beaten. At once Spain found her grasp slipping from those areas of Europe where she had gained preponderance simply through the absence of competition: Savoy, the Swiss cantons, northern Italy, north-western Germany. Spain's land communications between Lombardy and the Low Countries and her domination of Italy, both of

---

[1] For the chronology of the defeat of the *Ligue*, cf. the exemplary study of H. Drouot, *Mayenne et la Bourgogne: contribution à l'histoire des provinces françaises pendant la Ligue* (1587–96) (Paris, 1937).

[2] RA Arnhem, *Archief...Berg* 604, Archduke Albert to Count Frederick van den Berg, 21 Oct. 1597, ordering that he and his deputies in Gelderland were to surrender rather than risk capture or destruction.

[3] Paymasters-General Santesteban and Walther Zapata declared they had received almost 90 million florins from Spain in 1590–9 (AGS *CMC* 2a/840 and 869). It is notable that the third bankruptcy of Philip II (29 Nov. 1596) had little effect on the receipts of the *pagaduría*. In fact the king only suspended payments from his treasury when a large fleet arrived from the New World; he was able to transfer this money to the Netherlands because the Fuggers were exempted from the terms of the bankruptcy and therefore continued to serve the monarch who had abused them so often but owed them so much. The king's ability to manage without his *asentistas* enabled him to conclude a highly favourable agreement with them on 14 Nov. 1597 (formalized on 14 Feb. 1598). They immediately agreed to lend the crown a fresh *asiento* of 7.2 million ducats (AGS *CMC* 3a/78).

them dependent on French impotence, were soon at risk. In 1601 the Spanish Road all but fell into French hands (cf. pp. 68–9 above).

The ten years following the defeat of the Spanish Armada also saw the emergence of another formidable adversary for the Army of Flanders. The Dutch Republic put Spain's preoccupation with France to good use. Their armies secured a defensible frontier; their merchants, emboldened by the defeats of Spain's major warfleets in 1588 and 1596, built up a lively trade with the Mediterranean countries and with Africa, America and south-east Asia. The Dutch commercial bonanza after 1588 provided the capital, loans and taxes which enabled the Republic to run the war. Finally, it was in the 1590s that the 'rebels' at last evolved a form of government which permitted purposeful military action over a long period.

At the same time, the Army of Flanders itself had grown weaker. Dispirited by the defeats of the 1590s and restless from lack of pay, the troops' morale sank very low. The falling provisions from Spain in 1598–1601 (Figure 24) and the limitation of their right to free lodgings

Figure 24. The receipts of the *pagaduría*, IV: 1598–1608

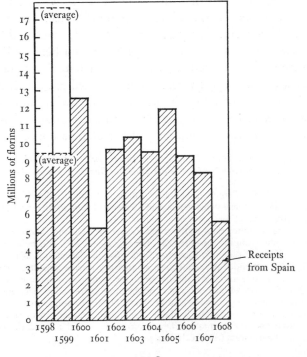

248

and service (cf. p. 144 above) pushed larger numbers of soldiers into mutiny for their wage arrears than ever before. It was during the decade 1597–1606 that mutiny really became the 'domestic remedy' of the Army of Flanders for the persistent problem of pay-starvation.

Between 1598 and 1604 every major campaign undertaken by the Army of Flanders was jeopardized or prevented by the mutiny of a large body of troops. In 1598, while the main army marched into the duchies of Cleves and Cologne in order to secure bridgeheads over the river Rhine, the Spanish garrisons of many important posts in the south mutinied (Lier, Antwerp and Ghent in particular). In 1599–1600, many of the troops who invaded the island of Bommel in the summer mutinied: 2,000 veterans from the main army based themselves on the walled town of Diest and demanded their arrears in full (Christmas 1599), while the garrisons which were left in the two forts built on Bommel by the Spaniards in 1599, St André and Crèvecœur, betrayed their posts to the Dutch early in 1600 in return for their back-pay. In July 1600, another part of the campaign army, again around 2,000 men, mutinied and made camp in the town of Weert. Encouraged by the 1½ million florins paid to the mutineers of Diest (February 1601) and the 1 million florins to those of Weert (March 1602), yet another major mutiny broke out among the Spanish field army in August 1602: this time no less than 3,200 men – about half the army – abandoned their units, made their base at the frontier town of Hoogstraten and laid claim to a further 1 million florins. This persistence of mutinies (and there were many more smaller ones) made nonsense of the Army of Flanders' attempt to besiege Ostend (June 1601 onwards). So many men were involved in mutinies and so much money was required to pay them that there was not enough of either to complete the blockade of the town. The Army's impotent efforts came to be something of an international joke.

To this stalemate situation came Ambrosio Spinola, descendent of great financiers and endowed with considerable military ability. As a fellow Genoese put it, Spinola could always raise a personal loan of 2 million escudos, and he could do it for half as much as the king of Spain.[1] By a curious contract, more in keeping with the *condottiere* of the fifteenth century than with the *grande guerre* of the seventeenth, he promised to recapture Ostend within a year provided he could control the financing of the siege and provided he had sole command of the troops around the town (29 September 1603). In the end unlimited credit, military ingenuity

[1] AGS *E* 634/73, paper of Juan Andrea Doria on the Netherlands, 1605.

and dogged perseverance paid off: the town, or what was left of it, surrendered to Spinola within the year (22 Sep. 1604).

This success was of very limited strategic value. Ostend was, arguably, less useful than the port of Sluis which the Dutch forced to surrender in August 1604, and it was certainly insufficient compensation for all the other towns which the Dutch had been free to take since 1601 thanks to the Army of Flanders' preoccupation with Ostend. Nevertheless, the capture was important. It demonstrated that, despite the failures of previous years, Spain and her Netherlands army were still powers to be reckoned with. It also consolidated Spinola's power in the Netherlands. He was made second-in-command of the whole army (*maestre de campo general*) and in March 1605 he was given the office of superintendent of finance, charged with absolute power over the military treasury.

The wisdom of this choice soon became apparent. Philip III had desired a truce in the Netherlands at least since the defeat of Nieuwpoort in July 1600 but, not surprisingly, the Dutch had refused (they were winning). In 1603, however, the death of Queen Elizabeth opened the way to an Anglo-Spanish peace (the Treaty of London, August 1604). This achieved what the Armadas of 1588 and 1596 had failed to do: the withdrawal of all official English aid to the Dutch. The capture of Ostend shortly afterwards left the Army of Flanders free to take the offensive again. The king felt that an invasion of Dutch territory would make the States more amenable to a truce. A large provision was sent in 1605 and Spinola was given express orders to invade Overijssel. Several towns were taken. The same strategy was employed in 1606. Although this time the chain of redoubts behind the IJssel and Maas (cf. p. 16 above) prevented the Army of Flanders from making a really effective thrust towards the heart of the Republic, Spinola still managed to capture more towns across the 'great rivers'.

The effort, however, proved too much. At the end of the campaign of 1606 a large part of Spinola's field army mutinied and made for the town of Diest which had already proved an advantageous base to other military revolts in 1590 and 1600. This time more men were involved than ever before, 4,052 veterans, and their arrears again totalled a million florins. Until they were paid there could be no further campaigns. Meanwhile in Madrid, Philip III and his advisers reluctantly concluded that their brave new strategy had failed: despite the high provisions of 1602–6 there was no peace-move from the States. On 14 December 1606 the Council of State therefore recommended, with regret, that the king should abandon 'Flanders': the size of the Army was to be drastically reduced and its annual provision from Spain cut from 9 million to 4½ million florins.[1] As this decision was about to be made public an unexpected offer arrived from the Dutch: they were willing to discuss a cease-fire. In Spain, the Dutch change of heart was regarded as nothing short of a miracle. The fighting ended on 24 April 1607.[2]

Despite the steady erosion of Spain's bargaining power (her involvement in a major confrontation with Venice; Haemstede's naval victory off Gibraltar; another Spanish decree of bankruptcy on 9 November 1607), negotiations continued and a Twelve Years' Truce was agreed in April 1609. The Army of Flanders was reduced to a peace-time force of 15,000 men and the provisions were cut back to 4 million florins a year. The arrears of the troops were paid off and the mutineers were outlawed.

1609–19

It was during the Twelve Years' Truce that the affairs of Germany first began to dominate the activities and the strategic thinking of the Army of Flanders. Of course an intimate relationship had long existed between the Netherlands and the Holy Roman Empire of which (after 1548) they formed a part. The emperor had offered his mediation in several vain attempts to bring the conflict in the Low Countries to an end (most notably in 1568, 1577, 1579 and 1591); and now and again Spanish forces had intervened in the political crises of north-west Germany in order to uphold the Catholic or the Imperial cause (at Aachen in 1581, in the electorate of Cologne in 1583–9 and so on). However, the death of the childless, Catholic, pro-Spanish duke of Cleves-Jülich in March 1609

Figure 25. The receipts of the *pagaduría*, v: 1609–19

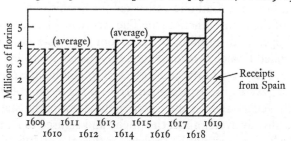

---

[1] AGS *E* 634/93, *consulta* of the special committee on foreign affairs, the *junta de los tres* (Franqueza, Idiaquez, Miranda), 14 Dec. 1606. The king appended his approval and ordered the marquis of Ayamonte to bear news of the cuts to Brussels.
[2] AGS *E* 2025/5, *consulta* of *los tres*, 16 Jan. 1607.

transformed this casual relationship. Gradually Spain, and her satellite government at Brussels, came to be convinced that the triumph of the Habsburgs and of their Catholic allies in Germany was crucial to the victory of Spain in the Netherlands. Unable to achieve victory in a limited conflict, Spain embraced the opportunity offered by the troubles in Germany to escalate her struggle with the Dutch into a general European war.

Cleves-Jülich was of great strategic importance to the Army of Flanders because the duchies formed a salient between the lands controlled by Spain and the States, and because they contained a bridge over the Rhine at Wesel (cf. Figure 2 on p. 15 above). The success of Spinola's campaigns in 1605 and 1606, for example, depended in large part upon ducal permission to pass through Cleves in order to invade Frisia and Overijssel. The death of Duke John William in 1609 left a disputed succession. The leading claimants, the palatine count of Neuburg and the elector of Brandenburg, were both Lutherans and as such unacceptable to Spain and to the emperor (because Cleves was a Catholic principality and was therefore, according to the Peace of Augsburg, entitled to a Catholic ruler). Faced with the hostility of the Habsburgs, the two claimants quickly mobilized support: the German Protestant Union, the States General of the Netherlands, and above all Henry IV of France, always anxious to add to the Habsburgs' difficulties. Open war seemed inevitable. Then in the course of 1610 Henry IV and the elector palatine, aggressive leader of the Protestant Union, died, both leaving minors to succeed them. War was narrowly averted but (almost as bad for Spain) Dutch, English and French forces overran the duchies and installed the two Lutheran claimants as joint dukes before the end of the year.

In 1613, still smarting from this reverse, Spain had an unexpected chance to regain her advantage. One of the Lutheran claimants, the count of Neuburg, became a Catholic and asked for Spanish help to make himself master of the entire inheritance. The Army of Flanders was only too ready to oblige. With nothing to fear from the pro-Habsburg regency which controlled French foreign policy, Spinola led his troops into Cleves early in 1614. Fifty-five towns and fortresses, including the crucial bridgehead of Wesel, were quickly occupied. In vain the elector of Brandenberg professed himself a Calvinist and called in the Army of the States General: Spinola had already overrun half the duchy and refused to fight the Dutch troops. 'The Truce must not be broken for the sake of Julich', he warned the king.[1] The *pax hispanica* was therefore preserved.

Apart from the Cleves emergency, the Army of Flanders was not put

[1] Paper of Spinola in June 1614 quoted by Rodríguez Villa, *Ambrosio Spínola*, pp. 299–300.

on alert during the first decade of the truce. Its cost to Spain remained at a manageable 4 million florins a year, and the Brussels government devoted itself to reconstruction in the south after the thirty years of war. Trade and industry were encouraged; Counter-Reformation orthodoxy was enforced; even the financial system was overhauled – in 1617, by some miracle, the year's provision from Spain was even paid monthly in advance.[1] This never proved possible again.

In May 1618 the estates of Bohemia, which had pre-elected the Archduke Ferdinand of Styria as their king the previous year, suddenly changed their mind and rebelled. Ferdinand's officials were expelled. The archduke urgently needed to regain control of Bohemia. Besides the affront to his dignity which demanded redress, Ferdinand was the Habsburg candidate to succeed to the imperial dignity when the ailing and childless Emperor Mathias died. Ferdinand's chances of election as emperor might well depend on the casting vote in the electoral college held, traditionally, by the king of Bohemia. Ferdinand had therefore to repress the rebellion quickly. In June 1618 he asked Spain for help.

There were strong arguments in favour of Spanish aid to the archduke: above all there was the secret agreement of 1617, the Treaty of Graz, whereby Spain would gain control of Alsace if the archduke became emperor (cf. p. 55 above). After the Treaty of Lyon put the Spanish Road in jeopardy, control of Alsace was vital to Spain's communications between Lombardy and the Low Countries, and if Ferdinand lost Bohemia, Spain would lose Alsace...Accordingly, early in 1619 Spain sent two armies to help Ferdinand; one from the Netherlands went direct to Bohemia, another from Lombardy marched to Alsace. It was almost too late. In August 1619 the Bohemian Estates solemnly deposed Ferdinand (although this did not prevent his election as emperor) and chose the elector palatine, Frederick V, as their king. He arrived in Prague in October. At Ferdinand's request, Spain prepared a third army for German intervention; this time the Army of Flanders was to invade and occupy the Lower Palatinate, commanding the middle Rhine. Far larger provisions were sent in 1619 and 1620 (cf. Figures 25 and 26) and, having obtained assurances that neither the Dutch, England nor France (again locked in civil war) would intervene, Spinola marched into the Rhine Palatinate in September 1620, rapidly gaining full control of the Rhine valley with its coveted communications between Italy and the Netherlands.

[1] AGRB *Audience* 1466/1, bundle i, unfol., Spinola to Pedro de Toledo, 28 Sep. 1619 (minute) describes the provisions of 1617.

Spain's victory in the Palatinate coincided with her refusal to renew the
truce with the Dutch which expired in April 1621. The Spanish government had been discussing the Netherlands question since March 1618,
evaluating all the arguments for and against renewing the truce. On
Christmas Day 1619 the die was cast: king and council were unanimous
that to renew the truce in its existing form would do irreparable damage
to Spain's trade with the Indies and to the Catholic faith. Since it was
considered (rightly) that the Dutch would not be willing to make further
concessions to Spain it was decided to provide the Army of Flanders with
enough men and money to enable hostilities to recommence as soon as the
truce expired. The death of Philip III made no difference to this decision:
the new king, Philip IV, formally announced that the truce would not be
renewed on 20 April 1621.[1]

The strategy followed in the first years of the new war was similar to
that of 1605–6. Spain made a concerted effort to force the Dutch by constant military pressure to beg for another truce, the terms of which Spain
could then dictate. Events favoured Philip IV. France was paralysed by a

Figure 26. The receipts of the *pagaduría*, VI: 1620–32

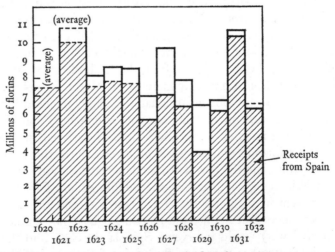

Note: The annual receipts from Spain for 1621–5 are averages estimated
from the total in Appendix K.

[1] AGS *E* 634/328, minute of a *consulta* of the Council of State, 25 Dec. 1619. The royal
announcement was recorded by the French ambassador in Madrid, Bassompierre in his
journal; cf. Gachard, 'Notice des manuscrits…à la Bibliothèque royale de Berlin', *BCRH*,
4e série i (1873), p. 36.

series of important revolts by certain nobles (1619–20) and by the Huguenots (1620–9) and James I of England conveniently refused to provide
open aid either to the Dutch or to the elector palatine. In Germany the
emperor's allies quickly overcame all opposition. Spain seemed to have
things all her own way. It is true that the marked and prolonged decline
in the Indies trade after about 1615 gave cause for concern, but since
Spanish forces were not committed elsewhere in Europe, the Army of
Flanders received full financial support from Madrid – 750,000 florins a
month (cf. Figure 26) – and Spinola was able to lead his troops to some
striking successes, notably the capture of Breda (June 1625).

The Habsburg successes continued. In the New World Spanish forces
recaptured Bahía from the Dutch (April 1625) and in Europe the emperor's Catholic allies advanced into north-west Germany. Alarmed, the
Dutch secured important military aid first from England (September
1625) and then from Denmark (December), but the emperor countered
this threat by raising an army of his own (under Wallenstein). In Spain
the English attack on Cadiz in October 1625 was a fiasco. In Germany
the Habsburg armies advanced relentlessly against their enemies,
driving all before them: by 1629 they were in Jutland and the king of
Denmark was forced to make peace. England followed in 1630.

Spain fully realized the possibilities opened up by this impressive
imperial advance to the Baltic. A new Habsburg navy might be created,
based on the ports of Mecklenburg captured by Wallenstein, or in alliance
with Catholic Poland, and this fleet could be used to attack the Dutch
where they were most vulnerable, in their trade to the Baltic, the foundation of the Republic's prosperity and consequently of its war-finance.
The Dutch Baltic trade had already been adversely affected by Sweden's
war with Poland (1617–29) and by the manœuvres of rival armies in the
German war. These political disturbances disrupted the great grain
commerce of Poland and east Germany on which, to a large extent,
Dutch prosperity depended. Dutch ships carried 103,000 lasts of grain
out of the Baltic in 1621, but only 30,000 in 1624 and 1625. A fleet of
Habsburg privateers might reduce the trade even further.[1]

Although this adventurous project came to nothing, Spain in these
years seemed very strong. Even another bankruptcy decree in February
1627 failed to affect the crown's credit: a new consortium of Portuguese
bankers stepped smartly into the shoes of the Genoese whose loans were

---

[1] F. Snapper, *Oorlogsinvloeden op de Overzeese Handel van Holland, 1551–1719* (Amsterdam,
1959), pp. 75–7. On Spain's plans for a Baltic fleet, cf. R. Ródenas Vilar, *La política europea de
España durante la guerra de Treinta años, 1624–30* (Madrid, 1967), part II.

frozen by the decree. The provision which reached the Army of Flanders in 1627 was one of the highest.[1]

Then, suddenly, there was a serious deterioration in Spain's position. The New Spain treasure fleet of 1628 was captured off Cuba by the warships of the Dutch West India Company: it carried silver worth 8 million florins. This was a welcome windfall to the Dutch war-chest, but it ruined the *asientos* which Philip IV had arranged for 1629 promising repayment from the silver on the fleet. The loss of the treasure fleet coincided with a perceptible decline in the revenues of Castile itself: there was a crisis in the cloth-production of Segovia and Toledo in 1625 from which they never recovered, and from 1628 onwards land values and internal trade (on which the crown's leading revenue, the *alcabala* or sales-tax was based) began a prolonged and marked decline. To cap it all, the harvest failed.[2] Spain tried to interest the Dutch in a new truce.

It was most unfortunate that in this situation Spinola was recalled for failing to relieve the town of Grol at the end of 1627. His vast financial resources and military skill might have preserved the Spanish Netherlands from the worst consequences of the fall in the military treasury's receipts. In the event, no money arrived from Spain between October 1628 and May 1629; no campaign could be prepared.[3]

Of course the Dutch fully realized their advantage (their admiral had captured the silver!) and they made haste to exploit it. Rejecting Spain's belated offer to negotiate, early in 1629 the Army of the States laid siege to the important town of 's Hertogenbosch, the gateway to Brabant. Spain could not raise an army of relief. Even so, all was not lost. In July 1629, fresh from his victory over Denmark, Wallenstein collected an army of 20,000 and sent it off to relieve 's Hertogenbosch and invade Frisia. Then suddenly the imperial forces were recalled. Urgent orders had arrived, Wallenstein explained to the government in Brussels, from Philip IV himself: all troops were required in another theatre, deemed to be more important to the interests of the Spanish Monarchy than the Low Countries – in Lombardy. 'S Hertogenbosch was doomed.[4]

---

[1] As in 1596–7, the crown's success in finding funds elsewhere encouraged the bankers whose loans had been confiscated (*los decretados*) to conclude a hasty agreement with their slippery creditor. The *medio general* signed on 17 Sep. 1627 (the decree was only issued on 4 Feb.) bound the *decretados* to provide a new loan to the crown of 1.89 million *escudos*. (AGS *CJH* 632 ant., various papers on the bankruptcy and its settlement.)

[2] Cf. on the treasure fleet the comprehensive yet neglected study of S. P. L'Honoré Naber and I. A. Wright, *Piet Heyn en de Zilvervloot* (Utrecht, 1928); on the falling revenues of Castile cf. the perceptive remarks of C. J. Jago, 'Aristocracy, War and Finance in Castile, 1621–1665...' (Cambridge Univ. Ph.D. thesis, 1969), chaps 4 and 5.

[3] AGS *E* 2322, unfol., Cardinal de la Cueva to the king, 13 May 1629.

[4] AGRB *Secrétairerie allemande* 471/278 and 362, letters of Wallenstein to the Infanta Isabella,

The war in Lombardy began in December 1627 with the death of the duke of Mantua-Monferrat. His heir was a Frenchman, the duke of Nevers. Spain was unwilling to admit a French duke and so, with the support of the emperor (suzerain of Mantua), Spanish troops overran the duchy. All went well at first, but the victory of Louis XIII over his last major domestic opponents, the town of La Rochelle (October 1628), left France free to challenge Habsburg dominance again. After agonizing discussion of the need for reform at home *versus* the need to challenge Habsburg supremacy abroad, in December 1628 Louis XIII pledged full support to Nevers. He led an army across the Alps to drive the Spaniards from Monferrat and Mantua in the spring of 1629.

It was to cope with this unforeseen escalation in the Italian war that Spain appealed to the emperor and to Wallenstein for help. In 1629 and 1630 the provisions sent to the Netherlands were reduced largely because more money was needed to fight the French in Lombardy. In the end, it was all spent in vain because in October 1630 the emperor, having dismissed Wallenstein and alienated his Catholic supporters in Germany, made a separate peace with France, agreeing to invest Nevers with the duchy of Mantua and to withdraw all his troops from Italy. Spain was left in the lurch and made the best terms she could (the Treaty of Cherasco, June 1631).

To sugar this bitter pill, in November 1630 the emperor renewed his offer to send an army to cooperate with the Army of Flanders in an invasion of Frisia, but again the promised assistance never materialized.[1] This time it was an emergency in the north of Germany which supervened. In July 1630 the king of Sweden, Gustavus Adolphus, landed at Peenemünde with a small army (14,000 men) to defend the Protestant cause. The Swedish army soon grew in size, and the imperial army intended for 'Flanders' was diverted to attack the invaders. The imperialists were defeated. In September 1631 Gustavus annihilated the main imperial army at the Breitenfeld, near Leipzig. Western Germany was quickly overrun. These traumatic events completely neutralized the effects of the large provision which Olivares managed to send to the Army of Flanders in 1631: nothing was achieved in the Netherlands and Alsace, the key to Spanish communications between Lombardy and the Low Countries, was lost.

The Dutch made only limited capital from Spain's prolonged em-

5 Jun. and 7 Jul. 1629, reporting the progress of Collalto's relief forces, and f. 393, same to same, 19 Jul. 1629, announcing receipt of Philip IV's urgent command, endorsed by the emperor, to send Collalto's army (18,000 foot and 2,500 horse) to Italy.
[1] AGRB *SEG* 203/283, Infanta Isabella to the king, 24 Nov. 1630, reporting the imperial offer.

barrassment. There was no attempt to follow up the successful campaign of 1629. Instead the Republic intensified its attack on Philip IV's overseas empire, capturing Pernambuco (north-eastern Brazil) in 1630. In 1632, the Dutch decided on a new attack on the Spanish Netherlands, and their army closed in on the town of Maastricht. Again the Army of Flanders was unable to relieve the town, this time because of the treason of its field commander, Count Henry van den Berg, who defected to the Dutch. There were further defections among the Walloon nobility in 1632 in protest against Spain's neglect of the Netherlands, and popular disturbances threatened the government's hold on Brussels. These events enabled the Dutch to capture two other valuable strongholds on the Maas: Venlo and Roermond. As its tide was ebbing fast, the Spanish court again condescended to negotiate with the Dutch, but without offering any real concessions. The Republic naturally refused.

1633–42

Once more, however, events in Germany strengthened Spain's position in the Netherlands. The invincible king of Sweden was killed as he inflicted yet another defeat on the emperor's troops (at Lützen, November

Figure 27. The receipts of the *pagaduría*, VII: 1633–42

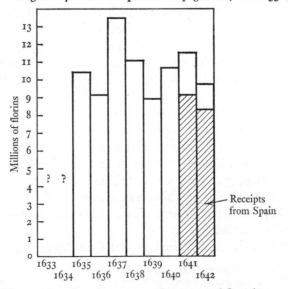

Note: The receipts for 1633–4 are unknown, and for 1635–40 the receipts from Spain could not be deciphered from the paymaster's accounts.

1632) and soon afterwards his army began to disintegrate because of inadequate financial support. Most of the campaign season of 1633 was wasted because the Swedish army refused to move without its pay.

The Habsburgs had a chance to recover from the trauma of the Swedish victories, and in adversity a closer collaboration than ever developed between the Spanish and Austrian branches of the family. A plan was evolved for the junction of a Spanish army from Italy with the armies of the emperor to expel the Protestants and the Swedes from south and south-west Germany. This would restore Spain's overland communications between Lombardy and the Netherlands as well as regain valuable Catholic areas from Protestant control. As early as 1631 Philip IV's chief minister, Olivares, had declared his intention of sending the king's brother, the cardinal-infante, Don Fernando, to govern the Netherlands.[1] In the course of 1633 it was agreed that the cardinal-infante should lead the Spanish army which was to operate in south Germany and re-open the land route to the Low Countries. The plan was triumphantly successful: the main Swedish army was routed at Nördlingen (September 1634) and the Habsburgs recovered almost all their losses in the Rhineland and south Germany. The cardinal-infante reached Brussels safely and Olivares, despite the steadily worsening economic situation of Castile, increased the provisions assigned to the Army of Flanders. With a truce in Germany between the emperor and his Protestant subjects (February 1635, expanded into the general Peace of Prague in May) it looked as if the joint Habsburg attack on the United Provinces, mooted since 1629, could at last take place.

These fine plans were overturned by the French declaration of war in May 1635. Communications between the Netherlands and Italy were again cut, and the forces collected for the reconquest of the north had to be moved down to the French frontier, as in 1590, to prepare for the new conflict. Philip IV became anxious for a peace with the Dutch at almost any price, but, since Spain no longer had the power to interfere with their overseas trade, they had no reason to wish for the war to end. As in the 1590s, war with France forced the Army of Flanders to move onto the defensive against the Dutch, reserving the heroic provisions arranged in Madrid for the war against France. Once again the proved strategy of Charles V was employed: France was to be attacked in the north in order to relieve the pressure on Spain and Lombardy. But times had changed. Even the invasion of 1636 by a joint Habsburg army, which almost reached

---

[1] AGS *GA* 1035, unfol., 'Copia de la consulta que hizo el consejo de estado...' 27 Feb. 1631 – this represented one of Olivares' major statements of future foreign policy.

Paris, failed to save Catalonia and, as always, Spain's intervention in France spelt the loss of more towns to the Dutch. Moreover, French armies entered Germany after 1637 and prevented the emperor from sending any further aid to the Army of Flanders.

At last the strain of war proved too much for Spain. The new struggle with France was fought not only in Picardy and the Netherlands but also in Spain. Even before the war began in 1635 Catalonia had been alienated by the policies of Olivares and by the new taxes they involved; the billets and the brutality of the Castilian troops sent to defend the principality from the French produced rioting and finally revolt in June 1640. Within a few months the rebels called in the French. Before the year was out Portugal, also restless under the heavy taxation and alien policies decreed by Castile, took advantage of the revolt of Catalonia to drive out the Spaniards and declare her own independence. Once again French aid was forthcoming. At the same time, Spain's Atlantic fleet was destroyed off Dover (the battle of the Downs, October 1639) and her Caribbean fleet was destroyed off Brazil (1640).

The *pagaduría* of the Army of Flanders did not immediately feel the effects of this acute crisis of the Spanish Monarchy because, as in 1572 in the face of the Dutch revolt, the central government could not easily concentrate all its resources in one spot – this was one of its chief weaknesses. Thus the provisions of 1640 and 1641 were very considerable, and even in 1642 there was enough money to maintain a strong defensive position in the Netherlands. A French invasion was decisively defeated at Honnecourt (26 May 1642). The débâcle came in 1643 and after, when Philip IV finally succeeded in focusing all his resources on the Catalan front, even moving his government to Zaragoza for greater effect.

1643–59

In large part, the Army of Flanders brought disaster on itself. The inability of Castile to maintain provisions at a high level after the revolt of Catalonia was obvious, yet in 1643 the captain-general of the Army of Flanders decided to invade France. There were those who pointed out that Richelieu was dead (4 December 1642) and the days of the tubercular Louis XIII were numbered (he died on 14 May 1643). Clearly, it was argued, France was already heading for civil war. The shrewdest counsel was to leave well alone. Don Francisco de Melo rejected this advice: he invaded France and laid siege to the town of Rocroi. The French despatched an army of relief which, with last-minute reinforcements, outnumbered Melo's troops 24,000 to 17,000. The result was the crushing defeat which ended a legend: at the battle outside Rocroi on 19 May 1643 the Spanish infantry resisted until it was cut down, the paymaster lost his treasure, the captain-general lost his papers.[1]

Such a mistake Spain could no longer rectify. The French armies and the Dutch fleets cut off almost all contact between the Spanish Netherlands and the outside world by both land and sea. The supply-routes of the Army of Flanders were all ruptured. In any case, Spain had few men and little treasure left to send; the wars in the peninsula required all her failing resources. In July 1644 Philip IV signed a general order to his ministers informing them that owing to the lack of men and money he was anxious that peace should be concluded on all fronts as soon as possible.[2] Above all, the king wished for peace with France, but France was not interested. The victory at Rocroi gave the new regency government in Paris sufficient authority to continue the war and, meeting with little resistance, the French armies captured one town after another in the south Netherlands. In August 1648 they routed the Army of Flanders again at the battle of Lens.

Philip IV's peace initiative was not wholly unsuccessful, however: peace was made with the Dutch in 1648. Of course the path to recognition of 'rebels' as a lawful sovereign state was not easy, but in the end Spain needed the services of the Dutch almost as much as she needed peace. Since 1644 it had been clear that the emperor was willing to cede Alsace to France in order to end the German war. This would automatically prevent Spain from sending men and money to the Army of Flanders by

Figure 28. The receipts of the *pagaduría*, VIII: 1643–53

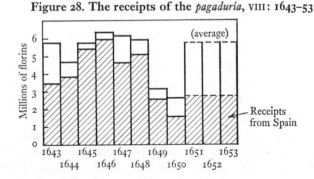

[1] BPU Geneva, *Ms. Favre* 39/277–88, opinion of the marquis of Velada on the 1643 campaign; BRB *Ms.* 12428–29/322, Certificate that the paymaster-general lost 40,688 *escudos* at Rocroy; AGRB *SEG* 43, a register of the captain-general's orders, records that it replaced the previous volume lost at Rocroi.
[2] AGS *E* 2162, unfol., *decreto* of Philip IV, 26 Jul. 1644.

land, and the sea-route depended absolutely on Dutch good-will after the battle of the Downs in 1639. Any peace in Germany would also allow the French to withdraw their armies from Alsace and use them against the Spanish Netherlands. On two counts, therefore, it was imperative for Philip IV to secure a settlement with the Dutch before peace was proclaimed in Germany, and for once Spain managed to make peace in time: the Eighty Years' War ended in January 1648, the Thirty Years' War in October.

Spain's fortunes continued to improve in 1648. The victory of Lens failed to protect the tottering regency government of France from collapse. The 'Te Deum' at Notre-Dame in honour of the battle ended in rioting, the rioting was taken as the excuse for a confrontation between the government and the Paris law courts, and the confrontation soon involved the nobility and became a serious revolt: the Fronde. In January 1649 the government was forced to flee Paris.

Here was a golden opportunity for Spain to recover all her lost territory, either by negotiation or by brute force. As usual she proved capable of neither. Reluctant as ever to negotiate on equal terms, Spain was nevertheless pitifully unable to send adequate provisions to finance an invasion of France from the Netherlands. Thanks to the exploitation of the taxes of the Low Countries themselves, a number of towns lost to the French in the 1640s were recovered after 1649, but the successes were of limited value. The Army of Flanders was still hamstrung by the financial shortage caused by unrest in other provinces of the Spanish empire. There were serious revolts in Naples and western Sicily in 1647–8 while riots caused by famine broke out in several major towns in Andalucia. At the same time, a new plague of unusual virulence broke out in Valencia in 1647, spreading irresistibly to the rest of Mediterranean Spain. The years of the Fronde therefore found a weakened Spain, concerned solely with the suppression of domestic rebellion. It was an exhausting process. In 1648, Spanish Italy was pacified, and Catalonia, abandoned by the French, was only regained in October 1652. Even then Portugal continued to resist. But in August 1653 Louis XIV too subdued the last of his major opponents, the town of Bordeaux. France was again ready to fight Spain. Worse still for Philip IV, in December 1654, without warning, England also declared war on Spain, taking the war into the Caribbean again (Jamaica was captured in 1655; the Indies fleets of 1656 and 1657 were destroyed by the English). Defeats followed fast for Spain on all European fronts: in Lombardy, Portugal and Catalonia as well as in the Netherlands. The campaign of 1658 was particularly disastrous, with another defeat for the Army of Flanders (the battle of the Dunes, 14 June 1658), the loss of Dunkirk (Spain's best port in the Netherlands and the base of her only remaining navy) and new reverses at the hands of the Portuguese. It could not last. In September 1658 Philip IV decided to sue for peace; a cease-fire was agreed with France on 8 May 1659, a firm peace, the Peace of the Pyrenees, was signed on 7 November 1659. Because France was almost as exhausted as Spain, the terms were lenient: in the south Philip IV surrendered only part of Catalonia, in the north he relinquished Artois and some frontier forts in Hainaut, Flanders and Luxemburg. It could have been much worse.

* * *

Although the contributions and protection system evolved since the 1590s preserved the Netherlands in the seventeenth century from the total destruction and dislocation which had characterized the earlier stages of the war, the utter impotence of Spain and her army were no longer open to question. The Spanish empire had clearly become the 'sick man of Europe'. It had become simply a matter of time before every stronghold in the south Netherlands fell to the French. After ninety-two years of fighting the Army of Flanders was unable even to defend the provinces it had been sent to dominate.

Peace, however, achieved the primary aim of Habsburg policy: Spain retained absolute control over at least a part of Charles V's Burgundian inheritance. In 1566 and 1577 the chances of that had looked rather remote. There was a second success to record: the Spanish Netherlands remained, and have remained to this day, the *Catholic* Netherlands. This was no mean achievement in view of the extent of Calvinism, Lutheranism and Anabaptism in the southern provinces – the cradle of the iconoclastic movement and the first consistories – before 1567 and under the rule of the States General (1577–85). It is arguable, however, that the preservation of the Roman faith in the south owed more to the persecution of the duke of Alva and the Council of Blood and to the work of religious reorganization undertaken by the archdukes during the Twelve Years' Truce than to any encouragement or example from the Army of Flanders.

It would not seem that Spain's protracted struggle in the Netherlands achieved any of her other objectives. Sending the duke of Alva did not, in the long run, save Spain money; the presence of a major army in the Netherlands failed to prevent the French from attacking Italy in the 1590s and Spain after 1635; the use of force against the rebels of the

Netherlands, involving such heavy financial pressure on the other parts of the Spanish empire, undoubtedly contributed to the unrest and eventual uprising of Catalonia, Portugal, Naples and Sicily in the 1640s; resuming the war in the Netherlands after 1621 did not keep the merchants of Holland and Zealand out of the Indies. And, in the end, the Revolt of the Netherlands was never suppressed.

The eventual failure was certainly not for want of trying. Spain's prodigious efforts to achieve her goal are unparalleled in early modern history. The consistently high receipts of the military treasury of the Army of Flanders, chronicled in Figure 29, and the heroic sacrifices made

Figure 29. The receipts of the *pagaduría* of the Army of Flanders, 1567–1664

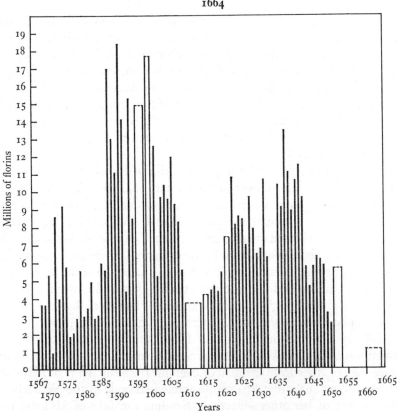

These totals record the pulse-rate of Spain's military activity in the Low Countries, with peaks in 1572–5, 1587–99 and 1635–41. The open columns with a dotted line represent the average receipt for a year estimated from a total for several years. Source: Appendix K.

for decades by Castile shown separately in Figure 30, testify to an awesome determination to succeed. In the interests of victory Spain evolved important new structures designed to improve the efficiency of the Army of Flanders: an entire network of military supply-routes was created to cope with the soldiers and specie which the Army constantly required; a series of new institutions was introduced to make the soldier's life more tolerable (medical care, marriage allowances and other free welfare services, with bread and clothing provided on credit); and more sophisticated machinery was set up to check the administration of public funds (the *sala de cuentas* in particular). This was an impressive organizational achievement, and one, moreover, which surpassed the capabilities of most other European states. Between 1585 and 1603, for example, Elizabeth of England sent to the Dutch almost 15 million florins, an effort which ruined her, and Henry IV of France with difficulty sent a further 10 million florins between 1598 and 1610 (both expected eventual repayment) – yet during the 1590s Spain sent almost as much as this every year![1] At a more practical level, the English government did not discover

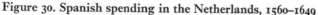

Figure 30. Spanish spending in the Netherlands, 1560–1649

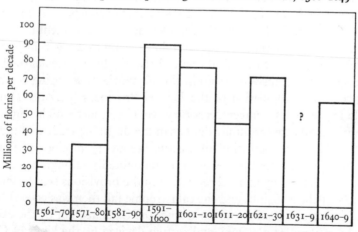

Years

A rough indication of the rhythm of Spanish spending in the Low Countries' Wars. Since the figures are taken from the money actually received from Spain by the paymasters-general, they represent the net or minimum expenditure (excluding interest charges and money sent to other officials). Annual fluctuations are given in Figures 21–8; these decennial totals reveal the general trend. Source: Appendix K.

[1] Cf. Parker, 'Spain, her enemies and the Revolt of the Netherlands', *Past and Present*, XLIX (1970), p. 90, n. 34.

the advantages of providing proper ancillary services for their armies until the New Model Army in the 1640s, the French not until the 1660s and '70s under the enlightened guidance of Michel le Tellier and Louvois. In the field of military organization the Spanish Habsburgs showed themselves to be well in advance of their rivals; it is doubtful whether any other European state could have managed so well in a war fought so far away for so long. This achievement contrasts strongly with the colours of rigidity, debility and incapacity in which the history of Golden Age Spain is so often painted.

Of course there were weaknesses, serious weaknesses, in the structure of Spanish military power, but they were by no means confined to Spain. Mutinies and bankruptcies were common to even the most advanced states: the Swedish army in Germany after Lützen and the New Model Army mutinied for their pay, and both ran the governments which employed them into deficit and unmanageable debt. The Dutch too, although they rigorously restricted their military activity to the Low Countries, ended their struggle with Spain owing their troops wage-arrears of 3.6 million florins, while the States of Holland alone were saddled with a consolidated debt of 140 million florins in 1651, bearing interest of 5 per cent. And even Holland acted with questionable honesty towards its creditors, arbitrarily lowering the interest rate on government bonds from $6\frac{1}{4}$ per cent to 5 per cent in 1644 and down again to 4 per cent in 1655.[1] There was indeed a world of difference between the finances of the Dutch Republic and of Habsburg Spain in the 1640s: the burgeoning commerce and prosperous population of the United Provinces (perhaps 2 million people in the mid-seventeenth century) could support a higher incidence of taxation and a larger public debt than the declining trade and industry and the faltering population of Castile (about $4\frac{1}{2}$ million inhabitants) where tax-yields after the 1620s were undoubtedly falling. Yet even so, one cannot detect any marked reduction in the provisions sent to the Low Countries before 1642–3, and the catastrophic fall then was caused by the need to concentrate all resources against the Catalans, not by the exhaustion of Castile. The governmental system devised by the kings of Castile seems to have been capable of squeezing its taxpayers almost indefinitely to pay for foreign war. Here again, the technical performance of the Spanish Habsburgs cannot be faulted.

The failure of Spain's attempts to suppress the Dutch Revolt was thus,

[1] J. A. Wijnne, *De Geschillen over de Afdanking van 't Krijgsvolk in de Vereenigde Nederlanden in de jaren 1649 en 1650* (Utrecht, 1885), pp. xiv–xv; and J. J. Weeveringh, *Handleiding tot de Geschiedenis der Staatsschulden. i, Nederlandsche Staatsschulden* (Haarlem, 1852), p. 6.

in essence, a political one. The end to which all these resources were so cleverly and so consistently mobilized turned out to be unattainable; Spain's chosen policy proved to be unrealistic. Given the military limitations imposed by the bastion, and given the large number of bastion-defended towns in revolt after 1572, repression was doomed to be a protracted and costly process; thus although Spain did possess the necessary resources to crush all Dutch resistance (cf. Figure 30) these resources could only be deployed effectively in the Low Countries when Spain was at peace on all other fronts. This, however, was impossible. As Philip IV observed in 1626: 'With as many kingdoms and lordships as have been linked to this crown, it is impossible to be without war in some area either to defend what we have acquired or to divert my enemies'.[1] No empire as far-flung as Spain's could confidently expect to be at peace for decades at a time. Although at certain periods (1582–7 and 1621–7, for example) a *pax hispanica* was achieved, it could never be preserved for long enough to permit total victory in the Netherlands by the conventional military techniques available. Even if Spain managed to restrain her viceroys and proconsuls from unprovoked aggression, the Dutch could usually prevail upon at least one of the Habsburgs' other enemies to provide support – either directly, with financial subsidies and military aid, or indirectly, by attacking Spanish interests elsewhere and thereby drawing Spanish resources away from the Netherlands. As early as 1574 the Ottoman sultan realized that the Dutch were his allies in the war against Spain and sent an ambassador to them; France, England and the German Protestants hardly needed reminding that a Spanish triumph in the Netherlands was the last thing they wanted.[2]

'The war in the Netherlands', observed a wistful councillor of Philip IV in 1623 (as he pleaded for hostilities to continue) 'has been the total ruin of this Monarchy'.[3] There was a measure of truth in this judgement, but it was perhaps one-sided. Subsequent events were to show that it was not the Dutch who destroyed the Spanish empire, but the French. The Low Countries' Wars were more like a weakening hold which, when long applied, debilitates a wrestler so that he will more easily submit under a more deadly attack from a different quarter.

Spain's use of force in the Netherlands coincided with the years when France, her great rival, was entirely occupied with domestic conflicts; instead of building up her strength ready for the inevitable resumption of

[1] Cf. pp. 128–9 above.
[2] Cf. Parker, 'Spain, her enemies and the Revolt of the Netherlands', pp. 82–3 and 85–6.
[3] AGS *E* 2037/11, *consulta* of the Council of State, 14 Apr. 1623, *voto* of Don Fernando Girón (a 'Flanders' veteran).

the Franco-Spanish struggle, the Spanish Habsburgs dissipated their resources so that when the internal divisions of France were healed again, after 1629, Spain had few reserves left on which to draw. In this lay the real folly of the medieval attitude of the Spanish court towards war and rebellion, a view in which only 'total victory' would do, a view which precluded any compromise solution and demanded massive financial sacrifices for an indefinite period. The French declaration of war in May 1635 sealed the fate of all Spain's hopes of reconquering the north Netherlands. The French pressure was relentless, seconded by the Dutch until 1648 and after 1654 by the English, and, although the French Monarchy itself almost perished in the attempt, Spain was beaten to her knees and was forced to sacrifice all her external commitments in a desperate effort to save herself. Spain's endeavours to suppress the Dutch Revolt by force were subject throughout to events independent of both the combatants. The Eighty Years' War remained to the very end the weathercock of international politics.

Appendixes

APPENDIX A

THE SIZE AND COMPOSITION OF THE ARMY OF FLANDERS, 1567–1661

Date	Total in Army	Infantry						Cavalry	Source
		Spaniards	Italians	Burgundians	British	Germans	Netherlands		AGS
Sep. 1572	67,259	9,100	—	—	—	24,440	19,500	14,219	E 550/47
Dec. 1573	62,280	7,900	—	—	—	16,200	33,400	4,780	E 554/172
Mar. 1574	86,235	8,016	—	—	—	27,449	38,110	12,750	IVdeDJ 68/309ter AGS
Jan. 1575	59,250	7,830	—	—	—	23,600	25,420	2,400	E 563/75
May 1576	51,457	6,125	—	—	—	21,226	22,616	1,490	E 566/23
Feb. 1578	27,603	4,993	—	2,100	—	8,680	9,692	3,038	E 573/111
Sep. 1580	45,435	—	384	—	—	13,000	29,678	2,373	E 582/88
Oct. 1582	61,162	4,636	4,754	1,500	—	26,438	20,295	3,539	E 585/64
Apr. 1588	63,455	9,668	5,339	1,556	1,722	11,309	30,211	3,650	E 594/192
Nov. 1591	62,164*	9,579	2,421	2,119	463	21,989	18,871	6,702	E 601/103
Mar. 1607	41,471*† (49,765)	6,545	3,679	1,145	2,442	16,776	5,724† (14,018)	4,164	E 2289/56–7

Date	Total in Army	Infantry						Cavalry	Source
		Spaniards	Italians	Burgundians	British	Germans	Netherlands		
Mar. 1609	15,259	6,528	2,613	848	1,699	—	3,571	1,500	E 2291
Aug. 1611	14,661	5,566	2,118	855	1,468	352	2,564	1,718	E 2293
May 1619	29,210	6,310	1,833	947	1,169	4,058	9,391	3,378	E 2307/41
Jun. 1620	44,200†	10,449	4,126	3,929	1,154	9,212	9,739	7,004	E 2309/265
Mar. 1623	62,606*	3,739	3,907	704	3,812	21,041	21,642	7,399	BM Addl. 14007/385 AGS
Apr. 1624	71,288*† (85,389)	7,354	8,212	4,127	3,926	21,062	19,039† (33,267)	7,568	E 2314/74-7
Jan. 1627	69,340*	6,077	4,137	2,013	1,772	20,132	27,412	6,815	E 2318
Sep. 1633	52,715† (63,258)	5,693	3,793	2,260	3,494	12,549	16,978† (27,521)	7,648	E 2048/158
Jan. 1640	88,280	17,262	3,872	1,067	2,692	14,929	37,111	11,347	AGRB CPE 1574/29–38
Dec. 1643	77,517	10,438	3,348	940	1,191	16,067	31,438	14,095	AGS E 2060
Feb. 1647	65,458	9,685	2,415	672	2,515	14,310	24,127	11,734	AHN E lib. 978
Sep. 1661	33,008	5,481	1,179	449	2,317	7,470	8,178	7,984	AGS E 2098

OBSERVATIONS

1. Totals marked * have been transcribed from the document studied even though, thanks to the defective arithmetic of the treasury clerks, they do not represent the sum of the columns.

2. Totals marked † do not include the Netherlands troops paid (and therefore mustered separately) by the *finances* department of the civil administration. As stated on p. 144, the *finances* paid roughly 20 per cent of the number paid by the *exercito*; the figures in the 'Total' and 'Netherlands' column in these cases have therefore been increased by one-fifth (the figures in brackets) to give a rough idea of the full strength of the Army.

3. Only formal musters of the entire army have been used, which means that for certain periods (1591–1607 or the 1650s, for example) no figures are available because the Army could not afford to muster all its troops.

4. The figures in the documents consulted have been transcribed literally because the musters of the Spanish army were fairly rigorous. However, it would be naïve to suppose that the actual number of effectives, especially for the German and Netherlands units, is accurate: I would suggest an overestimate of between 5 and 10 per cent for these units, an overestimate of under 5 per cent for the rest.

APPENDIX B

THE ORGANIZATION OF THE ARMY OF FLANDERS

The Spanish infantry

Throughout the Eighty Years' War, the Spanish infantry was organized in *tercios* of about 12 companies (the number was not fixed). The *estado coronel* (staff officers) of the *tercio* were:

> *maestre de campo* (colonel, and captain of the first company of the *tercio*), his page and 8 halbardiers;
>
> sergeant-major (and captain of the second company);
>
> two assistant sergeants-major (*ayudantes de sargento mayor*);
>
> a judge-advocate (*auditor*), clerk and two guards (*alguaciles*);
>
> *barrachel de campaña* (chief of the regiment's military police), a hangman and four horsemen;
>
> one chaplain-major and two ordinary chaplains;
>
> a quartermaster-general (*furier mayor*);
>
> a surgeon-major (*chirurgeano mayor*);
>
> a drum-major (*atambor mayor*).

From 1567 until 1636, the Spanish company in 'Flanders' consisted of 250 men in theory; either 11 officers, 219 pike-men (about half of them with body-armour – the *corseletes* – and half of them without) and 20 musketeers, or 11 officers, 224 arquebusiers and 15 musketeers. There were supposed to be two companies of arquebusiers for every ten of pike-men, making two companies of arquebusiers in a *tercio* of twelve.

After 1636 the company was reduced to 200 men and standardized: all had 11 officers, 30 musketeers, 60 arquebusiers, 65 *corseletes* and 34 other pike-men without body-armour (the *piqueros secos*).

The officers of the Spanish company (known as the *primera plana*) always remained the same: the captain and his page, lieutenant (*alferez*), ensign, sergeant, two drummers, one piper, a chaplain, quartermaster (*furier*) and barber. The men of the company were divided into *esquadras* (sections) of 25 men, each under a *cabo de esquadra* (corporal). The musketeers received double pay (6 *escudos* a month) and there were bonus-pays (*ventajas*) worth a total of 30 *escudos* per month distributed among the rest.

Source: AGRB *Contadorie des Finances* 4.

The German infantry

Throughout the Eighty Years' War the German infantry was organized into regiments which normally consisted of 10 companies. The *estado coronel* of the regiment comprised:

> the colonel (also captain of the first company);
>
> the lieutenant-colonel (also captain of the third company);
>
> the sergeant-major;
>
> judge-advocate, clerk, halbardier and 10 guards;

provost-general, deputy, clerk, chaplain, hangman, jailer, 8 servants and 6 halbardiers;
quartermaster;
chaplain-major;
victualler;
surgeon-major;
baggage master.

Each company of German infantry had 300 men during this period, half of them musketeers, the rest pike-men; all earned 3 escudos a month, but the 150 pike-men shared 323 bonus-pays (sobrepagas, doppelsolden) of 2 escudos each, and the 150 musketeers shared 225 bonus-pays of 1½ escudos each.

The officers of the company were: the captain (with ten servants paid by the treasury), lieutenant (with one servant), ensign (with one servant), the first sergeant (feltweybel, with one servant), two other sergeants, a clerk, 'fuder', quartermaster, barber, two drummers, two pipers, 2 halbardiers, a chaplain and interpreter. This made 31 places (18 officers and 13 servants) and all drew pike-men's pay and held pike-men's places in the company.

Source: AGRB Contadorie des Finances 4 and MD 3842/43 and 60.

The English and Italian infantry

These 'nations' first served in the Army of Flanders in 1582 and were organized in tercios modelled on the Spanish infantry.

The Burgundian infantry

Served in regiments like the Germans until 1598, thereafter in tercios on the same footing as the Spanish infantry, except that their companies were only 200 men: 11 officers, 67 arquebusiers, 15 musketeers, 67 corseletes and 40 other pike-men.

Source: AGRB Audience 964/5.

The Walloon infantry

Regimental organization until 1602, thereafter grouped in tercios. The companies were organized differently: there was one more sergeant than in the Spanish units and the company's theoretical strength after 1592 was only 200 men. After 1592 there were 11 officers, 25 musketeers, 35 corseletes and 129 others. In 1617 there were 11 officers, 50 musketeers, 99 arquebusiers and 40 corseletes in each company. In 1636 this was altered yet again to 11 officers, 142 musketeers and 47 corseletes. In 1643, because not enough men could be found capable of carrying the weighty musket, arquebusiers were again permitted.

Sources: AGRB Contadorie des Finances 4, Audience 2811 and SEG 43/128v.

The light cavalry

Organized into companies (only) for most of the war, usually of 100 men each, either lancers or mounted arquebusiers. The units were under the general command of the comisario general de la caballeria ligera.

The heavy cavalry

Organized in regiments and companies under individual military contractors for the German units (the 'Black riders' – zwarteruiters) and in bandes d'Ordonnance under local noblemen for the Netherlands heavy cavalry.

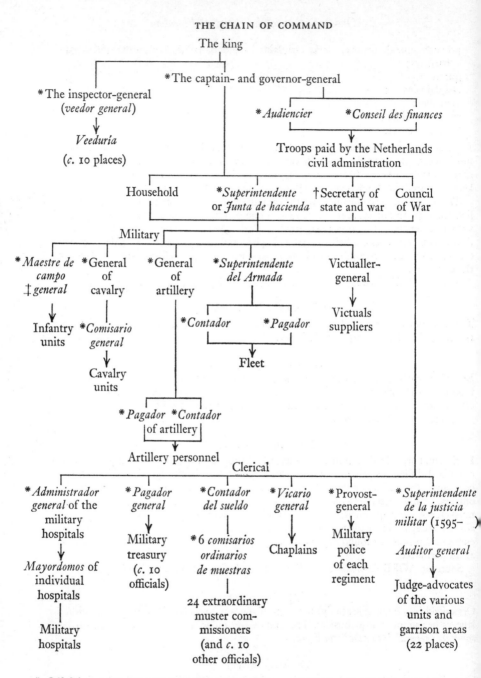

The king

*The captain- and governor-general

*The inspector-general
(*veedor general*)

*Audiencier   *Conseil des finances

Veeduría
(*c.* 10 places)

Troops paid by the Netherlands
civil administration

Household   *Superintendente   †Secretary of   Council
or *Junta de hacienda*   state and war   of War

Military

*Maestre de   *General   *General   *Superintendente   Victualler-
campo   of   of   del Armada   general
‡ *general*   cavalry   artillery

Infantry   *Comisario   *Contador   *Pagador   Victuals
units   general   suppliers

Cavalry
units

Fleet

*Pagador *Contador
of artillery

Artillery personnel

Clerical

*Administrador   *Pagador   *Contador   *Vicario   *Provost-   *Superintendente
general of the   general   del sueldo   general   general   de la justicia
military   militar (1595–)
hospitals

Mayordomos of   Military   *6 comisarios   Chaplains   Military   Auditor general
individual   treasury   ordinarios   police
hospitals   (c. 10   de muestras   of each
officials)   regiment   Judge-advocates
of the various
Military   24 extraordinary   units and
hospitals   muster com-   garrison areas
missioners   (22 places)
(and c. 10
other officials)

* Official appointed by the king (the others were appointed by the captain-general).
† Appointed by the king after 1594.
‡ Until 1630 the *maestre de campo general* was second-in-command of the Army. In that ye
new office, the *gobernador de armas*, was created to command the Army in the absence of the c
general. The *maestre de campo general* became third-in-command.

B : Organization of the Army of Flanders

UNIT ORGANIZATION: THE PRACTICE

(a) *The four Spanish 'tercios' in the Netherlands, 12 May 1571* (AGS E 547/99*bis*)

| | Number of companies | | Number of men | | | | | |
| | Total | Arque-busiers | Total | Officers | Musketeers | Arque-busiers | Corseletes | Other pike-men |
Tercio								
Naples	19	3	2,676	171	281	456	962	806
Sicily	11	3	1,642	99	165	543	430	405
Lombardy	10	2	1,588	90	150	345	563	440
Flanders	10	1	1,603	90	0	161	561	791
Total	50	9	7,509	450	596	1,505	2,516	2,442

Average size of company: 150 men.

(b) *Muster of the Army of Flanders, 24 March 1601* (AGS E 618)

| | Number of men | | | | | | Monthly cost per man (*escudos* of 50) |
Nation	Total	Officers	Musketeers	Arque-busiers	Corseletes	Other pike-men	
Spaniards	6,001	646	1,237	2,117	1,047	954	7.7
Italians	1,204	110	253	394	270	177	6.7
Germans	8,852	665	1,194	700	5,601	692	6.0
Burgundians	1,718	123	440	662	409	84	4.8
Walloons	4,678	375	1,237	1,242	1,125	699	4.4

The different cost of the 'nations' was the result of the large number of bonus-pays (*ventajas*) issued to the Spanish and Italian troops and the *doppelsold* system of paying the Germans.

APPENDIX C

SPANISH AND ITALIAN TROOPS SENT TO THE NETHERLANDS, 1567–1640

		Numbers and route			
Year	Commander	Spanish Road	Alsace	Sea	Source
1567	Alva	8,652 S 1,250 C	—	—	AGS *CMC* 2a/63
1568		—	—	2,427 S	AA 166/2
1572	Medina Celi	—	—	1,263 S	*Co.Do.In* xxxvi p. 5
1573	Acuña	5,052 S 300 C	—	—	AGS *E* 1236/98
1575	Valdes	—	—	430 S	*E* 564/139
1577	J. Manrique	4,093 S 2,138 C	—	—	*E* 573/111
1578	Figueroa	4,000 S 1,300 C	—	—	*E* 573/111
1578	Serbelloni	2,696 S 413 C	—	—	*E* 1249/153
1582	Paz	5,105 S 1,300 C	—	—	*E* 1256/110
1582	Carduini	4,754 I	—	—	*E* 585/64
1584	Tassis	4,915 S 500 C	—	—	BM *Addl.* 28392/105v
1585	Bobadilla	2,195 S	—	—	*ibid.*, f, 164 AGS
1586	A. Manrique	2,000 S	—	—	*E* 1261/105
1587	Spinelli	4,117 I	—	—	*E* 1262/26
1587	Zúñiga	2,662 S	—	—	*E* 1262/54
1587	Capizucchi	4,900 I	—	—	*E* 1262/59
1587	Queralt	1,900 S	—	—	*E* 596/87
1588	Medina Sidonia	—	—	1,300 S	*E* 598/22
1591	Toledo	3,087 S	—	—	*E* 1269/96–7
1593	Mexía	3,048 S	—	—	*E* 1272/244
1593	Treviso	2,038 I	—	—	*E* 1272/244
1596	Albert	5,400 S 2,600 I 636 C	—	—	*E* 611/15
1597	Dávalos	4,000 I	—	—	*E* 1283/36
1598	Leyva	—	—	4,000 S	*E* 615/99
1601	Spinola	2,000 S 6,000 I	—	—	AGRB *SEG* 20/42–43v
1601	Giron	—	—	1,500 S	AGRB *Audience* 1398/5

Year	Commander	Numbers and route			Source
		Spanish Road	Alsace	Sea	
1602	Spinola	8,759 I	—	—	AGS *CMC* 2a/875
1602	F. Spinola	—	—	1,000 S	AGS *E* 620
1603	Borja	2,500 S 1,200 I	—	—	BNP *Lorraine* 531/113
1604	Biamonte	—	2,000 S	—	AGRB *Audience* 1953/1
1605	Girón	—	2,877 S	—	AGS *E* 1294/30
1605	Avellino	6,000 I	—	—	AGRB *Audience* 1980/1
1605	Sarmiento	—	—	1,200 S	AGRB *SEG* 128/195
1606	Bravo de Laguna	3,000 S	—	—	AGS *E* 1294/170
1611	—	—	—	500 S	AGS *E* 627/117–8
1615	Vidalcanal	—	—	2,924 S	*E* 629
1620	Oliveyra	—	—	1,080 P	*E* 2308/306–8
1620	Córdoba	2,205 S 6,395 I	—	—	*E* 1924/120
1623	Claros de Guzman	—	1,889 S 4,969 I 393 C	—	*E* 1926/238–9
1623	Medina	—	—	1,500 S	AGRB *SEG* 28/325v
1631	Santa Cruz	—	9,782 SI 1,526 C	—	AGS *E* 3337/15–18
1631	Jacobssen	—	—	1,233 S	*GA* 1042
1631	Ribera	—	—	4,367 S	*GA* 1042
1634	—	—	—	1,200 S	AGRB *SEG* 33/173v
1634	Cardinal-infante	—	9,540 SI 2,044 C	—	AGS *E* 3341/254
1635	—	—	—	2,000 S	AGRB *SEG* 213/69
1636	Velada	—	—	3,671 S	IVdeDJ 85/781
1637	Hozes	—	—	4,000 S	RAH *Ms.* 11-5-1/8786 no. 20
1639	B. Wright	—	—	1,500 S	AGRB SEG 221/159
1639	Oquendo	—	—	9,000 S	BM *Addl.* 14007/71–5v

C = cavalry; I = Italian infantry; P = Portuguese infantry; S = Spanish infantry.
For diagrammatic representation, cf. Figure 7.

APPENDIX D

THE SPEED OF OVERLAND MILITARY EXPEDITIONS BETWEEN LOMBARDY AND THE LOW COUNTRIES

| Year | Commander | Approximate number | Date of departure from | | Arrived Namur | Total days |
			Lombardy	Savoy		
1567	Alva	10,000	20 Jun.	6 Jul.	15 Aug.	56
1573	Acuña	5,000	4 May	16 May	15 Jun.	42
1578	Figueroa	5,000	22 Feb.	2 Mar.	27 Mar.	32
1578	Serbelloni	3,000	2 Jun.	14 Jun.	22 Jul.	50
1582	Paz	6,000	21 Jun.	?	30 Jul.	40
1582	Carduini	5,000	24 Jul.	5 Aug.	27 Aug.	34
1584	Tassis	5,000	26 Apr.	6 May	18 Jun.	54
1585	Bobadilla	2,000	18 Jul.	25 Jul.	29 Aug.	42
1587	Zúñiga	3,000	13 Sep.	24 Sep.	1 Nov.	49
1587	Queralt	2,000	7 Oct.	15 Oct.	7 Dec.	60
1591	Toledo	3,000	1 Aug.	?	26 Sep.	57
1593	Mexía	3,000	2 Nov	23 Nov.	31 Dec.	60

OBSERVATION

The average speed for the 680 mile journey along the Spanish Road was thus 48 days. The record speed was held by the veteran troops of Don Lope de Figueroa in 1578 who not only completed the crossing in thirty-two days but managed to do it in the depths of winter. The sources for this table are the same as for Appendix C.

APPENDIX E

THE SENIOR OFFICERS OF THE ARMY OF FLANDERS, 1567–1659

THE CAPTAINS-GENERAL

Officer	Previous experience	Later career
Don Fernando Alvarez de Toledo, duke of Alva, Apr. 1567–Nov. 1573	Captain-general in Germany 1546–7 and 1552–3, and in Italy 1556–8	Commanded invasion of Portugal, 1580
Don Luis de Requesens, *Comendador Mayor de Castilla*, Nov. 1573–Mar. 1576	Adviser to Don John of Austria in war of Granada and at sea 1568–72; governor of Lombardy 1572–3	Died in office
Don John of Austria, Nov. 1576–Oct. 1578	Commanded Spain's Mediterranean fleet 1568 and 1571–6, and commanded forces to repress morisco rebellion, 1569–71; Philip II's brother	Died in office
Alessandro Farnese, prince, later (1586) duke of Parma, Oct. 1578–Dec. 1592	Present at Lepanto (1571), assisted Don John 1577–8; nephew of Philip II, son of Margaret of Parma who governed the Netherlands 1559–67	Died in office
Peter-Ernest, Count Mansfelt, Dec. 1592–Feb. 1594 (interim)	Governor of Luxemburg; *maestre de campo general* since 1577	Returned to previous offices d. 1604
Ernest, archduke of Austria, Feb. 1594–Feb. 1595	Commanded Habsburg forces in Hungary; nephew of Philip II	Died in office
Don Pedro Enríquez de Azevedo, count of Fuentes, Feb.–Dec. 1595 (interim)	Military commander in Portugal since 1587	Governor of Lombardy, 1600–10 (d. 1610)
Cardinal Albert, archduke of Austria, Dec. 1595–Aug. 1598	Viceroy of Portugal since 1583; nephew of Philip II	Cf. below
Cardinal Andrew, archduke of Austria, Jul. 1598–May 1599 (interim)	Nephew of Philip II	Returned to Germany
Archduke Albert and Infanta Isabella, May 1599–Jul. 1621 (joint sovereigns)	Nephew and daughter of Philip II	Albert d. 1621
Infanta Isabella, Jul. 1621–Dec. 1633	Daughter of Philip II	Died in office

Officer	Previous experience	Later career
Don Francisco de Moncada, marquis of Aytona, Dec. 1633–Nov. 1634 (interim)	Spanish ambassador in Germany, 1624–9, then in Brussels 1629–33	Principal adviser to cardinal-infante (d. 1635)
Cardinal Fernando, infante of Spain, Nov. 1634–Nov. 1641	Viceroy of Catalonia 1632–3; governor of Lombardy 1633–4; brother of Philip IV	Died in office
Don Franciso de Melo, marquis of Tor de Laguna, Nov. 1641–Aug. 1644	Spanish ambassador in Genoa and Germany; principal adviser to the cardinal-infante, 1641	Recalled in disgrace after Rocroi
Don Manuel de Moura y Cortereal, marquis of Castel Rodrigo, Aug. 1644–May 1647	Spanish ambassador in Rome and Germany	Recalled
Leopold-William, archduke of Austria, May 1647–Jun. 1656	Cousin of Philip IV	Recalled
Don Juan-José of Austria, Jun. 1656–May 1660	Son of Philip IV; commanded Spanish forces against Catalans	Commanded Spanish forces against Portugal, court politician, d. 1679

THE INSPECTORS-GENERAL (*veedores generales*)

I have been unable to find any personal details concerning many of these officers; it would seem that all but Necolalde (a secretary by training) were simply clean-ploughed *caballeros* with military experience. The frequent periods during which the office was vacant are obvious.

Don Antonio Galíndez de Carvajal, *comendador de la Magdalena*, 1567–9;
Jordan de Valdés, 1572;
Don Jorge Manrique de Lara, 1577–9;
Don Juan de Acuña Vela, 1579–80;
Don Pedro de Tassis y Acuña, 1584;
Juan Bautista de Tassis, 1586–91;
Don Diego de Ibarra, 1593–9;
Don Gerónimo Walter Zapata, 1600–3;
Don Francisco de Vaca y Benavides, 1603–10;
Don Francisco de Andía y Irrarazaval, 1615–17;
Don Crístobal de Benavente y Benavides, 1618–22;
Don Gaspar Ruíz de Pereda, 1623–30;
Don Luis Phelipe de Guevara, 1631–8;
Don Juan de Necolalde, 1641–7;
Don Diego Girón, 1648–57;
Don Antonio Melía y Paz, 1658–65.

E: Senior officers of the Army of Flanders, 1567–1659

Officer	Previous experience	Later career
Francisco de Lixalde, 1567–77	Acted as Philip II's treasurer in England, 1555–8	Died in office
Martín de Unceta 1577–9	Nephew of Lixalde and his *oficial mayor* after 1569; paymaster of the Flanders fleet 1574–7	Paymaster of the Army of Andalucia in the 1590s, and in Flanders again 1603–8
Juan de Lastur 1579–80	*Criado* of Philip II; experience in the treasury of Castile	Cf. below
Pedro de Olave 1580–5	Official of *Contador* Carnero in the Netherlands, 1576–7	D. 1586
Juan de Lastur 1585–90	Cf. above. Served as treasurer-general of Castile 1584–5	Treasurer-general of Castile, 1590–2, returned to Netherlands 1592–3, d. 1593
Gabriel de Santesteban, 1590–5	*Receptor de las penas de cámara* at the law courts of Valladolid until 1590; Valladolid oligarch family	Paymaster-general again 1600–3
Don Gerónimo Walter Zapata, 1595–1600	Page of Emperor Rudolf II, passed into Spanish service; on Council of War in Netherlands 1593, favoured by Archduke Ernest	*Veedor general* 1600–3 and *mayordomo mayor* of the archdukes 1602–6; recalled to Madrid, disgraced for fraud, d. 1612
Gabriel de Santesteban 1600–3	Cf. above	Recalled in disgrace for fraud
Martín de Unceta, 1603–8	Cf. above	Recalled to render his accounts
Hortuño de Ugarte, 1608–21	*Comisario de muestras* in Netherlands in 1590s; *contador de las galeras de España* until 1608	Advised the king on Netherlands military patronage in 1620s
Tomas de Mendieta, 1621–5	Nephew and *oficial mayor* of Ugarte	Died in office
Juan Antonio de Larrea, 1625	*Oficial mayor* of Mendieta	Died in office
Tomas López de Ulloa, 1626–32	Antwerp banker, Portuguese family; large legacy from father who died in Brazil	Cf. below
Antonio Wedell, 1633–4	Paymaster of the Flanders galleys 1607; *contador* of the *Sala de Cuentas* in Brussels until 1632	*Contador* of the *Sala* again
Don Juan de Lira, 1634–41	Son of Philip III's *cavallerizo* and trained in the *contaduría mayor de cuentas*	Giving accounts
Tomas López de Ulloa, 1642–8	Cf. above	Cf. below
Don Sebastián López Hierro de Castro, 1648	Antwerp banker; contacts with Amsterdam	Resigned because unable to deal with other *asentistas*
Tomas López de Ulloa, 1648–51	Cf. above	D. 1653

Officer	Previous experience	Later career
Hilario de Benero, 1651–3	Senior clerk in the *contaduría*	*Contador de viveres* 1652–; cf. below
Don Diego Henríquez de Castro, 1653–4	Antwerp banker, brother of Don Sebastián López	Cf. below
Hilario de Benero, 1654–6	Cf. above	*Contador de viveres*; served as paymaster-general again, 1674
Don Diego Henríquez de Castro, 1656–60	Cf. above	Served again, 1665–71

THE WAGE ACCOUNTANTS (*contadores del sueldo*)

Officer	Previous experience	Later career
Crístobal de Castellanos, 1567–74	Spanish *contador* in the Netherlands army, 1555–61	Died in office
Alonso de Alameda, 1567–77	*Criado* of Philip II working in the Treasury of Castile until 1566	*Contador* of the Army of Portugal 1579–83, died 1583
Juan de Navarrete, 1574–80	Official of *contador* Castellanos in the Netherlands 1559–60; *contador de resultas* in Castilian treasury 1560–7; paymaster of artillery in the Netherlands, 1567–74	Died as he returned to Spain (1580)
Pedro Coloma, 1580–95	Nephew and *oficial mayor* of Navarrete; paymaster of artillery, 1577–9	Dismissed for fraud
Balthasar de Gayangos, 1595–9	Pay-clerk in the Netherlands from 1583; relative and *oficial mayor* of Pedro Coloma; in charge of Spanish subsidies to the *Ligue* 1590–5	Dismissed for fraud
Alonso Carnero, 1584–7 and 1589–95	Official of *contador* Castellanos after 1567; acting *contador* in the Netherlands 1576–7; member of the *Tribunal de cuentas* in Madrid, 1580–4	Retired
Antonio Carnero, 1587–9	Private servant of the count of Olivares (*contador mayor de cuentas*) until 1584; nephew and *oficial mayor* of Alonso Carnero	*Contador* of artillery in Lombardy in 1610s, then in Netherlands 1622–31; wrote a history of the Revolt
Juan López de Aliri, 1599–1603	*Contador* of artillery 1583–90 and acting *veedor* of the Netherlands fleet 1590–3; judge of the *visita* 1593–4 and 1596–8	Returned to Spain
Asención de Eguigerem, 1603–10	*Comisario de muestras* in the Netherlands, 1590s	? Died in office?

Officer	Previous experience	Later career
Gonzalo Guerra de la Vega, 1610–22	An official of the *Contaduría* in 1591; rose to *contador* of the fleet in the Netherlands by 1610	Died in office
Luis de Casuso Maeda, 1622–30	Served in Spanish infantry 1592–7; official of the Flanders *veeduría* after 1605; acted as *contador* of the Spanish troops in Frisia until 1611; secretary of state and war to the duke of Feria, governor of Milan 1618–22	Died in office
Diego de Hernani, 1630–51	Official of Esteban de Ibarra in the Netherlands 1593–6 and in Spain 1596–9; *contador* of F. Spinola's galleys, 1599–1601; *contador* of the *Sala de Cuentas* after 1619 and *oficial mayor* of the *Contaduría*	Died in office
García Ossorio, 1652–71	Son of a *contador* of the *Sala*; a *comisario de muestras* and then (1647–52) *contador de viveres*	Died in office

THE SECRETARIES OF STATE AND WAR (*secretarios de estado y guerra*)

Officer	Previous experience	Later career
Juan de Albornoz, 1567–73	Replaced Juan Fernández de Ventosa as private secretary of the duke of Alva in 1565	Returned to Spain with Alva; died in his service 1580/1
Domingo de Çabala, 1573–5	Private secretary of Don Luis de Requesens from 1568	Became secretary of Requesens' brother Zúñiga, 1576–86; entered royal service; on government enquiry in Madrid 1599–1603
Balthasar López de la Cueva, 1575–6	Secretary of Requesens from 1568; deputy of Çabala	*Veedor* of the army of Andalucia in 1590
Juan de Escobedo, 1576–8	Cousin and servant of the duchess of Francavilla and then of Ruy Gómez de Silva in the 1550s; secretary of *consejo de hacienda* 1566–74; secretary of Don John 1575 onwards	Assassinated on the orders of A. Perez
Andres de Prada, 1578–80	Secretary of Don John from 1568; deputy of Escobedo	Returned to Spain 1580; secretary of *consejo de guerra* 1586–1600; joint secretary of *consejo de estado* 1600–11 (died)

Officer	Previous experience	Later career
Cosme Masi, 1580–92	Private secretary of the prince of Parma since 1568	Remained in Flanders with Parma's papers until 1595; lent money to the crown 1596; given two dukedoms for 'loyal service' 1627
Esteban de Ibarra, 1594–5	Servant of Alva 1567–8; secretary of state to Don Fadrique de Toledo 1568–73; with Alva to Portugal from 1579; *proveedor* of the Lisbon fleet in the 1580s; joint secretary of the *Consejo de Guerra* from 1591	Returned to be secretary of the *consejo de guerra* until death in 1606
Isidro Morán, 1595	Private secretary of the count of Fuentes since 1590	Continued to be secretary to Fuentes; died in Milan in office 1603
Juan de Mancicidor, 1595–1618	Secretary of one of the councils in Madrid by 1590	Died in office
Matheo de Urquina, (war only) 1618–25	Official of Esteban de Ibarra after 1594; *oficial mayor* of Mancicidor	Died in office
Pedro de San Juan, state only, 1618–25, state and war 1625–33	Official of Mancicidor after 1602	Retired with a pension when Infanta Isabella died
Gerónimo Vélez de Medriano, 1633–4	Private secretary of the marquis of Aytona	Returned to service of Aytona
Don Martín de Axpe, 1634–6	Appointed secretary to the cardinal-infante in or before 1632	Retired through ill-health
Francisco de Galaretta, 1636–8	Secretary of the Spanish embassy in Paris until 1633, then secretary of Prince Thomas of Savoy	Continued as secretary to Prince Thomas; cf. below
Don Miguel de Salamanca, 1638–41	*Procurador* for Burgos in the *Cortes* of 1633; *veedor* of artillery in the Netherlands 1635–8	Leading adviser of the Brussels government until 1649
Don Diego de la Torre, 1641–4	Official in the secretariat since 1622, then in the Spanish embassy in Rome, then *oficial mayor* of Axpe, Galaretta and Salamanca, 1636–41	Recalled
Francisco de Galaretta, 1644–8	Secretary of Prince Thomas cf. above	Died 1648–9
Dr Antonio Navarro Burena, 1648–55	Secretary of the Spanish embassy in Vienna	?
Martín de Galaretta Ocariz, 1655–69	Secretary of the Spanish embassy in Paris; brother and *oficial mayor* of Francisco de Galaretta	Died in office

APPENDIX F

PHILIP II's BUDGET FOR 1574: SOURCES

The Castilian Treasury estimated the revenues of 1574 at 5,978,535 ducats and expenditure on administration at 2 million, on debt charges at 2,730,943 ducats (IVde DJ 24/16–22). The paymaster of the Mediterranean fleet, Juan Morales de Torre, received 2,052,634 *escudos* of 10 *reales* (AGS *CMC* 2a/814) and the paymaster-general of the Army of Flanders, Francisco de Lixalde, received a further 3,688,085 *escudos* of 39 pattards in the year (AGS *CMC* 2a/55). The ducat has been converted at the rate of 37 pattards, the *escudo de a 10 reales* at 40.

The 3.69 million *escudos* received by Lixalde was far below the 702,727 *escudos* a month (or 8.4 million a year) estimated as necessary for victory by Captain-General Requesens (AGS *CMC* 2a/14, unfol., 'Relación' sent to the king).

APPENDIX G

THE FINANCING OF SPANISH IMPERIALISM IN THE NETHERLANDS, 1566–76
(in florins of 20 pattards)

Source	Received from the Netherlands by the central treasury	Year	Received from Spain	Source
AD Nord				AD Nord
B 2579	618,192	1566	886,162	B 2579
B 2585	851,302	1567	1,596,620 ⎫ +1,649,119 ⎭	B 2585 AGS
				CMC 2a/55
	?	1568	3,673,615	CMC 2a/55
B 2596	2,178,594	1569	3,462,208	CMC 2a/55
B 2602	3,871,865 (Jan.–Jun.)	1570	881,379	CMC 2a/55
B 2608	4,937,927 (Jun. 1570–Dec. 1571)	1571	229,999	CMC 2a/55
B 2614	834,782	1572	3,419,042	CMC 2a/55
B 2620	980,813	1573	3,491,196	CMC 2a/55
B 2626	1,300,430	1574	7,357,730	CMC 2a/55
B 2632	2,226,764	1575	4,957,661	CMC 2a/55
B 2638	1,819,284	1576	1,679,249	CMC 2a/55

APPENDIX H

ANNUAL EXPENDITURE BY THE 'PAGADURÍA' ON VICTUALS FOR THE TROOPS

Oct. 1577–Mar. 1580	£516,189 of 20 pattards	(AGRB *CC* 25767, account of Victualler-General Odrimont)
May 1585–Aug. 1590	1,014,557 *escudos* of 57 pattards	(AGS *CMC* 2a/879, account of Paymaster-General Lastur).
Nov. 1603–Mar. 1608	2,140,542 *escudos* of 50 pattards	(AGS *CMC* 2a/2, account of Paymaster-General Unceta)
Jul. 1621–Oct. 1625	2,792,342 *escudos* of 50 pattards	(AGS *CMC* 3a/961, account of Paymaster-General Mendieta)
Jan. 1642–Dec. 1645	2,819,637 *escudos* of 50 pattards	(AGS *CMC* 3a/993, account of Paymaster-General Ulloa)

APPENDIX I

THE 'TAIL' OF THE ARMY OF FLANDERS: WOMEN AND SERVANTS WITH THE TROOPS

Date	Unit	Men	Women	Servants	Total persons	Total non-military persons number	Total non-military persons %	Source
1577	1 company Spanish horse	110	8	117	235	125	53	AC St Jean de Maurienne *EE* I.4
1594	9 companies Italian horse	658	?	?	1,304	646	50	*Ibid.*
1594	11 companies Italian foot	1,458	?	?	1,638	180	11	*Ibid.*
1594	26 companies Spanish foot	3,131	?	?	3,534	403	11	*Ibid.*
1605	25 companies Spanish foot	2,995	?	?	3,245	250	8	*AD* Savoie *SA* 7570/1
1620	42 companies Spanish and Italian foot	6,975	85	458	7,518	543	8	*AD* Savoie *SA* 7461

Date	Unit	Soldiers	Women	% women to men	Source
1579–86	5 companies 'Low Germans'	480	72	15	Gemeente Archief Nijmegen, 2942 and 2943
1606	Spanish *tercio* of Juan Bravo	922	47	5	AGRB *Audience* 1896/2 portf. 6
1629	Walloon *tercio* of Count Hennin	1,043	289	28	AGRB *Audience* 2806

Note: All these figures come from enquiries by civil authorities connected with billeting: the women and servants noted had to be given lodgings. The figures are therefore a minimum. Cf. also p. 167 above.

THE MUTINIES OF THE ARMY OF FLANDERS

Mutiny centre	Dates	Duration Number of days	Number of men	Units involved	Total cost	Aver. mutin settler (in flo
Valenciennes	Oct. 1570	c.10	c.1,000	Lodron's German regiment	?	regime disban
Haarlem	29 Jul.–16 Aug. 1573	19	2,634	Spanish tercios	74,131 escudos of 39 pattards	5
Antwerp	15 Apr.– 30 May 1574	45	4,562	Spanish infantry	543,689 escudos of 39 pattards	23
Holland– Maastricht	7 Nov. 1574– 5 Mar. 1575	119	2,219	Spanish 'tercio of Italy'	65,923 escudos of 39 pattards	5
Brabant	Mar.–Apr. 1576	c.30	1,300	Spanish light horse	4,895 escudos of 39 pattards	
Aalst– Antwerp	2 Jul. 1576– 31 Mar. 1577	272	{ 1,329 4,005	light horse infantry (Spanish)	632,971 escudos of 39 pattards	23
Luxemburg	Mar. 1580– Jul. 1581	c.270	7,000	German foot	209,000 escudos of 39 pattards	5
Oudenaarde siege-works	Jun. 1582	?	?	German regiment	none	–
'Pays de Waes'	Oct.– Nov. 1585	c.15	2,000	Walloon infantry	4 months' pay	c.2
Bommelerwaard	30 Aug. 1589	1	1,500	Spanish tercio viejo de Lombardia	nil	nil (ter 'reforn
Kortrijk	23 Feb.– 26 Jun. 1590	124	1,800	Spanish tercio of A. de Zúñiga	197,783 escudos of 39 pattards	21
Diest (I)	27 Nov. 1590– 9 Nov. 1591	347	1,872	Spanish tercio of M. de Vega	300,000 escudos of 50 pattards	34
Rijnberg (I)	1 Dec. 1592– 29 Nov. 1593	364	446	German garrison	69,249 florins	15
St Pol	24 Jul. 1593– 18 Aug. 1594	389	{ 200 1,200	horse foot (Italian)	30,000 florins monthly sustento; plus settlement of 184,000 escudos of 50 pattards	32

| Mutiny centre | Duration | | | Units involved | Total cost | Average mutineer's settlement (in florins) |
	Dates	Number of days	Number of men			
t-sur-Sambre	23 Aug. 1593–14 Aug. 1594	356	1,500	horse and foot (mainly Italian)	45,000 florins monthly *sustento*; plus 188,600 *escudos* of 50 pattards	315
nkirk	25 Jul, 1594–Mar. 1595	c.240	c.400	Spanish garrison	225,000 florins	c.562
hem – Tienen	26 Jul. 1594–6 Jul. 1596	710 {	800 horse / 2,000 foot / all 'nations'		15,000 *escudos sustento* after Jan. 1595; plus 331,165 *escudos* of 50 pattards	297
Chapelle	5 Sep. 1594–Jul. 1596	c.672	c.800	Spanish and Walloon garrison	5,000 *escudos* monthly *sustento*; plus 80,000 *escudos* of 50 pattards	c.250
emburg	1595	?		German regiment of Biglia	?	?
ssels	1595	?		German regiment of Pernesteyn	?	?
is	25 Jul. 1595–18 Aug. 1596	389	c.500	Spanish garrison	85,000 *escudos* of 50 pattards	425
telet	Apr. 1597–Apr. 1598	c.365	c.300	Spanish and Walloon garrison	?	?
ais	30 Nov. 1597–18 May 1598	169	294	Spanish garrison	?	?
nbrai del	28 Dec. 1597–28 Mar. 1598	91	230	Spanish garrison	?	?
res	15 Jan–25 Jul. 1598	192	?	garrison (part Spanish)	?	?
llens	28 Apr.–30 Sept. 1598	156		Spanish garrison	?	?
r	28 Jul. 1598–5 Oct. 1599	435	?	Spanish and Walloon garrison	?	? outlawed
werp del	8 Aug. 1598–12 Feb 1599	189	600	Spanish garrison	63,714 *escudos* of 50 pattards	265 outlawed
ent	1 Oct. 1598–2 Feb. 1599	125	448	Spanish garrison	126,763 florins of 20 pattards	283 outlawed
berg (II)	26 Apr.–20 Dec. 1599	239	?	German garrison	?	?
enthals	13 Oct. 1599–3 Apr. 1600	173	?	garrison	?	?
nont–st (II)	25 Dec. 1599–22 Feb 1601	424 {	770 horse / 1,452 foot (Spanish, Italian, Walloon ...)		27,873 *escudos* monthly *sustento* after Mar. 1600; plus 518,000 *escudos* of 50 pattards settlement	582

Mutiny centre	Dates	Number of days	Number of men	Units involved	Total cost	Aver mutin settle (in flo
Weert	Jul. 1600–Mar. 1602	c.600	{ 758 1,169	horse foot – all 'nations'	*Sustento* of 25,249 *escudos*; plus c.150,000 *escudos* of 50 pattards	c.20
Crèvecœur fort	Jan. 1600	20	c.100	Walloon garrison	Betrayed fort to Dutch	?
St André fort	Jan.–26 Mar. 1600	c.70	c.100	Walloons	Betrayed fort to Dutch for 125,000 florins	1,25
Kerpen fort	May 1600–Feb. 1602	c.600	110	garrison	?	?
Maastricht	Jun. 1601	?	?	garrison	?	?
Fort St Isabella–Bergues	Jun. 1601–1602	?	?	Italian and Walloon garrison	?	?

(Scheldt forts of St Jacques, La Croix and St Philippe also suffered from mutinous garrisons in

Mutiny centre	Dates	Number of days	Number of men	Units involved	Total cost	Aver mutin settle (in flo
Hamont–Hoogstraten-Grave Roermond	1 Sep. 1602–18 May 1605	990	{ 1,200 2,000	horse foot – all 'nations'	Monthly *sustento* of 32,000 *escudos* after May 1604; plus 397,743 *escudos* of 50 pattards	31
Lier (II)	1603–4	?	513	garrison	?	?
Isendijk fort	May 1604	?	?	Walloon garrison	Betrayed to Dutch	
Sta Clara fort	1605	?	c.70	garrison	Betrayed to Dutch	?
Diest (III)	11 Dec. 1606 –27 Nov. 1607	351	{ 2,037 2,015	horse foot – all 'nations'	292,000 *escudos* paid in monthly *sustento*; 372,000 *escudos* of 50 pattards in final settlement	2,

Sources

For the duration and composition of the mutinies between 1570 and 1602 I have used the accounts prepared by the *contaduría del sueldo* for the final settlement. These accounts, in Simancas, are given in detail in my *Guide to the Archives of the Spanish Institutions* (Brussels, 1971), pp. 79–81. Other data are taken from the reports and letters sent to the king and preserved in AGS *Estado Flandes*. I have also consulted the studies of: L. de Torre, 'Los motines militares en Flandes', *Revista de Archivos, Bibliotecas y Museos*, XXV (1911)–XXXII (1915) (seven articles); and G. Wymans, 'Les mutineries militaires de 1596 à 1606', *Standen en Landen*, XXXIX (1966), pp. 105–21.

THE RECEIPTS OF THE MILITARY TREASURY OF THE ARMY OF FLANDERS, 1567–1665

Year	Total receipt	Currency	Receipt from Spain	Source
1567	845,702	*escudos* of 39	845,702	AGS *CMC* 2a/55
1568	1,887,552	,,	1,883,905	,,
1569	1,888,043	,,	1,775,491	,,
1570	2,751,781	,,	441,794	,,
1571	453,943	,,	117,948	,,
1572	4,409,497	,,	1,753,355	,,
1573	2,043,071	,,	1,790,347	,,
1574	4,726,593	,,	3,688,085	,,
1575	2,984,281	,,	2,485,043	
1576	946,129	,,	861,153	
1577	1,049,300	,,	845,845	AGS *CMC* 2a/55 and *E* 574/152
1578	1,474,351	,,	1,149,511	AGS *CMC* 2a/44
1579	{ 1,327,019	*escudos* of 39	1,327,019	AGS *CMC* 2a/44
	{ 1,225,493	*escudos* of 48	1,225,493	AGS *E* 579/101
1580	{ 799,999	*escudos* of 48	799,999	AGS *E* 582/147
	{ 1,084,826	florins of 20	} receipt from Spain Jul. 1580 –Apr. 1585 = 14,949,802 florins of 20	AGS *CMC* 2a/844
1581	3,480,059	,,		,,
1582	4,923,814	,,		,,
1583	2,867,462	,,		,,
1584	3,125,081	,,		,,
1585	1,596,497	,,		,,
	1,560,375	*escudos* of 57	} receipt from Spain May 1585 –Jul. 1590 = 15,678,229 *escudos* of 57	AGS *CMC* 2a/879
1586	1,969,645	,,		,,
1587	5,997,233	,,		,,
1588	4,580,801	,,		,,
1589	3,899,156	,,		,,
1590	4,245,348	*escudos* of 57		,,
	6,362,241	florins of 20	} receipt from Spain Aug. 1590–Mar. 1595 = 37,873,976 florins of 20	AGS *CMC* 2a/840
1591	14,136,642	,,		,,
1592	4,400,020	,,		,,
1593	15,301,137	,,		,,
1594	8,469,102	,,		,,
	1,120,240	,,		
1595	} total receipt of the military treasury Jan. 1595–Dec. 1597 = 42,310,175 florins	,,	} receipt from Spain Jan. 1595 –Dec. 1597 = 32,929,213	AGS *CMC* 2a/869
1596				
1597				

Year	Total receipt	Currency	Receipt from Spain	Source
1598	total receipt, Jan. 1598–Jan 1600 = 35,370,472 florins	florins of 20	total receipt from Spain, Jan. 1598–Jan. 1600 = 18,995,215	AGS *CMC* 2a/869
1599				

I have been unable to find complete accounts for the military treasury between 1600 and March 1608. The only fragments are – 1602 total receipt: 3,734,339 *escudos* of 50 (AGS *E* 2023/116); Nov. 1603–Mar. 1608, total receipt: 18,261,058 *escudos* of 50 (AGS *CMC* 2a/2). There is, however, a detailed statement by the Castilian treasury of the money sent to the Netherlands between 1598 and 1608: AGS *E* 626/43.

Year	Money sent by the Castilian treasury to the Netherlands
1600	1,717,985,533 *maravedís* (of which 375 made one Spanish ducat,
1601	714,935,424 ,, each ducat valued at about 55 pattards
1602	1,321,291,579 ,, in the Netherlands at this time)
1603	1,412,482,413 ,,
1604	1,304,945,840 ,,
1605	1,624,425,329 ,,
1606	1,483,378,867 ,,
1607	1,131,584,408 ,,
1608	762,616,935 ,,

The accounts of the paymasters-general begin again in April 1608.

Year	Total receipt	Currency	Receipt from Spain	Source
1608	total receipt Apr. 1608–Dec. 1613 = 8,672,683	*escudos* of 50	8,624,975	AGS *E* 634/369
1609				
1610				
1611				
1612				
1613				
1614	total receipt 1614–15 = 3,431,494	*escudos* of 50	3,431,494	,,
1615				
1616	1,780,385	,,	1,778,400	,,
1617	1,867,766	,,	1,778,400	,,
1618	1,755,820	,,	1,755,820	AGS *CMC* 3a/940
1619	2,181,277	,,	2,181,207	AGS *CMC* 3a/883
1620	total Jan. 1620–Jul. 1621 = 4,738,368	,,	4,738,368	AGS *CMC* 3a/881
1621				
1622	total Jul. 1621–Dec. 1622 = 6,125,161	,,	total receipt from Spain, Jul. 1621–Dec. 1625 = 15,622,798	AGS *CMC* 3a/951 and 961
1623	3,250,000	,,		,,
1624	3,440,691	,,		,,
1625	3,407,308	,,		AGS *CMC* 3a/951 and 953

Year	Total receipt	Currency	Receipt from Spain	Source
1626	2,799,880	*escudos* of 50	2,253,722	AGS *CMC* 3a/1438
1627	3,886,998	,,	2,819,401	,,
1628	3,170,918	,,	2,567,811	,,
1629	2,590,840	,,	1,539,938	,,
1630	?	,,	2,468,818	AGS *CMC* 3a/1763
1631	?	,,	4,152,635	,,
1632	?	,,	2,521,443	,,

The accounts of Antonio Wedell, paymaster in 1633–4, appear to have been lost; those of Don Juan de Lira are so damaged by humidity that only the total receipt can be discerned – it is probable that 90 per cent of this, if not more, came from Spain.

Year	Total receipt	Currency	Receipt from Spain	Source
1635	4,142,144	*escudos* of 50	?	AGS *CMC* 3a/975
1636	3,654,087	,,	?	,,
1637	5,379,717	,,	?	,,
1638	4,439,342	,,	?	,,
1639	3,565,087	,,	?	,,
1640	4,275,625	,,	?	,,
1641	4,604,349	,,	?	,
1642	3,890,618	,,	3,326,641	AGS *CMC* 3a/956
1643	2,319,891	,,	1,385,101	,,
1644	1,886,423	,,	1,533,743	,,
1645	2,310,717	,,	2,176,154	,,
1646	2,538,372	,,	2,390,892	,,
1647	2,317 874	,,	1,863,577	,,
1648	3,735,800	,,	1,913,098	AGS *CMC* 3a/956 and E 2072, *relación* of Fuensaldaña
1649	?	,,	1,033,043	AGS *CMC* 3a/956
1650	?	,,	677,714	,,
1651	Jan.–Jun.	,,	710,033	,,
1652	⎱ Jun. 1651– Apr. 1653 =	⎰ Jun. 1651 Apr. 1653 =		
1653	4,535,453	,,	1,752,277	AGS *CMC* 3a/1762

1654–60 no accounts found.

Feb. 1660–Jan. 1665 the military treasury received 10,618,738 florins (AGS *CMC* 3a/933) and from Jan. 1665 until Jun. 1671, it received 6,072,965 *escudos* of 50, only 2,376,826 of them from Spain (*CMC* 3a/1760).

OBSERVATIONS

1. The vast majority of the sources used to compile this table are the declared accounts of the paymasters-general of the Army of Flanders, submitted to the audit office of the Spanish exchequer (the *contaduría mayor de cuentas*).

2. Despite the apparent precision of these figures, they must be used with the utmost caution. The paymasters made a number of mistakes in compiling their accounts – some arithmetical errors, some fraudulent entries and omissions – and most of them did not compile annual totals, which means that further minor inaccuracies may have been committed in preparing them. The figures here therefore reveal only the *overall trend* of the receipts of the *pagaduría*, its total income and also its income from Spain (cf. Figures 29 and 30 for illustration of this). In the pre-statistical age, however, the trend is all-important.

A NOTE ON SOURCES

MANUSCRIPT SOURCES

The vast majority of my material on the Army of Flanders comes from the archives of the Spanish central government and of the various Spanish institutions in the Netherlands. These sources are described and in some cases inventoried in my book: *Guide to the Archives of the Spanish Institutions in or concerned with the Netherlands, 1556–1706* (Brussels, 1971). In addition I have used material from the French and German military and financial papers of the Brussels government: AGRB *Audience* 2769–2785 and *Secrétairerie d'Etat allemande* 199–201 and 471, and AD Nord (Lille), series *B, comptes de la recette generale des finances*. I have also consulted the archives of a sample number of garrison towns: Antwerp, Breda, Groningen, 's Hertogenbosch and Nijmegen.

On the movements of troops, particularly along the Spanish Road I consulted the correspondence, accounts and municipal deliberations of the various local authorities along the routes: AGRB *CC* 25667–25670, 25741–25797, 25805, 25811–25815 and some others (accounts of *étapes* in Luxemburg and Namur);

AGRB *Audience, lettres missives*, correspondence of the Brussels government with the governments of Namur, Luxemburg, Lorraine and Franche-Comté between 1567 and 1633, a large part of it concerned with the preparations for and the passage of Spanish troops;

AD Meurthe-et-Moselle, series *B*: 855, 2126, 3065, 3313, 3659, 5414, 5625, 5967, 5971, 6454, 6679, 6709, 7029, 8194, 8252, 9844 (accounts of government receivers of Lorraine communities through which troops using the Spanish Road passed);
series *3 F*: 203–204, 279, 429, 438–439 (papers on the neutrality of Lorraine);
series *4 F*: 1, 7, 9 (correspondence about the troops);

AD Doubs, series *B*: 578, 1351, 1767, 1803, 1826–1827, 1831–1832, 1849, 1955–1958, 1964–1966 (accounts of *étapes* for the troops);
series *2 B*: 1512–1518 (accounts and enquiries concerning the troops: very important);
series *C*: 263–265, suppl. 57 and 97 (accounts and enquiries about the troops made by the provincial estates);

AD Savoie, series *SA*: 6603–6605, 6664, 6720, 6792–6793, 6722–6826, 6912, 6915, 7388, 7392, 7415–7416, 7431, 7461, 7470–7472, 7530, 7551, 7570, 7573–7574, 7607, 7615, 7650 (accounts of *étapes*).

The correspondence of the central governments of Franche-Comté, Savoy and Lorraine has, unfortunately, largely disappeared, but I found some state papers in the following collections:

AM Besançon, *Ms. Granvelle* vols 87–89 (Correspondence of M. de Vergy, Philip II's governor of the Comté);

BNP *Collection de Lorraine*, vols 458, 490–491, 524–531 (papers of the marquis of Varembon, Spanish commander) and 598 (a volume entirely concerned with arrangements for the passage of troops through Lorraine to the Army of Flanders).

I also found considerable material on the organization of Spain's 'military corridors' in the following communal archives along the Spanish Road (those which are still in the commune are marked with an asterisk, the rest are in the departmental archives):

Dept. Vosges: AC Epinal, Rambervillers;
Dept. Haute-Saône: Gray, Gy, Luxeuil-les-Bains;*
Dept. Doubs: Baume-les-Dames,* Besançon,* Pontarlier;*
Dept. Jura: Arinthod,* Conliège,* Orgelet,* St Claude,* Salins-les-Bains;*
Dept. Savoie: Aime-en-Tarantaise,* La Chapelle, Lanslevillard, St Jean de Maurienne,* Termignon.*

There were inventories (of variable usefulness) of all these communal archives in the departmental archives; all were classed upon the same scheme: *BB* – municipal/communal deliberations, *CC* – communal accounts, *EE* – military papers. I consulted all papers in these classes between 1567 and 1620 in each of the above archives. I also consulted:

AE Geneva, *RC* 61, 62, 68, 72, 77, 79, 82, 96, 119 (registers of the deliberations of the Council of the Republic of Geneva);

 PH 1825, 1827, 1933, 1940, 1986–7, 2121, 2271–2, 2367, 2553–5, 2636, 2642–3, 2651–2, 2656 (correspondence of the Republic with its neighbours and others about the passage of Spanish troops).

Italian archives did not prove nearly as rich in detail concerning the movement of troops as those of France. I only found the following of help:

AS Torino, *Sezioni Reuniti* 172 and 256–257 (*étape* accounts);
AS Milano, *Militare P.A.* 165bis, 210–211, 406, 410–411 (military papers); *Autografi* 225/13;
AS Genova, *Archivio Segreto* 2738, 2412a–2416, 2745–2746 (correspondence of the Genoese ambassadors in Spain and of the Spanish ambassadors in Genoa with the Doge and Senate).

CONTEMPORARY SOURCES

A large number of the participants in the Eighty Years' War wrote about the events, people and institutions of the time. They are listed and described in the relevant chronological section of the following bibliographies:

J. Almirante, *Bibliografía militar de España* (Madrid, 1876);
H. de Buck, *Bibliografie der Geschiedenis van Nederland* (Leiden, 1968).

There are also excellent remarks on the merits of various historians in the bibliographical introductions to each volume of:

L. van der Essen, *Alexandre Farnèse, prince de Parme, Gouverneur-Général des Pays-Bas* (Louvain, 1933–7, 5 vols);
and in:
B. Vermaseren, *De Katholieke Nederlandsche Geschiedschrijving in de XVIe en XVIIe eeuw over den Opstand* (Maastricht, 1941).

OTHER SOURCES

The Eighty Years' War certainly caused a lot of ink to flow. Besides the chronicles and histories which poured from pens and presses all over Europe, there were the 'instant' compilations: the pamphlets, news-sheets (*avvisi*) and, in the seventeenth century, the first regular newspapers. The Dutch *corantos* were soon including weekly reports from their own army (news *vvt ons velt-leger* appeared from 1625) and also, after 1640, from the French army. Cf. the useful publication: F. Dahl, *Dutch Corantos, 1618–1650. A bibliography* (The Hague, 1946). Alas, there is no similar guide to the *corantos* of Belgium, although there were three weekly newspapers appearing at Antwerp by 1635 (one of them dating from 1605) and another started at Bruges in 1637.

Most of the major events of the Low Countries' Wars gave rise to visual as well as written records. There are medals, special coin-issues and siege-money which shed interesting light on the war and the passions it generated. The following illustrated guides provide an introduction:

H. van Loon, *Histoire metallique des XVII provinces des Pays-Bas* (La Haye, 1720–40);
H. Enno van Gelder & J. van Kuyk, *De Penning en het Munten van de Tachtigjarige Oorlog* ('s Gravenhage, 1948);
H. Enno van Gelder, *De Nederlandse Noodmunten van de Tachtigjarige Oorlog* ('s Gravenhage 1955).

Of the more conventional pictorial representations, the engravings of François Hogenburg (first printed in Aitzing's *De Leone Belgico*) and Jacques Callot (especially his gigantic engraving of the siege of Breda) are outstanding. The paintings of the Antwerp artists Sebastian Vranckx (1573–1647) and his pupil Pieter Snaeyers (1592–1667) are accurate and revealing; many of them are in the Prado in Madrid. For the Netherlands and its people on the eve of the troubles, there is the incomparable Breughel whose paintings and etchings give a vivid picture of life and customs in the 1560s. On his value as a historical source, cf.: C. Terlinden, 'Pierre Breugel le Vieux et l'histoire', *Revue Belge d'Archéologie et d'Histoire de l'Art*, III (1942), pp. 227–57.

MODERN PRINTED SOURCES

Because of their central importance in the affairs of western Europe at the time, the Eighty Years' War and the power of Spain are mentioned in a large number of history books and articles covering the western world in the century 1550–1650. Happily there are already a number of admirable bibliographical surveys of the material which make it unnecessary to provide a detailed list here of the works I have consulted. (Full references to all publications directly cited are given in the footnotes to my text.)

The Netherlands

H. de Buck, *Bibliografie der Geschiedenis van Nederland* (Leiden, 1968);
H. Pirenne, *Bibliographie de l'Histoire de Belgique* (3rd edn, Brussels, 1931).

Since 1947 there have been regular critical bibliographies of all publications on Belgian history in *Revue du Nord* and since 1952 also in *Revue Belge de Philologie et d'Histoire*. There is also the annual *Bulletin Critique d'Histoire de Belgique* (ed. J. Dhondt, Ghent, 1967 onwards).

Spain

B. Sánchez Alonso, *Fuentes de la Historia española e Hispano-americana* (3rd edn, Madrid, 1952).

Publications since 1952 are given brief critical notices in the quarterly *Indice Histórico Español* (Barcelona, 1952 onwards).

INDEX

Index

Index

Cleves-Jülich, German duchy of
strategic importance, 16
succession struggle (1609–14), 251–2
clothing, military, *see* uniform
Cologne, war of (1583–9), 156, 251
Coloma, Don Carlos (1566–1637), ambassador, military commander and historian, 118, 119, 188
Coloma, Pedro, *contador* of the Army of Flanders 1580–95, 284
company, army unit, 13–16, 19–20, 35–8, 274–5, 277
comradeship (*camarada*) in the Army of Flanders, 177
contador of the Army of Flanders
office of, 109
office-holders, 284–5
contaduría mayor de cuentas, audit office of the Castilian exchequer, 111–12
contributions-system in the Netherlands (after 1574), 142–3
council of war in Spain (*consejo de guerra*), 35 and n. 1, 111
crime in the Army of Flanders, 90, 178, 179–80
Curiel, Gerónimo de (d. 1578), Spanish factor at Antwerp and Paris, 238

'debauchers', agents paid to entice soldiers from one army to another, 214–15
decrees of bankruptcy (*decretos*), orders suspending payments from the Castilian treasury
mechanism of, 148–51
in 1575, 234–9
in 1596, 247 n. 3
in 1627, 255–6
demobilization, 222–7
depositario general, 'public trustee' for the Army of Flanders (after 1596), 172
desertion, 193, 206, 207–18
Deventer (Dutch town), fortifications of, 8, Pls. 2 and 3
Diest (Belgian town), mutinies at
in 1590–1, 186, 189, 290
in 1599–1601, 249, 291
in 1606–7, 186, 194, 197, 250–1, 292
discipline in the Army of Flanders
in a mutiny, 188–9, 193
in the ranks, 160, 179–80, 199–200, 216, 220
for senior personnel, 115–17
disease in the Army of Flanders, 167–9
Downs, battle of the (21 Oct. 1639), 46, 78, 260, 262

drill, lack of in the Army of Flanders, 13 and n. 1, 19–20, 33–4
Dunkirk (Channel port mostly controlled by Spain until 1658)
fleet of, 4–5
garrison of, 11–12
mutiny at, 291
port of, 57, 263
Duplessis-Mornay, Philippe, French Huguenot writer, urges attack on the Spanish Road (1584), 67
Dutch Republic, *see* United Provinces

Eguigerem, Ascención de, *contador* of the Army of Flanders 1603–10, 284
electo, leader of a mutiny, 188–206 *passim*
Elizabeth I, queen of England 1558–1603, 57, 231, 243–4, 250, 265
Empire, Holy Roman
opposition to invasion by Spanish troops (1599), 156
Spanish intervention in (1619–34), 251–9
used as military corridor by Spanish troops, 53–6, 73–4
engineering in the early modern period
civil, 80–2
military, 7–10, 18–19
England
foreign policy of, 57, 77–9, 243–4, 250, 255, 262–3
military practice, 145 n. 3 (15th century), 158 (17th century)
see also British soldiers
enterprisers, military, 38–9, 45
entretenidos (staff officers) in the Army of Flanders, 108, 109–10
Epinal (town in Lorraine), experience of the Spanish Road, 91, 92 n. 1, 218
Ernest, Archduke of Austria (1553–95), governor-general of the Netherlands, 281
Escobedo, Juan de (d. 1578) secretary of state and war in the Army of Flanders 1576–8, 225, 285
étape system, 88–96

fairs of exchange, 146–56 *passim*
Fawkes, Guy, soldier in the Army of Flanders and Gunpowder conspirator (1605), 41
Ferdinand, Archduke of Styria and later (1618–37) Holy Roman Emperor, 55, 253, 255–6, 257, 258–9
Fernández de Navarrete, Pedro, Spanish reformer of Philip IV's reign, 128–9

Index

Swiss Confederation
political neutrality of, 60–1, 62, 68
pro-Spanish Catholic cantons, 70–3

'Tenth Penny', tax imposed on the Netherlands (1572), 139–40
tercio, army unit, 13–16, 19–20, 274–5
tercio of Sardinia, 'reformed' in 1568, 219–20
tercio viejo de Lombardía, 'reformed' in 1589, 178, 188, 220–1
testaments of soldiers, 170–1, 172–4
Thirty Years' War in Germany (1618–48), 76, 253–62
Toledo, Don Fadrique de (d. 1585), son of the duke of Alva and commander of the Army of Flanders, 203
Toledo, Don Hernando de (d. 1592), natural son of the duke of Alva and Spanish military commander, 119
Toul, French enclave in Lorraine (after 1552), 62, 65
transport for the troops' baggage, 95–6, 182–3
tribunal de las cuentas de Flandes (1581–4), 114
Tromp, Maarten Harpertszoon, Dutch admiral, 78
tunnel, first Alpine (1480), 80
Turkish empire, threat to Spain, 107, 231–8, 267
Twelve Years' Truce, 1609–21
debate over, 25, 77, 129–30, 205, 250–1
renewal of, 129–30, 132, 226, 254
Tyrol, Habsburg dominion, recruiting ground of the Army of Flanders, 29, 53

Ugarte, Hortuño de, paymaster-general of the Army of Flanders 1608–21, 283
Unceta, Martín de, paymaster-general of the Army of Flanders 1577–9 and 1600–3, 283
uniform in the Army of Flanders, 19, 27, 46, 164–5, Pl. 6
'Union of Arms' scheme (1626–8), 156–7
United Provinces, the
costs of war to, 266
growth of, 16–17, 234, 236, 239–40, 245–6, 248, 258
overseas trade of, 130–1, 248
and Spanish deserters, 217–18
and the Spanish Road, 67
Urquina, Matheo de, secretary of state and war in the Army of Flanders 1618–25, 286

Valdes, Francisco de, Spanish maestre de campo and military theorist in the Netherlands 1567–80, 201

Valtelline, Alpine valley controlled by the Grisons, 70, 73, 74–6, 81, Fig. 9
veedor general (inspector-general) of the Army of Flanders
office of, 112–13
office-holders, 282
Veere (Dutch town), naval arsenal at, 4
Vélez de Medriano, Gerónimo, secretary of state and war in the Army of Flanders 1633–4, 286
venereal diseases in the Army of Flanders, 169
Verdugo, Francisco (1536–95), Spanish military commander and historian, 12 n. 2, 118
Vervins, peace of (2 May 1598), 68–9, 247
victuallers, military
on the march, 92–5
in the Netherlands, 162–4, 176–7
see also provisioning
Vigenère, Blaise de (d. 1596), French military theorist, 42, 162 and n. 2, 173
visita, government enquiry in the Netherlands 1593–1602, 115
Vitelli, Chiappino, marquis of Cetona (d. 1575), commander of the Army of Flanders, 142, 220 n. 2

wages of soldiers
in the Army of Flanders, 158–71, 182, 191
in the Dutch army, 159 n. 2
Wallenstein, Count Albrecht von (k. 1634), imperial general, 117, 255, 256, 257
Walloons, see Netherlands troops
Walter Zapata, Don Gerónimo (d. 1610), paymaster-general 1595–1600 and inspector-general 1600–3 of the Army of Flanders, 108, 283
warfare in the early modern period
armies, size and composition of, 6, 25–49, 272–3
battles, see under individual engagements
cost of, 134–7, 139–56, 231–67
methods of, 3–21
'war-game', made for prince Philip (IV) of Spain in 1614, 3–4
wartegeld (waiting money) system, 39
wastage of troops in the Army of Flanders, 207–11
Wedell, Antonio, paymaster-general of the Army of Flanders 1633–4, 283
Weert (Belgian town), mutiny at (1600–2), 186, 189 n. 3, 197, 249, 292
whores in the Army of Flanders, 175–6
Williams, Sir Roger (d. 1595), English soldier and military theorist, 11, 33

308

DH
186.5   Parker, Geoffrey, 1933–
P23   The Army of Flanders and the Spanish Road, 1567–1659
          the logistics of Spanish victory and defeat in the Lo
          Countries' Wars. Cambridge [Eng.] University Press, 197

               xviii, 309 p. illus. 24 cm. (Cambridge studies in early mode
          history) index.   B*

          Includes bibliographical references.

               1. Netherlands—History—Wars of Independence, 1556–1648.
          I. Title. 2.Spain-History-House of Austria, 1516-
               1700
298190 DH186.5.P28   949.2′03   76–18002
          ISBN 0-521-08462-8   MAR
          Library of Congress   ′2 [10–2]